T0094355

Equal Care

Equal Care

Health Equity, Social Democracy, and the Egalitarian State

Seth A. Berkowitz, MD, MPH

JOHNS HOPKINS UNIVERSITY PRESS   BALTIMORE

Johns Hopkins University Press

2715 North Charles Street

Baltimore, Maryland 21218

www.press.jhu.edu

Library of Congress Cataloging-in-Publication Data is available.

A catalog record for this book is available from the British Library.

ISBN 978-1-4214-4824-4 (hardcover)
ISBN 978-1-4214-4825-1 (ebook)

Special discounts are available for bulk purchases of this book. For more information, please contact Special Sales at specialsales@jh.edu.

Contents

That, I believe, is our basic function: to develop alternatives to existing policies, to keep them alive and available until the politically impossible becomes politically inevitable.

—Milton Friedman

For Avram, Nora, Katherine, Ruth, and Scott

Figures and Tables

Acknowledgments

My deepest thanks go to the patients I have been privileged to work with in Whitakers and Chapel Hill, North Carolina; San Francisco, California; and Revere, Massachusetts. Much of this book is abstract and technical, but its root is the real consequences our unjust system of social relations has on people's health.

For extremely helpful feedback (and pushback) on many of the ideas in this book, I thank Katherine Aragon, Sanjay Basu, Crystal Wiley Cené, Avik Chatterjee, Andrew M. Courtwright, Samuel T. Edwards, Somnath Saha, and Atheendar Venkataramani. Their generous help should not be seen as an endorsement of any of the ideas presented, and all errors are solely mine.

Robin Coleman, editor at Johns Hopkins University Press, has been enormously supportive during the writing of this book, especially given my unfamiliarity with the process. I am also thankful to two anonymous reviewers for Hopkins Press.

I am immensely grateful to Katherine Aragon for her love and support, not only as writing slowly unfolded on this project but throughout all aspects of my life. Having a supportive partner I admire so much is my greatest blessing. Nora V. and Avram A. Berkowitz, while of limited direct assistance, have proven to be enormously, if obliviously, helpful for maintaining motivation and focus. If I was ever having trouble writing from the heart, I thought about you. I hope you grow up to live in a time when everyone's fundamental moral equality is taken seriously. If I can slip in a bit of parental advice here: moral education for children often starts with what is sometimes called the Golden Rule. But one quickly notices that there seem to be two operative versions of the Golden Rule: "Love your neighbor as yourself," and "Those who have the gold make the rules" (you might think of these as the egalitarian version and the hierarchical version, respectively). My advice is that the version you prefer is a defining choice.

All figures and tables, with the exception of figures 3.1A and 3.1B, were prepared by the author. I thank Christina Berkowitz for preparing figure 3.1A and the Robert Wood Johnson Foundation for their permission to use figure 3.1B. Portions of chapter 5 and chapter 7 draw from "The Logic of Policies to Address Income-Related Health Inequity: A Problem-Oriented Approach," which was published in the *Milbank Quarterly* (2022 Jun;100[2]: 370–392, https://doi.org/10.1111/1468-0009.12558). I thank the Wiley Online Library for permission to reuse these sections.

My own family's story in many ways reflects the benefits of the approaches emphasized here. My Bubba, who died during the writing of this book, was born in 1931, just before the start of New Deal programs that brought some social democratic ideals into US policy, at least in a limited way. That era was deeply unequal and rife with racist and other oppression. But the social democratic policies of its time—policies that helped create extensive public education, a progressive tax system, social security, and a strong labor movement—did provide meaningful benefits that moved the United States in the direction of justice, at least for some. I was raised in a loving and financially secure home that taught me to embrace learning, work hard, and care for others. These values enabled, in the right social context, my parents' success. Their mobility was consolidated into an advantaged social position in my own life, and I have benefitted from public education at every stage of my career. This in turn has advantaged my children. Thus, my family's story is one of New Deal–era universalist policies and their generational benefits. But although it was made possible by policies that at least gestured toward universalism, my family's story is not a universal one—the opportunities we have had were not and are not open to everyone. That is our national failure.

Equal Care

1

Introduction

During the pandemic before COVID, 2009's H1N1 influenza outbreak, I was a resident in primary care internal medicine in San Francisco. In the hospital, we provided care that would have seemed like science fiction only a generation or two before. Almost any failing organ could be supported with the right equipment and expertise. Continuous venovenous hemodialysis (CVVHD) did the work of kidneys. Extracorporeal membrane oxygenation (ECMO) replaced the function of hearts and lungs. Blood-clotting proteins were replaced with "factor" made using recombinant DNA. Remarkably during that pandemic, many who came in critically ill not only survived but had excellent recoveries—soon returning to being a parent, having a career, living their normal lives. Being part of this inpatient care was thrilling, and the more I learned the more amazed I was by medical technology.

As another part of my residency, one or two afternoons a week I went across the street from the hospital to the outpatient clinic building, where I had visits with primary care patients. The experience there was different. Instead of being awed by what modern medicine could accomplish, I was often angered by how little it had to offer. I would see a man whose diabetes remained uncontrolled because he could not afford healthy food to eat. A woman who missed chemotherapy to take her son to the emergency department when his asthma was exacerbated by their moldy apartment. One man was listed as my patient, but in three years I never actually met him, as he could not afford the trip into the office. The contrast between advanced medical technology and unmet basic needs was so stark that as I learned more during my training about social medicine and social epidemiology—

how social conditions affect the health of individuals and populations—it resonated with me in a way that CVVHD and ECMO did not.[1-3]

Within social medicine and epidemiology, one frequently encounters the metaphor of "thinking upstream."[4] This term notionally comes from a story about two doctors walking along a riverbank. When one of them notices a drowning child, they both jump in, quickly saving the child and returning to the shore. A moment later, another drowning child appears, who is again quickly saved. Then another. This time, one of the pair starts running desperately upstream. "Where are you going?" the other doctor asks, diving into the river once again. "I'm going to see about whoever is throwing the kids in!"

As a primary care doctor and health researcher, my day-to-day work is decidedly "downstream." Mostly, it consists of trying to mitigate the consequences of adverse social conditions, which still show up just as they did during my residency: as food insecurity (insufficient or uncertain access to healthy food[5]), or diabetes, or missed treatments. These consequences occur predictably among those who have experienced racism, or economic exploitation, or myriad other injustices. Given these facts, working downstream has never bothered me. If people are being thrown in to drown, then the world needs lifeguards.

But, in many ways, such "lifeguard" work is emblematic of an era that has coupled an increasingly sophisticated understanding of how injustice harms health with policies of technocratic tinkering meant to palliate injustice rather than cure it.[6] This has been justified as tractable harm-reduction for times when socially transformative policies that could eliminate injustice are politically impossible. But using health equity work to avoid political confrontation over social inequality risks accepting, and even normalizing, the production of health inequity. Managing, rather than challenging, injustice ultimately just makes the problem harder to solve. Instead, what the field of health equity needs is an egalitarian politics that directly challenges social inequality.

Central Premise and Goals

The central premise of this book is that health inequity is social failure embodied, and the only true cures are political. Health equity, I argue, is an inherently normative and political project. It can be achieved only through a policy regime that translates an abstract vision of justice into concrete, salutary, material conditions of equality throughout the entire system of social relations: civil, political, and economic. The overarching goal of this book is to synthesize three elements necessary for this political project—normative justification, mechanistic knowledge, and technical proficiency—into a theoretically sound and practical vision of what to work toward.

When I say that health equity can only be achieved politically, I am thinking of politics, in the words of political scientist Adolph Reed, "as a discrete sphere of activity directed toward the outward-looking project of affecting the social order, most effectively through creating, challenging or redefining institutions that anchor collective action with the objective of developing and wielding power."[7] The political project that I think is capable of achieving health equity is *social democracy*.

What is social democracy? The term has been used in various ways since it emerged in the 1800s. In this book, I use "social democracy" to mean a political project that seeks justice by bringing democratic relationships to all sites of human cooperation: in civil society, in political processes, and in economic activities.[8-11] Democratic relationships are egalitarian, meaning that they are based on a premise of the fundamental moral equality of all individuals. In a democratic relationship, everyone has a real say in matters that concern them, everyone's view counts for something, and everyone's interests are considered. Cooperation is undertaken because it is mutually desired, not because superiors impose their terms and inferiors resignedly acquiesce. A democratic relationship contrasts with a hierarchical one, where some have unaccountable authority or inherent esteem that subordinates others to them. Social democracy emphasizes what philosopher Elizabeth S. Anderson calls *relational equality*—equality of status or standing—as opposed to equality of, for example, well-being or income.[8,12,13] Though other forms of equality may reflect relational equality or help achieve it, these other forms of equality are not themselves the goal.

Democracy is concerned with making moral equality concrete through political practice—establishing a government that "secures the conditions of everyone's freedom."[8] In democratic government, everyone stands as an equal, and the state has a *duty of equal care*—an obligation to show equal concern for all of the lives over which it has dominion.[14] Democracy is not majoritarianism. In democracy, conflicting interests are adjudicated by a body that takes all interests seriously, whether in the majority or minority, using fair procedures that all could agree to. Moreover, a democratic state needs not only to protect the interests of those in the minority but to coordinate with those in the majority to further the interests of those in the minority.[9]

A key motivating question for this book is why, despite formal political and civil equality, there is substantive inequality in the United States. An important part of the answer is that despite formal civil and political equality, there is formal inequality in the economic sphere, particularly in laws and institutions related to the private ownership of productive assets and the employer-employee relationship. Social democracy seeks to bring democracy beyond its current limits so that it extends throughout the conditions in which people are "born, grow, work, live, and age"[3]—and so that all people have the freedom to participate in society as equal partners.

The mechanism to do this is the *egalitarian state*. The egalitarian state consists of all the aspects of the state that help fulfill the state's duty of equal care. One key part of the egalitarian state is the "welfare state"—policies and programs that provide income support and social services necessary to meet basic needs.[15] But the egalitarian state is broader than the welfare state and also includes aspects related to economic production, along with civil and political rights. A major concern of the egalitarian state is that society's distributive institutions—such as labor markets, tax-and-transfer systems, and property rights regimes—distribute the national income in ways consistent with equality of social standing.

Health Equity and the Special Importance of Health

A book about health equity invites reflection on its importance. Why does health, of everything injustice can affect, deserve special attention? In short, health is of special importance because good health helps people live the lives they want to live. Poor health can shorten a life span or foreclose the chance for a person to pursue their vision of a good life. Health is fundamentally freedom enhancing—it facilitates the exercise of other capabilities people may have.[16] In the words of economist Amartya Sen, "removing deprivations of health and addressing issues of health injustice is, thus, central to expanding significant human capabilities and freedoms that we have reason to value."[16(pviii)]

Achieving health equity is primarily about justice in a system of social relations, not about personal health care. This is not to say that health care is unimportant. The unfair way we allocate access to health care in the United

States contributes greatly to health inequity. Universally available health care of equal quality for all should be a central goal of social policy. Moreover, health care delivery in the United States is often discriminatory and reproduces systems of oppression, and this, too, must be addressed to achieve health equity. But as important as these issues are, the factors that occur outside of health care, which pattern living conditions, opportunities, and expectations about what kind of life is achievable, are more important.

Plan of the Book

The three sections of this book provide a normatively justified vision of health equity, describe the pathophysiologic and social mechanisms that link injustice to poor health, and discuss how policy that can achieve the goals of social democracy works.

Chapter 2 begins the first section by critiquing the predominant way of thinking about health inequity—as differences in health outcomes across categories of individuals, or the subset of those differences that are avoidable and unfair ("disparities").[17,18] It proposes an alternative approach that views health inequity as *injustice that harms health*.

Chapter 3 provides an analysis of what type of equality should be sought and critiques several common conceptions of equality. The chapter also introduces a theme that will recur throughout the book: the idea that the economy is essentially a government program, created and maintained by state institutions.[19-21] Those institutions, such as property rights, need to be justified by producing just outcomes. A major impediment to policy that can achieve health equity is the mistaken belief in a natural (external to the state) entitlement to wages and other market income, with the implication that taxation means expropriation.[19]

Chapter 4 provides a detailed explication of the normative underpinnings of social democracy, drawing in particular from Anderson's "democratic equality."[8] Democratic equality emphasizes a system of social relations that both recognizes people as equals and distributes resources to help make such equality substantive. This is important because these issues compound each other, with lack of social standing often leading to material deprivation, and material deprivation reinforcing the perceived inferiority of those denied social standing.

Chapter 5 begins the second section of the book by introducing epidemiologist Nancy Krieger's idea of health as an "emergent embodied phenotype," which arises from an individual's history as an organism enmeshed within both a biophysical world and a system of social relations.[22] I then discuss epidemiological theories and common mechanisms—pathways of embodiment—that clarify how unjust social relations harm health. Ultimately, chapter 5 provides empirical support for the idea that achieving the normative goals of social democracy will improve health.

Chapter 6 gives special focus to issues of inegalitarian ideologies, exemplified by racism, as forms of oppression that harm health.[22-27] It further discusses the concept of intersectionality in the context of health equity.

Chapter 7 begins the third section of the book. It opens with a discussion of why the welfare state is essential to the egalitarian state. In a market economy, income is principally distributed through ownership of productive assets or working for wages. This income provides individuals with purchasing power that lets them consume the products needed for health. Without that purchasing power, poor health results. However, people frequently inhabit roles, such as older age, childhood, and disability, such that they are unable, and not expected, to earn income from wages. In fact, at any given time, about 50 percent of the US population falls into such roles, and over the life course everyone does.[28] In these situations, the welfare state can provide *transfer income* (income received without the exchange of goods or services) for those who do not receive *factor income* (income from land, labor, or capital—the factors of production), enabling all individuals to obtain the products needed for health. Chapter 7 also discusses two approaches to implementing the welfare state, *universalism* and *residualism*, which reflect fundamentally different values.[8,29-32] Universalism creates "first-line" programs to be used by all who need them, framing program access as social rights.[31-34] Residualism views state benefits as backup plans, to be used for "residual" needs not met through the market, family support, or private charity. In many ways, residualism is a form of public charity. A hallmark of residualism is *means testing*, meant to help ensure a program is only used by those below a certain level of income and/or assets. This creates two ways that people meet needs—a "regular" way used by those who are better off, and a "safety net" for those who are worse off. Such stratification undermines equal social standing. A recurring theme in this book is that residualism does not show equal care for individuals.

Chapter 8 discusses concepts from economic theory that are important for a technical understanding of how the egalitarian state is to pursue its goals. It also describes basic types of policy instruments and introduces a way to think about which products necessary for health are best allocated by the market, and which are best provided publicly.

Chapter 9 discusses public finance, including taxation. A key point is that taxes are not a necessary evil. Instead, they are elegant solutions to difficult collective action problems. This chapter also introduces the idea of the social wealth fund, an important policy tool that can help achieve social democratic goals.

Chapter 10 discusses issues of policy implementation, including state legitimacy and policy design choices that can make policies more likely to achieve their intended effects—or more likely to fail.

Chapter 11 marks a shift from general policy concepts to specific policy areas. It covers transfer income policy and considerations about when transfer income should take the form of in-kind services rather than cash benefits. It further discusses three products best provided as in-kind services: education, health care, and personal care.

Chapter 12 continues the discussion of transfer income policy, focusing on approaches to cash benefits, such as social insurance and universal basic income.

Chapter 13 discusses factor income policy, including the fundamental policy goal of redressing the structural imbalance of power between workers and employers that a regime of private property in productive assets creates. It further discusses labor market institutions, including collective bargaining, and issues related to full employment.

Chapter 14 addresses, briefly, civil and political rights, including how the failure to achieve substantive economic rights undermines formal equality in the sphere of civil and political rights.

Finally, Chapter 15 concludes with a restatement of the main arguments in the book and offers specific policy areas where it may be possible to make practical progress.

Knowledge Problems and Power Problems

Every society has a set of institutions that allocate power and distribute resources. When those institutions are unjust, health inequity results. The crucial normative questions we should ask are about what makes those institutions just, and the crucial technical questions we should ask are about how those institutions should be configured to achieve their normative goals. Rather than focusing on particular policy recommendations, which I believe should instead derive from a specific context and result from democratic deliberation, the aim of this book is to provide a basis for thinking through questions about how to structure a society's institutions to achieve health equity. In other words, this book is intended in a spirit economist John Maynard Keynes meant when he wrote, "the object of our analysis is, not to provide a machine, or method of blind manipulation, which will furnish an infallible answer, but to provide ourselves with an organised and orderly method of thinking out particular problems."[35(p297)]

I began this chapter by reflecting on a strange juxtaposition I experienced at the beginning of my career: the exceptional technological achievements of modern biomedicine contrasted with an inattention to the basics that everyone needs for health. At that time, I viewed this as a knowledge problem—a problem of not knowing how best to address people's basic needs when they go unmet. There is, no doubt, still much to be learned in this regard. But I no longer see health inequity as primarily a knowledge problem. Instead, it is a power problem. What we lack are people with the power and will to apply the knowledge we do have to the problem of health inequity. My hope, probably a naïve one, is that this book will contribute to the development of a coalition that will solve this power problem. A system of social relations that we have reason to value shows equal care for everyone's life, and health equity would be one of its finest achievements.

2

What Is Health Equity?

The World Health Organization defines health equity as "the absence of unfair and avoidable or remediable differences in health among population groups defined socially, economically, demographically or geographically."[1] In the United States, the Healthy People 2020 project[2] influentially defined healthy equity as "attainment of the highest level of health for all people," and the US Centers for Disease Control and Prevention's (CDC) Office of Minority Health and Health Equity says that "health equity is when everyone has the opportunity to be as healthy as possible."[3]

These definitions all seem similar, but they hide within them two distinct approaches to the concept of health equity. Both approaches assess health equity by comparing observed health to some reference standard. However, the approaches differ in what standard is used. The first approach—*disparitarianism**—compares the health of categories of individuals who have experienced injustice to the health of categories of individuals thought not to have experienced the same injustice. The second approach—*health justice*—compares the health of individuals or categories of individuals thought to

---

* My concern throughout this book is to use terminology carefully and precisely, but not in a doctrinaire way. That is, I will try to introduce terms to indicate what I think are substantive rather than merely semantic distinctions. This point is relevant to health equity terminology like "disparities" and "inequities." I use the term "disparitarian" to describe a point of view that emphasizes difference in some health outcome between individuals in one category compared with individuals in another category as the metric of health equity. In the United States, this kind of difference, if it is also unjust, is commonly called a disparity owing, I think, to the influence of the "disparate impact" standard in US civil rights law. In Europe, my sense is that unjust differences of this kind are generally termed "inequities"

have experienced injustice to what their health would have been had they not experienced injustice.

If we take a disparitarian perspective, health inequity involves a difference in health outcomes between categories of individuals. If we take a health justice perspective, though, health inequity is an injustice that harms health, without requiring a comparison to another category of individuals. Thus, disparitarianism emphasizes using other observed categories of individuals for comparison, while health justice emphasizes making counterfactual comparisons—comparisons between an observed health state and the health state that would have been observed under more just conditions (figure 2.1). In this chapter, I will describe these two approaches in more detail, highlight problems with disparitarianism, discuss why health justice presents a workable solution to those problems, and give examples of how to conduct health equity inquiry using the health justice approach.

Before moving on, I want to be clear that health equity practitioners using the disparitarian and health justice approaches frequently have the same goals and motives, and often the same individuals employ the different approaches in different circumstances. This is not a case of "disparitarianism bad, health justice good." Disparitarian health equity inquiry has been critical for calling attention to the problem of health inequity. However, disparitarianism also has limitations, which have become increasingly apparent. At this point, not adopting alternative approaches that overcome those limitations is likely to hinder progress toward health equity.

Disparitarian and Health Justice Approaches to Health Equity

Disparitarianism is currently the dominant approach to health equity inquiry and praxis. Central to disparitarianism is the concept of disparity. Disparities are differences in health outcomes between categories of individuals defined socially, economically, demographically, or geographically (for

---

rather than "disparities." Whether the term "disparity" or "inequity" is preferred, the point of agreement is that differences between categories of individuals are the key indicators of injustice. Thus, the point of view I describe as disparitarian encompasses work that is fundamentally about making between-category comparisons, whatever the term used to describe differences found after making those comparisons. On the other hand, when those adopting the health justice perspective use the term "health inequity," the meaning is a health state that has resulted from injustice, not necessarily a difference in health states across categories of individuals (although such a difference often does result from injustice).

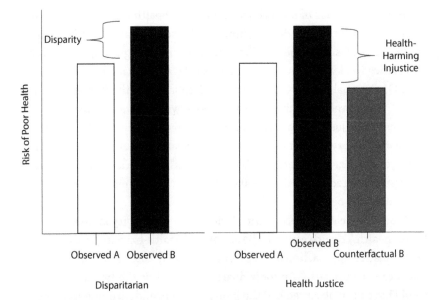

Figure 2.1. The difference between the disparitarian approach, which compares observed health outcomes across two different categories of individuals (observed A and observed B), and the health justice approach, which compares an observed health outcome to a counterfactual health outcome—the health outcome that would have occurred for the same individuals in the absence of injustice (observed B and counterfactual B). Information about observed A may be useful for estimating counterfactual B, but observed A and observed B are not directly compared.

example, between men and women or between Hispanic and non-Hispanic individuals) that are, in the words of an influential early definition, "unnecessary and avoidable, but in addition are considered unfair and unjust."[4,5] What I term *disparitarianism* is the idea that disparities are the lens through which one should study, and the primary metric of, health equity.[6,7] Because disparities are a subset of differences in health outcomes between categories of individuals, between-category differences are a necessary component of health inequity under disparitarianism. Therefore, the key disparitarian health equity questions are whether there are differences in health outcomes between categories of individuals, and whether those differences are avoidable and unjust (although in practice this second question is not always given due emphasis). On the disparitarian account, when disparities exist, health inequity exists. When disparities are reduced, health equity has improved. Examples of disparitarianism in US health equity discourse include the Institute of Medicine's (now the National Academy of Medicine) landmark 2003 study Unequal Treatment: Confronting Racial and Ethnic Disparities in Health Care[8]; the Agency for Health Research and Quality's (AHRQ) National Health Care Disparities Report[9]; Healthy People 2020 and 2030[2,10,11]; and health equity reports from nongovernmental organizations.[12,13]

The health justice approach differs from disparitarianism by not using between-category difference as its metric of health inequity. Instead, health justice emphasizes counterfactual comparisons between an observed health state that resulted from injustice and what health state might have occurred had conditions been just.

From the health justice point of view, health inequity is injustice that harms health.* Health equity is the absence of health-harming injustice. The health justice approach makes use of a particular counterfactual outcome that I call "just health." An individual's just health is the health state that would have been observed had the individual's life and its influences** been spent in a just system of social relations. When conceptualizing just health, the health state must be feasible given the resources, knowledge, and technology available to the society in question. This follows from the principle that "ought" implies "can." Further, just health is not the highest possible level of health. Better levels of health that could be obtained through luck or injustice, for example, do not figure into just health.

Both disparitarianism and health justice require a working theory of justice. In disparitarian approaches, this is used to determine whether a difference is a disparity; in health justice approaches, this is used to determine whether a system of social relations is just (theories of justice are discussed in chapters 3 and 4).

The key questions for health equity inquiry using a health justice approach are whether an injustice has occurred and whether the observed health state, which resulted from that injustice, is different than an individ-

---

*Again, the distinction between the disparitarian and health justice approaches is that under disparitarianism the meaning of "inequity" is a difference (literally an inequality), while for health justice the meaning of "inequity" is an injustice.

**Influences are conditions that affect an individual's life even before they were alive. For example, if one's mother, prior to conception, was exposed to a mutagen that subsequently affected one's health, the mutagen exposure would be an "influence." Injustice can have intergenerational effects.

ual's just health. Health equity is achieved when there is no health-harming injustice.* When injustice has occurred and harmed health, (just) interventions can seek to mitigate those harms and eliminate recurrence of injustice. If they succeed, they reduce health inequity. This is a gradient conception of health equity—a society gets closer to health equity when its system of social relations changes in a just way and results in a health state that is closer to an individual's just health. Health equity for any category of individuals can be considered the aggregated form of this definition—in other words, health equity for a category of individuals occurs when its members do not experience injustice that harms health.

The Trouble with Disparitarianism

The hallmark of disparitarianism is the assessment of between-category difference.[14] Differences are the disparitarian metric of health equity—when there are no differences, the distribution of the health outcome cannot be judged to be unjust. This is where the fundamental problem with disparitarianism lies. Disparitarianism explicitly seeks parity rather than explicitly seeking justice. But there is no inherent relationship between parity and justice—parity is only important if it reflects that the pattern of outcomes arose justly. Some differences in outcomes will result from injustices and should be remedied. Some differences will be just and should not be. And some injustices will not result in a difference, which disparitarianism misses entirely. Health outcomes that are equally bad can still be unjust. Thus, between-category difference has substantial limitations as a metric of injustice.

This section details six common problems with disparitarianism.

Parity Hiding Injustice

Because parity in health (or other) outcomes between categories of individuals can hide other types of injustices, a situation judged to be just by a disparitarian standard may still involve injustice. One way this occurs relates to disparitarianism's reliance on a reference category, thought to be better off in some way than individuals in the category of interest, for mak-

---

*Logically, health equity under this definition could occur in the presence of injustice that is not health harming. There would, of course, be reasons besides health to work against those injustices.

ing comparisons. This can ignore the level of health experienced by those in the reference category. For example, by March 2021, the COVID-19 mortality rate for non-Hispanic Black individuals in the United States was 179.8 per 100,000 population.[15] For non-Hispanic White individuals, the mortality rate was 150.2 per 100,000 population. Since these differences (29.6 deaths per 100,000 population on the absolute scale, or a risk ratio of 1.2—20 percent more—on the relative scale) in mortality rates are likely due to avoidable and unjust differences in social circumstances, they are disparities. But at the same time, the COVID-19 mortality rate in Canada, for the population overall, was 62.9 per 100,000 population.[16] Even if COVID-19 mortality for non-Hispanic Black individuals in the United States had been exactly the same as for non-Hispanic White individuals in the United States, mortality would still have been more than twice as great as it might have been, as there is no reason to think that the mortality rate achieved in Canada could not have been achieved in the United States under more just conditions. Thus, parity between non-Hispanic Black and non-Hispanic White individuals would still have hidden an important injustice.

Of course, disparitarianism could accommodate this. There could be a separate account of disparities between the United States and Canada added to the account of disparities between non-Hispanic Black and non-Hispanic White individuals in the United States. But disparitarianism does not inherently focus on the level of health experienced by those in the reference category, which makes it easy to ignore. Disparitarianism can produce a kind of tunnel vision that misses unjustly low levels of health for individuals in the reference category. By focusing on only one aspect of injustice, the between-category difference, disparitarianism may ignore other parts of the total injustice. Moreover, this will tend to *underestimate* the injustice experienced by individuals in the category of interest.[17] This is not simply a theoretical concern. As an example, an official webpage from the CDC about health equity in COVID-19 outcomes focuses only on between-category differences in health outcomes in the United States.[18]

Another way that parity can hide injustice relates to injustices that occur within a given category of individuals. Disparitarianism frequently frames health equity questions as comparisons between categories defined by a single aspect of identity (or a small number of aspects). For example, AHRQ's National Health Care Disparities Report publishes disparity data only by single category characteristics (e.g., race and ethnicity, or gender, or income).[9]

But framing comparisons in this way can hide injustice that is equipropor-tional within categories. In other words, parity (independence between cat-egory membership and a health outcome) does not imply a just distribution of that outcome.

Consider the following example. There is a disparity in age-standardized mortality between non-Hispanic Black adults (1,307 per 100,000 standard population in 2017) and non-Hispanic White adults (1,137 per 100,000 stan-dard population in 2017).[19] Further, income is very unequally distributed be-tween non-Hispanic Black and non-Hispanic White households.[20] In 2017, for non-Hispanic Black households, 58.3 percent have income below $50,000 a year, and 3.1 percent have income above $200,000 a year, while for non-Hispanic White households the numbers were 37.6 percent below $50,000 and 8.9 percent above $200,000. Given the strong connection between in-come and mortality,[21] the income distribution may explain part (though cer-tainly not all) of the mortality disparity between non-Hispanic Black and non-Hispanic White adults.

Now, imagine two hypothetical interventions to address this dispar-ity. Intervention A reshuffles incomes such that the income distribution for non-Hispanic Black individuals now matches the income distribution of non-Hispanic White individuals—37.6 percent of non-Hispanic Black indi-viduals now live in households with incomes below $50,000 and 8.9 percent in households with incomes above $200,000 (and the other particulars of the income distribution all match). As a result of intervention A, the mor-tality gap between non-Hispanic Black and non-Hispanic White individuals improves.

Intervention B compresses the income distribution—increasing the in-come of everyone (regardless of race and ethnicity) with less than $50,000 and reducing the income of those with incomes above $200,000. Given the pre-intervention income distribution, intervention B would disproportion-ately, though not exclusively, benefit non-Hispanic Black individuals, and so also reduces the mortality disparity. Suppose that the specifics of interven-tion B were such that it reduced the mortality disparity to exactly the same extent as intervention A. Given the effect of intervention B on incomes for poorer non-Hispanic White individuals, it would likely have additional benefits not captured by examining the non-Hispanic White/non-Hispanic Black disparity alone. With a similar impact on parity and a greater impact on overall mortality, intervention B seems preferable to intervention A.

However, a disparitarian approach may well be insensitive to the advantages of intervention B. Some might even say that intervention B is not an intervention for non-Hispanic Black individuals at all. If the metric of health equity is a difference between non-Hispanic Black and non-Hispanic White individuals, one would have no reason to prefer intervention B over intervention A on health equity grounds—one would be indifferent. Figure 2.2 provides a more detailed examination of this problem.

One response to this issue is to create more nuanced categories—perhaps creating four categories defined by income along with race and ethnicity (lower income non-Hispanic Black, lower income non-Hispanic White, higher income non-Hispanic Black, and higher income non-Hispanic White). Indeed, health equity work often considers questions in this way, based on one interpretation of the concept of *intersectionality*, sometimes called inter-categorical intersectionality.[22-25] Understanding how racism and income combine to shape health is an important topic, as is intersectionality more broadly (the concept is discussed in more detail in chapter 6). However, inter-categorical intersectionality, like disparitarianism, emphasizes between-category comparisons and thus presents many of the same limitations.[26]

Between-category comparisons are forms of stratified analysis. But stratification is not well suited for studying the joint effects of racism and income on health.[27] Stratification-based approaches work by limiting the variation of some factors in order to better understand the consequences of variation in other factors. As an example, examining mortality disparities between lower income non-Hispanic Black and lower income non-Hispanic White individuals would limit the variation in income. But since the intersectional question is not "How does racism, independent of income, affect health?" but rather, "How do racism and income jointly affect health?" this approach will be of little use. Indeed, to the extent that aspects of racism (say, employment discrimination) lead to lower income for non-Hispanic Black individuals, a stratified analysis would misunderstand how racism and income affect health by omitting the role of employment discrimination in causing lower income. Moreover, it would say nothing about the justice of the income distribution, even if that distribution were equiproportional across racial categories.

This limitation of disparitarianism can be put to use by those with inegalitarian motives who want to "equity-wash" their actions. For example, disparitarian analysis could serve as misdirection by focusing attention on a

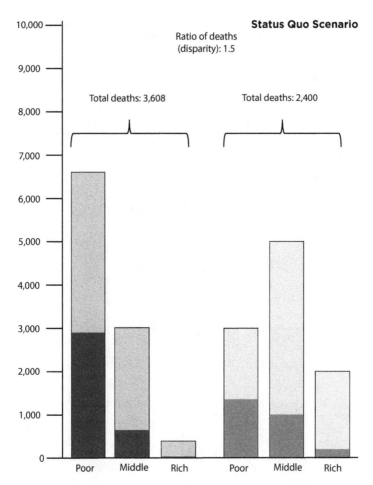

Figure 2.2. A key problem with disparitarianism is parity hiding injustice. In this three-part stylized example, there are two categories of equal size at the start of an observation period: those with blue eyes (*left in each figure,* representing a disadvantaged category) and those with green eyes (*right in each figure,* representing an advantaged category). The height of the bars in each instance represents the proportion of the population by income levels (poor, middle income, or rich), and the darker shaded areas represent the proportion of individuals within that income level who die during the observation period. Risk of death is highest for those with the lowest income and lowest for those who have the highest income. Given discrimination in the status quo, a greater proportion of blue-eyed individuals (compared with green-eyed individuals) are in lower income categories. At every income level, risk of death is 10% higher for those with blue eyes than green eyes, reflecting that the disparity has additional causes beyond income. Total mortality in each category and the ratio of deaths between blue-eyed and green-eyed individuals (a measure of disparity) are listed above each scenario. Figure 2.2A depicts the status quo, while on subsequent pages 2.2B depicts intervention A and 2.2C depicts intervention B.

Continued

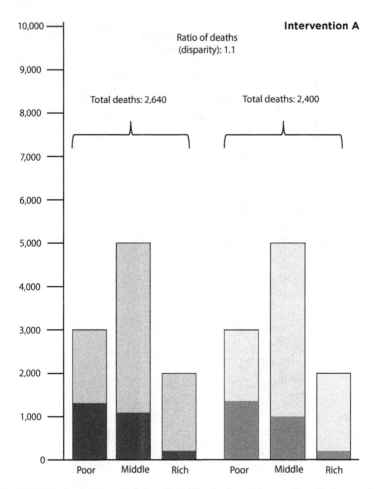

Figure 2.2B. Intervention A shows the effect of an intervention that equalizes the income distribution across categories (i.e., it puts blue-eyed individuals into the same income distribution as green-eyed individuals).

particular disparity (or lack thereof) in order to divert attention from other injustices—particularly in cases where addressing those other injustices might require a more substantive reassessment of power relations.[14] In other words, one form of equity-washing is pointing to the lack of disparity to legitimate remaining injustices.

Overall, the disparitarian vision of justice is often piecemeal, focusing on pairwise comparisons between categories of individuals rather than being more encompassing.

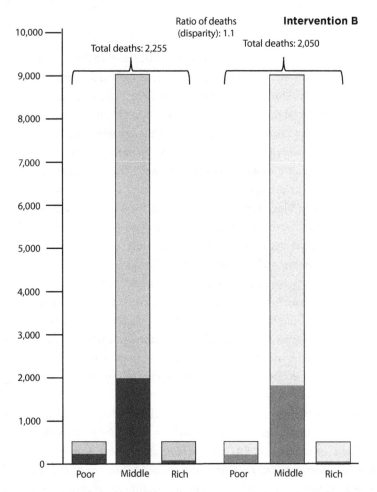

Figure 2.2C. Intervention B shows the effect of addressing the income distribution directly, improving the disparity to the same extent as intervention A (2.2B) while also lowering total mortality compared with intervention A or the status quo (2.2A).

Indifference to How Parity Occurs

Mathematically, a reduction in disparity can occur when worse-off individuals get better, better-off individuals get worse, or some combination of both. Of course, health equity practitioners generally recognize that "leveling down"—a reduction in disparities caused by better-off individuals getting worse—is not desirable and would prefer to reduce disparities by "leveling up"—that is, differentially improving the health of worse-off individuals. However, this distinction is sometimes elided. For example, in response to racial disparities in health outcomes during the COVID-19 pandemic, the state of Michigan issued a press release[28] on September 28, 2020, that contained the following statement praising "the administration's efforts to tackle racial disparities": "While Black residents only make up 15% of Michigan's population, they represented a staggering 29.4% of the cases and 40.7% of the deaths in the early days of tracking COVID-19 data based on race. In the past two weeks of available data, the state has seen significant progress in limiting the disparate impact of COVID-19 on communities of color, with Black residents accounting for 8.2% of cases and 9.9% of deaths." But this statement omitted that through April 12, 2020,[29] the first six weeks of the pandemic in Michigan, there were 24,635 confirmed coronavirus cases (approximately 8,130 in Black individuals) and 1,483 coronavirus deaths in the state (594 in Black individuals).* By September 27, 2020, just before the statement was released, there had been 134,373 confirmed cases (27,260 in Black individuals) and 7,044 deaths (2,683 in Black individuals). Thus, the improvement in disparities the statement mentions occurred in a setting where cases and deaths had increased dramatically for all categories of individuals. It is not clear that such a scenario represents a meaningful improvement in health equity.

The problem of leveling down could perhaps be corrected by adding a condition that improvements in disparities only count when they do not result from leveling down. But while seemingly sensible, this would run into another problem: not only is disparitarianism indifferent to changes in disparities achieved by leveling down versus leveling up, it cannot distinguish between situations where leveling down is problematic and when it is not. For example, imagine a situation where heart failure outcomes are better among individuals in one racial category, compared with another. This difference stems from discrimination, whereby those in one category are differentially less likely to receive heart transplants despite having similar clinical characteristics, because they are thought likely to "waste" the transplant through "non-compliance." The difference in outcomes is avoidable and unjust. Further, imagine that demand for heart transplantation greatly exceeds supply—this is a zero-sum game. Removing discrimination as a barrier to

---

* The press release does not give an exact time frame for the "early days," but these numbers yield percentages that are close to those quoted.

heart transplantation will have the effect of worsening health for individuals from the favored category, as, owing to scarcity, fewer individuals in that category will now receive a heart transplant. This will appear as if an improvement in disparities has been, at least partially, achieved by leveling down the health of those in the better-off category.

There is a difference between this scenario and the Michigan COVID-19 scenario, however. In the COVID-19 scenario, a more just policy response might have improved outcomes for Black individuals and White individuals alike. For the heart transplantation example, however, favored individuals essentially received ill-gotten gains—they unjustly benefited from discrimination. Leveling down is unjust in the COVID-19 example, but in the heart transplantation example it is consistent with justice. Disparitarianism, however, does not provide a clear way to distinguish these situations.

Just Difference

The third problem with disparitarianism is that sometimes parity, or even a gap that is too small, can represent injustice. For example, women suffering acute coronary syndrome are more likely to be subjected to diagnostic errors than men—their symptoms are often attributed to less serious conditions, and they may not receive lifesaving therapy.[30-34] Sexism, operating in this case as stereotypes about unreliable symptom reporting and somatization, is a likely explanation for this phenomenon. Since any differences in health outcomes caused by this sexist treatment would clearly be avoidable and unjust, this would seem to be a classic case of disparity. But women do not have greater heart disease mortality than men. For example, in 2017 heart disease mortality for men was 216.9 per 100,000, whereas for women it was 181.2 per 100,000.[35] But what if, in the absence of sexism, women would have even better cardiovascular health outcomes—perhaps the mortality rate for women would have been 160 per 100,000? In this case, parity of outcomes, or even outcomes that are still better for women, might result from injustice. Surely this should count as health inequity, but the disparitarian approach may ignore it. It is hard to explain, in disparitarian terms, the injustice in a difference being too small.

This problem also arises when category membership is inherently correlated with health outcomes owing to reverse causation. For example, poor health can cause lower education or lower income. Thus, there may be differences in health outcomes across categories defined by education or income, even in the absence of injustice. This makes examining injustice experienced by individuals with lower education or income using disparitarian approaches difficult, if not completely infeasible.

Requiring a Comparison Category

A fourth problem with disparitarianism is that assessment of parity may simply not be possible. For example, imagine that a particular genetic abnormality occurs almost exclusively in those of one ethnicity, as, for example, Tay-Sachs disease occurs almost exclusively in Ashkenazi Jews. Further, imagine that people with this ethnicity are treated unjustly, such that they are frequently poor, lack health insurance, and suffer discrimination when they do access health care. All of this results in worse health outcomes. Now, imagine a study that compares this usual state of poverty and discrimination to an intervention that provides income support, health care access, and compassionate care—and finds that those who receive the intervention have much better health outcomes. By improving health through combating injustice, it would seem that the intervention has improved health equity. But the disparitarian approach cannot account for this. As the genetic condition occurs almost exclusively in members of the particular ethnic category, there is no better-off category to compare against. The disparitarian approach breaks down when it is unable to make between-category comparisons, but not all types of health-harming injustices can be measured by between-category comparisons.

Category-Level Analysis

A fifth problem is that not only does the disparitarian approach require at least two categories to compare, but it is only relevant for describing the experience of categories of individuals, not individuals as individuals. In other words, disparitarianism is only applicable at the category level. But this is a reification. Categories do not experience injustice or poor health—individuals do. This means that gaps between categories, in and of themselves, may not be meaningful outcomes. It is the injustice experienced by individuals, or the intervention that addresses it, that is meaningful. Further, a category-level focus inherently means aggregating the experience of many individuals—individuals whose personal experience may differ substantially from the central tendency. This can ignore heterogeneity of experience within a given category. The heterogeneity ignored could be at a finer level of the category—for example, those working on issues of Hispanic and Asian American health equity often highlight the need to disaggregate these categories.[36] Moreover, an individual who is a member of a category that, on average, experiences injustice may not have themselves experienced an injustice that harms their health. Conversely, a member of a category that, on average, experiences little injustice may nevertheless have experienced injustice that harmed their health. These are health equity issues that disparitarianism cannot recognize.

Emphasizing Description over Explanation

A sixth problem of disparitarianism is not inherent to the method but is a common problem in its everyday use by health equity practitioners. In practice, the bread and butter of disparitarian scholarship is to document differences in health outcomes between categories of individuals. But beyond demonstrating these differences, there may be little motivation to explain what causes those differences. In fact, a common methodological approach in disparitarian research is to demonstrate that a difference exists even after investigators adjust for some of the very mediators that help explain why the difference exists. For example, a study examining the difference in hemoglobin A1c levels between individuals with diabetes who primarily speak English versus Spanish might find that there is a difference after adjusting for health insurance coverage and report that there are disparities "independent of" health insurance. This could be useful, because it might be understood as indicating that addressing health insurance differences alone may not bring the outcomes to parity. But the tendency for many studies to simply conclude with the fact that unspecified residual factors must account for some of the difference works against understanding and intervening on the forces that create the differences in outcomes.

Some of this tendency may come from the relationship between disparitarianism and the disparate impact standard in civil rights law.[37] Demonstrating a difference in outcomes is often easier than elucidating the causes of that difference (for example, in the legal context, establishing that a racial animus caused differences in hiring). Thus, the disparate impact standard makes civil rights enforcement more tractable than applying a standard where discriminatory intent has to be proven. This is an important advantage in the legal context, but it may be a disadvantage in the scientific context, where the goal is to understand and explain. Because the categories used for disparitarian analysis (e.g., race or gender) do not have causal power, finding that health outcomes vary across these categories does not establish the causes of those differences. Instead, it is injustices experienced by individuals in those categories (e.g., injustices that may fall under the broad heading of racism or sexism) that can have explanatory power. However, specific interrogation of these mechanisms is often omitted in disparitarian studies. This tendency to emphasize description over explanation is not insurmountable—explanatory work is done sometimes—but it is worth reflecting on whether the approach encourages this tendency by not putting specific injustices front and center.

Moving on from Disparitarianism

The above examples highlight six problems with disparitarianism—that is, framing health equity as a question of between-category difference. These problems are: (1) parity hiding injustice, (2) indifference to how parity occurs, (3) just difference, (4) requiring a comparison category, (5) category-level focus, and (6) emphasizing description over explanation. Taken together, these problems mean that the concept of disparities is less useful for health equity work than typically assumed. This is not to say the concept is never useful—demonstrating disparities has been an important way to call out injustice, and certainly disparitarian inquiry has pushed the field forward. But disparities are an imperfect metric because there are many health-harming injustices that they do not detect. This can occur when the health of individuals in the oppressed category is harmed by injustice but still better than the health of individuals in the reference category, when there is no relevant reference category, or when there is also injustice that harms the heath of individuals in the reference category (or both categories) that is hidden within the disparity metric. Moreover, and perhaps more importantly, reducing disparities is an imperfect target for interventions. Disparities can indicate injustice, but it does not follow that eliminating disparities achieves justice. This is because a reduction in disparities need not imply a reduction in injustice, and in fact it can be consistent with increasing injustice.

Health Justice

Health justice approaches health equity counterfactually—as a comparison between what was observed and what might have been observed under more just conditions. This helps to avoid the problems of disparitarianism.

Advantages of Health Justice

First, as the name implies, the health justice approach places issues of justice front and center. For example, using the health justice approach, the issue of COVID-19 mortality for non-Hispanic Black individuals could be cast not as a comparison between non-Hispanic Black and non-Hispanic White individuals but as a comparison between observed mortality for non-Hispanic Black individuals and the mortality that would have been observed had social conditions been just. To investigate that, one could draw not only from mortality observed among non-Hispanic White individuals in the United States, who might provide information about what would be observed in the absence of anti-Black racism, but also mortality observed in other societies with different patterns of social relations. Of course, any attempt to estimate what might have occurred will have important uncertainty. But making counterfactual comparisons is helpful because it means considering what the level of health should be, rather than defaulting to the level of health of individuals in another category (under conditions that may not have done justice to those individuals either).

In addition, health justice helps avoid the issue of ignoring within-category injustice because it encourages examination of all injustice that harms health. In the income distribution example above, health justice would recognize the greater improvement in health equity offered by the second, compared with the first, intervention.

Moreover, health justice can distinguish leveling up from leveling down. If presented with a change in a between-category difference in health outcomes, one can use the health justice approach to examine whether the change was caused by less injustice for those who are worse off or more injustice for those who are better off. Further, one can use the health justice approach to distinguish when leveling down is acceptable and when it is not. In the organ transplantation example, the high level of health for individuals who benefitted from discrimination was unjust. Since that level of health would not occur under just conditions, moving away from it is no injustice.

Another advantage of health justice is that it can handle situations of "just difference"—where injustice might result in a difference that is too small rather than too large. The case of diagnostic error for acute coronary syndrome in women illustrates this. Working with a health justice approach, one could investigate what women's heart disease mortality would be if they did not experience sexist disbelief of their symptoms. To do so, one could estimate rates of misdiagnosis for men and women, the number of deaths attributable to misdiagnosis of this type in women, the number of those deaths that occur due to "excess" misdiagnosis (owing to sexism), and subtract those excess deaths from the observed deaths. Information about achievable levels of diagnostic error could be learned from studying men, but then applied to estimating a heart disease mortality rate that is still sensitive to reasons for lower heart disease mortality in women that are not unjust. Though simplified, this example suggests possibilities for meaningful health equity inquiry that are hard to frame under disparitarianism.

An additional advantage is that the health justice approach does not require a comparison category. In the genetic abnormality example, comparing outcomes under conditions of discrimination to conditions without discrimination makes clear that health equity has improved.

Finally, one more advantage of the health justice approach is that it can be applied to the individual, as well as the category, level. It is perfectly sensible to ask how a particular injustice harmed the health of a specific individual.

Health Justice and Health Equity Inquiry

Health justice works to reorder the workflow of health equity inquiry in important ways. With disparitarianism, an investigator compares health outcomes for individuals in one category to outcomes for individuals in a reference category (often presuming that such categories are meaningful). If a difference is present, the investigator judges whether that difference is unjust and avoidable.* For example, an investigator might first evaluate whether there is a difference in diabetes outcomes between men and women, and then determine whether that difference is avoidable and unjust. This

---

*Although the idea of avoidability and injustice are central to determining that a difference is in fact a disparity, these aspects often are implied rather than explicit in disparitarian studies. For example, a study may document a difference in diabetes prevalence between individuals in advantaged and disadvantaged categories, and call that difference a disparity. The study may not, however, provide an explicit account of why that difference is avoidable and unjust. Despite the common omission of such arguments, I think disparitarian studies generally do report differences that are truly disparities.

workflow does not require the specification of any injustice in advance, and so such studies may not seek to uncover specific injustices that explain the disparity; may only consider injustice in a speculative, post hoc, fashion; and may not engage with prior scholarship.[38] Although using a disparitarian approach could identify a problem, it is not inherently connected to identifying causal mechanisms in either an etiologic sense (to understand what caused the outcome, specifically) or an interventional sense (to understand what intervening on the mechanism would do). Empirically, identification of disparities in research has often borne little relationship to improving them.

Using the health justice approach, investigators select injustices to study and make comparisons between the observed health outcome and the health outcome that would have been observed had the injustice not occurred. For example, one might judge food insecurity an injustice and then estimate whether diabetes outcomes are worse for those who had experienced food insecurity, compared with a counterfactual situation in which they had not. This focuses squarely on injustice as an explanation for health outcomes. It also facilitates both elucidating etiology and intervention, and it motivates engagement with prior scholarship on the topic of the specific injustices studied.*

Traits versus States

Another way to understand this issue is that disparitarianism often focuses on *traits* that are not directly modifiable, while health justice focuses on temporally located *states*. For example, examining disparities by race or gender uses these traits as categories of analysis. This can give rise to misperceptions that the trait (e.g., race) is somehow causally related to the disparity, prompting the needed clarification that it is racism, not race, which explains the observed difference in health. By contrast, a health justice analysis focuses on the experience of injustice, such as discrimination or food insecurity, as a state at a given time. By focusing on a potentially changeable injustice rather than a fixed trait, the health justice approach accords with the ultimate goal of health equity inquiry—achieving health equity. For example, if studying homelessness using a health justice approach,

---

*In focusing on workflows applicable to quantitative epidemiological or health services research, I do not mean to slight other methods, such as qualitative inquiry, ethnography, or historical analysis.

the focus would not be on whether health outcomes are equal for those experiencing homelessness and those who are housed, but on understanding how homelessness harms health and that fewer people experience homelessness in the first place.

If a particular injustice is ubiquitous (i.e., if all individuals racialized in a particular way have experienced discrimination), the health justice approach may examine the same individuals as the disparitarian approach would. However, the health justice approach would still be advantageous for two reasons. First, the comparison would be to a counterfactual situation in which those who had experienced injustice had not experienced it, rather than to other individuals. Second, the analysis would focus on an injustice experienced in common among individuals in the category, rather than assuming an essential sameness (or that the aggregated category is inherently meaningful).

Comparing Disparitarianism and Health Justice

Table 2.1 presents a stylized example to help clarify some of the differences between the disparitarian and health justice approaches (here, all factors not mentioned, such as cost or ease of implementation, can be considered equal).

In this example, there are two equally sized populations, one advantaged and one disadvantaged. The disadvantaged population experiences, under the status quo, a greater risk of a poor health outcome than the advantaged population, and this greater risk is both avoidable and unjust—a disparity. There are also three intervention scenarios: 1, 2, and 3. In scenario 1, the intervention lowers risk for individuals in both categories, but it lowers risk more (in absolute terms) for advantaged individuals than for disadvantaged individuals. In scenario 2, the intervention lowers risk equally (in absolute terms) for both categories. In scenario 3, the intervention lowers risk for both categories, but it lowers risk more (in absolute terms) for disadvantaged individuals.

When the goal is health equity, how would these scenarios be ranked? From the health justice perspective, there are three possible metrics: in which scenario would the disadvantaged individuals be better off, in which scenario would the advantaged individuals be better off, and in which scenario would the overall population be better off? Under disparitarianism, there is only a single evaluation metric—which scenario presents the lower disparity?

Table 2.1. Comparing disparitarianism and health justice

	Status quo: Risk of Poor Health Outcome	Scenario 1: Risk of Poor Health Outcome	Scenario 2: Risk of Poor Health Outcome	Scenario 3: Risk of Poor Health Outcome
Overall	0.25	0.18	0.15	0.10
Disadvantaged category	0.30	0.25	0.20	0.10
Advantaged category	0.20	0.10	0.10	0.10
Disparity	0.10	0.15	0.10	0.00

From the health justice perspective, and considering disadvantaged individuals, scenarios 1, 2, and 3 would all be preferred over the status quo because risk is lower. Further, disadvantaged individuals are at lower risk under 2 than 1, 3 than 2, and 3 than 1. Considering all individuals, the patterns are the same. If only considering advantaged individuals, any intervention is preferable to the status quo, but there is no clear preference between the interventions, as the risk of a poor health outcome for advantaged individuals is the same in scenarios 1, 2, and 3.

Viewing the question through a disparitarian lens, however, leads to counterintuitive conclusions. Under disparitarianism, scenario 3 would be preferred over the status quo, scenario 1, and scenario 2. Further, scenario 2 would be preferred over scenario 1. However, one would be indifferent between scenario 2 and the status quo. Even more counterintuitively, one would prefer the status quo to intervention 1, even though individuals in both the disadvantaged category and the advantaged category would be better off with intervention 1.

This example is simplistic, but it highlights core problems of disparitarianism. In several scenarios, using a disparity metric might lead one to conclude that some interventions did not improve health equity because disparities worsened, even when there were gains in health for individuals in all categories. This occurs because disparity can be an *essentializing* metric— it assumes an essential commonality among category members such that a disparity is a category-level harm apart from any specific injustice an individual experiences. The health justice approach, in contrast, encourages a more nuanced position. For example, using a health justice perspective, one can explain that the scenarios where health improved to a lesser extent for disadvantaged individuals were somewhat beneficial; but further investigation is also needed to ensure that there was not injustice in implementation that explains the lesser benefit, and to determine if there is remaining injustice to remedy.

Objections to Health Justice

For those first encountering counterfactual thinking, the health justice approach may sound fanciful. Isn't the scientific method about the observable, not what might have been observed had things been different? How could the health justice approach ever be applied?

One way of expressing the apparent problem with health justice is as follows. One would like to observe the outcomes of the same individuals who experienced (at least) two different situations at the same time, for example, the outcome that would have been observed in some scenario X, and the outcome that would have been observed in some scenario Y. These are sometimes called the *potential outcomes*. But, at most, only one of these potential outcomes can be observed—either the outcome under scenario X or scenario Y—not both. This apparent impasse can be resolved by casting counterfactual problems as missing data problems—the unobserved potential outcome is treated as missing. Then, scientific methods to deal with missing data can be applied, typically by imputing missing observations by making use of other observed data.

In modern biostatistics, epidemiology, and econometrics, counterfactual thinking underlies the entire field of causal inference.[39-43] For example, consider a randomized clinical trial that compares the health outcomes of participants who receive an intervention to those who receive "usual care." In such a trial, the potential outcomes that the intervention group would have experienced if they had received usual care instead are not observed. Using appropriate methods, however, researchers can draw causal conclusions about the treatment effect of the intervention even though those potential outcomes are missing. For example, the design of randomized clinical trials allows researchers to use the experience of those who received usual care to impute the missing potential outcomes of those who received the intervention. The observed data in the usual care group stands in for the experience that those who received the intervention would have had, had they received usual care. This is a counterfactual method. And there are counterfactual methods beyond randomized clinical trials. Indeed, counterfactual methods are already standard in many areas of health research. Counterfactual thinking can be applied by using techniques like instrumental variable analysis, difference-in-differences, regression discontinuity, matching, outcome regression models, and propensity score methods. So, there is no methodological barrier to applying counterfactual thinking to questions of health equity.

While there may be no methodological barrier, can these methods be applied in practice? If no society is fully just, are the data necessary to estimate counterfactual outcomes really available? Certainly, no society is fully just. But this does not mean that no relevant information is available. Both health justice and disparitarianism can make use of information from situations where conditions are more just, but the approaches do so differently. The example of heart disease mortality for women, described above, illustrates this well. For estimating the effect of a particular type of injustice (e.g., the effect of sexist diagnostic errors), borrowing information from the experience of men can help estimate what heart disease mortality outcomes in women might be if they did not suffer this injustice. But using information from observations made about men to estimate what the experience of women would have been like had they not experienced injustice is different than, and avoids problems that come from, directly comparing the outcomes of women and men.

Finally, it is important to separate conceptual and implementation concerns. The ideal data to answer a particular question are rarely available in scientific inquiry. No matter what approach is used, investigators will have to make the best use of the data they have, be explicit about their assumptions and uncertainties, and update findings and conclusions as better data become available. And even if the health justice approach faced implementation challenges disparitarianism did not, it would still be preferable, because it gives a clearer way to think about the issues of health equity inquiry than disparitarianism does.

Summary

This chapter has focused on how to think about health equity. The currently dominant approach—disparitarianism—has at least six important problems. Rather than thinking of health inequity as primarily about differences in health between categories of individuals, it is more useful to think of health inequity as primarily about how injustice has harmed health.

Disparities are a byproduct of injustice. When individuals are treated unjustly, that can show up as differences in health between categories of individuals—but it need not in all cases. The mistake of disparitarianism is to focus on the difference and not the injustice. This means that the goals of disparitarianism can be satisfied by achieving parity in the amount of injustice experienced across categories of individuals, rather than by achieving justice. And as the examples of this chapter show, there are injustices that disparitarianism simply cannot detect, so the absence of a disparity cannot be taken to indicate lack of injustice. Ultimately, disparitarianism often undercounts the harm done to oppressed individuals both through comparisons to others who are themselves harmed by injustice and by missing some injustices entirely. Moreover, even though the presence of a disparity often indicates an injustice, resolving a disparity does not imply resolving an injustice.

For all of these reasons, disparitarianism offers a more limited conception of health equity than health justice does. What the health justice approach makes clear is that health equity is not fundamentally about making the health of one category of individuals similar to that of another's. Instead, the heart of health equity work is in substantively addressing the unjust conditions that lead to poor health.

Working from a health justice perspective, the following chapters will provide the normative grounding for judging conditions as unjust, examine how unjust conditions harm health, and detail the policy approaches needed to work against injustice and achieve health equity.

3

Equality of What?

A common genre of health equity cartoon aims to distinguish the terms *equality* and *equity*. One version (figure 3.1, *top*) shows three people of varying heights attempting to watch a baseball game blocked by a fence. Giving everyone a box of the same height to stand on, taller individuals are able to see the game, but shorter individuals are not. When height is taken into account and boxes are distributed accordingly, all can watch the game. Another depiction (figure 3.1, *bottom*) illustrates the same idea with bicycles. If given the same bicycle, some can ride comfortably but others cannot. With bikes suited to people's differences, all can ride. The point is the same in both cases: formally equal interventions can result in unequal outcomes.

I find forcing a distinction between the terms *equality* and *equity* unhelpful, as the plain meaning of each word is equivalent, and I use the terms synonymously throughout this book. However, these images relate to a sound question—famously phrased by economist and philosopher Amartya Sen as "equality of what?"[1] Different kinds of equality (or equity) can have very different implications. Therefore, it is critically important for egalitarian theories to define the space in which to seek equality—to make clear what they suggest should be equal.*

In the last chapter, I argued that health inequity is injustice that harms health. Operationalizing this idea requires what I call a working theory of justice. This informs judgments about whether the social relations that

---

*There is irony in that a theory of equality can be thought of as a theory of what inequalities to tolerate, and a theory of liberty can be thought of as a theory of which liberties it is acceptable to restrain.

EQUALITY   EQUITY

Figure 3.1. These images depict different answers to the "equality of what?" question. The images labeled "equality" reflect equality of resources (everyone has the same box or bicycle). The images labeled "equity" reflect equality of capabilities (everyone is able to watch the game or ride the bicycle comfortably). I think it is clearer to specify what type of equality one is talking about (e.g., equality of resources or equality of capabilities) rather than use similar words to indicate different concepts. *Top*, Used with permission of Christina Berkowitz, 2023. *Bottom, Visualizing Health Equity: One Size Does Not Fit All* infographic (copyright 2017); used with permission from the Robert Wood Johnson Foundation.

produced a particular health state are just. If social relations are just, according to a particular theory, then a health state that results, even if it is a state of poor health, is not an inequity. Poor health is always unfortunate, but to represent health inequity, it must result from injustice. For an egalitarian theory of justice, a system of social relations is just if it is consistent with some specific kind of equality. But theories differ on what that equality is.

A working theory of justice relevant for health equity is not necessarily one that tries to equalize health. Instead, it is one that clarifies what should be equalized so that resulting social relations, and the health states they produce, are just.

Explicating a theory of justice is no small task. Entire books are devoted just to defending a particular theory of justice. It is not my goal to do that here. Instead, this chapter will introduce several common theories of justice, highlight their key critiques, and help to answer the question of the space in which equality should be sought to achieve health equity. In the following chapter, I will give a more detailed account of the working theory of justice that underlies the arguments in the remainder of this book.

The Abstract Egalitarian Principle

This book is premised on the fundamental moral equality of individuals—the idea that people should be recognized to be and treated by others as equal.[2-4] An acceptable working theory of justice, then, must be an *egalitarian* theory. By egalitarian, I mean a theory of justice that calls for establishing political and other social institutions that translate moral equality into substantive equality within people's lives. An acceptable theory specifies the kind of equality, in the realm of social relations, needed to reflect individuals' underlying moral equality.

Some well-known theories of justice, such as those in the school of Aristotle[5] or Nietzsche,[4,6] are not egalitarian. Neither are theories that suppose inherent or essential racial or caste differences, such as those that supported slavery in the United States, or revanchist Jim Crow laws after the egalitarian reconstruction amendments, or the apartheid regime in South Africa. These all posit fundamental inequalities in moral status between individuals that should be reflected in political structures. An apt description of this hierarchical, rather than egalitarian, idea comes from Frank Wilhoit: "Conservatism consists of exactly one proposition, to wit: There must be in-groups whom the law protects but does not bind, alongside out-groups whom the law binds but does not protect."[7] Under these theories, differences in health between those with more versus less moral worth, or that result from social stratification reflective of the rightful superiority some possess, would not represent health inequity.

Given the premise that individuals have equal moral worth, I reject inegalitarian theories out of hand. Further, across the ideological spectrum, politicians and the larger public at least pay lip service to equality as a political ideal. That ideal underlies recognition of democracy, a system in which each individual has an equal (at least in some sense) say, as a just system of government. Philosopher and jurisprudentialist Ronald Dworkin called this broad, if nonspecific, commitment to political equality the "abstract egalitarian principle"[2] and expressed it as the idea that the state must show equal care for the life of each citizen.* Dworkin called this the "sovereign virtue," as showing equal care legitimates a state having dominion over individuals' lives.[2]

As with any abstraction, however, the devil is in the details. There may be broad agreement that a just political philosophy is egalitarian, but there are vehement disagreements as to what showing equal care would mean, concretely. Describing these disagreements forms the bulk of this chapter. But before discussing different egalitarian theories and the space in which to seek equality, it is important to think through how sufficiently broad agreement on any theory might be reached.

Reasonable Pluralism and the Democratic Society

Democratic societies are "systems of fair cooperation between free and equal citizens over time."[8(p7)] As philosopher Elizabeth S. Anderson notes, democratic societies are not ethnocultural nation-states where the views of one group are imposed on all others. Instead, democratic societies are characterized by the self-determination of a community of equals, in accordance with rules that can be justified to all.[3(p313)]

There are, broadly, two types of justification available. One type, the

---

*Throughout this book, I use the term *citizen* to mean something along the lines of a "member" of society—the individuals a society's rules are meant to apply to. This is different from the legal idea of citizenship, with formal rules about immigration, how one becomes a citizen, and so on.

"third-person" standpoint, provides an external, impersonal reason to accept an argument. Examples of third-person justifications include arguing that a particular conception of justice is right in a deductive, logical sense, or is a revealed religious truth, or is fitting for the kind of society under discussion.[9,10] Another third-person justification, the communitarian approach, appeals to a shared sense of identity, tradition, or community.

The alternative is the "second-person" standpoint.[9,10] The idea of the second-person standpoint is that justice needs to be justified interpersonally—that is, it needs to be justified on terms others can (or would) accept, and that can be willed collectively. This is not an issue of simply deriving valid conclusions from correct premises but of being able to explain to others why they should accept one's claims.

Here it is useful to mention two logics that can guide human behavior—the rational and the reasonable.[11-13,14(p121)] These logics are equivalent in status, one is not reducible to the other, and they motivate different concerns. The rational concerns what is in one's interest and how to achieve it. It may be rational to pursue certain ends no matter their effect on others. The reasonable concerns proposing and abiding by rules that others have no reason to reject, conditional on those individuals seeking to strike a general agreement.[13,14] A principle is reasonable if one is willing to abide by it, providing others do the same. The reasonable is not altruism—the pursuit of another's interest without regard for one's own. It is a principle of reciprocity and entails recognizing that one is in a system of social relations with others, who all also seek to pursue their own rational ends and have just as much right to do so as anyone else.[8,15] Any system of social cooperation then must be agreeable, at least in principle, to all parties. As historian R. H. Tawney said, "the test of a principle is that it can be generalized, so that the advantages of applying it are not particular, but universal."[16]

As an example of the distinction between the rational and the reasonable, consider a situation in which a person is drowning. At the side of the pond is a life preserver on a rope, and a bystander happens upon the scene. The bystander could easily throw the life preserver and save the drowning person. It may be rational for the bystander to demand that the drowning person agree to pay $10,000 for the life preserver. It may be rational for the drowning person to accept. But there is a clear sense in which such a demand is unreasonable, as individuals would have good reason to reject a system that conditioned a minimal amount of lifesaving effort on ability to pay. As Anderson notes, consenting to an option within an option set does not justify the option set.[17] Reasonableness makes sense of why that is. Both rationality and reasonableness can be invoked in second-person justifications.

One reason it is important to emphasize second-person justifications relates to what philosopher John Rawls called "the fact of reasonable pluralism."[8] This is the idea that, within a society, there are many reasonable views about how one should live one's life. Thus, there may be no single "comprehensive doctrine," no single conception of what a good life would be, that everyone must accept. Some may live their life in the Jewish faith, some may follow a utilitarian moral philosophy, and others may have no specific comprehensive doctrine. In a democratic society, people free to form their own judgments about how to live their life will often come to different conclusions. Recognition of this fact underlies, for example, the principle of religious toleration.

Given the fact of reasonable pluralism, the question then is what working theory of justice could different people, holding different comprehensive doctrines, all agree on? One way forward is to limit the terrain where agreement is sought to a small subset of issues more suitable for broad consensus. For example, agreeing on a comprehensive doctrine may not be possible, but it may be possible to agree on fundamental principles like the moral equality of all individuals. From this starting point, there might be agreement on how individuals' interests should be represented to others and how institutions should adjudicate competing interests.[8] Rawls calls this a "political" conception of justice, as it focuses only on the rules necessary for individuals to live together, rather than a "comprehensive" conception of justice that might tell people how to live their lives overall.[8] A political conception of justice does not ask those with differing comprehensive doctrines to agree on anything more than they have to. If one is willing to respect others as free and equal, to tolerate their way of life as long as it likewise tolerates that of others, then the institutions of society can be agreed on those terms, without needing everyone to endorse the same comprehensive doctrine. In other words, if one can agree to the idea of oneself and others as free and equal citizens, then one is otherwise free to live in accord with any comprehensive doctrine not in conflict with that agreement.

If the idea of freedom is understood to mean, broadly, the capability to live as one wills,[3(p315)] then such an agreement is the minimum agreement necessary to form a democratic society with a stable political system that guarantees the conditions of everyone's freedom.[8]

Even a restricted agreement of this kind may be too much for some. It is not compatible with all comprehensive doctrines, particularly non-egalitarian ones. However, this type of political agreement does give the broadest space possible for comprehensive doctrines, and it does not require commitment to any particular comprehensive doctrine. In the absence of such a political agreement, the alternative would be that those holding one particular doctrine "clobber, coerce, or overawe" those who hold other doctrines into submission.[18(p18)] Such a situation can only characterize oppression of those with nondominant views, not freedom and equality.[8]

Since no one comprehensive doctrine can unite everyone in a democratic society, a democratic society's unifying idea can instead be that social institutions should treat everyone fairly. This is an idea that free and equal members of society can all endorse (even if they disagree profoundly about other issues). This also helps explain why showing equal care for the lives of each citizen is the sovereign virtue.[2] Treating people fairly shows equal care for their lives, and thus helps legitimate the power a government has over them.

Of course, specifying what exactly it means to have social institutions that treat people fairly is an enormous task. Simply agreeing to treat people in this way does not, by itself, get very far. But it is an idea that can be endorsed by many individuals holding differing comprehensive doctrines (or no particular comprehensive doctrine).

Overall, in order to reach the broadest agreement possible, it is desirable that the working theory of justice used to pursue health equity be justifiable from a second-person standpoint and not require accepting any particular comprehensive doctrine.

Quasi-Egalitarian Theories

This section discusses quasi-egalitarian theories of justice, specifically libertarianism, meritocracy, and utilitarianism. I term these *quasi-egalitarian* theories because although they may accept the fundamental moral equality of individuals, they seek social institutions that concern themselves with equality in people's lives in only a thin and formal, rather than a substantive, way. Charitably, these theories are egalitarian theories over a very restricted space. More cynically, they use a veneer of egalitarianism to cover over deeply inegalitarian ideas.

Knowing the historical context in which these theories emerged helps make sense of them (but is not needed to assess them normatively). In Western Europe, these theories emerged during (and helped shape) a period of political and economic transition.[16,19,20] At the beginning of the period, the civil, political, and economic spheres of people's lives were formally inegalitarian. A hierarchical structure privileging nobility, aristocracy, and certain religions translated into both formally different legal rights and rigidly stratified social systems, with a feudal economy.

This period saw calls for greater (or any) popular representation in government and religious toleration, intertwined with the emergence of democratic government, the capitalist economic system, colonialism, and slavery on a global scale. Conservative thought, perhaps epitomized by Edward Burke,[21,22] defended established hierarchies, both political and economic, against rule by the rabble. This thought emphasized that a "traditional" economic system included both obligations for the lower classes to perform work and entitlements to receive some duties of care from the upper classes.[16,21,23]

The thought that opposed these traditional social relations was termed "liberal." In the United States today, "liberal" is often used to indicate the political left, but here it meant an individualistic ethos emphasizing freedom, for some individuals,[24] from traditional hierarchies, and the ability to seek one's fortune.

The more fully egalitarian theories that I discuss subsequently primarily emerged during a later time when the quasi-egalitarian theories were more dominant and problems with them had become clearer.

Libertarianism

The work of John Locke is a key reference point in the history of liberal political thought.[25,26] A modern theory that takes pains to emphasize its connection to Locke is libertarianism. Also called classic liberalism, and related to the economic idea of laissez-faire capitalism, the libertarian interpretation of Locke's work and its related body of scholarship is an important contemporary political philosophy that has inspired slogans like "taxation is theft" and "small government." Libertarianism sees justice in social arrangements that strongly value "negative" freedoms[27]—freedom from being "coerced" to do things that individuals would not choose to do. Though libertarians accept that coercion might be required in some cases (e.g., to prevent violations of others' rights), libertarianism overall views society as being more just the less such coercion occurs.

Philosopher Robert Nozick offered an influential expression of how a libertarian state might be structured so as to require the minimum amount of coercion necessary.[28] Nozick's theory of justice as entitlement accepts that a state is necessary to protect rights, and it must have the resources needed to do its work. But he was concerned with limiting the extent to which individuals can be coerced to provide the resources the state needs. He does this by introducing the idea of self-ownership: individuals naturally own themselves and whatever they produce with their labor.[28,29] Further, he presents a *procedural* justification of property holdings: one is entitled to property that results from following fair procedures in acquisition (claiming natural resources never previously possessed by humans), transfer (from another person in free exchange), or rectification (redress for past wrongs). As a consequence, being stripped of property (e.g., by taxation) represents unjust coercion. Nozick, however, does make an exception: taxation is legitimate when used to establish and maintain a "minimal state" (sometimes called a "night watchman state") that provides defense and security services. Nozick argues that prior to state formation, a free market would spontaneously emerge, and security agencies would arise in that market. Through competition and merger, one security agency would dominate, ultimately achieving a monopoly on the legitimate use of force. This would establish the minimal state, which would be justified in collecting taxes to finance security services, as these would effectively be no different than what individuals paid voluntarily prior to the state.*

Libertarianism does, I think, accept the abstract egalitarian principle and its duty of equal care. The libertarian state emphasizes, for example, formal equality in the right to hold property. Libertarianism can thus be thought of as an egalitarian theory over a very small space—namely a small set of rights, liberties, and some version of what might be termed "equality of opportunity" (in the libertarian formulation, absence of any formal bar preventing one from competing for material resources and power on the free

---

*Why the same argument would not apply to education or health care is, in my opinion, not sufficiently addressed.

market). However, I believe that libertarianism's commitment to equality is very restricted, which ultimately prevents it from supporting a substantive egalitarianism.

The libertarian argument commonly makes use of two concepts worth explaining (and rebutting): (1) the natural and self-regulating market, and (2) coercion avoidance.

THE MARKET IS NEITHER NATURAL NOR SELF-REGULATING

The idea of the natural and self-regulating market is that "free" markets arise spontaneously, are natural and separable from the state, and regulate themselves, serving as nexuses where people express freely chosen preferences without state involvement. However, this idea is both ahistorical and conceptually unsound—no "natural" version of markets exists outside of systems of social relations established by human beings.[30] Historically, conditions of market exchange arose as the explicit policy choices of centralized states.[19,31] And a body of work dating back to late 19th- and early 20th-century legal realists and institutional economists, such as Robert Lee Hale, Wesley Hohfeld, and Walton Hamilton, and social liberals such as Leonard Hobhouse and Thomas Hill Green, serves to, in the words of legal scholar Barbara Fried, "debunk the notion that the market is natural (pre-political) or neutral (apolitical)."[30]

Beyond this history, markets—tools to facilitate the fair exchange of property—simply require substantial state involvement to function as intended. This includes the legal, police, judicial, and carceral systems that establish and enforce the terms of "free trade," transportation, energy, and communication infrastructure, and the currency with which exchange is facilitated. Further, markets need constant tending to avoid monopolies, externalities, and other problems that impede their intended function.[32] This all means that there is really no separation between the state and the market—a market economy is a government program.[33]

COERCION CANNOT BE AVOIDED

The second idea relates to coercion avoidance and negative liberty. Libertarians argue that the regime of libertarian rights (including property rights) is necessary to avoid coercion. Any other system of social relations would be coercive—it would use state violence (or its threat) to force compliance. But in fact, there is coercion inherent to any system of rights—it cannot be avoided, only managed.[30,34] The essence of any legal right is to restrain others' behavior under threat of violence. This is true not only for rights such as a right not to be assaulted but also for property rights. Property rights provide the ability for an owner to exclude others from using their property unless the other party agrees to terms.[30,35]

To illustrate, consider a person who needs to eat. They may need land and equipment to farm, forage, or hunt; or they may need raw materials and equipment to work for wages, which can then be exchanged for food. This person can be coerced by an owner's threat, backed by state power, to withhold the use of their property unless the person agrees to their terms. At the same time, an asset owner who needs their property put to use can be coerced by the laborer's threat, backed by state power, to remain idle unless wages will be paid. The laborer works because wages will be withheld if they do not, and the employer pays wages because work will be withheld if they do not, all backed by the state. In any exchange made under a system of rights, the threat of state violence exists in the background.

LIBERTARIAN PROPERTY RIGHTS

The ideas of the natural and self-regulating market, and coercion avoidance, are often employed in libertarian arguments to justify a special status for factor income (income that results from wages, ownership of land and other natural resources, and/or capital assets: the "factors" of production[36]) and other property acquired through market-based exchange. In such arguments, these holdings serve as a normative baseline for measuring state interference (e.g., the more the state decreases one's market-derived holdings, the more the state has interfered in private affairs). The idea of people's natural entitlement to market holdings is widely accepted, even among those who may not describe their political philosophy as libertarian. Philosophers Liam Murphy and Thomas Nagel describe this idea as "everyday libertarianism" to indicate its "common sense" status.[37]

There are two common justifications for the special status of factor income in "everyday libertarianism." One justification, exemplified by Nozick's theory, is procedural. Another justification arises from seeing market-derived holdings as the just deserts that reward productive efforts. However, understanding the problems with the ideas of the natural and self-regulating market and coercion avoidance help make clear why everyday libertarianism is incorrect.

PROCEDURAL JUSTIFICATIONS

The procedural justification for everyday libertarianism is based on the idea that government should not interfere with the outcomes of free exchange. If people follow the correct procedures to obtain property, taking some of it (e.g., via taxation) would be infringing on their freedom. Procedural justifications face two main problems, however. First, they cannot justify the process of property formation—the allocation of initial property holdings that precedes exchange. This is a major problem because property rights, rather than being constitutive of liberty, decrease it. As Fried notes, "If liberty is absence of government constraint, then any system of property rights cannot be reconciled with liberty, as property rights can only be to impose, through the agency of the state, correlative restraints on the universe of non-owners."[30] Philosopher G. A. Cohen puts it similarly when he says that "the distribution of . . . property-entitlements amounts to a distribution of freedoms and unfreedoms."[38] Moreover, property formation cannot be settled "once and for all," as new individuals are always being born, and thus their liberty is infringed upon by the property rights of others. Therefore, a general claim that libertarian property rights are an unmitigated defense of freedom cannot be sustained.

As a broader point, this example makes clear that rather than always decreasing freedom, state involvement can increase or decrease freedom, depending on the specifics of a given situation, the concept of freedom used, and the assessor's point of view. State provision of services everyone needs, such as education or health care, can readily be viewed as increasing freedom in both the positive and negative sense.[27] For instance, provision of these services not only creates capabilities people may not otherwise have had—a positive sense of freedom,[39] but frees people from the threat of having these essential services withheld if they do not agree to someone else's terms, backed by state authority—a negative sense of freedom.

Second, because a market economy is in fact a government program, property holdings arising through market exchange are not qualitatively different than property holdings arising in other ways. Market exchange is one institution for distributing *rivalrous* resources (resources that cannot be possessed by more than one person at a time), put in place by the state. But taxes and income-support programs can be described the same way. If following the institutional rules of market exchange justifies property holdings, following the institutional rules of tax payments and state pension programs should as well.*

DESERTIST JUSTIFICATIONS

The desertist view is that property derived from market exchange should enjoy a special status because it represents the just deserts of one's labor. One is entitled to such deserts as recompense for the real cost, or sacrifice, involved in the labor.[30] However, it is mistaken to think that what an individual receives in market exchange necessarily bears any relation to their labor. Factor income is distributed by markets to owners of natural resources and capital, which by definition is not related to labor. And for income that is connected to labor, markets do not allocate resources based on the sacrifice made by any individual but by the value placed by others on the product sold. In a modern economy, in which everyone is engaged in a complicated web of joint production, it is typically impossible to attribute specific proportions of that value to any one individual.[40] Further, even if some portion of such value could be attributed to the productive ability of one individual, that productive ability itself largely stems from influences that the individual cannot be said to deserve. Such influences include knowledge and technology produced by previous generations and now held in common (sometimes called "total factor productivity"[41]), unearned care received as a child, and state efforts that help everyone, such as reducing air and water pollution, management of natural resources, the building of infrastructure, and the establishment of markets. Further, state creation and enforcement of property rights and regulation of trade itself creates value.[42] For example, the imprimatur of FDA approval for a medication can make it worth more than a huckster's snake oil. Thus, the argument that the state swoops in, after the work has been done, to tax away hard-earned income is mistaken. Instead, the state facilitates the entire process of production and exchange, creating value all along. If desertist arguments were to be taken

---

* It is of course also true that property held by real individuals right now did not come about through a history that a libertarian would view as fair. No property currently held has escaped the countless acts of violence and injustice that have accompanied acquisition and transfer since time immemorial. Libertarian principles, even if accepted, cannot justify any currently existing property distribution—doing so would merely consolidate ill-gotten gains, not serve justice. Taking seriously libertarian theory would require a massive effort of rectification.

seriously, the state would have a strong claim to deserve, as a silent partner, at least some of the exchange value of a transaction.[36,43]

THE IMPOSSIBILITY OF THE LIBERTARIAN IDEA

To sum up a brief case against libertarianism, I have argued that markets are in fact government programs, that any entitlement to market earnings can only result from a system of social relations, not stand apart from it, and that coercion is inevitable in social relations.

What understanding state creation of property rights and markets, and the ubiquity of coercion, means is not that anything goes; instead, the rules a state puts in place to manage these issues need to be justifiable with regard to fulfilling the state's duty of equal care. Fundamentally, property rights are not about relationships *between* people and objects but about relationships *among* people. For instance, owning a house is principally about the power to say who can or cannot use the house, rather than the ability to do what one wants to the house. Because property rights structure relations between people, a property rights regime, as with all laws, is a manifestation of political power[30] that forms part of a system of social relations. And as with any other part of a system of social relations, a property rights regime should be justifiable to everyone. Otherwise, it would not recognize everyone's equality.

Taxes, transfers, in-kind services, and the regulations that establish property rights and enable market exchange are tools used by the state, guided by a theory of justice, to achieve desired ends.[37] Property holdings are the *outcome* of a set of institutional arrangements and are defined by those arrangements. They do not exist external to the arrangements. Thus, debates about what set of institutional arrangements we should have cannot be resolved by reference to some external standard of holdings—that would be question begging.

Economic historian Karl Polanyi explained the impossibility of the libertarian idea by analogy to a quest for immortality.[19] Wanting to avoid death is so understandable that seeking immortality seems unobjectionable. But because death is inevitable, seeking immortality can only lead to quackery. Once one realizes immortality is impossible, one can focus on how best to find meaning in a life in which death is inevitable.

Similarly, one might, naïvely, think it desirable that everyone spend their life pursuing their own rational self-interest free from coercion by others.

But that is as much a fantasy as immortality. Instead, once one accepts that life necessarily involves coexistence with others whose interests have equal standing to one's own, then one can focus on how that coexistence should be managed. The question is not how to avoid coercion, which is as inevitable as mortality, but how the necessary coercion can occur in a manner that still respects everyone's fundamental equality. The principle of reasonableness offers one solution.

The problem with inegalitarian, hierarchical thought can be summed up as "false difference"—imagining there are differences in moral status between individuals when there are not.[44] The problem with libertarianism can be summed up as "false equivalence"—pretending that because people have formal equality in a restricted set of rights, they have similar substantive freedom, and the state need not involve itself further. But in fact, rather than showing equal care, policy that only addresses the areas libertarians think appropriate would often leave people at the mercy of historical circumstances, bad luck, or oppression. In short, it would be unjust.

Meritocracy

I define meritocracy as a theory of justice that views *opportunity* alone as the space in which equality should apply. Equality of opportunity can be thought of as the idea that social positions, especially those that provide welfare, resource, or status advantages, should be open to all, with selection based on aptitude.[45] I distinguish meritocracy from theories of justice that use the principle of equality of opportunity as one element of just social relations, rather than the only determining factor.

Meritocracy arose from similar impulses as libertarianism—the idea that individuals should not be bound by hierarchical systems that distributed social positions by pedigree. Instead, anyone can have talent, and that talent should be rewarded. The capitalist economic system provided another justification for meritocracy—using the scarce resource of talent wisely raises society's level of production.

On its face, meritocracy has some appeal. Clearly, basing social positions on family connections is unfair, and society overall may indeed benefit from putting people in positions for which their talents are best suited. Moreover, meritocratic equality of opportunity might go further than libertarian equality of opportunity. For example, it might include provision of education, health care, and child allowances to help individuals develop their innate talents, or policies to prevent discrimination in hiring by private employers that a libertarian system might allow.

Despite these appealing features, the equality that meritocracy offers is still thin. Though it rejects the idea of familial hierarchy presumed by feudal societies with formal aristocracy, it does not reject hierarchy generally. Instead, meritocracy posits an innate hierarchy of talent and uses the mechanism of market or other social competition to reveal it. In this way, meritocracy, while paying lip service to moral equality, allows—indeed, is predicated on—arranging society to reflect inequalities of ability.

Meritocracy is also importantly incomplete, because it does not establish a position on how unequally the rewards of filling certain social positions should be distributed, or which positions should be highly rewarded. Meritocracy says that people should have an equal chance to fill advantageous social positions, but which positions should be advantageous, and how should the rewards for winning the competition to fill them be determined?

Meritocracy finds social hierarchy acceptable if individuals have a fair chance to occupy the upper echelons. Therefore, meritocratic social policy focuses on education, cultural recognition and acceptance, and other ways to provide a fair shot at success—all of which is good.[46] But it might offer little material aid to those who have lost in a "fair" competition, thereby proving themselves "unworthy." If assistance were offered, it may be as charity from one's betters, rather than a fair share owed to an equal.[3] Meritocracy can justify showing lesser care for some individuals on the basis of their demonstrated lesser ability.

These criticisms would hold even if succeeding in society were a fair test of one's abilities—but of course it is not. A truly fair competition is not possible, owing to myriad undeserved differences in upbringing and endowments that would be impossible to rectify. At some level, it is simply impossible to deserve one's talents, which calls into question whether the results of those talents can be deserved.[12]

Finally, though not inherent to the idea, there is a sense in which meritocracy uses "mobility as an excuse for inequality,"[47(p127)] disingenuously reinforcing hierarchical social structures that result in widely varying levels of welfare, resources, and social standing within a society. Pointing to what an exceptional individual achieves can be used to undermine collective action that "seeks to narrow the space between valley and peak."[16]

Given these limitations, I do not think that meritocracy is a suitable theory of justice. But although opportunity is not *the* space in which to seek equality, opportunity is *a* space in which to seek equality. Everyone does deserve a fair chance to compete for social positions they find desirable. This is clearly part of showing equal care, but as a component of a more comprehensive system.

Utilitarianism

Jeremy Bentham provided the first systematic account of utilitariansm,[48] which shared with classical liberalism a goal of sweeping away outdated social practices. Though developed in many ingenious variations, the heart of utilitarianism as political philosophy is that the rightness or wrongness of state action, whether specific acts or general rules, is judged in reference to the maximization of total utility (or welfare) that follows from the action.* Utilitarianism is a form of consequentialism, which holds that the rightness of an action can be judged by its consequences. Utilitarianism and similar consequentialist theories have been very influential in both political philosophy and economics.

I highlight two important critiques of utilitarianism. The first was perhaps best expressed by Rawls, who argued that utilitarianism does not respect the distinction between persons.[12] Theories that seek to maximize total utility within a society would allow some individuals to suffer in order to improve the utility of others. This means that utilitarianism could accept slavery, were it to make the life of slave owners sufficiently good, or torture, were it to sufficiently gratify sadists. Although it may be rational for an individual, when making a decision, to select the option that maximizes their utility, it does not follow that the same principle ought to guide the assessment of social relations, as the utility of different individuals is incommensurate.

The second key objection, as highlighted by Sen,[1] concerns the fact that individuals have different utility functions. For a given quantity of resources, some individuals will derive more utility from them than others. For example, someone with a disability may need more resources to achieve the same utility as someone without that disability. In these cases, utilitarianism would

---

*A later-developing expression of utilitarianism seeks to maximize the average level of utility rather than the total, but this will be the same as maximizing the total utility for the same number of individuals.

argue that, all else being equal, the person who is better able to convert resources into utility should receive more resources. Thus, someone already disadvantaged by a disability could be doubly disadvantaged by receiving, on account of this disability, fewer resources—even if such resources might make up for the disadvantage.

These critiques make clear that, although utilitarianism is egalitarian in the sense that it incorporates everyone's utility, weighted equally, into its calculus, its conception of showing equal care is much too thin.

Egalitarian Theories

I consider the next set of theories of justice to be true egalitarian theories, in that they call for social institutions that seek substantive equality in people's lives. These theories differ, however, in that they seek that equality in different spaces: welfare, resources, or social standing.

Equality of Welfare

Equality of welfare theories improve on classical (total) or average utilitarianism by their concern with the distribution of welfare (the "utility" of utilitarianism being one conception of welfare), not simply its maximization. These theories hold that there is some meaningful measure of the subjective states of individuals, their welfare, and the way to judge a system of social relations is to examine the distribution of welfare—a just distribution being one where welfare is equalized. Equality of welfare theories are typically secondarily concerned with the total (or average) level of welfare but are unwilling to trade off equality for increasing this level. For example, using an equality of welfare standard, a situation in which everyone had 11 units of welfare, however conceived, would be preferred over one in which everyone had 10 units of welfare. However, a situation in which, from a starting point of everyone having 10 units of welfare, one individual would climb to 12 units, at the cost of another individual falling to 9 units, would be rejected. In social choice theory,[1] this is sometimes called "leximin," with equality "lexically prior" to maximization, such that maximization is considered after equality (as words beginning with B are listed strictly after words beginning with A in a lexicon).

At first glance, equality of welfare seems appealing. However, equality of welfare has important problems. The first is sometimes called the problem of expensive tastes.[2] Some individuals may require more resources to achieve the same level of welfare. For example, one person may be satisfied seeing an independent band in a dive bar, while another requires viewing an Italian opera company in a box seat to achieve the same level of welfare. This difference in welfare (or utility) functions between persons is the same issue encountered with utilitarianism and disability. However, for equality of welfare theories, the situation has opposite implications. In utilitarianism, resources would preferentially go to the individual without expensive tastes, as they would convert the same amount of resources into more welfare. Under equality of welfare, resources would preferentially go to the person with expensive tastes as they would need more resources to achieve the same welfare.[1]

Though it may sound somewhat silly, the issue identified by the problem of expensive tastes can have real consequences for the level of welfare achieved within a society. Aiming to increase welfare for a few individuals could divert a large amount of resources, and consequently societal welfare could be substantially lower than it might be with only a little welfare inequality. For example, a large share of US health care spending occurs after poor health (one aspect of welfare) has developed—as an equality of welfare approach might support.[49] However, some argue that this has resulted in shortfalls in spending on public health and preventive health care—services that may substantially boost average health across the life course.[50]

Equality of welfare is further complicated by feasibility concerns. First, there is unlikely to be consensus on any particular conception of welfare.[2] Some may think welfare should be operationalized as happiness, but others may think happiness is worth giving up to achieve the satisfaction of completing a difficult task. Second, even if a particular welfare construct could be agreed upon, it may be difficult to measure. And even if welfare could be agreed upon and measured, it is a personal preference. It is likely impossible to make interindividual trade-offs for personal preferences, as they may be incommensurate between two (or more) different people.[51-53] But equality of welfare theories rely on just such comparisons. So, if whether two individuals have equal welfare cannot be determined, the approach is impracticable.

Finally, equality of welfare considers only the level of welfare, not how it was produced.[1,54] For example, there may be some individuals whose welfare is increased by torturing others, or by committing racist acts. Even if the welfare of those who were tortured or oppressed could be made equal to the welfare of the torturers and racists, it is hard to understand how such a system would be justifiable to everyone. Given all these concerns, I do not think that welfare is the right space in which to seek equality.

Equality of Resources and Distributional Egalitarianism

The next family of theories of justice are those that seek equality in the space of resources, such as income, rights, and opportunities.[2,55–57] Given the focus on distribution of resources, this school of thought is sometimes called distributional egalitarianism.

Distributional egalitarian theories are often keen to distinguish outcomes that result from people's considered choices, for which they can be held responsible, from outcomes that result from undeserved chance, for which they should not be held responsible.* These theories recognize that when individuals pursue lives in accordance with their own conception of the good, varying outcomes result. Respecting these choices means that the resources people have at a given time may be unequal for reasons that are not unjust. However, lives are also influenced by factors beyond individuals' control, and distributional egalitarian theories posit that individuals should have a claim on resources necessary to meet undeserved hardship. Distributional egalitarian theories also take seriously issues with expensive tastes and disabilities.[2] An individual who requires more resources through no fault of their own (a disability) has a valid claim on extra resources. But if the requirement for more resources stems from deliberate choice (an expensive taste) then others are under no obligation to provide them.

To help delineate deservingness in an uncertain world, distributional egalitarian theories often distinguish between two types of luck: "brute luck" (outcomes unrelated to a person's choices) and "option luck" (outcomes that result from a choice consciously made, even if the outcome is undesirable).[2] Bad brute luck is undeserved, and thus eligible for compensation, but bad option luck is deserved, and thus compensation is not required. Bad brute luck can pertain to many circumstances, some of which call into question common ideas about merit and deservingness. For example, as discussed in relation to meritocracy, above, one's innate talents, abilities, and work ethic could be considered the results of brute luck, which one cannot

---

* For this reason, they are also sometimes called "luck egalitarian" theories, although they do not aim to equalize luck.

meaningfully deserve. Thus, the potential scope for compensation under distributional egalitarian theories is broad.

To provide compensation, distributional egalitarian theories again invoke the distinction between deserved and undeserved outcomes, this time focusing on resources that those who are well-off might possess. Some portion of what the well-off possess might be fully deserved as the result of choices they are responsible for. But another portion might result from good fortune—perhaps a natural talent. Distributional egalitarian justice would distribute the underserved portion of the resources the well-off possess to compensate the less well-off for misfortunes beyond their control.

Distributional egalitarian theories are deeply egalitarian theories. Recognizing the equal moral worth of all, they argue that one should not be condemned to avoidable bad outcomes on account of bad brute luck. And many policies that would improve health can be framed in distributional egalitarian terms, such as access to health care to prevent and treat maladies for which one is not responsible, education to develop one's talents, and income supports to protect against undeserved misfortunes, like unemployment or lack of marketable skills.

Despite their appeal, however, distributional egalitarian theories have important drawbacks. First, distinguishing between situations a person is responsible for versus situations they are not would require the state to make intrusive, and in some cases impractical, judgments about deservingness.[3] For example, is one entitled to medical care after a car crash resulting from intentionally risky driving? Could the state distinguish between the bad option luck of choosing to drive too fast, and the bad brute luck of being a born thrill-seeker? Should it?

Moreover, it is difficult to understand individuals' choices without reference to the circumstances in which they make the choice.[2] During periods of the COVID-19 pandemic, when stay-at-home orders were in place, some individuals may have left the house to have fun, but others did so to put food on the table. Did those who worked to support their family and subsequently contracted COVID-19 experience bad brute luck or bad option luck? Should they receive health care?

Finally, there is a sense in which distributional egalitarians conflate dissimilar circumstances. Consider three undeserved harms an individual might experience: having their arm broken by a falling tree limb, having their arm broken by someone committing a hate crime, and having their arm broken in a fall from a dilapidated subway staircase, which was poorly maintained owing to segregation and systemic underinvestment. In all cases the bad outcome is undeserved, and compensatory resources needed might be similar, so a distributional egalitarian could view these situations as all the same. But from another perspective, harm caused by random natural phenomena is different than harm caused by racist violence, and both are different than harm stemming from structural oppression.[58] By focusing on the role of chance, distributional egalitarian theories de-emphasize the role of injustice perpetrated by others or channeled through institutions. To be sure, distributional egalitarians are against injustice such as racism, sexism, and economic exploitation. But by emphasizing the role of impersonal chance, and de-emphasizing the extent to which injustice is done to individuals by other individuals, and the social structures they create, distributional egalitarianism under-recognizes the role of social relations in injustice.[3] This could lead to policies overly focused on compensation and mitigation, rather than policies that address causes more directly, such as by improving social standing for those who experience injustice. Indeed, distributional egalitarian policy may reinforce rather than redress social stratification by creating classes of "losers" who need to be compensated from the surpluses of those for whom things have gone well.[3] Despite its appeals, then, I think distributional egalitarianism is undesirable as a theory of justice.

Equality of Standing and Relational Egalitarianism

The last family of theories of justice to discuss are those that focus primarily on how people relate to each other.[3,9,16,47,59] These "relational egalitarian" theories emphasize social standing as the space in which to seek equality. Social standing refers to how the interests of individuals are counted in a democratic society. A hierarchical society in which the interests of superiors count for more than the interests of inferiors does not reflect equal social standing.[17] Relational egalitarians reject hierarchies that grant some individuals arbitrary and unaccountable power over others, or allow them to extract tokens of deference.[17] One way to think about relational egalitarian theories is that they are about the kinds of power people can have over others, and what makes having that power legitimate or illegitimate. Sociologist T. H. Marshall expressed a vision of relational egalitarianism when he discussed one strand of political reform in the United Kingdom as moving toward "social citizenship" that aimed to level existing hierarchies of status through social policy.[47]

A particularly influential relational egalitarian theory was proposed by Rawls.[12] Rawls viewed the object of justice as arranging the basic structure of society so as to facilitate cooperation between free and equal citizens.[12] The "basic structure" is the "way in which the major social institutions distribute fundamental rights and duties and determine the division of advantages from social co-operation."[12(p6)] This includes the "political constitution, legally recognized forms of property, and the organization of the economy."[60]

Rawls explored intuitions about how individuals holding different comprehensive doctrines could fairly construct a system of social relations by imagining something called the "original position," in which individuals are asked to derive principles of justice that will govern their society. In the original position, individuals are under the "veil of ignorance," meaning they do not know the particulars of their situation—such as their race, ethnicity, gender, or comprehensive doctrine. They know they may have these attributes, but not any specific realization of them. The veil of ignorance is a striking embodiment of the abstract egalitarian principle. Without knowledge of the particulars of their situation, one suspects individuals would be inclined to agree on terms that treat everyone with equal care.

Using the device of this thought experiment and other considered reflection, Rawls proposed two principles of justice: "(a) Each person has the same indefeasible claim to a fully adequate scheme of equal basic liberties, which scheme is compatible with the same scheme of liberties for all; and (b) Social and economic inequalities are to satisfy two conditions: first, they are to be attached to offices and positions open to all under conditions of fair equality of opportunity, and second, they are to be to the greatest benefit of the least-advantaged members of society (the difference principle)."[8(pp42–43)] Rawls conceived of the resources that the basic structure of society distributes as "social primary goods": "things which a rational man [sic] wants whatever else he [sic] wants,"[12] and gives as examples civil and political rights, liberties, opportunities, income and wealth, and the social bases of self-respect.[12] Some of these, like basic liberties, must be strictly equalized in accordance with the first principle, while for others, like income, some inequality might be permitted. Rawls argues that inequity with regard to social primary goods would be acceptable only if those individuals who are least advantaged, relatively speaking, are better off, in an absolute sense, than they would have been without the inequality (and only for things that do not require a stricter equality).

Rawls also notes that the first principle is lexically prior to the second and that fair equality of opportunity (sometimes called "careers open to talents") is lexically prior to the difference principle, such that people must have a fair chance to compete for the jobs and other opportunities that allocate social primary goods, before inequality in social primary goods could be allowed. Under the Rawlsian theory, a just society would protect liberty, give everyone a fair chance at earning the subset of social primary goods that might be distributed unequally, and, after that, only countenance inequalities if those inequalities work to the benefit of the least advantaged (for example, if the profit motive can be used to increase production to such an extent that the least advantaged individuals have a greater standard of living than they would have had with less inequality).

Although Rawls's theory, libertarianism, and meritocracy all involve equality of opportunity, they treat equality of opportunity quite differently. Both libertarianism and meritocracy believe that the inequality of individuals, with regard to certain abilities, rightfully allows for great differences in health, welfare, and resources. The mechanism of equality of opportunity serves both to reveal the inequality in abilities and justify the inequality of outcomes.

Rawls, in combining fair equality of opportunity with the difference principle, recognizes (as no one disputes) that there are differences in abilities across individuals, but he regards those differences as irrelevant for social standing. The abilities can be put to use, both for the benefit of the individual and society overall, but even those not fortunate enough to possess profitable abilities are still entitled to stand in a relationship of equality with others. This is why superior abilities can only command superior rewards if those least advantaged also benefit. Because the benefits available to those with superior abilities only arise from social institutions, those institutions must be justifiable to others under a standard of reasonableness.

Anderson and others[9] have emphasized that in examining how to structure the basic institutions of society so as to reflect individuals' underlying moral equality, Rawls's theory is primarily about egalitarian relationships. There are aspects that focus on resource distribution, of course, but they do so in service of equalizing social relations.[12] The rest of this book is shaped by the fundamental insight that the normatively justifiable form of equality is relational equality. The following chapter will provide an extended account of relational equality and its implications for a just system of social relations.

Capabilities as Metric

Before moving on to a more thorough discussion of relational egalitarianism, I want to discuss issues of how to assess equality. Both distributive egalitarians and Rawls's relational egalitarianism use resources as a metric of equality—that is, these theories assess equality, at least in part, by making comparisons regarding the resources available to different individuals. This makes sense if equalizing resources is the goal, but for relational egalitarian theories that emphasize equality of social standing, such a metric can miss the mark.

Sen raised a powerful objection to resources as metric, arguing that doing so is a type of fetish in that it seeks equality of inanimate objects rather than equality in the lives of actual human beings.[1] Sen's point was that resources are valued instrumentally—that is, for what they enable a person to do, such as being able to pursue one's conception of the good life, rather than intrinsically.

Sen makes a case for a different metric: capabilities.[61,62] Capabilities (and in particular those capabilities closely related to one's social standing) are an important concept for the purposes of health equity and social democracy. In the formulation of Sen, a capability is the substantive freedom to engage in a "functioning."[62,63] In turn, "functionings" consist of activities that people can undertake ("doings," such as receiving an education) or states they can be in ("beings," such as being well-nourished). A person's capability set is the set of functionings a person has a substantive (as opposed to merely a formal) freedom to engage in (whether or not they exercise that freedom). For example, a person might suffer from undernourishment as the result of a famine or as the result of going on a hunger strike. In the former case, being well-nourished is not in the person's capability set; in the latter, it is.[39]

Capabilities are unlike purely subjective welfare, as capabilities are not personal preferences. For example, one person might view the right to vote as extremely important, such that their life would be much worse if they could not vote, while another person may be totally indifferent. If neither had the right to vote, both would have the same (lack of) capability but different levels of welfare. Further, capabilities are not resources, which are the means one might use to achieve a particular functioning. For example, if two people each have $100, but one lives in an area where food is abundant and cheap and the other in an area where food is scarce and expensive, the two will have equal resources but different capabilities for nourishment.

Thinking about capabilities explains the intuition of the cartoons described at the beginning of this chapter. In those cartoons, equality of resources (boxes or bicycles) does not lead to equality of capabilities (watching the game or riding the bicycle). Instead, it takes different resources to produce equal capabilities. This insight is important as oppression often deflates the value of resources, meaning that those who experience oppression may need more resources to achieve the same level of capabilities.[64]

In later work,[8] Rawls emphasized what he called the "fair value" of political liberty and equal opportunity—emphasizing its substantive rather than merely formal aspects. I understand this fair value interpretation as being very similar to Sen's capabilities approach.

Sen has primarily discussed capabilities as a metric that might be used by other theories, rather than developing a full-fledged capability theory of justice. However, other philosophers have developed such theories. Perhaps the most prominent is that of philosopher Martha Nussbaum. I do not discuss her theory in detail because it is less useful for this project. It is a comprehensive doctrine with a particular perspective on what living a good, or flourishing, life consists of, rather than a political theory of justice.[65] Also, philosopher Jennifer Prah has developed a capability theory specific for health care and public health. I do not discuss it in detail because it specifically limits its focus to health care delivery and public health, rather than an entire system of social relations.[66]

Fundamentally, I think using capabilities as the metric of equality is the correct approach. Welfare is inherently incommensurate between people. Resources are only instrumentally valuable—they have no real value apart from what they allow individuals to do. Capabilities speak to what we really care about: the kinds of lives people are able to lead.[63]

One way to think about the egalitarian project is to think about "securing the social conditions of everyone's freedom."[3] Thinking of this freedom in terms of capabilities helps to set both normatively defensible and practical goals for egalitarian social transformation.

Summary

In this chapter, I have examined several approaches to political justice, rejecting inegalitarian, libertarian, meritocratic, utilitarian, equality of welfare, and distributive egalitarian approaches. I have also argued that given the fact of reasonable pluralism, a limited, "political" conception of justice should be sought, which individuals holding different comprehensive doctrines could agree to. Further, I have stated briefly that the kind of egalitarianism we should seek is a relational egalitarianism, with capabilities as the metric of equality. But I have not yet provided a more detailed description of a relational egalitarian political theory of justice. This is the focus of the next chapter.

4

Democratic Equality

The goal of this chapter is to introduce and argue for a specific working theory of justice called *democratic equality*, which underlies the normative arguments I make throughout this book.

Democratic Equality

Philosopher Elizabeth S. Anderson detailed the principles of democratic equality in her seminal article "What Is the Point of Equality?"[1] Anderson was a student of philosopher John Rawls, and I interpret democratic equality as broadly accepting Rawls's two principles of justice for determining the "basic structure" of society—its fundamental institutions. But democratic equality offers modifications, extensions, and clarifications of Rawls's arguments that help make more clear what a system of social relations that could achieve health equity would look like. Democratic equality is a relational egalitarian theory using capabilities as metrics. For democratic equality, the important form of equality is equality of social standing. The measure of that standing is specific capabilities in the civil, political, and economic spheres that permit individuals to be free and equal members of democratic society. These capabilities are underlain by capabilities related to meeting the basic needs all human beings have (e.g., food and housing). Since capabilities operationalize the concept of freedom, democratic equality attempts to ensure that all people have specific substantive freedoms. Democratic equality does not seek to guarantee all capabilities people might desire—instead it focuses specifically on arranging institutions to equalize those particular capabilities needed to stand in a relationship of equality with other citizens of a democratic state. The corresponding duty of citizens in a democratic society is to, acting through government, arrange their institutions so as to guarantee these capabilities for all. As Anderson says, under democratic equality "the basic duty of citizens, acting through the state, is not to make everyone happy but to secure everyone's freedom."[1] Here, freedom can be thought of as the capability to live as one wills (subject to the constraint that it not impede others' freedom).[1(p315)]

Because democratic equality is a relational egalitarian theory, it seeks to ensure that people stand in a relationship of equality with each other, rather than in a hierarchical relationship of superiority and inferiority.[1,2] It is concerned with the distribution of resources because resources can be critical for equal social standing, and because resource distributions often reflect the relationships, egalitarian or hierarchal, that people have. However, democratic equality does not view the distribution of resources, in and of itself, as something to be equalized or a metric of the equality of social relations.

Democratic equality is a "contractualist" theory in the sense that it takes the idea of principles people could agree to, or not reasonably reject, as the grounds of normative force,[3] and can be justified from a second-person standpoint.[4] Democratic equality is also a liberal theory in the sense that the state does not take a substantive position on any particular conception of the good.[5] The state does, however, need to take a substantive position, in the affirmative, on providing for its citizens the specific capabilities needed for equal social standing.

Democratic equality has both a negative aim (which can be thought of, following Isaiah Berlin's famous distinction between negative and positive liberty,[6] as establishing "freedom from"), and a positive aim ("freedom to").* The negative aim of democratic equality is freedom from oppression.[1] The positive aim is freedom to stand in a relationship of equality with others. As Anderson says about the egalitarian goals of democratic equality:

> Egalitarians base claims to social and political equality on the fact of universal moral equality. These claims also have a negative and a positive aspect. Negatively, egalitarians seek to abolish oppression—that is, forms of social relationship by which some people dominate, exploit, marginalize, demean, and inflict violence upon others. Diversities in socially ascribed identities, distinct roles in

---

* In addition to negative and positive freedom, political philosophers also sometimes discuss "republican" freedom, which can be thought of as having a say in things that affect you, without others exercising arbitrary power over you.

the division of labor, or differences in personal traits, whether these be neutral biological and psychological differences, valuable talents and virtues, or unfortunate disabilities and infirmities, never justify the unequal social relations listed above. Nothing can justify treating people in these ways, except just punishment for crimes and defense against violence. Positively, egalitarians seek a social order in which persons stand in relations of equality. They seek to live together in a democratic community, as opposed to a hierarchical one. Democracy is here understood as collective self-determination by means of open discussion among equals, in accordance with rules acceptable to all. To stand as an equal before others in discussion means that one is entitled to participate, that others recognize an obligation to listen respectfully and respond to one's arguments, that no one need bow and scrape before others or represent themselves as inferior to others as a condition of having their claim heard.

Democratic equality is particularly suitable for the project of health equity because it is directly concerned with inegalitarian social arrangements that, empirically, produce poor health outcomes (chapters 5 and 6). Those social arrangements all involve ideas of hierarchy and subordination, often based on factors like ascriptive identity (e.g., race or gender), or natural talents, or ability to earn a market income.[1] Whatever the specifics, these hierarchies not only result in unequal distributions of the resources needed to be healthy, but they are based on social relationships of dominance and subordination, not of equality. Thus, even if resources were similar, those viewed as inferior would nevertheless be second-class citizens, unequal in social standing even if equal in, for example, income or wealth. Democratic equality gives a clear way to think about these kinds of injustices. Under democratic equality, an injustice occurs when a circumstance "reflects, causes, or embodies" inferiority in their standing as a member of society.[2] Combining this with the definition of health inequity I proposed earlier, if this injustice harms health then it causes health inequity. This understanding of injustice does not mean social institutions must work to make everyone equal in every way. For example, institutions that result in income inequality could be permitted if they made everyone better off while maintaining relationships of equality— that is, if they worked to everyone's advantage. But the standard that should apply, to the basic structure of society (not necessarily to every specific policy or decision), is not whether inequalities help more than they hurt, or whether the inequalities advantage the "right" people. It is whether the structure of society permits only those inequalities that make everyone better off—that advantage everyone and disadvantage no one.[5]

Under democratic equality, the state fulfills its duty of equal care by guaranteeing to members of society "the social conditions of their freedom at all times"—the capabilities needed to "avoid or escape entanglement in oppressive social relationships" (both public and private) and to "function as an equal citizen in a democratic state."[1(p316)] At the same time, by focusing only on those capabilities needed to avoid oppression and function as an equal citizen, and by guaranteeing capabilities rather than requiring their use in any particular way, democratic equality can be justified to those who hold a wide range of ideological beliefs, and it avoids requiring that individuals hold any particular comprehensive doctrine.

Democratic equality guarantees the conditions of equality throughout individuals' lives. That is, it is not a "starting gate" theory where individuals receive an initial stock of capabilities or resources and are then held responsible for whatever outcomes emerge. This is because the capabilities democratic equality emphasizes are the capabilities needed to function as an equal in society, not all the capabilities that one might desire. As such, it is difficult to see what actions one could take to deserve, for example, to lose the capability for adequate nutrition. Under democratic equality, no one is owed luxuries. But one's fundamental moral equality means that one *is* owed, throughout one's life, the basics needed to stand as an equal in society.

By focusing only on those capabilities that are necessary for equal social standing, democratic equality still upholds the idea that individuals bear responsibility for pursuing their own conception of the good (e.g., individuals who hope for a vacation home in retirement should save now); but it does so without resorting to intrusive judgments about whether someone deserves their particular outcomes.[1]

Another important aspect of democratic equality is the manner in which it guarantees particular capabilities. As discussed in chapter 1, there are two distinct approaches to the welfare state. In universalism, goods and services are distributed by virtue of one's equal citizenship. In residualism, goods and services are provided in the spirit of charity from one's betters, once one has proven to be incapable of securing needed goods and services on one's own. Democratic equality is firmly universalist. This means that, under democratic equality, one can make claims for goods and services as an equal, not as a supplicant who needs charity. This avoids the creation of a hierarchy between those who are thought to provide for themselves and those who are thought to be dependent on others.[1]

One final aspect of democratic equality relates to "non-ideal" theory. No real society ever looks like a philosopher imagines. Some philosophical approaches are relevant even when the real is not the ideal, but others are not. A strength of democratic equality is that it is applicable in non-ideal cases. Using the principles of democratic equality to make policy decisions in an unjust society is likely to move toward a more just society. For example, policies to facilitate equal social standing are sensible (especially) when current social standing is characterized by relationships of superiority and inferiority. In contrast, other theories of justice may not make sense in non-ideal settings. For example, in a setting in which fair holdings did not apply, libertarian prohibitions against taxation would make little sense.

Essential Capabilities

A key task for a system of social relations governed by democratic equality is to specify the set of capabilities it seeks to guarantee. I have discussed these in a general sense, but when moving toward more specific formulations, there are two considerations to keep in mind. First, can the capabilities be objects of collective willing—that is, can they be justified to others as reasonable? Second, are these capabilities of special interest to egalitarians? As noted above, capabilities of special interest to egalitarians can be thought of in both a negative and a positive form. Negatively, these are capabilities needed to "avoid entanglement in oppressive relationships" (both public and private). Positively, these are capabilities needed to "function as equal citizen in a democratic state."[1(p316)] Collectively, I refer to the set of capabilities needed to ensure equality of social standing and that the state has a duty to guarantee across the life course as the "essential capabilities."

The goal of this section is not to give a perfectionist list of capabilities that must be guaranteed in every society, but to draw examples, from past egalitarian movements, of what capabilities have been regarded as essential. Ultimately, of course, the capabilities a society guarantees should be settled democratically.*

---

*There is a tension in this, as people need certain capabilities in order to stand in relation to each other in such a way that the result of a democratic process has normative force. This can have the effect of constraining what can result from the process. However, the justification for such capabilities is not so that people with them will generate the "right" outcomes,

In any event, the capabilities I enumerate below are meant as examples that illustrate the idea of democratic equality, and I do not here argue that each capability is one that everyone must agree on.

Civil, Political, Economic, and Basic Capabilities

I find it helpful to think about essential capabilities as existing in one of three spheres of social relations—civil, political, and economic—underlain by a sphere relating to basic needs.

The civil sphere refers to social life open to the general public and not part of the state bureaucracy. The relevant capabilities within the civil sphere involve effective access to the goods and relationships of civil society.[1,7] This could include freedom of speech and association; liberty of conscience with regard to religion and other comprehensive doctrines; liberty of person and movement; and being equally able to own property, enter into contracts, and take up employment on offer. It also could include substantive equality before the law, both criminal and civil, in terms of enforcement, due process rights, bringing claims and petitioning for redress, and hearings to resolve disputes. It could also mean that individuals can make use of public spaces and businesses that are open to the public, being able to use services like the mail and utilities (e.g., electricity or internet connectivity), and to buy, sell, and trade goods on the market.[1] Discrimination in these aspects of social life would represent unequal capabilities.

The political sphere involves both activities that influence who enters government (as an elected official, political appointee, or in the larger state bureaucracy, such as the civil service), and the actions that government takes.[1,7] Relevant capabilities within the political sphere might include rights to political participation, such as freedom of political speech and the franchise (both being able to vote and that each person's vote counts equally), the ability to run for and hold elected office, the ability to be considered for government positions, and the ability to compete for government contracts and grants.[1]

In the economic sphere, relevant capabilities could include access to systems of production, careers being open to talents, occupational choice, to

---

but that these are the capabilities that allow people to substantively participate in the process. Thus, any capabilities specified outside of a democratic process must be justified as providing freedoms that allow people to participate meaningfully in that process.

have one's interests represented within an organization in which one may be employed, and sufficient financial security to permit striking a fair bargain in accepting work and negotiating wages.[1,7] Another important capability in the economic sphere relates to participation in a division of labor that works to everyone's benefit.[1] This may entail unequal remuneration, but it should be interpersonally justifiable—that is, all individuals can recognize that such a division of labor works to their advantage.[1] Employment discrimination, financial insecurity, and imbalances of power such that some are open to economic exploitation represent unequal capabilities in the economic sphere.

Underlying the civil, political, and economic spheres of social relations are capabilities that are basic in the sense that they make possible participation in the other spheres. Some of these capabilities relate to biological needs, such as those regarding food and nutrition, shelter, housing and clothing, and health care and public health services. Others are social but nonetheless basic. These include education, both to function in one's society and to develop one's talents in order to have fair equality of economic opportunity, and capabilities that relate to, in the words of Rawls, the "social bases of self-respect,"[8] or, in the words of economist Adam Smith, "the ability to appear in public without shame."[8] These capabilities allow individuals to present themselves as equals.

The Importance of Economic Capabilities

Capabilities in the economic sphere are the least well developed or protected in contemporary American life, and they may be more controversial than those in the civil or political sphere. However, they are critical nonetheless. From the libertarian point of view, government needs strict regulation because its great power can overwhelm the relatively powerless individual. This concern is sensible, but private organizations within modern economic systems, holding power delegated by the state, can exercise an indistinguishable power. This power needs to be regulated as well. Just as civil and political rights help ensure freedom against malign government power, economic rights related to health care, education, and financial security can help ensure freedom against the power of private organizations. Historian R. H. Tawney described the how economic, along with civil and political freedom are interrelated with equality:[9(p168)]

Hence, when liberty is construed, realistically, or implying, not merely a minimum of civil and political rights, but securities that the economically weak will not be at the mercy of the economically strong, and that the control of those aspects of economic life by which all are affected will be amenable, in the last resort, to the will of all, a large measure of equality, so far from being inimical to liberty, is essential to it. In conditions which impose co-operative, rather than merely individual, effort, liberty is, in fact, equality in action, in the sense, not that all men perform identical functions or wield the same degree of power, but that all men are equally protected against the abuse of power, and equally entitled to insist that power shall be used, not for personal ends, but for the general advantage. Civil and political liberty obviously imply, not that all men shall be members of parliament, cabinet ministers, or civil servants, but the absence of such civil and political inequalities as enable one class to impose its will on another by legal coercion. It should not be less obvious that economic liberty implies, not that all men shall initiate, plan, direct, manage, or administer, but the absence of such economic inequalities as can be used as means of economic constraint.

Capabilities, Desert, and Personal Responsibility

The essential capabilities are to be guaranteed across a lifetime. This does not mean that each capability is relevant at all points in one's life (for instance, older adults likely no longer need the capability to receive elementary education). But it does mean that some capabilities are market inalienable (i.e., one cannot sell one's right to free speech), and are, at most, subject to forfeit only for serious crimes. For example, while one might forfeit liberty of person as punishment for a crime, one would not forfeit the right to adequate nutrition through financial mismanagement, or to health care through smoking cigarettes. Of course, members of society, acting through government, could discourage, say, cigarette smoking through taxation or legislation. But under democratic equality, members of society, acting through the state, still have a duty to provide essential capabilities, like the capability to receive health care, without making intrusive judgments about whether one "deserves" those capabilities. A key tenet of democratic equality is that ideas of desert should not enter into questions about essential capabilities.

When thinking about what capabilities democratic equality would guarantee, it is important to remember that the essential capabilities are only a subset of all capabilities. People may be unequal in other capabilities, and for any capability people may choose not to make use of it. This is in keeping with an understanding of capabilities as freedoms. For example, while everyone might be owed a capability of sufficient nourishment, which would require strict equality in that capability, people may vary in their capabilities to consume various expensive delicacies, with those capabilities dependent on earned income.[1] This also relates to personal responsibility. Individuals are ultimately responsible for pursuing their life as they prefer. The freedom that democratic equality provides means that people are able to pursue this life (whatever it may be), but the freedoms democratic equality guarantees are not provided as a means to do this—they are provided as an expression of equality.[10] Some approaches to distributive justice focus on determining if public support is justified for a given individual on the basis of their deservingness, responsibility, or past behavior.[11-13] But this requires paternalism and intrusive judgments, which do not treat people with respect.[1] Democratic equality takes a different approach: it specifically restricts the capabilities it seeks to guarantee to those necessary to stand as an equal citizen, rather than those needed to live a full and complete life as an adherent to any particular comprehensive doctrine would see it. Democratic equality also takes seriously everyone's role in a system of production with a fair division of labor, and thus it both expects and supports individual effort to contribute to production as a mutual activity.[1] Those contributions could be in the form of employment, or in unpaid caregiving, or other unpaid, but socially useful, roles. But it should not be thought that by guaranteeing certain capabilities democratic equality seeks to create a society where some live off the effort of others.[1]

Duties of Recognition and Duties of Distribution

Under democratic equality, the institutions of society provide for and respect two distinct but interrelated categories of claims that citizens can make on each other: claims about recognition and claims about distribution.[1] The first type of claim relates to recognition of one's equal social standing. Duties of recognition have to do with power, prestige, and social connections. Social relations that move individuals or groups away from equal social standing, without good reason, represent forms of oppression. Duties of recognition are duties to prevent or counter this oppression. The second type of claim relates to material resources. Duties of distribution relate to distributing society's resources so as to support the material basis for the essential capabilities. Varying levels of resources, across persons, may be needed to do that. Distributions of resources that are insufficient for essential capabilities represent a form of poverty. As a shorthand, one can think of duties of recognition as regarding power and duties of distribution as regarding resources.

Duties of recognition and duties of distribution are different forms of the state's duty to show equal care for the life of each individual. As Anderson notes, duties of recognition and distribution work together as part of democratic equality[1(p289)]:

> In seeking the construction of a community of equals, democratic equality integrates principles of distribution with the expressive demands of equal respect. Democratic equality guarantees all law-abiding citizens effective access to the social conditions of their freedom at all times. It justifies the distributions required to secure this guarantee by appealing to the obligations of citizens in a democratic state. In such a state, citizens make claims on one another in virtue of their equality, not their inferiority, to others. Because the fundamental aim of citizens in constructing a state is to secure everyone's freedom, democratic equality's principles of distribution neither presume to tell people how to use their opportunities nor attempt to judge how responsible people are for choices that lead to unfortunate outcomes.

Power and resources are often interrelated. Unequal social standing may be used to distribute resources unequally, as in the case of economic exploitation. Alternatively, resource distribution may be an important policy tool to help counter unequal social standing. Policies that meet duties of distribution might help counter, for example, stereotypes that result from living in poverty and undermine duties of recognition, and policies that help meet duties of recognition may help meet distributional goals by, for example, enabling people to work for wages. Meeting duties of recognition may require stricter equality than duties of distribution.[5] In fact, in meeting duties of distribution, it may take unequal resources to produce equal capabilities, because people may vary in their ability to convert resources into capabilities.[14]

Fulfilling Duties of Recognition and Distribution

In cases where social standing is unequal, relational egalitarians would prefer to change social norms rather than distribute material resources in compensation. For example, if some members of society are thought to be racially inferior, and this leads to impoverishment through employment discrimination, it would be preferable to combat the ideology of racism rather than to offer only compensatory payment for experiencing racism. In practice, meeting duties of recognition may be more difficult than duties of distribution. Doing so will likely require both state involvement (e.g., passage and enforcement of antidiscrimination laws) and egalitarian social movements. The specific expertise these movements can provide—related to the experience of the particular form of oppression being combated—is an important part of efforts to meet duties of recognition. However, different movements may vary in their effectiveness and the timescale over which they can enact change. While changes to social norms that meeting duties of recognition requires are pursued, however, resource distribution programs can help guarantee the essential capabilities. In the long term, the goal should be to "integrate duties of recognition and distribution" so that policies both effectively guarantee the essential capabilities and do so in a way that does not express disrespect.[1] This means that it is important not only to examine the effects of policies but also their rationale. Policies should be based on the conception of citizens as equals and should not be grounded in ideas of inferiority.[1] As Anderson says, "goods must be distributed according to principles and processes that express respect for all. People must not be required to grovel or demean themselves before others as a condition of laying claim to their share of goods. The basis for people's claims to distributed goods is that they are equals, not inferiors, to others."[1(p314)]

Social Democracy and Income Inequality

The concept of duties of recognition and duties of distribution helps explain why income equality is not in and of itself a goal of social democracy. The distribution of material resources, particularly income, figures prominently in social policy, and rightly so. Mechanisms to distribute income fairly are central to attempts to equalize social standing, and any approach toward equalizing social standing that does not rank income distribution highly among its aims is unlikely to succeed. Further, as a practical matter, income distribution is something that the state can do well. But ultimately, income distribution alone will not achieve equal social standing. Fundamentally, the inegalitarian social theories that democratic equality opposes are based on suppositions of superiority and inferiority, and take as perfectly

natural a hierarchy of unequal social relations that both justifies and generates unequal distributions of power, resources, and health. The goal of social
democracy is not to address income inequality per se. Instead, the goal is
to address the relational inequality that results in income inequality and
other manifestations of injustice. And in turn, this is what will achieve health
equity.[1,15]

Oppression

Unequal social standing that occurs when duties of recognition are
not met represents oppression. An obvious form of oppression is formal
legal inequality, such as existed in Europe under feudalism,[9] and in America
under slavery and the Jim Crow laws. But oppression still occurs despite formal legal equality.

Drawing on the work of political scientist and philosopher Iris Marion
Young,[16] this section discusses in an illustrative (rather than exhaustive) way
some types of oppression still present despite formal legal equality.

The first type of oppression is *exploitation*, which can be thought of as
occurring when one's vulnerability is instrumentalized for another's en-
richment.[17]

The next is *marginalization*.[16] Marginalization occurs when one does not
get to develop or exercise one's capacity for productivity or social participation. This can occur through discrimination (e.g., being actively kept out of
the labor force) or more structurally (e.g., growing up in neighborhoods with
poor schools).

A third type of oppression is *powerlessness*.[16] Powerlessness relates to issues like respectability and autonomy over decisions at work. Powerlessness
reflects a difference in status that may not correlate with material resources.
Consider two roles in a workplace—one of a professional, and one of what
is sometimes called an "unskilled" laborer. Even if both were to be paid similarly, the professional may be treated with respect, listened to, or shown
deference, while the unskilled laborer may have little control over their working conditions and be ordered around. This is an example of powerlessness.

A fourth type of oppression is called by Young *cultural imperialism*. Cultural imperialism relates to living in a society whose dominant meanings
render the particular perspective of one's own group invisible, stereotyped,
and marked as not just different but "other." Under cultural imperialism, the
experience and culture of the dominant group is universalized.

A phenomenon that sometimes goes along with cultural imperialism is *essentialization*.[18-20] This occurs when individuals are not seen as individuals but instead are stereotyped or homogenized on the basis of some aspect of ascriptive identity—all individuals in that category are seen as all being the same in some way. Essentialization plays a key role in the contemporary American ideology of racism.[19] In fact, the idea of race for many in the United States is that of an essence—in other words, that a racial ascription carries some deeper meaning about who a person is or what they are like.[20] Even among those who disavow a biological view of race, the idea of culture can serve a similar role—implying that those with a particular racial, ethnic, or ancestry-based identity still share something essential that renders members of that group homogenous in some way.[21] Imputing a shared culture to heterogeneous individuals thought to be joined by race is a form of essentialization. Essentialism can facilitate oppression by providing a justification for why someone is inherently different from other individuals and thus does not deserve equal social standing. Ultimately, inegalitarian ideologies rely on some form of "othering," which invariably implies inferiority and justifies subordination. Essentialization can be a step in the process of othering.

A fifth type of oppression is *violence*.[16] Of course, anyone can experience violence. But violence as a form of oppression is used in particular ways. Oppressive violence is used to humiliate or dominate or degrade (for example, a person in a position of authority slapping someone in a position of servitude). Oppressive violence is often legitimated or excused in some way (e.g., "they had it coming," "it's the only thing they can understand, you know what they're like," or "what did they expect would happen if they talked to me like that?"). Violence committed by those in dominant positions against those with lesser social standing is often more tolerated, with cases being overlooked or lenient punishments handed out (often justified by the negative consequence punishment would have for the perpetrator). Oppressive violence is often meant to stifle egalitarian social movements (such as the dogs and firehoses used against US civil rights activists in the 1960s). Oppressive violence can also include petty harassment (e.g., shoving someone who is loath to fight back because they know the authorities will side with the instigator), street attacks (e.g., as experienced by individuals with Asian ancestry in the midst of the COVID-19 pandemic), and pogroms (e.g., those that occurred against Jews in Europe, or the 1898 Wilmington Insurrection in the United States).

A sixth type of oppression is *draconianism*. Draconianism relates to applying laws and policies severely to certain categories of individuals, assuming the worst about them, or not giving them the benefit of the doubt. When those in positions of power exercise judgment, draconianism may result in those with lower social standing being treated more severely (e.g., given a custodial sentence at the longer end of a range), denied second chances others might have received, considered in a less favorable light, or reduce the opportunities, benefits, or assistance individuals receive.

A seventh type of oppression is *exclusion*. Exclusion occurs when social circumstances are arranged so that some are unable to participate even though they have every right to do so. Examples of this are public structures that do not allow access for those with disabilities, or proceedings that those of particular language communities cannot understand. Exclusion can co-occur with cultural imperialism, but it can also occur among individuals who share the same culture. For example, lack of ramps to enter buildings excludes those with mobility limitations even if they are members of the dominant culture.

An eighth type of oppression is *discrimination*. Discrimination can be thought of as not treating like cases alike, or using what should be irrelevant features as determining factors. Although formally barred in some contexts and for some protected characteristics, discrimination nevertheless occurs in many settings.

A ninth type of oppression is *stigmatization*, which occurs when behavior or cultural practice becomes associated with inferiority.[22,23]

Equality Supports Freedom

These examples of oppression are helpful, not only for beginning the discussion of how injustice can harm health (the focus of the following two chapters) but also for understanding the important point that democratic equality seeks to integrate ideas about freedom and equality. Some argue that freedom and equality conflict—or more specifically that efforts to support equality inherently reduce freedom. Democratic equality's understanding of oppression as reduced freedom that results from inequality helps make clear why that is not the case. As Anderson says[1(p315)]:

> This claim might seem paradoxical, given the prevailing view that represents equality and freedom as conflicting ideals. We can see how it is true by consider-

ing the oppressive relationships that social equality negates. Equals are not subject to arbitrary violence or physical coercion by others. Choice unconstrained by arbitrary physical coercion is one of the fundamental conditions of freedom. Equals are not marginalized by others. They are therefore free to participate in politics and the major institutions of civil society. Equals are not dominated by others; they do not live at the mercy of others' wills. This means that they govern their lives by their own wills, which is freedom. Equals are not exploited by others. This means they are free to secure the fair value of their labor. Equals are not subject to cultural imperialism: they are free to practice their own culture, subject to the constraint of respecting everyone else. To live in an egalitarian community, then, is to be free from oppression to participate in and enjoy the goods of society, and to participate in democratic self-government.

In closing this section on oppression, it is important to note that those who have not experienced a particular form of oppression are often unaware of it. This means that accounts of oppression from those who are oppressed should be taken seriously, and those who are oppressed should be actively included in key roles that help design solutions to oppression.

Collective Action

As Young discusses, the idea of injustice entails a conception that some person, or people, committed the injustice and/or have power to change it.[24] This means that justice and injustice are fundamentally about actions that individuals took and should take. But this does not necessarily mean that acting justly entails working individualistically.

Acting as individuals, people are called upon to act justly in many ways—for example, by not committing racial discrimination when in a position of authority. However, a tenet of democratic equality is that justice is providing "the social conditions for equal citizenship."[1(p332)] This is an obligation that can only be fulfilled collectively. Injustice is always the product of human action, but a specific injustice may result from ways human actions are aggregated, such as through institutions and other social structures. Thus, an injustice may neither have been intended nor even fully under the control of any one person. Instead, injustice may be an effect of a system of social relations in which individuals are enmeshed. These systems are produced and reproduced by human actions but may have effects that were not deliberate or volitional.

This means that in many instances it is beyond the power of any one individual, working as an individual, to end or remediate an injustice. Acting justly as an individual, though important, will generally not be enough. At the same time, however, discharging one's duty to act justly must be within the realm of ordinary possibility, not a superhuman endeavor. Thus, it is important to think of justice as something people can work toward in the course of their normal lives (though this does not mean that the lives of those who benefit from injustice might not have change). The principal way to do this is through collective, political action. Concrete examples not only include voting, but also public service, political organizing, issue advocacy, and participation in egalitarian social movements. In sum, it is important to act justly as an individual while also engaging in collective action to discharge the duties of justice. Everyone has a duty to contribute to securing the conditions of everyone's freedom, even if doing so is not directly under any one individual's control. In other words, "you are not obligated to complete the work, but neither are you free to abandon it."[25(v2:16)]

The Priority of the Right over the Good

An important aspect of democratic equality, and other contractualist theories of justice, is what might be called the priority of the right over the good. The priority of the right over the good comes from the idea of society as a system of fair cooperation. In such a system, there must be rules all can abide by, provided that others do the same. For that reason, the right (how people need to act as part of a system of fair cooperation) must take priority over the good (what people would like to do or have for themselves). For example, some actions, like murder or enslavement, can be rejected out of hand, even if they might be profitable.

In contrast to contractualist theories, utilitarian and other consequentialist theories of justice, which determine what action to take by considering the outcomes the action produces (for example, in terms of utility, welfare, or resources), typically do not distinguish between the right and the good. Some actions that would simply be off the table for contractualist theories, like slavery or murder for profit, become questions of trade-offs between the amount of disutility (or another metric of consequences) caused to the victim (and other affected parties) and the amount of utility that accrues to the perpetrator (and other affected parties).

One implication of the priority of the right over the good is that questions about maximization and distribution of outcomes like welfare or income should only be considered by comparing normatively acceptable options, not all possible options. Equal citizens pursue their concept of the good from within the normative constraints imposed by the conditions that provide that equality.*

There is an important question as to the level at which the principle of the right over the good applies. The principle does not necessarily imply that for every specific action, or even for every particular policy, there may not be winners and losers. But, at least at the level of the basic structure of society, core institutions cannot be premised on inequality for some individuals so that others can better pursue their conception of the good. The priority of the right over the good has important implications for policy approaches that will be discussed later in this book.

Equal Care: A Restatement

In light of the discussion about theories of justice, and in particular democratic equality, over the last two chapters, I want to restate the idea of the state's duty of equal care. Democratic equality is a contractualist, relational egalitarian theory of justice. The state's duty of equal care stems from the contractualist idea: institutions that everyone is required to accept and participate in must be justifiable to everyone, and showing equal care for the life of everyone is part of what makes the institutions justifiable.[26] Further, the duty of equal care is essential to democratic government. In other words, the essence of democracy is not just that citizens comprise or are represented in the government but that the government accepts its duty to show equal care for each citizen. The democratic state exists to protect and advance the interests not of some elite or favored group, but of everyone.[26,27] Further, in a democratic state, when the interests of citizens conflict, the state should adjudicate that conflict in a way that recognizes and preserves the fundamental equality of its citizens. The institutions of a state that adjudicate these conflicts must take the interests of all parties seriously.

In some cases, a society's institutions will result in an unequal distribution of resources and capabilities. If this does not undermine overall equality

---

*Similarly, the goal of policy is to create option sets so that choices made within them are among justified options. Arguments against interfering with freedom of contract are not meaningful unless parties to the contract are in normatively justifiable bargaining positions when negotiating.

of social standing, measured by the essential capabilities, this may be justifiable. Such justification would need to include at least three aspects: an institutional justification (i.e., a good reason to have an institution that gives rise to inequality), procedural fairness (i.e., that the process that assigns positions with varying levels of benefits is fair), and substantive opportunity (i.e., that people have a fair chance to be qualified to be selected for positions with greater benefits).[26]

Critics can, sometimes disingenuously, misrepresent what relational equality means in order to paint it as impossible. Given everyone's differences and the need for some hierarchies to organize and coordinate society, the argument goes, relational equality is magical thinking. But relational equality is not quixotic. Equality in the space of political capabilities does not require that everyone be a senator, but rather that everyone have a say in who should comprise the government. Likewise, equality in the space of economic capabilities may not mean that everyone has the same income, but rather that everyone can meet their needs such that economic circumstances do not serve as a significant constraint on their freedom.[9]

The idea of equal care helps guide policy that guarantees essential capabilities. A person without a particular essential capability provides evidence that the state is failing to meet its duty of equal care. An individual in such a situation is justified in making a claim on the state (representing their fellow citizens) to remedy this. Further, the idea of equal care helps explain why policies need to provide equal, rather than "sufficient," essential capabilities. If there is substantial inequality in the essential capabilities, it would be hard to understand how the state has shown each individual equal care.[26]

The way the state (and by extension all of us, collectively) meets its duty of equal care is to guarantee the essential capabilities needed to stand in a relationship of equality with others. The principles of democratic equality help identify what those capabilities are. This is the normative substance of social democracy. The technical substance of social democracy is understanding how to guarantee those capabilities. The aspects of the state that guarantee these capabilities are the egalitarian state. When functioning well, the egalitarian state creates a system of overlapping and complementary policies—a regime—such that there are no "spaces" within the social structure where people experience poverty, or oppression, or other forms of political injustice.

Summary

Fundamentally, health equity is not about finding more or better ways to provide personal health care, though that is important. It is about ending the injustices that harm health. This chapter has sought to present and argue for a working theory of justice that can guide the pursuit of health equity. The purpose of such a theory is not to create some kind of utopia but to provide direction for designing policies that are just. As the coming chapters will show, being able to set normative goals is a prerequisite for using knowledge and methods from epidemiology, economics, public administration, and other fields that allow a society to translate normative principles into material realities. The theory of justice that helps do this, Anderson's democratic equality, is an egalitarian theory that seeks equality of social standing, measured by essential capabilities, to create "the social conditions for equal citizenship."[1(p332)] It is a contractualist, relational egalitarian theory. It is also a liberal theory in that it is neutral with regard to comprehensive doctrines and the conceptions of the good that equal citizens might pursue. However, it is definitely not neutral with regard to guaranteeing, throughout the civil, political, and economic spheres of social relations, the capabilities needed to stand as free and equal citizens.

Democratic equality integrates questions of recognition and distribution—not only seeking a fair distribution of resources but seeking to ensure that that distribution occurs in ways that recognize the moral equality of all citizens. This is part of why democratic equality is particularly suitable for health equity work, because injustices in power and resources, the types of injustice democratic equality is particularly concerned with, are fundamental causes of poor health.[28,29] This means that the normative framework of democratic equality works in concert with empirical observations about the causes of health. When power and resources, as determinants of health, are distributed unjustly, the result is injustice that harms health.

The state fulfills its duty of equal care by, subject to the technological, resource, and geopolitical constraints of its time, establishing a regime that regulates society as a system of fair cooperation. Though equality is fundamentally about the relationships people have with each other—avoiding unjust power relations—resource distribution is also important, as unequal power often results in unequal resources and unequal resources often sustain inequalities of power. Thus, the state's duty of equal care includes both duties of recognition (i.e., treating people as equals) and duties of distribution (i.e., distributing resources so that people are substantively equal) with regard to a set of essential capabilities. An individual's duty is to work collectively in a political project to establish and maintain a state that can fulfill its duty of equal care.

The conditions that determine health are not ones that occur naturally, or by chance. Democratic equality applies "judgments of justice to human arrangements, not to the natural order. This helps us see that people, not nature, are responsible for turning the natural diversity of human beings into oppressive hierarchies" that harm health.[1(p336)]

5

How Injustice Harms Health

So far I have argued that health inequity should be thought of as injustice that harms health, which invited the question: what is an injustice? I then argued that, under the normative approach called democratic equality, an injustice occurs when a person is not guaranteed the capabilities needed to stand as an equal citizen—when their life is not shown equal care. This chapter moves from normative questions about injustice to empirical questions about how injustice harms health. Its purpose is to make clear that the issues of normative concern—social standing and its relationship to the distribution of power and resources—are also empirically important for health.

The causes of health that concern health equity are fundamentally about the relationships people have with one another. This is because health equity relates to justice, and justice has to do with how people relate each other. In the words of philosopher and political scientist Iris Marion Young, "to judge a circumstance unjust implies that we understand it to be at least partly as humanly caused, and entails the claim that something should be done to rectify it."[1(p95)]

Empirical sciences like social epidemiology and social medicine do not make normative claims. Instead, their uses are technical: to document health states (description), to establish that particular social relations affect health (etiology), to understand how particular social relations affect health (mechanism), and to determine whether changes to social relations change health outcomes (intervention). The technical knowledge produced can be used to help achieve normative goals.

The organizing principle I use to understand how social relations affect health is epidemiologist Nancy Krieger's idea of embodiment.[2] She defines embodiment as "how we literally incorporate, biologically, the material (bio-physical) and social world in which we live."[3] The health state of any individual at any particular time is an "emergent embodied phenotype"—which is a product of their entire history as an organism.[4] This history results from dynamic and reinforcing processes that interlink one's actions, the direct actions of others, and the indirect actions of others (e.g., those that produce and reproduce institutions and other social structures) in a system of social relations. Embodiment is to understanding human health and disease as evolution by natural selection is to understanding biology. Social epidemiology and medicine identify the pathways of embodiment, that is, how social conditions literally get under the skin.[5]

This chapter discusses several epidemiological perspectives useful for understanding processes of embodiment. This chapter also discusses common mechanisms—pathways of embodiment—that link unjust social relations and poor health. Together, these perspectives and mechanisms provide ways to explain how the distribution of power and resources in a society helps determine the distribution of disease, or, in the words of Krieger, how "health and disease are socially produced within evolving and socially-conditioned biologic parameters."[5(p229)]

Epidemiological Perspectives

Medical perspectives seek to explain the health of individuals, while epidemiological perspectives seek to explain the distribution of health and disease in populations.[5] As a field of scientific inquiry, epidemiology is rooted in empiric data—observations about the world. However, data are not self-interpreting. Data are understood—marshaled to create a coherent story—by use of theory. This section sketches out some common theoretical perspectives, indicating their relevant strengths and limitations (figure 5.1). An aphorism often attributed to statistician George Box is that "all models are wrong, some are useful." The theoretical perspectives presented here are models: simplifications to aid understanding, or approximations to guide action (that must be checked and possibly revised against empirical results).

Sociological Insights Regarding Human Behavior

To understand population health, it is important to understand the behaviors that people engage in that affect their health and that of others. The behaviors that people adopt can generally be understood in reference

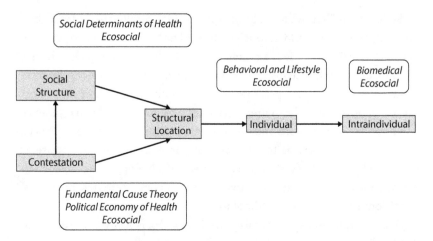

Figure 5.1. A simplified illustration of areas of focus for different epidemiological perspectives. The behavioral and lifestyle perspective and the biomedical
perspective emphasize individual or intraindividual factors. The social determinants of health perspective emphasizes how social structures and locations
within them affect individual health. Fundamental cause theory emphasizes
the importance to health of individuals' location, as it relates to others, within
social structures and the attendant resources of those locations. Political economy of health emphasizes contested relations that help determine social structures, which in turn distribute power and resources. The ecosocial perspective
synthesizes individual, relational, and structural foci. The life course perspective, not shown, can be combined with the perspectives depicted to provide
mechanistic explanations for how exposures at one point in time subsequently
affect health.

to their *interests* (or *incentives*), the *ideas* that they hold, and/or the *institutions* they are embedded in. But while ultimately human agency determines
behavior, people are not typically making decisions about behaviors to engage in under conditions of their own choosing. This means that social
structures, which help arrange people's interests and incentives, which affect the ideas they are exposed to and adopt, and which are formed, at least
in part, by institutions, provide critical context for understanding behavior
(figure 5.2).

Social structures comprise the social environment in which people are
enmeshed. "Macro" level social structures are aggregations and emergent
phenomena of relations between "micro" level agents—in this case, indi-

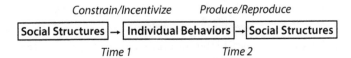

Constrain/Incentivize   *Produce/Reproduce*

| Social Structures | → | Individual Behaviors | → | Social Structures |

Time 1   *Time 2*

Figure 5.2. Social structures can be thought of as the aggregated relations (and emergent properties thereof) between individuals that constrain and/or incentivize individual behaviors at a particular time. Subsequently, those behaviors result in the social structures of the next time period, and so on.

viduals.[6] These relations include processes of contestation that both shape social structure and locate people within those structures (with attendant power and resources).

The social structures of a particular time impose constraints on the practices of individuals, and in turn the practices of individuals maintain, transform, or reproduce social structures for the next time period.[6] Institutions are an important type of social structure. Institutions are relatively stable formal and informal rules, regulations, policies, and norms that influence, constrain, channel, and/or regulate the actions of individuals, organizations, and other actors.[7] Institutions help define the legitimate actions an actor can take, and they often represent historical arrangements made to settle specific issues or competing interests.[8] In this sense, institutions represent "congealed power."[9]

Social structures are an analytical abstraction. They should not be reified and do not have causal force—only individual agency does.* But the concept of social structures is useful for thinking about why people adopt particular behaviors. Social structures set the "rules of the game," constraining an individual's actions, shaping their interests and incentives, and defining conditions under which they can "go with the flow" or pay a cost for going against it. Structures can be thought of as influencing the menu of actions people might choose from, and which version of the menu any specific person is shown. Structures can also be viewed as part of a process of socialization whereby individuals internalize expectations, customs, values, norms, and practices ("culture").

Ultimately, people's actions and the effects of those actions on others

---

*This is the premise of methodological individualism.

determine whether and how social structures are maintained, reproduced, and/or altered. Social movements can work to change formal and informal rules. People can also recognize the culture and ideas they have internalized, and work for change, both for themselves and others.

Individual, Structural, and Relational Foci

The above discussion of social structure is helpful for understanding a key distinction among the epidemiological perspectives—their focus: individual, structural, relational, or a synthesis. A given perspective could emphasize characteristics of individuals, characteristics of the social structure individuals are in, power relations between individuals in different structural positions, or synthesizing all of these contributors to population health. To help illustrate the difference between these foci, imagine a game of musical chairs. Individual explanations for why some win and others lose may focus on factors like individuals' speed or reflexes. Structural explanations may focus on the number of chairs relative to the number of players, how long the music plays, or second chances offered. Relational explanations may focus on how the rules were made and who those rules might favor.

Outcomes that seem to be determined by chance at the level of the individual can be shaped by social structures—a concept sometimes called structured chance.[4] Imagine a game, like a quincunx or pachinko, where a disc slides down a peg board and falls into one of 10 bins (figure 5.3). Though each disc's path will be random, the distribution of many discs across the bins will be patterned by where the discs start and the arrangement of pegs. The chance outcome of each disc is structured. Changes to the starting point or the arrangement of the pegs would change the distribution of outcomes. The structured chances that health equity work is concerned with result from sociological processes that both produce and reproduce a system of social relations (arrangement of pegs) and locate individuals in social positions within it (starting point).

To help make each of the following epidemiological perspectives more concrete, I provide a running example of how one might, using each perspective, understand and intervene on the problem of type 2 diabetes mellitus.

Individually Focused Perspectives

The two individually focused perspectives I discuss are the biomedical and the behavioral and lifestyle perspectives. The biomedical perspective

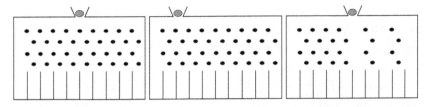

Figure 5.3. Structured chance. Though the path of an individual disc through the pegs may be determined by chance, the board's structure will affect the distribution of a "population" of discs across bins. Compared with the arrangement on the left, changing the starting point (*center*) or arrangement of the pegs (*right*) is likely to alter the overall distribution of disc outcomes.

focuses primarily on processes that occur within the body, while the behavioral and lifestyle perspectives focus on actions that individuals take.

BIOMEDICINE

The biomedical perspective is the dominant paradigm for understanding health and illness in the United States today. Emphasizing genetics, molecular biology, (patho-)physiology, microbiology, and related "basic" sciences, the biomedical perspective seeks "to understand normal and abnormal function from gene to phenotype and to provide a basis for preventive and therapeutic intervention in human disease."[10] A key metaphor is the body as an intricate machine, with thousands of molecular processes, best understood by principles of chemistry and physics, working in conjunction to produce a given state of health.[5(p138)] The biomedical perspective views changes in health as caused by changes in intraindividual biology, and it is unrivaled for understanding how, mechanistically, biology relates to health. Manipulation of biological processes through medical technology has prolonged life and reduced suffering across many conditions.

The biomedical perspective focuses within individuals, but human health cannot be understood without reference to social relations. To illustrate, imagine two individuals with the same inborn error of metabolism—a mutation that results in decreased ability to metabolize phenylalanine, and causes the condition phenylketonuria (PKU). PKU can result in intellectual disability if even small amounts of phenylalanine are consumed.

Someone with PKU living in a society that has not produced the knowledge about the condition and dietary modification as treatment, or that does not screen for this condition soon after birth, or does not guarantee the capability for appropriate food, could suffer poor health. However, someone with PKU who lives in a society that has produced this knowledge, and does screen, and guarantees appropriate treatment, may suffer no ill effects.

Therefore, a key limitation of the biomedical perspective is not considering the system of social relations in which the individual it focuses upon lives. The same biological processes can produce different health outcomes in different environments. As such, the biomedical perspective is an incredibly useful, but incomplete, way to understand health.

An example biomedically informed explanation for type 2 diabetes mellitus is that it results from loss of β-cell function such that residual endogenous insulin secretion cannot overcome insulin resistance. An example intervention is administration of glucagon-like peptide 1 (GLP-1) agonists to improve insulin sensitivity and reduce hyperglycemia.

BEHAVIORAL AND LIFESTYLE PERSPECTIVES

Behaviors describe the actions people take, and lifestyle refers to patterns of those behaviors. Behavioral and lifestyle perspectives focus at the level of the individual[5,11,12] and often emphasize risk factors for poor health, such as dietary patterns, cigarette smoking, and sexual activities.[13] Behaviors individuals undertake, once or accumulated over time, are important in the process of embodiment—they can help explain why the biological changes that the biomedical perspective focuses on occur. Behavioral and lifestyle perspectives can help link social conditions to intraindividual biology, but often these perspectives pay little attention to why particular behaviors and lifestyles are adopted, ignoring the social conditions that can constrain and incentivize behavior.

An example behavioral and lifestyle informed explanation for type 2 diabetes mellitus is that it arises from unhealthy diets and sedentary lifestyles such that resulting obesity damages pancreatic β-cells. An example intervention is an intensive lifestyle program to promote a healthful diet, weight loss through dietary modification, and physical activity.

Structurally Focused Perspectives: Social Determinants of Health

Structurally focused perspectives are concerned with the "social determinants of health." The World Health Organization defines the social determinants of health as "the conditions in which people are born, grow, work, live, and age, and the wider set of forces and systems shaping the conditions of daily life. These forces and systems include economic policies and systems, development agendas, social norms, social policies and political systems."[14]

There is a vast body of work on social determinants, which has been reviewed in detail.[15-21] Some social determinants work focuses on particular sets of determinants. For example, sub-perspectives of political determinants of health, legal determinants of health, and commercial determinants of health all give important specificity to ways that their area of focus affects health.[22-26] Other work focuses on particular mechanisms that link social conditions and health. Examples include sub-perspectives focusing on how culture and norms influence health (often by shaping behavior and lifestyle),[27] how material conditions (such as food insecurity, housing instability, or health care access) influence health,[28-30] and how psychosocial processes influence health.[31,32] Psychosocial here refers to how people perceive and experience their social circumstances, and how their circumstances shape their goals and expectations.[33-35]

A common metaphor used by structurally focused perspectives is that in processes of embodiment there are downstream (or proximal) factors that are at or close to the individual level, and upstream (or distal) factors at the level of social structures. Structurally focused perspectives have provided a much-needed countervailing influence to individually focused perspectives, and social determinants of health has become the international consensus frame for discussing effects of social structures on health.[36] Further, structurally focused scholarship has provided an invaluable understanding of the processes of embodiment.

Nevertheless, an important criticism is that structurally focused scholarship often places little emphasis on how the social conditions studied are produced and maintained. Further, structurally focused perspectives can be vulnerable to "downstream drift"—justifying interventions on the basis of structural factors but actually intervening on behavioral or other "downstream" issues.[36] An example of downstream drift is identifying the cause of food insecurity as unjust distributive institutions but intervening with behavioral interventions, like education about purchasing healthy foods.

A social determinants of health informed explanation for type 2 diabetes mellitus is that it results from material hardship such as food insecurity, political failures that limit access to preventive health care, and commercial determinants such as marketing of obesogenic food to low-income populations. An example intervention is using the Supplemental Nutrition Assistance Program (SNAP, a means-tested food subsidy) to help individuals experiencing food insecurity afford foods they can use to help manage their diabetes.

Relationally Focused Perspectives

Relationally focused perspectives emphasize cooperation and contestation over positions within social structures, and the forms of social structures themselves. Two important relational perspectives are fundamental cause theory, which focuses on contestation between people with differential resources needed for health (which stem from occupying different locations in the social structure), and political economy of health, which focuses on processes of contestation that shape the social structures that influence health.

FUNDAMENTAL CAUSE THEORY

Sociologists Bruce Link and Jo Phelan[37,38] proposed fundamental cause theory to explain why the gradient between socioeconomic status and health persists across contexts with very different threats to health.[39] The central tenet of fundamental cause theory is that flexible resources, defined within the theory as "money, knowledge, prestige, power, and beneficial social connections"[38] are able to protect health (that is, be used to avoid disease and mitigate consequences if disease occurs) "no matter what mechanisms are relevant at any given time."[38] In contrast to the upstream/downstream distinction, fundamental cause theory makes a "fundamental/surface" distinction.[40] The fundamental cause patterns the outcome, even as the surface (or superficial) causes may change. For example, at the turn of the 20th century, when tuberculosis was a major cause of death in the United States, greater resources enabled less crowded and better ventilated housing that lowered the risk of exposure.[41,42] In the 21st century, when cardiometabolic diseases are major causes of death, greater resources can be used for healthier food and exercise opportunities to avoid developing type 2 diabetes mellitus, or better treatments to avoid complications if it develops. And whatever the major causes of death are at the turn of the 22nd century, greater resources are likely to help avoid them as well.[42]

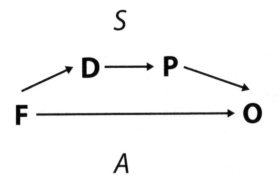

Figure 5.4. A stylized relationship between fundamental cause *F* and health outcome *O*. Whether specific pathway *S* is addressed through proximal cause *P* or distal cause *D* (or both), the relationship between *F* and *O* can persist through alternative pathway *A*. This suggests that either the fundamental cause should be addressed, or all possible pathways between *F* and *O* must be addressed. If alternative pathway *A* is not apparent prior to intervention (e.g., because specific pathway *S* is dominant and *A* is dormant), knowing all pathways to address a priori may be difficult.

Fundamental cause theory has several important implications. First, addressing only a surface cause may not meaningfully change the distribution of health outcomes as other pathways can become more salient when one pathway is blocked. For example, access to healthcare is one mechanism that links income to health—a surface cause. But providing universal healthcare access, by itself, may not remove the connection between income and health, because income may still pattern exposures to unhealthy environments, or uptake of treatments once in care (figure 5.4).

From a fundamental cause perspective, policies to improve health equity could either address a fundamental cause directly or address all possible pathways between the fundamental cause and poor health. The latter approach is likely complex and may be impossible if some pathways are unknown, so addressing the fundamental cause directly is often preferable.

Another insight of fundamental cause theory is that in an unjust system of social relations, new technology to improve health will cause new injustices to emerge. For example, for an unavoidable disease with no treatment, there may be little relationship between resources and health outcomes for that disease.[38] However, if knowledge about prevention or treatment becomes available, a relationship between resources and health outcomes becomes possible. When resources are unjustly distributed, every new advance in health knowledge or technology can be preferentially taken up by those who are unjustly better off. The injustices of the COVID-19 vaccination rollout provide a vivid example.

Despite its important insights, fundamental cause theory has meaningful limitations. Because it regards surface causes as less important, it can deemphasize mechanistic investigation. Also, fundamental cause theory may not examine what causes the fundamental causes (i.e., the factors that lead to unjust distributions of income or unequal social standing). Given these limitations, other perspectives are helpful complements to fundamental cause theory.

As alluded to above, an explanation for type 2 diabetes mellitus informed by fundamental cause theory is that lesser resources might preclude healthier food and exercise opportunities, which those with greater resources enjoy preferential access to.[42] An example intervention might be a basic income program.

POLITICAL ECONOMY OF HEALTH

The political economy of health perspective focuses on the institutions and other social structures that affect health through the distribution of social standing, power, and material resources.[5(p167),43,44] A central tenet is that interrelated political and economic systems—the values they emphasize, the structures that constitute them, and the factors they prioritize, in combination with the suite of technology available—generate the material conditions and social relations that people live in. This produces a society's profile of health and disease. As Krieger notes[5(p167)]:

> In each case the "what" these [political economic] systems produce refers not only to their literal economic output (financially and in material goods), but also to:
> 1. Their particular societal structure, including its constituent social and economic groups and their relationships with each other (whether adversarial or supportive);
> 2. The means and materials these social groups use to reinforce or challenge their social position and to sustain and reproduce themselves in the

daily course of life (involving paid and unpaid labor outside and in the home); household, family, and childrearing structures; and access to and use of needed goods and services; and

3. The norms, values, and ideologies justifying—and challenging—their political and economic priorities.

The political economy of health perspective focuses clearly on how health is actively produced by society's institutions. It investigates why those institutions and other social structures came to be, whose interests they serve, and what forces maintain and reproduce them. However, it is limited in its ability to elucidate biological processes of embodiment. Thus, questions from the political economy of health perspective are complementary to those of structurally focused perspectives, which often examine mechanisms whereby those institutions and other social structures cause particular health outcomes.

An example explanation for type 2 diabetes mellitus informed by political economy of health is that it results from government captured by agribusiness, leading to artificially cheap, ultra-processed, diabetogenic foods dominating the food supply. An example intervention is anti-corruption laws and campaign finance reform to reduce corporate influence in policy making.

Synthesizing Foci: The Ecosocial Theory of Disease Distribution

To affect health, social conditions must somehow "get under the skin." Thus, synthesizing individual, structural, and relational foci can help examine the entire process of embodiment, rather than particular elements alone.

Krieger's ecosocial theory of disease distribution does this.[5] In short, the theory concerns itself with how individuals embody their societal and ecological contexts.[5] As Krieger puts it, ecosocial theory "explicitly incorporates constructs pertaining to political economy, political ecology, ecosystems, spatiotemporal scales and levels, biological pathways of embodiment, and the social production of scientific knowledge."[5(p203)]

The theory is ecological in that it views people, as organisms, interacting with their environment (both natural and socially constructed, and including both other people and non-human organisms) at different levels or scales of analysis, and in specific times (i.e., a historical milieu) and places (i.e., geographies).[5(p208)] Further, it is ecological in the sense that people, as organisms, can be thought of as belonging to "populations" that both shape and are shaped by their environment in a dynamic process.[5(p208)] Ecosocial theory views levels or scales of analysis (e.g., global, national, regional, small area, household, individual) as vital to accurately conceptualizing population health dynamics, but it does not view these as inherently nested hierarchies—there can be non-nested relationships or cross-level interactions. Four core propositions of ecosocial theory are worth highlighting[5(p215)]:

> "People literally embody, biologically, their lived experience, in societal and ecological context, thereby creating population patterns of health and disease."

> "Societies' epidemiologic profile are shaped by the ways of living afforded by their current and changing societal arrangements of power, property, and the production and reproduction of both social and biological life, involving people, other species, and the biophysical world in which we live."

> "Determinants of current and changing societal patterns of disease distribution, including health inequities, are (1) exogenous to people's bodies, and (2) manifest at different levels and involve different spatiotemporal scales, with macrolevel phenomena . . . more likely to drive and constrain meso- and microlevel phenomena than vice versa; to the extent genes are relevant to societal distributions of disease, at issue is gene expression, rather than gene frequency."

> "Explanations of disease distribution cannot be reduced solely to explanations of disease mechanisms, as the latter do not account for why rates and patterns change, in complex ways, over time and place."

In sum, ecosocial theory pays "attention to levels, pathways, and power, in historical, social, and ecological context."[4] These factors together produce an emergent embodied phenotype—not a static health state but an expression of one's history that both influences and may be influenced by subsequent social and ecological context.[4] An essential insight of ecosocial theory is the idea of embodiment, which is indispensable for understanding how social relations affect health. Another cardinal precept is that the processes that shape health are ecological—individuals are shaped by and shape their environment, dynamically. Finally, ecosocial theory makes clear the need to understand health and disease in relation to a specific geographies and historical milieus, at multiple, not necessarily nested, levels.

An explanation for type 2 diabetes mellitus informed by the ecosocial perspective is that globalization and 21st-century US trade and domestic food policy affect the food environments people are exposed to, while the decline of labor unions and corporate capture of state legislatures influence declining real wages, putting increased pressure on food budgets and constricting dietary choice. These phenomena are embodied through an allostatic loading process as increased insulin resistance and declining β-cell function. An example intervention is a regime with voting rights enforcement, living wage policies, and universal health care that provides lifestyle interventions and prescription medications.

Life Course Epidemiology

The life course perspective emphasizes a mechanistic understanding of the relationship between time and health.[45] It helps explain how exposures at any point in time, even before birth, can influence subsequent health. Three concepts are particularly relevant.[46] The first is *critical periods*. Critical periods are developmental windows that irrevocably pattern future health.[42] As an example, in vision development, if the brain does not receive visual input from the eye during a critical period, it may never learn to process vision, even if visual input is later restored. A second concept is *path dependence*—a trajectory set in motion.[42] Trajectories can be self-reinforcing via feed-forward loops such that the impact of an initial exposure is magnified. For example, imagine that rich exposure to language in early childhood boosts a child's verbal reasoning skills above that of their peers. An aptitude test identifies this, which results in tracking to more enriching education. This further differentiates the child from their peers, resulting in additional education opportunities, affecting the child's educational attainment and health many years in the future. A third concept is *cumulative effects*. Although any particular exposure may not be enough to determine a health outcome, cumulative exposures may nevertheless result in a particular health outcome, either by crossing a threshold or probabilistically. For example, eating one unhealthful meal may have little impact on health. Repeated exposures to such meals, perhaps owing to unjustly low material resources, may result in diabetes.

The life course perspective makes clear that injustice at any time, even before an individual was born, can produce irreversible effects on health.

An example explanation for type 2 diabetes mellitus that incorporates a life course perspective is that in utero exposure to conditions of material deprivation fall during a critical window for metabolic gene regulation, increasing type 2 diabetes mellitus risk in midlife. An example intervention is prenatal nutrition support policies.

Integrating Epidemiological Perspectives

Each of the epidemiological perspectives has important lessons to offer. Biomedical and behavior and lifestyle perspectives give important insight into how differences in biology and behavior impact health. However, these perspectives can be limited by a decontextualized focus on individuals. Structurally and relationally focused perspectives—social determinants of health, fundamental cause theory, political economy of heath, and the ecosocial theory of disease distribution—provide this context. These perspectives support, each in their own way, the centrality of social standing, power, and resources in explaining how social conditions relate to health. Finally, the life course perspective helps understand how exposures affect health over time. More than one theoretical perspective can be useful in understanding and explaining how an embodied phenotype emerges.

In synthesizing these perspectives, it is important to avoid common pitfalls. First, though I have presented these perspectives as distinct, they overlap. The substantive points raised by the various perspectives are more important than trying to assign a particular point to particular perspective. Second, figure 5.1 presents for explication a neat and linear relationship at a single time point. A more accurate depiction would include non-linearity, feedback loops, and other complexities. Third, it is important not to conflate the conceptual ordering in figure 5.1 with time ordering. For example, although poverty may be patterned by institutions that took shape long ago, someone with hypoglycemia related to food insecurity is experiencing poverty simultaneously with the physiological derangements poverty causes. Finally, although common and sometimes helpful for understanding processes of embodiment, the upstream/downstream metaphor has limitations. An upstream factor is not necessarily more important to address than a downstream one, nor is addressing it necessarily more likely to have an impact. Further, people experiencing harm need help, and if addressing a downstream factor (e.g., providing nutritious food) is a more expedient than addressing an upstream factor (e.g., fomenting a substantive change in the political economic system that produces food insecurity), downstream-ness is no valid criticism—and there may be no reason to choose. Finally, downstream factors (like people's actions) can influence upstream factors (like social structures), standing the metaphor on its head.[4]

Pathways of Embodiment

Epidemiological perspectives help explain how social relations, just and unjust, are translated into levels and distributions of health in populations. They help marshal data points into explanations but are not necessarily mechanistic. The purpose of this section is to provide an overview of some common mechanisms—pathways of embodiment—whereby unjust social relations harm health. It is meant to illustrate why a fair distribution of power and resources matters for health, rather than as a comprehensive list of mechanisms.

This section comes with two important caveats. First, for explication, I will discuss these mechanisms in a reductionist, isolated way. In reality, they form parts of complex, nonlinear systems with self-sustaining loops that can make isolating the effect of any particular mechanism challenging. Second, as discussed above, understanding how one mechanism affects health under the status quo does not imply that intervening on that mechanism alone will inevitably improve health. If injustice continues, its effect on health could leak through via other mechanisms.

Oppression

Oppression, inferior social standing in a system of social relations that fails to meet duties of recognition (chapter 4), is a major injustice that harms health. A substantial body of heath equity scholarship in the United States relates oppression stemming from anti-Black racism to poor health,[40,47,48] and there are of course many other forms of oppression and studies of its harms.[3] Given the importance of the topic, chapter 6 is devoted to a detailed discussion of the effects of oppression related to inegalitarian ideologies on health. Such oppression can harm health through both material conditions and psychological impacts. Systems of oppression often perform an extractive function, siphoning income and other material resources from those who experience oppression to those who benefit from it. Moreover, oppression that inflicts trauma, creates stigma, and erodes the social bases of self-respect creates psychological harm,[49,50] including depressive symptoms, anxiety, and stress.[51,52]

Income (and Wealth)

Material resources are a fundamental cause of health, and three important concepts related to material resources are income, wealth, and consumption.[53(pp105-106)] Wealth is a stock of resources, income is an inflow of resources, and consumption is the use of goods and services. A bathtub helps illustrate their interrelationship. Income is represented by water that flows from the faucet in a given period. Wealth is represented by the volume of water the bathtub is holding. Spending to enable consumption, an outflow of resources, is represented by the water that flows out the drain during the same period. Income not converted to consumption is saved and adds to the stock of wealth—water that does not flow out adds to the volume the bathtub is holding.

Income and wealth can provide purchasing power (and thus consumption power) for the goods and services needed for health that are sold on the market. One way to understand wealth is as the present value of transferable future income flows.[54]

Hundreds of studies have documented an association between lower income and worse health.[32,55-58] Wealth is also important for health—it can help smooth consumption if income shocks occur and provide social standing that influences the power and resources available to an individual even without being converted directly into income. I focus this section on income because methodologically rigorous studies typically find income to have more explanatory power for health outcomes than wealth, but I do not mean to downplay the importance of wealth.[59,60]

Underlying the association between income (and wealth) and health is that consumption of various goods and services is needed for health. In market economies, lower incomes typically mean less consumption power, so lower income, on average, leads to worse health.

This stylized fact raises several questions. The first is whether reverse causation occurs—does poor health also cause lower income, along with lower income causing poor health? Evidence does suggest such a bidirectional relationship between income and health, but with asymmetric magnitudes.[15] Lower income has a large effect on health, and worse health has a small, but real, effect on lower income (chiefly by interfering with the ability to earn labor income).

The next question relates to the shape of the income-health relationship.

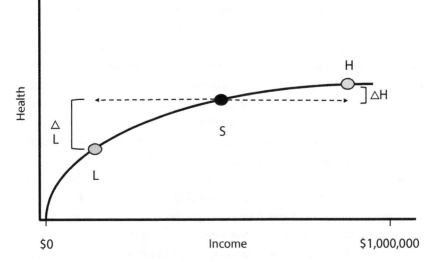

Figure 5.5. Simplified illustration of the absolute income hypothesis. From starting point (S), decreasing to lower income level (L) results in a decrease in health (ΔL) of larger magnitude than the magnitude of the increase in health (ΔH) caused by an increase in income, of the same magnitude, to higher income level (H). Thus, for a fixed level of income and population size, a more equal income distribution will tend to result in greater total health than a less equal distribution of income.

Specifically, is the relationship that of a threshold (for example, a poverty level), with a distinct change in health status above some income level, or is it a gradient, such that health increases steadily with income? Evidence supports a gradational relationship, rather than a threshold.[32,61,62] Specifically, this relationship seems to be monotonically increasing (health is better when income is greater) and concave—there are diminishing returns between income and health (figure 5.5).[62] When income is low, a small increase in income may greatly improve health. But when income is high, a large increase in income may not improve health much. Underlying this relationship may be that the advantages of higher income are primarily relational. Higher income enables individuals to outbid others for salubrious products. Those with high incomes may already be able to outbid others sufficiently, so further increases in income bring few benefits. For example, going from an income level where a nutritious meal is unaffordable to an income level that permits a nutritious but plain meal will improve health greatly. But going from an income level that permits only a nutritious but plain meal to one that allows for a nutritious and gourmet meal may have little effect on health.

So low income leads to worse health, and the relationship between income and health is a concave gradient.[62-64] This raises a final set of questions, not about income per se, but about income *inequality*. Many studies have found that countries (or subnational units like states) with greater income inequality have worse population health.[32] Several hypotheses have been proposed to explain this relationship. The first is the absolute income hypothesis.[62] The absolute income hypothesis notes that the greater the income inequality, the greater the proportion of people with low income. With a fixed national income and population size, from any starting distribution, an increase in income inequality implies that some people will now have more income and others less. As an example, imagine a two-person society, with a total income of $100,000 that is equally distributed—each person has an income of $50,000. For income inequality to increase with constant income, one person must receive more (say, $51,000) and the other person less ($49,000). But given the concave relationship between income and health, the gain of $1,000 will improve health much less than the loss of $1,000 will harm it. Thus, compared with the level of health in a completely equal distribution, the level of health in any unequal distribution with the same total income will be lower. Under the absolute income hypothesis, one's health depends on one's income (including any pooling in households) but not directly on the income of others in the local community or broader society. The evidence supporting the absolute income hypothesis, particularly from studies that examine individual-level income, is strong.[62,65,66]

However, the absolute income hypothesis may not explain the entire association between income and health.[32,62] There are different ways to express the idea that one's health depends not only on one's own income but also on others' income. One is the relative income hypothesis, which states that one's health depends on how one's income deviates from the mean or median income in one's local community or broader population.[62,67] This implies that if everyone else's income rose, but one individual's remained constant, that individual's health would worsen. A related idea is the relative position hypothesis. In this formulation, health depends both on one's income and where that income falls in the ranking of incomes.[67] Compared with the relative income hypothesis, the relative position hypothesis emphasizes the rank ordering and its perception rather than the dollar amount of difference. A final hypothesis relates to income inequality itself, and is thus called the income inequality hypothesis.[62] This hypothesis is that a person's health depends not only on their own income but also on the magnitude of income inequality in their local community or broader population (as indicated, for example, by the income range, or standard deviation, or Gini coefficient), with greater magnitude implying worse health.

Investigators working within the psychosocial sub-perspective of social determinants of health have proposed a number of mechanisms for why income inequality may be directly harmful. In general, these are related to one's perception of inequality and social position, competitive access to scarce resources, and social cohesion or social capital.[32,67] There is some empiric support for the importance of more relative or positional aspects of income inequality.[59] One explanation for these findings may be that relative measures are capturing the existence of a social hierarchy that results in an unequal distribution of income. Thus, it may not be that the difference in income per se harms health but that income inequality reflects, or results from, a hierarchy that harms health in other ways.

In interpreting evidence about income and health, it is important to remember that it is ultimately context dependent.[68] In societies where access to the products necessary for health depends less on income, there is likely to be a weaker connection between income, or income inequality, and health. Thus, observed associations should be seen as specific to particular social conditions rather than universal.

The empirical findings about the relationship between income and health have policy implications. Compressing an unjust income distribution is likely to be health improving. This would both raise absolute income and reduce income inequality. Policies that do this are likely to have small, if any, negative effects on health for those with higher incomes. And since health benefits that accrue from having unjustly high income are themselves unjust, any negative effects would not worsen health equity.

How strictly a society should pursue income equality is not entirely clear. Empirically, the concave relationship between income and health suggests that, *for a given level of income*, health is maximized by a perfectly equal distribution of income. However, this relationship, by itself, does not negate the possibility that everyone's health, even those at the lower end of the distribution, might be better in society with a greater amount of income to distribute, even if it were distributed slightly more unequally.

Ultimately, the question of what, if any, level of income inequality a society might permit must be made on normative grounds and through a democratic process. But it can be informed by empirical findings. If income inequality inherently worsens health, then this is important to consider. However, neither maximizing health nor making income equal is a goal of social democracy per se. Instead, the goal is to guarantee the capabilities essential for standing in a relationship of equality with others. Given people's varying capacity to convert income into capabilities, some income inequality may be needed to guarantee the essential capabilities, and any society will have to make decisions about how to optimize guaranteeing the entire set of essential capabilities under the specific constraints it faces.

Overall, this means that income inequality that results from unjust social relations, as it typically does now, should be addressed. But within a just system of social relations, some income inequality may be permissible.

Education

The level of education one attains has strong associations with health—with greater levels of education typically associated with better health.[69–71]

The association between education and health may have elements of reverse causation—specifically that healthier individuals may pursue greater education.[71] Further, the level of education one pursues is also shaped by one's social environment, such that those who experienced injustice themselves as children, or come from families harmed by injustice, may pursue less education.[70] Therefore, education can be a principal way those from advantaged backgrounds reproduce that advantage in their adult life.[70]

Nevertheless, education likely does causally improve health, through at least two pathways.[69,71] First, education directly affects health, primarily through imparting knowledge and skills. These include cognitive skills, knowledge about disease prevention, when to seek treatment, and health literacy needed to navigate receipt of health care. Further, education socializes individuals such that they can interact to their own advantage with others who influence their health outcomes.

Second, education has a strong influence on one's social position through credentialing and signaling (or filtering) effects that influence subsequent occupation, income, social connections, and the social and biophysical environment in which one lives. Education helps situate individuals in contexts that can promote healthful behaviors and that lessen the pressure to trade off long-term health to meet immediate needs for themselves and their families.

Educational opportunity is a key component of fair equality of opportunity—educational chances should not depend on family background, race, gender, or other irrelevant factors. And greater absolute levels of education may indeed translate into better health for everyone, through directly salubrious effects. But although education can be a pathway to social mobility for some, educational opportunity cannot provide social transformation overall. The effect of education on social position is primarily related to one's level of education relative to others, rather than in an absolute sense. A credential that everyone has does not bring differential economic rewards. Nevertheless, social policies that provide appropriate levels of education, and educational opportunity, for everyone, are important goals of social democracy.

Health Care

Far more goes in to producing health than health care, but health care is an important determinant of health. The relationship between health care and health is complex,[72-77] but there are at least three important aspects: access, agency, and quality.

Access to care (including acute, outpatient, and long-term care[78]) encompasses a number of facets. First, there is physical proximity. Next, there is the ability to have a long-term relationship with a clinician providing primary care. Primary care–based health care systems create better health outcomes, including lower mortality rates.[79-82] Other facets are the availability of specialty care and the ability to sustain treatment plans over time. In the inpatient setting, consultation with physicians, diagnostic testing, and delivery of treatment coincide. But most health care over one's life occurs as an outpatient. Outpatient access requires being able to see physicians and other clinicians, receive diagnostic testing, and engage with treatment plans, including taking prescription medications and receiving skilled services such as physical and occupational therapy. Finally, user fees are important barriers to access. These include fees related to clinician consultation, health care facility use, diagnostic services, and medications. Further, there can be costs related to transportation and opportunity costs of seeking care (e.g., for hourly wage workers). Thus, even public finance of health care does not necessarily mean everyone can access care.[83]

A second aspect is what philosopher Jennifer Prah calls health agency.

Health agency is the "ability to engage with and navigate the health system and [one's] environment to avoid mortality and morbidity and meet health needs."[84(p9)] Health agency can be supported, or frustrated, by the social structures one is enmeshed in.

The quality of health care received greatly affects health.[85] The problems of quality measurement in health care are well known and may be insurmountable.[86-91] Nevertheless, even if difficult to measure, health care certainly can vary in quality and this variation can affect health. Poor health care quality can represent oppression in its own right and exacerbate other injustices, as, for example, when those with unjustly low income are unable to afford high-quality care and suffer doubly. For example, unjustly low income can increase diabetes risk.[92,93] Newer diabetes treatments, such as GLP-1 agonists and sodium glucose cotransporter-2 inhibitors, have important health benefits beyond those of older glycemic lowering therapies such as sulfonylureas. But these treatments are often unaffordable for those with unjustly low income, even with health insurance coverage.[94] Health care quality is also worsened by discrimination.[95] For example, racist and sexist ideologies often lead to lower quality treatment.[95-97]

Health care plays an important role in producing health inequity and has a key role to play in improving health equity. Aspects of health care related to access, agency, and quality are all important pathways of embodiment.

Material Insecurity

Material conditions, including conditions related to food, housing, heating and cooling, safe drinking water, transportation, and telecommunications, are primary pathways of embodiment.[29,30,98-102] The concept of insecurity encompasses a spectrum including change in quantity of consumption, change in quality of consumption, and worry about meeting needs (even without change in consumption). Considering the full spectrum is important because uncertainty prompts compensatory actions that have their own health consequences. Thus, material insecurity can impact health even without changing consumption.

The relationship between different types of material insecurity and health shares common patterns but also has elements specific to each type. For example, food insecurity harms health in at least three ways.[103,104] First, there is a nutritional "quality and quantity" pathway. For example, there may be financial pressure to purchase inadequate amounts of food and/or to purchase cheaper, less nutritious foods. Importantly, because of the "quality" component, this nutritional pathway can impact health even if calorie and macronutrient consumption is sufficient to avoid malnutrition. Second, people make trade-offs as they seek to meet their overall set of needs, for instance by decreasing consumption of medications.[105] This is the compensatory pathway. Finally, uncertainty about meeting basic needs increases stress, depressive symptoms, and anxiety, and it can lower self-efficacy. This is the psychological pathway.

Similar pathways are relevant for other material needs. For example, housing insecurity also has a "quality and quantity" pathway. Housing insecurity may lead to homelessness (insufficient "quantity" of housing) or may pressure people into accepting lower quality housing (which can worsen respiratory health), analogous to the way food insecurity worsens cardiometabolic health through lower quality food. Further, housing insecurity also induces trade-offs (compensatory pathway) and stress (psychological pathway). In fact, most types of material need insecurities have compensatory and psychological pathways, and quality and quantity pathways analogous to the nutrition pathway for food insecurity. Examples include cold exposure and/or using more dangerous forms of heating (e.g., ovens or space heaters) for those experiencing insecurity relating to heating costs,[106] use of water contaminated by lead or pathogens when safe water is not accessible, and missing needed health care or other appointments when transportation is not available. A growing issue is telecommunications insecurity, especially as broadband-speed connectivity becomes, like electricity and indoor plumbing became in the early 20th century, an integral part of modern life.[100] Finally, material insecurities are interrelated. Those experiencing, say, food insecurity are likely to have other unmet needs.[107] At the same time, assistance with one type of need can free up resources to meet others. For example, reductions in rent burden, a type of housing insecurity, can free up resources to be spent on food.[108]

Stress, Allostatic Load, and Weathering

Stress is conceptualized as events (or perceptions) that lead to biological or behavioral change in an organism.[109,110] Stress can affect health through the sympathetic-adrenal-medullary system (a pathway of autonomic nervous system activation) and the hypothalamic-pituitary-adrenal axis. Differential activation of these systems, both acutely and over time, can result in poor health through chronic inflammation, metabolic changes, effects on the cardiovascular system, dysregulation of the immune system, and changes in gene expression.[111] Further, stressful experiences and attendant biological changes can alter health behaviors.

The concept of allostatic load is helpful for understanding the embodiment of stressful experiences.[33] The term allostasis denotes "stability through change." Allostatic load refers to a stressor that causes an organism to change one parameter or process to maintain stability in another. For example, consuming a meal with a high glycemic index causes blood sugar to rise, and the body secretes more insulin to maintain blood glucose in a normal range. This action to preserve glycemic stability begets a change—the additional insulin increases adipose tissue, which in turn increases insulin resistance. At the next meal, even greater insulin secretion is required to maintain glucose homeostasis, perpetuating the cycle. Eventually, the ability to secrete sufficient insulin may be lost—leading to the clinical phenotype of diabetes. Therefore, the cumulative effect of allostatic loading, the wear and tear on one's biological systems, helps explain one's current health state. Allostatic load is implicated in cardiometabolic conditions such as atherosclerosis and diabetes, and immune dysregulation.[34]

The "weathering" hypothesis of public health researcher Arline Geronimus relates the concepts of stress and allostatic load to social conditions.[35] The metaphor of weathering explains why worse health is observed at younger ages among those who experience material deprivation, social exclusion, discrimination, and other forms of injustice. Injustices increase exposure to allostatic load. Sustained exposure to stressful conditions prematurely erode or weather away one's health, effectively accelerating processes associated with aging.[112] This causes biological changes with health consequences in their own right, and it uses up the body's capacity to cope, leaving the individual more susceptible to poor health outcomes from future exposures.

One biological indicator of weathering is telomere length.[113] Telomeres can be thought of as aglets, or protective endcaps, on chromosomes, which are used up and shorten as cells divide. Shorter telomeres, relative to individuals of similar age, reflect a history of greater allostatic loading and greater risk for subsequent illness. More recent iterations of this concept have combined telomere, other biomarker, and anthropomorphic assessments to calculate multidimensional allostatic load scores, which help quantify the embodiment of social relations.[114]

Mental Health, Stigma, and Psychological Mechanisms

Oppression and material deprivation harm mental health, causing depressive disorders, anxiety symptoms, sleep disorders, loneliness, social isolation, and serious mental illness. Although there may be an element of reverse causation, as worse mental health can result in lower income, research studies with strong designs support a causal relationship between adverse social circumstances and worse mental health.[115,116] One way oppression may worsen mental health is through stigma and the erosion of the social bases of self-respect.[49,50] That is, those who experience oppression may be bombarded with messages about their inferiority.

Beyond its own importance, mental health also affects other aspects of health.[117-119] The connection between depression and worse outcomes in cardiometabolic disease and cancer is particularly strong.[117-119]

Situations of inadequate material resources, or scarcity, may induce more negative evaluations of other experiences, and constrain the "cognitive bandwidth" one needs to attend to complicated circumstances that can affect health.[120-122] A further potential behaviorally mediated pathway of embodiment is that long-term exposure to oppressive and/or deprived conditions can result in changes in outlook that can affect health.[123-125] Said differently, conditions that give reason for hope may exert benefits by inspiring it.

Working Conditions

Working conditions are a major pathway of embodiment, as they can expose people to injury risk (both acutely and over time), toxic substances, and irregular working hours.[126-129] Further, an extensive body of literature relates to the psychological impact of workplace relations.[15,127,130] Working conditions characterized by low control over one's tasks and relationships of inferiority clearly worsen both mental and physical health. Further, informal work arrangements, such as gig economy work, are characterized by precarity that can be both exploitative and stressful.[131]

Criminal Justice and Other Government Services

Justice system involvement has become an increasingly salient pathway of embodiment.[47,132-134] Such involvement exerts health effects directly (e.g., police violence, consequences of incarceration including psychiatric illness and communicable disease exposure) and indirectly though economic extraction and constrained ability to earn an income.[135,136] Other government services including public health efforts, the prehospital care system, and fire services also have direct effects on health. Variations in the quantity and/or quality of these government services are all potential pathways of embodiment.

Substance Use

Use of substances such as alcohol or opioids is generally not more common among those experiencing injustice (tobacco is an exception).[39,137,138] However, there is evidence of a "harm paradox" such that those with, for example, fewer material resources come to harm at lower levels of exposure than better-off individuals.[39] This suggests that substance use may interact with other pathways of embodiment, including nutritional status, access to treatment, and social exclusion, to produce poor health despite similar, or even lower, levels of substance use.

Area-Level and Environmental Exposures

So far, I have focused on factors that can be thought of as occurring at the level of the individual. Another set of pathways relate to factors that are relevant to larger levels of spatial and social aggregation—such as households, neighborhoods, municipalities, states, regions, countries, and globally. These levels are also characterized by their existence at a specific time, and exposures over time can be aggregated. The interrelationship between these levels is complex. While the social ecological model[139] (related to the ecological systems model of psychologist Urie Bronfenbrenner[140] and distinct from the ecosocial perspective[5]) conceptualizes these levels as nested within each other, in reality they do not nest neatly; there may be level skipping, and people may have multiple environments at the same level (e.g., different communities based on whether someone is at home or at work).

Area-level and environmental exposures consist of social environments, such as exposure to violence, social cohesion, laws and policies, the commercial environment and marketing, and government services; biophysical environments, such as exposure to toxins and pollutants,[141] communicable diseases, and risks of climate change including extreme heat, cold, storms, and flooding[142]; and their interrelationship, such as the built environment, including housing conditions (crowding, ventilation, exposures to toxic substances like lead and asbestos, structural integrity, cold and damp conditions), sanitation, utility services, greenspaces, recreation facilities, light and noise exposure, and transportation networks.[143]

An important concept for environmental exposures is segregation, particularly residential segregation.[144-147] Most clearly illustrated by de jure racial segregation policies in the US Jim Crow era, segregation can be thought of as the concentration of those experiencing injustice into particular areas. De facto segregation by race, ethnicity, and/or income ("concentrated poverty") remains commonplace in the United States.[145,146] Sociologists David Williams and Chiquita Collins identify segregation as a fundamental cause of worse health for Black individuals.[144] As sociologist Rogers Brubaker puts it: "Residential segregation has been the 'structural linchpin' of racial inequality. Segregated neighborhoods have entailed not just segregated schools, churches, associations, and networks but also segregated experiences. And since this segregation has been imposed rather than chosen, and produced in tandem with a process of 'sociospatial relegation' to systematically disfavored spaces, it has generated and perpetuated massive, cumulative, and mutually reinforcing inequalities in housing, education, amenities, public safety, municipal services, trust, social capital, job opportunities, and exposure to environmental hazards, crime, delinquency, and stress."[148]

Segregation is a form of social exclusion that makes it harder to access the resources needed to stay healthy, reduces social standing, and narrows one's social networks. Segregation spatially separates individuals from jobs and other economic opportunities, and it can make social networks more susceptible to shocks (such as a factory closure) with less ability to diversify risk. Further, repeated experiences of injustice in one's social network makes it difficult to get ahead, as individuals are more frequently called upon to assist others.

Segregation often goes hand in hand with political disenfranchisement. This may be formal disenfranchisement, or de facto disenfranchisement resulting from voter suppression, gerrymandering, and unresponsive public officials. This can yield government services of lower quantity and quality (e.g., fire protection, building inspection, sanitation, public health), undermining state legitimacy and worsening social cohesion.

Economically, segregation can work against the ability to gain financing and investment,[149] and it can also lower purchasing power as products on offer may be more expensive and/or of lower quality.[144] Further, transportation availability may be poor, and marketing of toxic substances may be intensified.

While the problems related to residential segregation are clear, they should not be viewed as deterministic. The same conditions that harm health can also inspire egalitarian social movements that seek justice in resolving them, and the experience of intensified injustice should not be mistaken for deficient agency on the part of those who experience it.

Summary

This chapter has sought to describe theories ("epidemiological perspectives") and specific mechanisms ("pathways of embodiment") that can help explain how the injustices that the normative framework of democratic equality is concerned with harm health. The purpose of this is to make clear why public policy to achieve the normative goals of social democracy is likely to improve health. To summarize: power and resources are distributed by a system of social relations, which may be just or unjust. Unjust distributions of power and resources harm health—causing health inequities. The idea that health equity is purely an issue of individual-level factors like behaviors, opportunity, or rising above one's circumstances, what one might call health entrepreneurialism, is a social myth.[150] Moreover, it is a distraction from the need to confront structural and relational issues.

As a goal of this chapter was to examine how injustice could be embodied in the form of poor health, the focus was necessarily on adverse circumstances. This should not be understood, however, as taking anything away from the resilience of and assets possessed by the people and communities whose health is worsened by injustice. Those experiencing injustice do not deserve the adversity they face, but neither are they helpless victims. Moreover, injustice does not only cause harm to some—it can also work to the benefit of others.[151] The conditions described here as health harming for some may make possible unjustly health-promoting conditions for others. The focus in working toward health equity should be on ways to improve health by which all can benefit, and to eliminate those pathways of embodying good health that can only come at others' expense.

The perspectives offered here help make clear why it is important to attend to duties of recognition and duties of distribution directly. It may seem more politically feasible to enact policies that address specific causes or "midstream" issues, rather than attempting to improve more fundamental issues

of power and resource distribution. But such a strategy is likely to be inef-
fective, as even if the policies are successful, the specific pathways of embodiment that connect injustice to poor health may shift. Further, those who
are better off may have differentially better uptake of new technology or
may be better able to turn a new policy or program to their advantage. Ultimately, trying to avoid the difficult work of contestation over society's basic
institutions is likely to make the problem of health inequity harder to solve,
not easier.[36] This is a lesson that harkens back to the emergence of public
health as a discipline, which recognized social transformation as the key to
improving health and health equity.[152]

6

Inegalitarian Ideologies and Health

Inegalitarian ideologies such as racism, sexism, and heterosexism cause unjustly worse health for many individuals and confer unjust advantages on others.[1,2] Health equity work, especially in the United States, is closely tied to understanding, preventing, and correcting the health harms that inegalitarian ideologies, especially anti-Black racism, cause.[3,4]

Ideology* can be considered a system of beliefs that explains what exists, what is possible, and what is good.[6] Inegalitarian ideologies posit a natural and unchangeable inferiority of some individuals such that worse health and other outcomes are both unavoidable and justifiable. This motivates oppression, which can become a self-fulling prophecy of inferiority. Inegalitarian ideologies exist as misdirection or mystification to shift attention away from social causes by presenting differences as natural and inevitable. In the words of legal scholar Dorothy Roberts: "Race is not a biological category that naturally produces health disparities because of genetic differences. Race is a political category that has staggering biological consequences because of the impact of social inequality on people's health."[7(p129)]

Understanding inegalitarian ideologies and their effect on health makes clear why achieving the normative goals of social democracy are likely to improve health for those who experience oppression. In this chapter, I will use the ideology of racism, specifically anti-Black racism in the United States, as an archetype for health effects of oppression driven by inegalitarian ideologies. I will also consider issues of intersectionality.

---

*An alternative, perhaps more cynical definition is that "ideology harmonizes the principles one wants to hold with what advances one's material interests."[5]

Other inegalitarian ideologies are also harmful and wrong, but I do not provide an in-depth discussion of them owing to space constraints, and even the discussion of anti-Black racism and health is necessarily incomplete. The works cited in this chapter, and other work by the cited scholars, provide more in-depth treatments of these issues, which are critically important for health equity.[1,3,4,8–11]

Racism as Ideology

There are many ways to think about what racism is. One way, put forth by historian Barbara J. Fields and sociologist Karen E. Fields in their seminal work *Racecraft: The Soul of Inequality in American Life*, is that at its heart racism is simply the belief that races exist—that human beings can be meaningfully categorized into races.[9] This view makes clear that it is the ideology of racism that constructs the idea of races, and not the other way around.

Owing to the ideology of racism, race is commonly seen as a biological category—a natural way to subdivide humanity. Indeed, there is a long history of "scientific racism" that seeks to determine the biological basis of race—and the innate inferiority of certain races.[7,12,13] Anthropological and genetic scholarship demonstrates unequivocally, however, that racial categories do not correspond to biologically meaningful categories.[7,14–16] Those who start with conceptions of "race" can use statistical techniques to reproduce "racial" categories in genetic analyses, but this does not establish race as a meaningful way to categorize people.[17–20] In fact, a consistent observation is that there is more genetic variation within than across racial categorizations, and that human genetic variation is better characterized as gradational or clinal, rather than neatly clustering into any particular racial classification.[7,15,16,20]

This means that unlike, for example, different categories of rocks (e.g., igneous, metamorphic, sedimentary) that exist in the world and are described by science, races are not inherent properties of human beings waiting to be discovered. Instead, the ideology of racism constructs race by taking a collection of inherently meaningless biological features (e.g., skin color, hair texture, facial physiognomy) and attributing to them social significance.

Sociologists recognize race as an "ascriptive identity," that is, a social category that is neither earned nor chosen, but nevertheless has broadly accepted rules about how categorizations are made.[21] Although socially constructed, ascriptive identity has very real effects on people's lives. Just as the rules of peerage under an ideology of aristocracy create categories of people like dukes, earls, and peasants—which shape all of their lives—ideologies of racism create categories of people as Black, White, or Asian. But these categories are produced by the ideology, not discovered by it.

Racism is an essentializing ideology—ascribed race is thought to reflect something essential about the person. Not all categorizations, even when biological, are essentializing. For example, the ability to roll one's tongue or whether the inferior part of one's earlobes dangle are both biological traits that could categorize people. But they are not thought to reveal anything essential—they are not taken to have any deeper meaning about the person's abilities, personality, or how their life will turn out. No social significance is attributed to them.

Since the idea that there are meaningful differences between races is a premise of racism, rather than a conclusion, the ideology persists even though a biological basis for race has been disproven. Instead, the supposed basis of race can shift from biological to cultural, while maintaining the same essentializing structure.[22] The idea, for example, that individuals ascribed a particular race must share a common culture, which then explains social outcomes, is a cultural repackaging of biological race.[23] Nonracial ascribed identities can also be used, analogously to race, to provide an essentialist justification for oppression.[21] Examples of this include ethnic identity (based more explicitly than race on a shared cultural, linguistic, or possibly genealogical connection), such as that possessed by Hispanic, Jewish, or Roma individuals, or religious identity, such as anti-Muslim oppression in the United States or sectarian oppression on the island of Ireland.

Racism is not transhistorical and unchanging. It is a historical phenomenon, modified and refined to respond to the concerns of the moment. There are different racisms at different times and places, each specific to a historical milieu.[9] In the United States currently, racial thinking often involves "continental" categories (e.g., Black individuals are "from" Africa, White individuals are "from" Europe). But across geographies and/or over time, the boundaries of racial categories shift, and who is considered White or Black, or even which races exist, change. The same person may be classified as belonging to different races in different societies.[12,24,25] At any time, however, racial categorization is heavily influenced by power relations within a society.

Ideologies play important roles within systems of social relations. For example, the ideology of racism emerged in the American colonies as an extractive ideology, meant to justify slave labor and economic exploitation.[9] But over time, ideologies can be modified and reproduced to maintain a political economic hierarchy. In doing this, ideologies shape social structures that uphold the ideology, but also, through processes of institutionalization, make it possible for actors to produce the ideology's intended effects without explicitly endorsing it. Such structures can in turn reinforce the ideology by making individuals targeted for oppression appear inferior—a self-fulfilling prophecy.

Injustice and Categories of Ascriptive Difference

Inegalitarian ideologies often harm health through processes that use ascriptive identity to locate individuals into specific positions within a system of social relations. A position can be formal, like a job, or an informal role, like a confidant. A position confers benefits and burdens, which can set individuals down pathways of embodiment. Sociological processes affect how people are located in these positions and the benefits and burdens associated with the positions. Sociologist Rogers Brubaker refers to three of these processes as the social production of persons, the allocation of persons to positions, and the structuring of positions.[21]

The social production of persons refers to "the full range of processes that generate agents endowed with particular self-understandings, dispositions, aspirations, skills, experience, human or cultural capital, and ways of thinking and acting. The persons so produced subsequently present themselves at points of selection—or refrain from presenting themselves—as differently qualified candidates."[21] In this way, a system of social relations stratifies the positions people seek by shaping the people they are.

The allocation of persons to positions refers to processes that influence and gatekeep selection for positions. Differential allocation can result from formal categorical exclusion, informal categorical exclusion, categorically inflected selection, and category-neutral screening on category-correlated, position-relevant characteristics.[21] Formal categorical exclusion refers to explicit bans on holding specific positions. One example of this in US history was racial covenants, which prohibited Black individuals from buying houses in certain neighborhoods.[26] Informal categorical exclusion refers to unwritten rules about who fills various positions (such as de facto exclusion of Jewish students from some university programs in the early to mid-20th century). Categorically inflected selection skews allocation of positions by conflating assessment of individual-level characteristics with assumed category-level characteristics. This might occur if an interviewer views, for example, a particular Hispanic applicant positively but thinks "Mexicans" do not have a strong work ethic. Category inflected selection processes may not prevent all members of a particular category from being selected. Instead, they may shift distributions such that only exemplary individuals from certain categories are selected, but mediocre members of other categories are. Finally, category neutral screening on category-correlated characteristics occurs when a formally neutral criterion is nevertheless highly correlated with categories of ascriptive difference. For example, university admissions officials may give extra points to applicants for having a parent who matriculated there. This may be a formally neutral selection mechanism, but it will likely, in the contemporary United States, select disproportionately more White than Native American individuals. Thus, the effect is differential position allocation, even if category membership was not a formal criterion.

A nuance to this discussion is that two positions may be superficially similar but hide meaningful differences. For example, two people may both be offered, say, a staff physician position at a hospital, but those positions may differ in terms of salary, work hours, or prestige. The processes described above may drive which individuals are allocated to more desirable and less desirable versions of similar-seeming positions.

The structuring of positions refers to the benefits and burdens attached to particular social positions. For example, consider the positions of physician and home health worker. The social production of persons may influence who seeks to become a physician, and the allocation of persons to positions may influence who is allowed to become a physician. But why, across the life course, is the health of a physician likely to be better than that of a home health worker's? The answer relates to the structuring of positions within a society. In the contemporary United States, a person who works as a physician is likely to be paid more, have better benefits, and have more control of their working conditions—all of which contributes to better health. Differentially rewarding positions that are differentially allocated can compound injustice in processes of allocation.

Once social positions are allocated and structured, the associated health outcomes can be understood with reference to the pathways of embodiment discussed previously. Social democratic policies address injustice in the processes that allocate and structure positions, and thus are likely to prevent unjust health consequences that can result from inegalitarian ideologies. The capabilities social democracy seeks to guarantee are strongly related to the social production of persons. Further, fair equality of opportunity, conceived in a substantive rather than merely formal way, helps address all four sub-processes of allocation to positions. Finally, social democracy works to ensure that differential benefits attached to particular social positions, if any, work to the advantage of all.

Racism and Health

Racist oppression as a cause of poor health has been documented in an extensive body of scholarship going back centuries.[3,4,7,12] In the United States, racist oppression frequently harms the health of individuals ascribed to Black, Hispanic, Indigenous, Asian, and Pacific Islander racial and ethnic categories. Sociologist David Williams and colleagues note that "the persistence of racial inequities in health should be understood in the context of relatively stable racialized social structures that determine differential access to risk, opportunities, and resources that drive health."[3(p107)] The roots of racist oppression are extractive, and lower levels of material resources among those who experience racist oppression remain common.[27] This worsens health through pathways of embodiment previously discussed. However, racism presents harms to health separate from those that stem from economic arrangements.

Individual studies of the connection between racism and health often emphasize phenomena that can be described as one of three types of racist oppression: internalized (intrapersonal), interpersonal (personally mediated), or institutional.[3,11,28]

Internalized racist oppression occurs in a context of cultural transmission of racist ideology, including through symbols, imagery, and language.[3,11] This context heavily influences the social production of persons. An example of this is the stereotype threat phenomenon where, among individuals who have received cultural messages of their inferiority, anxiety about confirming a stereotype diminishes performance on tests or other measures.[29]

A second type of racist oppression relates to interpersonal interactions.[3,11] Racist ideology shapes the attitudes and beliefs of those in a position of superiority. Studies that emphasize interpersonal racist oppression often focus on connections between experienced racial discrimination and health outcomes, or connections between the attitudes, beliefs, and behaviors of those in positions of power and health in racialized categorizes of individuals.[30] Interpersonal racist oppression can be conscious and intentional or unconscious and unintentional. Distinguishing between the two can be difficult, particularly as honest reporting of prejudice suffers from social desirability bias. Although false positive findings are likely rare, false negatives are probably common, and many investigators attempt to sidestep the issue by assessing only implicit forms of bias. Nevertheless, even though illegal in many settings, interpersonal racist oppression is very common in the United States and causes harm across many sectors, including health care, housing, finance, and criminal justice. Within health care, interpersonal racist oppression worsens care.[30] A common example is clinicians making substantively different decisions for individuals perceived to be of different races but who are clinically similar.[31] Interpersonal racist oppression is strongly connected to the allocation of social positions, which in turn impacts the social production of persons.

A third type of racist oppression relates to institutions and other social structures. Institutional racist oppression includes policies and practices of both state (e.g., police departments) and non-state (e.g., employers) actors that either formally discriminate or, perhaps more insidiously, are formally neutral but produce oppressive effects.[31] The infamous 100-to-1 sentencing disparity between possession of crack versus powder cocaine, "stop-and-frisk" policing policies, and employer practices of offering fewer interviews to applicants with names racially coded as Black all exemplify institutional racist oppression.[32-34] Institutional racist oppression is connected with the social production of persons, the allocation of persons to positions, and the structuring of positions.

Contemporary scholarship of racism and health emphasizes understanding the above phenomena as elements of structural (or systemic) racism, rather than in isolation.[35,36] An influential expression of this idea comes from physician and epidemiologist Camara Phyllis Jones, who says, "Racism is a system of structuring opportunity and assigning value based on the social interpretation of how one looks (which is what we call 'race'), that unfairly disadvantages some individuals and communities, unfairly advantages other individuals and communities, and saps the strength of the whole society through the waste of human resources."[37] Another expression is offered by epidemiologist Zinzi Bailey and colleagues: "Structural racism refers to the totality of ways in which societies foster racial discrimination through mutually reinforcing systems of housing, education, employment, earnings, benefits, credit, media, health care, and criminal justice. These patterns and practices in turn reinforce discriminatory beliefs, values, and distribution of resources."[4]

Structural racism is a way to think about forms of oppression that are not necessarily caused by individuals' beliefs (although it is inclusive of that).[38] However, focusing on a single category of ascriptive difference may be incomplete in that there are myriad ways people come to be targeted by oppression. The next section focuses on thinking through how systems of oppression combine to shape an individual's health.

Intersectionality

Inegalitarian ideologies typically focus on one category of ascriptive difference, but the experience of individuals is shaped by a combination of factors ("identities").[39] Intersectionality is an approach to analyzing the ways that several aspects of identity can combine to yield varying experiences of oppression and privilege.[40] Intersectionality is not in itself a theory about health or health equity, but rather it is a concept that can be used to help understand the types of health-harming injustices people may face. Intersectionality has theoretical links to "simultaneity" as expressed by members of the Combahee River Collective,[41] and the term was coined by legal scholar Kimberlé Crenshaw in 1989.[42]

In an influential 2005 article, sociologist and political scientist Leslie McCall described three intersectional perspectives.[40] The first is the *anti-categorical* perspective. This perspective makes the point that any amount of aggregation is inherently a simplification and questions how relevant the approach of studying categories of difference really is. That aggregation into categories is a simplification is certainly true. However, it may not be an *oversimplification*, but rather a useful simplification. Nevertheless, the anti-categorical insight to question whether the aggregations being used are meaningful is an important one.

A second intersectional perspective is *intra-categorical*.[40] In this perspective, the goal is not to make comparisons between different strata of identity categories but to understand deeply the experience of those in a single stratum (with strata constituted by multiple aspects of identity), often using ethnographic or other qualitative research methods. In her famous speech "Ain't I a Woman?," abolitionist and women's rights activist Sojourner Truth made the point that her experience was uniquely constituted by the combination of being Black and a woman—her experience of being a woman was very different than a White woman's experience of being a woman.[43] The idea in the intra-categorical perspective is that one's experience does not consist of discrete racial, gender, and other experiences added together, but that one's experience is created holistically through the full combination of the aspects of one's identity. These together produce the individual's particular history, which results in their emergent embodied phenotype. As an (oversimplified) analogy, if different aspects of one's identity could be described by the colors blue and yellow, one's full identity would not be variegated—discretely half-blue and half-yellow—but green. The intra-categorical perspective is very useful for health equity work adopting the health justice approach. Because of its deep investigation into the experience of individuals with a specific combination of identities, it can yield a clear picture of particular injustices faced and how those injustices affect health.

A third intersectional perspective,[40] perhaps the most common in health equity research currently, is *inter-categorical*.[44] This perspective focuses on making comparisons between categories of individuals and is frequently implemented in scholarship by delineating fine strata for comparison. For example, instead of comparing Black and White racial categories and, separately, men and women as gender categories, on some particular health outcome, one might compare Black women, Black men, White women, and White men on this outcome. This is often referred to as "disaggregation" (relative to single categories), though proponents of the anti-categorical perspective may view it as simply a different form of aggregation. The inter-categorical perspective can reveal heterogeneity of experiences concealed within category means or obscured by the greater number of individuals in some strata than others. For example, disaggregation of the "Asian" racial category or the "Hispanic" ethnic category can reveal highly varying experiences related to the nation individuals within the category trace their ancestry to.[45] Increasingly sophisticated quantitative methods to investigate inter-categorical intersectional questions are available. These move beyond simple product terms in regression equations and include analysis of individual heterogeneity and discriminatory accuracy (AIHDA) and multilevel analysis of individual heterogeneity and discriminatory accuracy (MAIHDA).[46–48] However, analyses adopting an inter-categorical perspective often also adopt a form of disparitarianism and face the problem of emphasizing parity rather than justice (chapter 2). By simply comparing several strata, rather than taking an explicitly counterfactual perspective, inter-categorical comparisons may not be asking the right questions. That is, they may be asking "are the experiences of individuals in different strata similar?" rather than "has injustice harmed health?" Examining patterns of differences in outcomes may not say much about why the patterns came to be, or if they are unjust. Further, similar outcomes may occur for different reasons in different strata, but inter-categorical analyses may have difficulty recognizing this.

Intersectional perspectives are important for health equity work in several ways. First, the axiom that what one sees (or experiences) depends upon where one sits is certainly true (although this perspective is not unique to intersectionality). Second, anti-categorical intersectionality reminds us that categorization is a simplification. Whether it is a useful simplification or an oversimplification has to be determined on a case-by-case basis. Third, health equity research using the health justice approach can benefit from adopting an intra-categorical perspective. Fourth, the intra-categorical approach shows that questions of primacy (e.g., is race or gender more important for health?) do not have a general answer.[49] At most, they may be answerable for specific outcomes, and often the premise—that one specific factor can be more important—is not true. Instead, it is often more relevant to examine how factors interact to produce an outcome, which is the hallmark of intra-categorical intersectionality.[50] Finally, it is important to investigate possible heterogeneity in the effect of policies and programs on health outcomes.

At the same time, some intersectional viewpoints may be less useful. It is sometimes implied that any person categorized as a member of a given stratum is representative, or can speak on behalf, of other individuals categorized in that stratum.[51] This does not follow, as the anti-categorical perspective makes clear, because within any given stratum there is still considerable interindividual variation. In particular, one's beliefs, values, and politics are not synonymous with or reducible to an identity category. Additionally, some proponents of intersectionality take the epistemic standpoint that only individuals from a particular stratum can understand the experiences of those from that stratum. This would imply that diverse perspectives are not valuable, as they could not be understood by anyone else. Instead, it is important to listen to those with diverse perspectives because they may reveal experiences of injustice overlooked by those personally unaffected.[52] A diversity of perspectives is valuable precisely because others *can* understand the harmful effects of injustice they did not themselves experience— and thus share the motivation to change systems of social relations that caused them.

Racism: Cause or Outcome?

One issue that complicates understanding the relationship between racism and health is that the term racism is commonly used in two distinct ways.* In the first way, racism is an assessment made of a motive that caused someone to engage in a particular action. In this sense, racism refers to situations where the decisions made or actions undertaken by individuals are influenced by a view that someone's racial categorization indicates, in some relevant way, their inferiority. A hiring manager who chose not to hire a Black candidate because they believe individuals racialized as Black are inherently less competent is an example of racism in this sense.

The second way in which the term racism is used is as a description of outcome patterns—when outcomes vary by race. This description could apply when the outcome's cause is also racism (in the racism-as-motive sense describe above). But it could also apply when racially disparate outcomes are present but the cause is known not to be racism (in the racism-as-motive sense), or when the cause is unknown. Thus, describing a situation under the heading of racism-as-outcome, that is, noting that an outcome is racially disparate, does not necessarily provide any information as to the outcome's cause. Addressing the injustices that create racism-as-outcome could require pushing further into causal explanation. Such explanations might inform concrete interventions, such as policies directed against specific processes, institutional practices and forms, or behaviors that cause the outcome. For example, both high maternal mortality among Black women and low prescribing of anti-coagulation for Black adults with atrial fibrillation are examples of racism-as-outcome—but improving these outcomes may require different interventions.[53-55] This is a case where an ecosocial

---

*The points raised in this section also apply to forms of intersectional oppression commonly studied using inter-categorical intersectional perspectives (e.g., misogynoir—the intersection of racist and sexist oppression that harms Black women).

perspective, with an emphasis on understanding pathways of embodiment at multiple levels, may be particularly useful.[14]

The Persistence of Racial Injustice

Despite substantial progress toward formal civil and political equality that accompanied the US civil rights movement and the fall of Jim Crow, racial injustices continue to harm health. A critical question for health equity then is how to explain and address these continuing injustices.[56]

Two perspectives on the persistence of racial injustice are the psychological account and the political economy account. Both the psychological and the political economy accounts recognize that despite formal civil and political equality, there is not substantive equality throughout the system of social relations, and that that substantive inequality negatively affects health. In other words, both recognize that though some things have changed since the civil rights movement, others have not. But the explanation of what has not changed differs.

The psychological account postulates that what has not changed is the psychological characteristics of individuals, such as their aesthetic preferences, values, attitudes, beliefs, and practices, which shape and are shaped by a larger culture. These unchanging psychological characteristics explain why health outcomes continue to be patterned by categories of ascriptive difference. Psychological accounts emphasize the need for introspection and cognitive change as key to overcoming racism.[57] Thus, proposed remedies often focus on changing thoughts, beliefs, attitudes, language use, and preferences through acknowledgment, self-awareness, and reflection. The chief antagonism, under the psychological account, is between people designated as superior within the racist system and people designated as inferior.

The political economy account postulates that what did not change after Jim Crow were economic relations, and in particular that the civil rights movement did not result in a change in economic rights. Thus, the failure to secure economic democracy means that everyone's struggle over material well-being occurs under unreconstructed economic institutions.[58] Structural conditions, such as those that force people to compete for economic survival where success is uncertain and destitution is a real risk, can provide the context for adaptation and adoption of racist ideology as a strategy for alliance making and a pathway to power—especially when the possibility of success via that route seems greater than structural transformation.[59] In other words, people might prefer to try to rig the system in their favor, rather than try to make it fair for everyone. The ideology of racism presents the idea of race as a tool for both political division across racial categories and solidarity within racial categories. This has served to prevent the development of economic rights that civil and political rights might otherwise have helped achieve, and ultimately harmed health. The political economy account does not view issues of oppression based on race, gender, sexual orientation, or other categories of ascriptive difference as reducible to economic inequality or secondary in importance to it. Nor does it argue that economic interests drive all oppression. But it does emphasize the centrality of political and economic institutions in shaping the context in which oppression continues to occur. And it emphasizes that structural transformation, for example, through a robust set of economic rights, would both undermine some incentives to adopt inegalitarian ideologies and help limit the harms those ideologies cause. In the political economy account, many of the expressions of racist ideology, from political disenfranchisement to cultural messages of Black inferiority to "zero sum" thinking that pits "White interests" against "Black interests," emerge in service to an economic order that seeks to exploit both Black and White individuals.

Because the way social relations are structured and the way people are positioned within that structure create motives to reproduce systems of oppression, the way to bring about egalitarian social transformation is with concrete policies that restructure those relations. Moreover, economic security helps shape people's ability to make progress on other, noneconomic concerns. Notably, the political economy account does not posit that the key antagonism is between those designated as superior within a racist system versus those designated as inferior. Rather, the political economy account suggests that a small number of individuals who benefit from an overall inegalitarian system seek to divide the larger group of those who do not by using, among other things, racist and other inegalitarian ideologies to stave off challenges to systems that benefit them.

This helps explain why partially reconstructing institutions (e.g., along lines that address only one form of oppression) may diversify the elite but would not achieve equality of social standing.[9] Instead, a full program of economic democracy would reconstruct distributive institutions in ways that would eliminate racial along with other forms of injustice. The following chapters focus on how to do this.

I prefer the political economy account to the psychological account for several reasons. First, the psychological account is individually focused and has little to offer for changing structures and institutions that shape people's behavior and beliefs. Biases do substantial harm and should be addressed, but as part of a more comprehensive approach that also attends to the factors that structure positions in society.

Next, without invoking material interests, psychologically focused accounts can come to rely on essentializing ideas as motives. For instance, psychologically focused accounts may posit that people categorized as belonging to particular races have a fundamentally similar culture, a shared set of experiences, and/or that their interests predominantly relate to their racial categorization. This is an essentialist idea and ultimately reinforces the ideology of racism.

Third, psychological accounts can be used, perhaps inadvertently, to shore up some systems of oppression even as they work to address others. This operates similarly to the issue of emphasizing parity over justice discussed in chapter 2. A focus on improving outcomes in one or a small number of circumscribed contexts can serve as pretext to avoid addressing a more deeply inegalitarian system of social relations. In other words, the contribution of material conditions to racial injustice can be ignored when the issue is framed as psychological. Further, a focus on psychological fixes for those enmeshed in systems of oppression that offer them benefits can let the architects of the system off the hook—a diversion that powerful interests may well seek to effect. Individuals should, of course, be held blameworthy for inegalitarian ideologies they believe and act upon. But doing so should not come at the expense of the overall egalitarian project. In some cases, the "good" may wind up being used as the enemy of the "perfect."

Finally, psychological accounts can make uniting individuals for social change more difficult. The political economy account is useful as it provides a way for individuals with different ascriptive identities to make common cause over shared interests—it can emphasize that inegalitarian ideologies are part of a system that works to the material disadvantage of many people. In other words, it can place blame on the positions people are in, rather than defects in their character. Psychological accounts, however, can wind up furthering conflict between individuals who have already been made to compete as a strategy to prevent unity.

A political economy approach has been borne out historically by the successes of egalitarian social movements. Typically, these movements did not emphasize combating an abstract racism or the psychology of racists.[60,61] Instead, they pursued concrete policy interventions to address material conditions and the system of social relations that produces outcomes patterned by categories of ascriptive difference.[3] As Williams and colleagues note:

> Because racism is a system that consists of a set of dynamically related components or subsystems, disparities in any given domain are a result of processes of reciprocal causality across multiple subsystems. Accordingly, interventions should address the interrelated mechanisms and critical leverage points through which racism operates and explicitly design multilevel interventions to get at the multiple processes of racism simultaneously. . . . The civil rights policies of the 1960s are prime examples of race-targeted policies that improved socioeconomic opportunities and living conditions, narrowed the Black–White economic gap between the mid-1960s and the late 1970s, and reduced health inequities. Interventions to improve household income, education and employment opportunities, and housing and neighborhood conditions have also demonstrated health benefits.[3]

Summary

Inegalitarian ideologies that create categories of ascriptive difference cause injustice that harms health. Understanding these causes both individually and structurally is important for the project of social transformation. In particular, it is important to identify both inegalitarian ideology and specific institutions and other social structures that have the effect of producing injustice even if current actors are no longer motivated by racist ideology, so that egalitarian social movements can work to change them. Further, highlighting that people can be subject to multiple forms of oppression paints a truer picture of individual experiences than focusing on a single form of oppression. And recognizing that how oppression harms health may vary based on multiple aspects of one's identity helps move away from homogenization of heterogeneous experiences.

In combating the effects of racism on health, it is important not to lose sight of the fact that individuals shape institutions even as they are shaped by them. It is true that social structures created by those holding inegalitarian ideologies can continue even in the absence of that ideology. But oppressive social structures cannot continue in the absence of individual agency, because no social structure can. Thus, whatever the relevant structures, they must be reproduced and maintained by real individuals (even if the influence of any one individual is small). Institutions are changeable. Metaphors about racism being "in the DNA of" or "baked in to" or the "original sin of" the United States capture the pervasiveness of racist ideology, but they deemphasize how ideologies of racism have changed over time in response to varying social conditions, the role that contemporary individuals play in reproducing these structures, and egalitarian movements' ability to change them.

Social democracy views the causes of outcomes patterned by racist, sexist, and other forms of oppression as inegalitarian social relations that unjustly distribute power and resources. Social democratic policy approaches are heavily focused on restructuring those social relations, which will improve health for those who experience injustice. The capabilities social democratic policies seek to guarantee offer important ways to combat both inegalitarian ideologies and their effects. Guaranteeing these capabilities would interrupt the processes that assign social positions on the basis of ascriptive differences. This would remove the connection between categories of ascriptive difference, social standing, and the distribution of material resources. Further, social democratic policies seek to restructure the positions of society— allowing all individuals to stand in a relationship of equality with others. Therefore, addressing the role inegalitarian ideologies play in harming health is a major way that the social democratic political approach will help achieve health equity.

7

The Theory of the Welfare State

This book began by examining how to think about health equity, arguing that health equity occurs when injustices that harm health are eliminated. I then discussed the state's duty to show equal care for the life of each individual. Practically, the state fulfills this duty by guaranteeing a set of essential capabilities needed to stand in a relationship of equality with others throughout the different spheres of social relations: civil, political, and economic. This is the aim of social democracy as a political project. I then discussed empirical reasons why many unjust social conditions are health harming. This next section of the book turns to practicalities involved in achieving the normative goals of social democracy. Questions covered include what the underlying logic of the policy regime should be, what the economics of such policies are, how to finance these policies, and how to implement these policies successfully.

The Egalitarian State

The normative goal of the social democratic state is to fulfill its duty of equal care, such that it creates social conditions in which people enjoy substantive freedom and are situated in a relationship of equality with each other. Practically, the state needs to turn these ideals into concrete policy that establishes the material conditions in which people live. What I call the "egalitarian state" is the collection of state functions that relate to fulfilling the state's duty of equal care. The egalitarian state thus institutionalizes the ideal of equality at the heart of social democracy.[1]

Types of Income

Many of the functions of the egalitarian state involve ensuring just distribution of income. As discussed in chapter 5, income is an inflow of resources. Income can be characterized by its form: money (or pecuniary) income, and nonmoney income (such as the "housing services" that a home-owner receives). It can also be characterized by its source. *Factor income* comes from a market-based payment related to labor or assets an individual holds (such as land, real estate, or capital investments)—the "factors" of production (labor, land, and capital).[2] Factor income is sometimes called "pretax" or "market" income, and the institutions that distribute it form the "factor payment system." *Transfer income* refers to income received without the exchange of goods or services, such as through state payments or support within families.[2] *Net income* (sometimes called "disposable," "posttax," or "postfisc" income) is all the income that actually belongs to an individual—factor and transfer income received, minus the portions that do not actually belong to the person who initially received them (e.g., tax payments).

Policy Arenas of the Egalitarian State

The egalitarian state has three main policy arenas. The first is civil and political rights. The second is factor income policy.[3] Factor income policy relates to the conditions under which people receive income from labor, land, and capital. The third is the tax-and-transfer system.[2] It is important to remember that taxation is both a mechanism of finance and a way to achieve normative goals in its own right.

Since economic activity undergirds fulfillment of basic survival needs, economic activity is of primary interest to the egalitarian state. Some commentators frame the question of how the state should be involved in economic activity as one of "big" versus "small" government. This is misleading, as all economic activity occurs within a system of social relations regulated by the state. Terming some state actions big and others small reflects only ideology. As discussed in chapter 3, even "free market" systems rely on a strong state apparatus of property rights and enforcement that distributes property and the advantages that come with it to some rather than others.[4] Markets are political before they are economic,[5] and "all incomes are determined by our politically-constructed economic institutions."[6] There is no true choice between big and small government. Rather, the question is how the state should act to achieve its normative goals. Some of this involves state activity in the civil and political sphere. And in the economic sphere, necessary state activity includes creating a regime of property rights, labor regulations, providing in-kind services, making transfer payments, taxation, and establishing other policy that sets the conditions under which economic activity occurs. Misunderstanding markets as natural rather than artificial creates a number of problems, which are discussed throughout the remainder of this book. These include reluctance to set appropriate background conditions for markets to function in a way that results in just outcomes, and misconstruing state involvement as being inherently "second best" or unlikely to achieve just outcomes. Another common misunderstanding is presuming individual entitlement to factor incomes. Instead, it is important to understand that factor income is a "gross" form of income, a "first pass" distributed for administrative convenience, not yet reconciled to the prevailing property rights regime.

The subsequent sections of this chapter will make these ideas clearer.

The Welfare State within the Egalitarian State

Within the egalitarian state, the welfare state can be thought of as a set of functions that relate to the distribution of resources needed to guarantee the essential capabilities. The welfare state is concerned with basic capabilities such as those that involve food, housing, education, and health care. Further, the welfare state is concerned with providing financial security throughout the life course—especially during times people may not be able to earn factor income, such as childhood, old age, sickness, and unemployment. Economist Howard Glennerster defines welfare as "remaining in good health and 'sufficiency.' "[7(p3)] He further notes,

> Life brings risks. Most of us will pass through periods of sickness and old age, many through periods of joblessness, and some through long periods of disability. All of us will be dependent on parents or partners for part of our lives, and we shall need to invest in some kind of training or advanced education not just early in our lives, but increasingly throughout them. It might be possible, if we are lucky, to survive such adversity by insuring ourselves during our working lives, or it might be possible to borrow to meet temporary needs. However, both are expensive. The costs fall heavily on families during periods when they are also trying to bring up children. Moreover, private insurance and capital markets

do not work well for these purposes, if at all in some cases. As a consequence virtually all modern advanced economies have evolved ways to spread the costs of meeting these risks over lifetimes and across income groups.[7(p228)]

The welfare state involves functions of the state that helps people face these risks.

The welfare state is a major component of the egalitarian state and thus deserves extended discussion—particularly regarding the arena of tax-and-transfer policy. However, the welfare state is necessary but not sufficient to fulfill the state's duty of equal care—welfare state policies in isolation will not achieve substantive equality.

The welfare state helps fulfill both duties of distribution and duties of recognition. Welfare states can vary dramatically in how, and how well, these duties are met. But because everyone values the products* of human labor needed for the essential capabilities, arrangements to provide them will occur one way or another. In some instances, the state may delegate production and allocation to private parties, but that should not be misconstrued as a lack of state involvement. There is no question, then, of whether there will be a welfare state. Instead, the question is how to arrange the welfare state so the state can best fulfill its duty of equal care.

The Problems the Welfare State Has to Solve

The welfare state exists to help the state fulfill its duty of equal care by ensuring essential capabilities for all citizens at all points in their lives. Some essential capabilities require consuming particular products, and thus individuals need to have the power to consume those products. Markets are useful ways to distribute at least some of the products needed for those capabilities.** But for markets to be part of guaranteeing the essential capabilities, people must have a source of purchasing power—or else they may not have the necessary consumption power. The market can provide purchasing power, but it does so by distributing income in relation to productive activity (i.e., either through paid labor or owning assets used in production). A problem with this approach, however, is that most people own few produc-

---

*Throughout, I use the term products as shorthand for goods and services.

**Some products are better supplied by the state directly; I will discuss considerations about when products should be supplied via markets rather than by the state directly in more detail in the following chapters.

tive assets and are only able to work at some points in their lives (and others never are).

At the same time, an economic system with distributive institutions that emphasize earning factor income through labor* and market allocation of products needed for essential capabilities has important advantages. And the state does have an interest in encouraging productive economic activity, when people are able to engage in it, as that is what makes it possible to guarantee the essential capabilities for everyone. Thus, the problem that the welfare state must solve is how to guarantee the essential capabilities for everyone (or at least those essential capabilities the welfare state is concerned with), while supporting the economic activity that makes doing so possible.

Stating the problem this way has two important implications. First, during the times in people's lives when they can work, it argues for a system in which factor income from labor is the primary source of income, perhaps even allowing some income inequality to incentivize work (subject to normative constraints). Transfer income may supplement factor income in some situations, but it would not be the primary source of income. Second, market institutions face an inescapable structural problem—productive capacity, and thus the ability to earn factor income from labor, varies considerably over a lifetime. Further, some roles, necessary for social reproduction, do not command factor income. Thus, on their own, market institutions are incomplete solutions to fulfilling the state's duty of equal care. Therefore, the state must create mechanisms to guarantee the necessary consumption power aside from the factor payment system.

Production over the Life Course

A typical human life includes three periods with respect to productive capacity. These are childhood, the working years, and older age. During the working years, one's productive capacity is at its peak, and during childhood and older age it is typically lower.**

---

*Though factor income can come from labor or capital, in societies in which most people do not own capital receiving factor income hinges on the capacity to perform paid labor. Further, capital cannot generate income without labor, so the economic system overall must emphasize labor, at least for some.

**This is only a common pattern—it does not mean everyone will have these periods of their life or that having these periods is "normal."

In the United States at present, childhood is often operationalized as being below 18 years of age and older age as being 65 years of age and above. There are exceptions, and these thresholds represent specific historical labor policy developments, but the underlying idea is that below and above a certain age, an individual will not have the productive capacity necessary to earn factor income (even leaving aside questions of whether they should be expected to).[2]

Further, during the working years, people may have periods where work is interrupted.[2] First, some individuals may be disabled, either temporarily or permanently, in the sense of being unable to work to earn factor income. Second, individuals may become unemployed—that is, looking to work but without a job. Third, individuals might be students, such that their current educational activities preclude working (typically with the goal of earning factor income later). Finally, individuals may be engaged in productive activity that is socially necessary but unpaid. A common example of this is caregiving, such as raising young children.

It is important to understand the distribution of these situations in the United States (figure 7.1). In 2019,[8] out of approximately 325 million Americans, about 73 million (22.5%*) were under 18 years of age, and about 55 million (16.8%) were age 65 and older. For those between 18 and 64 years of age, about 11 million (3.5%) reported being disabled and unable to work, about 2 million (0.5%) reported being unemployed the entire year, about 9 million (2.9%) reported being full-time students, and about 12 million (3.7%) reported being caregivers without any labor income. This leaves about 163 million (50.1%) who might be expected to work. In other words, only about half of the population would be expected to perform paid labor at any given time.

Why the Welfare State Is Essential

Understanding productivity across the life course facilitates a more in-depth discussion of the problem the welfare state has to solve. The market can get income directly to people who are supplying factors of production (labor, land, and capital). However, few people own enough land or capital to provide a sufficient stream of income, and the ability to engage in labor varies greatly across a typical life course. So, relying on factor income to provide

---

*Percentages are of the entire population.

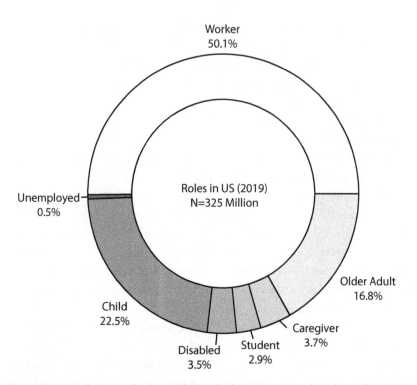

Figure 7.1. Distribution of roles in the United States using data from the 2020 US Census Current Population Survey Annual Social and Economic Supplement (covering calendar year 2019). Individuals were categorized into mutually exclusive roles as follows: Age < 18 years ("child") or ≥ 65 years ("older adult") using variable "A_AGE." Then, if aged 18 to 64 years inclusive, an individual was considered a caregiver if they reported that the main reason they did not work in 2019 was "taking care of home" (variable "RSNNOTW" = 3), then considered disabled if the main reason they did not work in 2019 was "ill or disabled" (variable "RSNNOTW" = 1), then considered a student if the main reason they did not work in 2019 was "going to school" (variable "RSNNOTW" = 4), then considered unemployed if the main reason they did not work in 2019 was "could not find work" (variable "RSNNOTW" = 5). If none of these applied, the individual was considered a worker or able to earn factor income, regardless of whether they were currently working. Berkowitz SA. The logic of policies to address income-related health inequity: a problem-oriented approach. *Milbank Q*. Published online March 22, 2022. doi:10.1111/1468-0009.12558.

purchasing power will not guarantee the essential capabilities for all people at all times. Therefore, the state needs to create additional distributive institutions that can guarantee essential capabilities for individuals who are in a variety of situations.

These situations can be divided into problems related to periods when one is not engaging in paid labor—childhood and older age, and periods of disability, unemployment, being a student, and caregiving—and periods when one is. To make clear why there is no alternative to the welfare state for guaranteeing the essential capabilities, I delineate seven potential distributive solutions for providing needed resources.[9,10]

The first four potential solutions are individually focused and market based: (1) earning sufficient factor income contemporaneously to consumption needs to purchase needed products, (2) stockpiling needed products during times of greater productivity to meet needs during times of less productivity, (3) accumulating sufficient wealth during times of greater productivity to permit purchase of needed products during times of less productivity (self-insurance), and (4) purchasing private insurance during times of greater productivity to establish a claim on needed products during times of less productivity. The next solutions are primarily family and/or community based: (5) receiving transfer income from family or friends during periods of less productivity, and (6) receiving transfer income from private charitable organizations during periods of less productivity. The last solution is: (7) receiving transfer income from the state during periods of less productivity— the welfare state.

Considerations for Those Not Receiving Factor Income

When one is not receiving factor income, a combination of solutions 1–6 cannot guarantee the essential capabilities in a normatively acceptable way without solution 7.

The first solution, earning factor income and using it to buy what one needs, clearly fails when productive ability is low or interrupted. It is simply not possible to earn sufficient factor income to guarantee the essential capabilities in childhood, older age, and periods of illness or disability.

The second solution, stockpiling needed products, could work in some instances. For example, one could attempt to accumulate and store, during one's working years, food and water, and secure a house that would not need repairs, all to provide for older age. However, stockpiling presents practical problems, including spoilage and the need for some products that cannot be stockpiled (e.g., health care). Further, stockpiling is not possible for childhood needs. Thus, stockpiling is, at best, an incomplete solution.

The third solution is to accumulate assets that can be used to provide consumption power during less productive times. For example, a stock of savings from factor income could yield a flow of income, or assets could be sold off to raise funds, and then needed products could be purchased on the market. However, this is also an incomplete solution. First, this will not work during childhood or other periods that precede the ability to accumulate adequate savings. Second, there is substantial uncertainty as to the amount and timing of savings needed, and inflation could occur such that assets that had been sufficient no longer are.

The fourth solution is to use factor income to purchase private insurance. Purchasing private insurance can guarantee essential capabilities in some cases. But, for technical reasons that will be discussed in chapter 8, markets for needed insurance often fail.[10] And again, this solution is not feasible for childhood or other periods that precede the ability to accumulate adequate funds to purchase such insurance. Thus, private insurance is another incomplete solution.

The fifth solution is to receive interpersonal transfers of income or assets from family and friends. This is, of course, a common way people have met their needs throughout history. But it is an incomplete strategy on its own. There is substantial heterogeneity in whether individuals have family or friends who can, or are willing to, provide such support. Making essential capabilities contingent on the resources and generosity of an individual's family and friends does not fulfill the duty of equal care. As an example, consider a situation in which a working-age man earns factor income while a working-age woman provides caregiving to young children, and receives sufficient income, through household pooling of resources, to provide her with the essential capabilities. Without an option to receive resources needed for the essential capabilities outside the current arrangement, her essential capabilities are not *guaranteed*. If the woman wanted to leave the relationship owing to, for example, domestic violence, she might hesitate to do so if there was no mechanism to support her (and possibly her children) financially until she could find employment. This would violate the state's duty of equal care. Given these risks, relying on transfers from family and friends is not justifiable public policy on its own, even though such transfers are completely unobjectionable.

The sixth solution, similar to the fifth, is to rely on voluntary associations or private charities. This is also an unobjectionable but incomplete solution. As the essential capabilities are owed to all citizens by virtue of their fundamental equality, requiring people to rely on charity is not justifiable.[11] First, it would place individuals receiving charity in a relationship of inferiority with those who provide it. Second, since charity is discretionary, it cannot *guarantee* essential capabilities. Further, empirically, for reasons related to externalities and lack of coordination (discussed further in chapter 8), this approach is typically not capable of providing the necessary level of support to guarantee the essential capabilities, even were it normatively justifiable.[10,12] Charity is often promoted as an alternative to state action, but it is, at best, supplemental. Moreover, pursuing only the charitable projects that most interest them, without additionally participating in a system that can guarantee essential capabilities, does not fulfill an individual's duty to work collectively toward justice.[13]

It is worth reiterating that the fifth and sixth solutions are not objectionable in themselves. The issue is that the state cannot fulfill its duty of equal care without creating other approaches that ensure an individual will have the essential capabilities even in the absence of transfers from family, friends, or charities. Further, calls for reliance on the family and charity are often used to stave off calls for state action. This can be motivated by the ideology and material interests of those who stand to benefit from systems of social relations that do not guarantee the essential capabilities for all.

As the problems with solutions 1 through 6 make clear, guaranteeing essential capabilities for all individuals during times when they are not able to earn factor income from paid labor is not possible without the welfare state. Since around half of the people in the United States are in this situation at any given time, and everyone is at some point in their life, the welfare state is essential to meeting the normative goals of social democracy.

Considerations for Those Receiving Factor Income

Individuals engaging in paid labor do not have the same inherent need for the welfare state as those who are not engaging in paid labor, as their essential capabilities could be guaranteed through factor income. This does not, however, imply no role for the state. First, the state still needs to ensure that factor income is earned under conditions that respect everyone's equality. Thus, the egalitarian state must work to provide equal opportunity, prevent discrimination in the labor market,[14] establish a justifiable property rights regime with respect to ownership of productive assets, and so on. Factor income policy to address these issues will be discussed in detail in chapter 13.

Second, the welfare state can still be useful for those who are engaging in paid labor. For example, for reasons to be discussed in chapters 8 and 11, it is often preferable on technical grounds for capabilities related to health care to be guaranteed through the welfare state, even for those earning factor income.[7,10]

Third, as will be discussed in more detail in the next section, those who are engaging in paid labor often live in households with individuals who are not. In the absence of welfare state programs to support individuals who are not engaging in paid labor, the standard of living for those earning equal amounts of factor income will vary depending on the number of individuals in the household who are not receiving factor income. This can even mean that an individual earning sufficient factor income to avoid poverty as a single person winds up in poverty because they need to support others.

Fourth, individuals will not receive factor income from paid labor throughout their lives. The same person for whom factor income was sufficient today was in need of transfer income earlier in their lives, and likely will be in need of it later in their lives.

For these reasons, individuals who are receiving factor income from paid labor still have an interest in, and good cause to support, the welfare state.

Individuation and the Welfare State

Fundamentally, the essential capabilities need to be guaranteed to individuals. However, people often pool resources within households. This can make it tempting to design welfare state policies at the household level. However, while sensible in some circumstances, this can also lead to problems. Household-level income is the aggregation of the income of all individuals within the household. This means that household composition strongly influences the standard of living a given level of household income can provide. For example, consider two households with the same household factor income: a household with two working-age adults earning factor income, and a household with one working-age adult earning factor income, one working-age adult who is disabled, three children, and one older adult. Clearly, the per-person consumption power a given amount of factor income provides differs between the households. Thus, given the need to guarantee each person's essential capabilities, it is generally better for policy to treat each person primarily as an individual, rather than a member of a household. This principle is sometimes called "individuation,"[15] and it is the perspective I adopt throughout the book. Individuation is often particularly important for ensuring women are treated justly by the state.[16]

The Welfare State as Property Rights Regime

A key question for any society is what system of property rights, a "property rights regime," it will have. One can think of property rights, or perhaps more broadly, economic rights, as enforceable claims individuals have about the distribution of natural resources, products, and income.

Property rights are established by the state as part of an overall system of social relations—they do not, and cannot, exist externally to the state.[4,17,18] Property held, income earned, taxes owed, transfers paid, and in-kind benefits received are all interdependent parts of the same system.[17] Any one element cannot be understood in isolation, and ownership is an inherently political claim about resource distribution.[4,19] Fundamentally, the economy is a government program.[20] More specifically, it is a government program meant to address allocation under conditions of scarcity (i.e., there may not be enough of a particular resource to satisfy everyone's desires) and rivalrousness (i.e., for many resources, more than one individual cannot possess the same resource).

Two examples help clarify this point. The first examines how the market (or "exchange") value of any asset (including labor-power) arises from social relationships and is thus endogenous to a system of social relations—it is not "natural" or external to the system. This undercuts the idea that the state inherently "takes" something from individuals when it, for example, levies taxes. The second example clarifies why, within a property rights regime, state actions like taxation do not represent redistribution (taking someone's property and giving it to someone else) but distribution (allocation of jointly produced products according to justifiable rules).

Asset Values Are Endogenous

Consider an upscale apartment building in an affluent neighborhood.[19] One might think that its physical amenities and location are the primary determinants of its market value. But imagine that there is a regime without property rights—no one can legally claim ownership of the building or the stream of income it generates, and the state will not enforce any such claim. In such a situation, the building's market value is likely to be low. Now, imagine a property rights regime where ownership is permissible and rent can be collected. However, eviction for nonpayment of rent is not allowed. Under such a regime, the building's market value is likely to be greater than in the regime with no ownership. This would be due entirely to the different system of social relations, not any difference in the building itself. Now, imagine a third regime—the owner can set any level of rent, and the state enforces evictions for nonpayment of rent. The building's market value is likely to be greater than under the other two regimes—again, due solely to state action.

Of course, within any particular system of social relations, attributes of the building itself figure into the value placed on it. But those attributes generate, at most, part of the building's market value. The "full" value, within any given system of social relations, is inextricably linked to that system of social relations and is not independent of it.

The same principle applies to income received from labor rather than capital. For example, building managers are likely to be paid more when the building can generate more income, even if the actual labor performed is the same.

No "Redistribution," Only Distribution

For the second example, imagine a salesperson working at a shoe store. The salesperson agrees to work for $20 an hour. Over the course of eight hours on the first day, the salesperson collects $800 in revenue from shoe sales.

Though the salesperson collected $800 in revenue, they receive only $160 in wages. $640 is not "taken" from the salesperson, nor is it "redistributed" from the salesperson to store accounts. Instead, the entire income is simply distributed according to the rules of the agreement—$160 to the salesperson and $640 to the store (on behalf of its owners). The salesperson's claim to $160 in factor income from wages was determined by the property rights regime at the same time as the lack of claim on the other $640.

Now imagine further that, under the prevailing property rights regime, the salesperson owes $32 (20%) in taxes on $160 in wages. That $32 in taxes is not taken from the salesperson by the state any more than the $640 in revenue was taken from the salesperson by the owners of the store. Under the prevailing property rights regime, the salesperson has a claim on $128 of labor income, and no claim on the other $32. Distributing $160 in gross income, to be later reconciled to $128 through tax payment, was simply an administrative decision—not one that implied entitlement to $160, any more than having the salesperson initially collect revenue implied entitlement to $800.

Recognizing that income received and assets held arise as part of a system of social relations is critical for understanding the workings of the egalitarian state. The egalitarian state emphatically does not intervene on pre-existing conditions, redistributing from the rich to the poor. Instead, the egalitarian state establishes the conditions under which income is earned and wealth is accumulated in the first place. This means that there is no "redistribution"—only distribution.[1,17]

Justifying a Property Rights Regime

That the state is inextricably involved in all economic activity does not mean that anything goes, or that the state could rightfully confiscate anything from anyone.[18] Instead, it means that a given system of social relations, including its property rights regime, needs to be normatively justified.[17] This justification must consider both the outcomes achieved and the means used to achieve them—whether such a system meets duties of distribution and recognition. The state does not appropriate and redistribute what citizens already own, it sets the rules that determine what citizens own.[11,17] Fundamentally, policies that affect the production and distribution of income and wealth are justified (or not) by their contribution to an overall system of social relations that is just—one that shows equal care and situates everyone in a relationship of equality.[18,21]

To help make these ideas more concrete, consider justifications that advocates of a property rights regime privileging market distributions of resources (e.g., libertarians or those who support laissez-faire) might provide.

In chapter 3, I discussed the *proceduralist* justification—that voluntary

market-based exchange represents a fair process and thus property holdings that result from it should be respected whatever the specific outcome.
As noted in chapter 3, this might justify some particular exchange, but it
cannot justify the overall system, including initial property formation. Given
the facts of scarcity and rivalrousness, any property rights regime inherently
limits the capabilities of some while enhancing the capabilities of others. To
take everyone's equality seriously given this state of the world, a property
rights regime must be justifiable to everyone. Thus, proceduralist justifications of a property rights regime are, at best, partial. They cannot fully
justify the starting positions individuals hold when coming into a potential
exchange.

I also discussed in chapter 3 the *desertist* justification—that markets allocate resources on the basis of people's productive contributions, and thus
market outcomes should be respected as representing people's just deserts
for productive efforts.[22] But as noted in chapter 3, this justification is both
empirically false and infeasible. Markets distribute income to owners of
natural resources and productive assets without requiring labor on the part
of the owner. In the case of natural resources, these assets were not even
created by any person. This income cannot be deserved through effort. Further, a key component of production is accumulated knowledge and technology (often from past generations)—"total factor productivity."[23] It is difficult
to see how a person producing now could deserve the results of total factor
productivity, either. Finally, because modern production is effectively a joint
enterprise with many contributors, it is generally not possible to assign a
particular value to any one person's contribution.[24] As will be discussed further in chapter 13, marginal productivity accounting (quantifying how output changes for a unit change in input) cannot determine whether any particular input (e.g., a person's labor) caused the change in output, which would
be necessary for a desertist claim to make sense.

A third justification for a market-privileging property rights regime
might be *consequentialist*—such a regime provides the greatest incentive to
increase production, and thus maximizes the output (or some other priori-
tized outcome) available to society. Even if empirically true (which is debat-
able), such a justification would not be acceptable as it does not respect the
distinction between persons. Such a regime would not necessarily guarantee
the essential capabilities to all individuals, and thus would not respect their
fundamental equality.

Proceduralist, desertist, and consequentialist arguments cannot justify a property rights regime. This leaves another option—an *institutionalist* justification. This justification argues that rules about property formation, property transfer, and property holding—the elements of a property rights regime—are part of the distributive institutions of a society and should be judged on the basis of how well they help fulfill the duty of equal care. The facts of resource scarcity and rivalrousness mean that property rights regimes can negatively affect—lessen the capabilities of—some individuals within a society. Thus, to respect everyone's fundamental moral equality, a given property rights regime must be justifiable to all members of society. Some inequality in property rights (and in *non-essential* capabilities that stem from them) might be permissible, but only in a way that works to everyone's advantage. Thus, an acceptable property rights regime gains its justification by helping to guarantee the essential capabilities.

Updating the Lockean Proviso

Property rights regimes are policy tools—ways for the state to establish society as a system of fair cooperation over time. The welfare state updates the Lockean Proviso emphasized by Nozick,[25] the idea that individuals can justifiably acquire property from nature through their efforts "at least where there is enough, and as good, left in common for others."[26(chap2:5:27)] Given scarcity and rivalrousness, the Lockean Proviso cannot literally be satisfied. Instead, however, an appropriate welfare state can satisfy it in spirit by ensuring that one's claim to property enhances, rather than impedes, others' essential capabilities. Such a normatively justifiable regime of property and other economic rights could involve both rules about what property one may claim (e.g., what factor income one may keep) and rules about what one is entitled to receive (e.g., an older-age pension).

Justifiable and Unjustifiable Property Rights Regimes

To sum up the idea of the welfare state as a normatively justified property rights regime, it is instructive to compare an unjustified property rights regime with a normatively justified one. Consider a libertarian property rights regime, in which the state establishes and enforces the conditions necessary for market exchange, security and defense, and a tax code necessary to finance these efforts. Under this regime, individuals are not entitled to the entirety of the factor income they receive (when they are

earning any) but to a portion of it. Individuals must rely only on factor income, accumulated assets, transfers from family and friends, and charity
to meet their needs. Given the problems with those approaches previously
identified, many individuals in this system would lack essential capabilities.
Such a regime would not be normatively justified, as it would not guarantee
essential capabilities across the life course for all. A state that implemented
such a regime would violate its duty of equal care.

Now consider an alternative regime. Under this regime, the state establishes and enforces the conditions necessary for market exchange, security,
and defense, as before. It further establishes policies that guarantee the essential capabilities to each individual across their life course, such as a system
of transfer payments and education and health care services. As before, it
establishes a tax code. Under this regime, an individual retains a lower proportion of factor income than under the libertarian system (when they are
earning any), but they again are entitled to a portion. This system guarantees
the essential capabilities to all, and it is thus justified. Therefore, the welfare state and the mechanisms that finance it—what might be considered
the entire tax-and-transfer system—are an important part of what makes
a property rights regime justifiable.

Welfare State: Robin Hood and Piggy Bank

Understanding the welfare state as a normatively justifiable property rights regime helps make sense of two commonly discussed functions
of the welfare state. Economist Nicholas Barr describes the "Robin Hood"
function of the welfare state as making interpersonal transfers—that is,
taking from those earning factor income and giving to those who are not.[10,27]
But understanding the welfare state as a property rights regime clarifies why
this view is mistaken. Because an individual is not inherently entitled to the
factor income they receive, the state does not "rob from the rich to give to
the poor." Instead, the rules of the system in total, including the tax code,
define what portion of factor income one is entitled to. As above, the welfare
state distributes income, but does not "redistribute" income. Through participating in such a system, people can discharge their duty to work toward
justice. Thus, the welfare state solves an important collective action problem that would be difficult to solve in its absence.

Barr also discusses the "Piggy Bank" function of the welfare state.[10,27]
Here, the welfare state can be thought of as distributing resources from a

person at one point in time to the same person at a different point in time—an intrapersonal transfer to smooth consumption and insure against risk. Such intrapersonal transfers are of course, *notional*, not actual. As political scientist Pieter Vanhuysse and colleagues explain: "The particular solution offered by welfare states uses taxes and promises to exploit the sectional nature of the lifecycle. At any given point in time, people who have been born in different years (different cohorts) live together (as age groups) in the same society. . . In other words, the welfare state solves the endemic problem of lifecycle consumption smoothing given inherently incomplete contracts about the future by arranging resource reallocations [*sic*] between age groups in cross-section."[28]

Capitalism, Socialism, and the Welfare State

People commonly question how the welfare state, as a system of distributive institutions, relates to systems of economic production. Two points to emphasize about this relationship are that (1) the welfare state is not synonymous with socialism as a system of economic production, and (2) the welfare state is not only compatible with but essential to both capitalism and socialism as systems of economic production.[29]

The terms *capitalism* and *socialism* have been used in many ways over a long period of time. I use the terms here to refer to ways of organizing economic production, specifically regarding ownership of productive assets. One might divide assets into three categories*: natural resources, not produced by anyone, to be used in production (e.g., land or minerals); products of human labor that are to be used for production (e.g., factory equipment); and products for personal consumption (e.g., clothing).[30]

The main difference between capitalism and socialism is that capitalist systems, overall, emphasize institutions of private productive asset ownership (natural resources and products used for production), whereas socialism emphasizes institutions of public productive asset ownership. Private ownership of products used for personal consumption is typical in both capitalist and socialist systems.

There can be exceptions within these broad outlines, of course. Capital-

---

*There are some gray areas (e.g., one may use specialized work clothes, such as steel-toed boots, to serve as both protective equipment in one's construction job and as one's regular daily footwear).

ist systems frequently include public ownership of some natural resources and products used for production (e.g., fighter jets used in the public production of defense services). And there are forms of socialism that favor collective, but private, ownership of products used in production (e.g., the assets of worker-owned cooperatives).

Normatively, I think either a broadly capitalist or a broadly socialist economy could be compatible with the principles of democratic equality and result in fulfilling the state's duty of equal care. Clearly, there are many examples of both capitalist and socialist systems that do not do this. These include right-wing dictatorships, laissez faire capitalism, and totalitarian communist states. But many other versions of capitalism or socialism are likely acceptable. Thus, a case-by-case approach that considers, for particular situations and sectors of the economy, the benefits and drawbacks of private versus public ownership of relevant assets is reasonable. The important thing is that decisions are made democratically and that the state meets its duty of equal care.

While capitalism and socialism relate primarily to production, the welfare state relates primarily to distribution and consumption.[29] That is, the goal of the welfare state is to distribute resources that provide consumption power, to guarantee the essential capabilities. The welfare state is essential, whatever system of production a society chooses, because the essential capabilities need to be guaranteed for everyone, even if they are not engaged in production. So, for example, a socialist system of worker-owned co-ops still needs the welfare state to guarantee the essential capabilities for, say, older adults and children.*

To sum up, the discussion about capitalism and socialism is principally about systems of production, and in particular about private versus public ownership of natural resources and productive assets. The welfare state is

---

* A term sometimes used in this context is *decommodification*, but that term can create confusion because it is used in at least two ways.[30] The first way refers to guaranteeing the essential capabilities for those not able to participate in the labor market.[31] The second way refers to not using markets as allocative mechanisms for certain essential products, such as food and health care. In the first sense, decommodification is a central goal of the welfare state. However, I see little inherent appeal to decommodification in the second sense. Whether or not markets are used to distribute particular products should depend on the specifics of the product (i.e., markets may be more useful in some cases than others, as will be discussed in chapter 8),[10] and not on a general preference against markets.

principally about consumption and the distribution of income and in-kind services needed to guarantee the essential capabilities. As the problems that the welfare state solves in order to guarantee the essential capabilities occur whether a society's system of production is capitalist or socialist, the welfare state is essential in either case. Furthermore, a strong welfare state is not indicative of either a capitalist or socialist system of production.

The Normative Case for the Universalist Welfare State

The welfare state is an essential aspect of the egalitarian state, but there are different approaches to welfare state design. The underlying logic of different welfare states designs varies considerably, which has important implications for the policies and programs that comprise it, and ultimately whether they are normatively justified. The goal of this section is to give an overview of two common welfare state approaches, universalism and residualism, and explain the normative arguments for and against them.

The focus in this section is on *normative* arguments for universalism. There are also important *technical* arguments to be made for universalism. Because these arguments rely on additional exposition, they will be presented in chapter 10.

Types of Welfare States

There is often a coherence to the logic that underlies welfare state policies in a given country, partly shaped by its historical development. Sociologist Gøsta Esping-Andersen described three predominant approaches in his seminal work, *Three Worlds of Welfare Capitalism*.[31] The first is sometimes called the corporatist-statist or conservative welfare state. This approach, associated with continental European countries such as Germany and France, emphasizes establishing loyalty to the state with generous benefits for civil servants ("statism"), formal incorporation of sectoral interests (e.g., businesses, the church) in the administration of benefits ("corporatism"), and a normative view of family relationships such that benefits target a (typically male) primary earner with a heavy emphasis on family transfers.[31,32] The conservative welfare state approach is neither compatible with the normative goals of social democracy nor commonly advocated in US policy debates, so I do not discuss it further.

The other two approaches are the universalist approach (exemplified by the Swedish, Danish, Norwegian, and Finnish welfare states) and the residualist (sometimes called the "liberal") approach (exemplified by the United States, Canada, the United Kingdom, Australia, Ireland, and New Zealand).[1,31] In considering different countries, however, it is important to note that particular policies or programs may not exhibit the same logic as predominates in the country overall—for instance, there are some universalist programs in the United States.

The universalist approach creates "first-line" programs—that is, the default expectation is that everyone would use them, as a right of citizenship.[33-36] Eligibility is typically "categorical," such as being an older adult (e.g., age 65 or older), and universal (in the set theory meaning of the term) within that category. For example, a universalist approach for older-age pensions would aim for participation by all older adults. Universalist programs need not involve the entire population—primary and secondary education can be universal for school-age children, and excluding older adults does not make them less universal. Further, within a given policy or program, benefit levels may vary—for example, there could be earnings-related pension benefits. However, the key to the universalist approach is that the policy or program is meant to include everyone within the relevant category in the same program. Programs are also meant to be sufficient—beneficiaries should not require additional, often private, programs to meet their needs. The universalist approach creates benefits as social rights that serve as the primary way to guarantee particular capabilities, not backup plans if family transfers or market mechanisms fail. Therefore, universalist programs are not safety-nets that catch individuals when they fall, but they are measures to prevent individuals from falling in the first place. The moral logic of the universalist welfare state is that it shows equal care for all and thus everyone, being reasonable as well as rational, has reason to support it.[33]

In contrast to universalism, residualism views welfare state programs as backup plans, to be used only when there are leftover, or residual, needs that cannot be met in other ways.[33,34] "Whereas universalism 'sees the public welfare services as normal, "first line" functions of modern industrial society,' residualism considers that they 'should come into play only when the so-called "normal" institutions of supply—the family and the market—break down.'"[34,35] The residualist approach views institutions like market exchange, enterprise benefits offered by employers, family transfers, and charity as the proper way for people to receive the products they need, with the welfare state only a last resort. This is the safety-net view of the welfare state. A hallmark of residualist programs is means testing—basing eligibility on having low income or assets—to ensure that only those who "really need" state benefits receive them. Residualist programs are often meant to reinforce social differences and not interfere with social inequality produced by market outcomes. Universalism, instead, is premised on the idea of relational equality and works against hierarchy and social differentiation.

Universalism Embodies Equality, Residualism Embodies Hierarchy

Universalism embodies relational equality by designing policies and programs for everyone to use as a matter of right, on terms acceptable to all. Universalism helps to meet duties of distribution *and* recognition simultaneously. In contrast, residualism creates and reinforces social stratification with a two-tiered structure: first-line programs for people who are doing well, and safety nets, inherently stigmatized, for people who are not.[11,37,38] A classic example of residualism in public policy was the English Poor Laws.[11] Residualist thinking emphasizes the idea that the need for assistance represents a personal failing.[11,33] Therefore, the aim of that assistance should be to help people put their lives in order, with "perfectionist" impulses that often include intrusive oversight and behavioral monitoring in program design.[11,33] A current example of this thinking is attempts to redesign the SNAP program so that benefits can only be used to purchase "healthy" foods.[39,40] Further, residualist programs often mean to help only the deserving and so include discretionary mechanisms to withhold or revoke benefits from those thought to have proven themselves "undeserving," even to the point of leaving people without essential capabilities.[11]

Residualist programs can be motivated by a sense of pity, rather than equality, which is normatively objectionable.[11] Here, welfare state benefits are seen as charity granted to inferiors, rather than rights due to equals. Even if such a welfare state met duties of distribution, it would do so in a way that does not meet duties of recognition, by not recognizing individuals' fundamental moral equality.[11,41]

Two-tiered systems lead to stigmatization of those who use second-tier benefits.[33,38] Residualist approaches that require people to grovel to prove their deservingness for assistance, restrict benefit spending in ways that all of us would not accept, or are punitively administered, cannot be part of how the state meets its duties of distribution.[11] As political scientist Bo Rothstein notes, to be normatively justified, "social policy should take the form of specified rights, not favors for which individuals have to petition, cap in hand. The idea [is] to replace discretionary poor relief with social policy as a right of citizenship."[33(p180)] But instead of guaranteeing essential capabilities as the right of citizens, under residualism individuals effectively give up their rights as full citizens for a second-class status with extensive oversight and supervision.[38] As sociologist T. H. Marshall said in his famous examination of the concept of citizenship, rather than being about equality, residualism is in some ways an attempt to make hierarchy "less vulnerable to attack by alleviating its less defensible consequences."[38(p33)] What residualism offers are "alternatives to the rights of citizenship, rather than additions to them."[38(p33)] Residualism stratifies individuals into second-class citizenship and subordinates meeting their needs to complying with conditions set by those in a position of superiority. Thus, a function of the residualist welfare state is to accommodate those who require its services to second-class citizenship and to shore up support for a system that does not offer equal standing to all.

Residualism Hides the State

Beyond creating a hierarchical system of social programs, residualism often submerges the involvement of the state in programs used by the well-off. Residualist systems give the appearance that only worse-off individuals require assistance from the state, but in reality the state assists the well-off too. For example, in the United States, "private," employer-sponsored health insurance is often presented as the normal approach to obtaining health insurance for working-age adults, with Medicaid insurance being the safety-net. However, employer-sponsored health insurance is heavily subsidized by federal tax expenditures (specifically, exempting employer health care spending from an individual's income tax base).[42] As another example, US housing policy includes both the home mortgage interest deduction and the housing choice voucher program (Section 8), but these hold very different places in US discourse about "welfare." Using multiple programs, stratified by income, to accomplish similar policy objectives contributes to making second-class citizens of worse-off individuals by pretending they are the ones who need government assistance while well-off individuals get by on their own. Reliance on state action may be hidden by locating programs in different parts of the government code, but that reliance is nonetheless real. Though the logic of residualism is that the state should be a last resort, this is of course impossible. The state is involved in all aspects of production and consumption. Universalism embraces that fact, residualism hides it.

Universalism and Income Inequality

In preferring universalism to residualism, it is important to remember that the goal is equality of standing, not equality of income. Universalist programs may help equalize income, but they may not. For example, the implementation of a universalist program may provide capabilities those who are less well-off might not have had, but it could also free up income for those who are better-off. This could conceivably increase the gap in income between these groups. But whether that gap increases or decreases is not the point. The point of universalist policy is to equalize treatment for everyone as a single class, instead of creating a population broken up, segmented, and stratified by different policies and programs.[38] Extreme income inequality is a symptom of a system of social relations in which the state does not fulfill its duty of equal care. Working toward a more equal distribution of income can help fulfill that duty in many cases. But income equality is not a goal for its own sake, and welfare state policy should recognize this.

Contrasting Universalism and Residualism

Differences in three areas help contrast universalism and residualism: the relationship between the welfare state and labor, how the welfare state can work against racist oppression, and the concept of poverty relief.

A supposed virtue of residualism is placing value on paid labor. In residualist programs, coupling benefits with work requirements is a common tactic to sort the "deserving" from the "undeserving." But residualist policies do not promote work equally. Under residualism, an individual who receives family transfers or a large inheritance may choose not to work without penalty, but such a choice is not open to an individual without this good fortune. Further, a residualist welfare state with means-tested programs inevitably creates poverty traps that serve as disincentives to labor,[10,43] because benefits are withdrawn as one's factor income increases (discussed further in chapter 10). This particularly affects those in the middle of the income distribution, who may find themselves with income levels too high for means-tested programs but too low to provide the essential capabilities, and it is another way the residualist welfare state undermines norms of reciprocity and reasonableness that the welfare state should exemplify.[33] In contrast, the universalist welfare state seeks to support individuals' productive abilities, as their production makes universalism possible.

A second contrast between universalism and residualism lies in how each approach interacts with racist ideology held by individuals. Residualism inherently creates hierarchy that can be weaponized by those who wish to use racism to divide individuals facing similar material circumstances.[44,45] Because a residualist welfare state paints some individuals as "makers" and others "takers," the "taker" category can be racialized for political gain. Indeed, this has been an enduring strategy in American politics. Universalism works against "divide and conquer" racism. By creating programs for everyone, as an expression of common equality, it undermines attempts to paint some individuals as inferior based on their supposedly aberrant use of state assistance.

Regarding poverty, the contrast between residualism and universalism is analogous to the contrast between treatment and prevention. From the residualist perspective, the rationale for the welfare state is to help "the poor," with everyone else getting by on their own. Residualism tries to "treat" poverty once it occurs. From the universalist perspective, "the poor" is not a meaningful category of people—rather, poverty is a risk to be prevented. The universalist approach tries to make it impossible to be poor in the first place, by creating policies that provide resources when people are in situations with high poverty risk—like childhood, older age, or periods of disability. Thus, the goal of the universalist welfare state is to ensure there are no "spaces" within the social structure that do not come with the essential capabilities.[46] The universalist welfare state sees the need for means-tested benefits as a form of state failure,[43] and it views its purpose as supplying products everyone needs, rather than providing relief to a certain few.[27]

Differences in perspective between universalism and residualism can shape policy. Questions of universalist policy can be framed as "what is fair to everyone?," or "what should we do overall?," or "how should we solve our common problems?"[33] In contrast, questions of residualist policy are framed as "what is to be done about the needy?," or "how should we solve their problems?" Thus, the moral logic of residualism does not focus on what is generally fair—it focuses on where to draw the line about who needs help.[33] To deserve help in a residualist system means to be different in some way, but being different suggests one is not really an equal citizen.[33,38]

For these reasons, a focus on poverty can provide cover for an inegalitarian structure that allows poverty to exist. Further, it creates a tension with the egalitarian idea that invites exploitation by forces aiming to undermine solidarity and reciprocity.

Summary
Market mechanisms as distributive institutions face predictable, structural problems as, at any given time, about half of society is unable to earn labor income.[47] Thus, a state must establish a complete set of distributive institutions, complementing the factor payment system with other institutions that ensure there are no locations within the social structure without equal standing.

In understanding the welfare state, it is crucial to remember that property rights regimes exist to help societies meet their normative goals—they do not exist external to them.[17] Thus, the welfare state should be understood as part of a normatively justified regime of property and other economic rights—helping to distribute the national income justly, not redistribute it.

Not only must welfare state institutions guarantee the essential capabilities, but they must do so in a way that reflects equality in social relations. The universalist welfare state embodies norms of reasonableness and reciprocity, treating the essential capabilities as due to all citizens in recognition of their fundamental equality. The residualist welfare state creates and reinforces hierarchy, social stratification, and exclusion.

An ongoing question in this book, discussed further in subsequent chapters, is why inequality of social standing—substantive inequality—persists despite formally equal civil and political rights. The concepts in this chapter offer one explanation in private property rights for natural resources and productive assets, along with a residualist welfare state. As the heart of private property rights is the ability to exclude others from the use of those assets, such rights inherently create some inequality. Without a counterbalancing regime of economic rights—for example, a universalist system of income supports and in-kind services, along with regulations governing the use of productive assets—equality of social standing will be impossible. We do not currently have such rights in the United States, which helps explain existing inequality. But this also helps explain why the welfare state is an essential part of the egalitarian state.

Specifically, the universalist welfare state is a vital part of a system that meets duties of recognition (and thus fights oppression) as well as distribution. First, welfare state policies can create material conditions that help people stand up to oppression. Second, the structure of the universalist welfare state can itself help to overcome oppression. Framing policies as rights rather than discretionary charity creates leverage points to push back against supposed inferiority. This does not mean discrimination and other forms of oppression cannot happen within a universalist welfare state—they can and do. But the universalist welfare state embodies equality, whereas a residualist welfare state embodies hierarchy. Attitudes and beliefs cannot be legislated, and ideals must be translated into policy to affect the material conditions under which people live. To combat oppression, individuals need power and resources. Thus a tractable approach, one readily addressable by policy, is to emphasize policies that combines formal equality with material security. Formal equality increases the power oppressed individuals have to make demands of others, and material security provides a basis for the struggle for substantive equality to succeed.

For the state to fulfill its duty of equal care, it must establish a policy regime that ensures the national income is produced and distributed in such a way as to guarantee the essential capabilities for everyone over their life course. Given this normative goal, the next question is how, technically, to achieve it. As Glennerster notes, "the costs of sustaining our well-being as individuals and families take a large share of our incomes, whether we do so through the public purse or otherwise. Indeed, because there are failures in the private insurance and health markets, private costs are larger than public ones, and in some cases, private markets do not work at all."[7(p227)] The next chapter begins a discussion of economic concepts that help explain why the universalist welfare state is not only normatively justified but an economically efficient way to guarantee the essential capabilities.

8

Economics of the Welfare State

The goal of this chapter is to discuss topics in economic theory relevant for welfare state policies. These topics include types of economic policies and their effects on economic behavior, conditions needed for real-world markets to operate as economic theory expects, and the importance of social insurance. Discussing these topics helps inform answers to a recurring policy question: whether the institutional form used to allocate the products needed to guarantee essential capabilities should be *market provision* or *public provision*. Market provision typically uses the price mechanism to coordinate consumption and production—with consumption choices made by a consumer under a budget constraint, and with profit as the rationale for production.[1] Public provision typically involves coordination of production and consumption using administrative rules, set politically.

The economic soundness of the welfare state has long been recognized. For example, economist Adam Smith wrote,

> The first duty of the sovereign, that of protecting the society from the violence and invasion of other independent societies. . . . The second duty of the sovereign, that of protecting, as far as possible, every member of the society from the injustice or oppression of every other member of it. . . . The third and last duty of the sovereign or commonwealth is that of erecting and maintaining those public institutions and those public works, which, though they may be in the highest degree advantageous to a great society, are, however, of such a nature that the profit could never repay the expense to any individual or small number of individuals, and which it therefore cannot be expected that any individual or small number of individuals should erect or maintain.[2]

As discussed in chapter 7, people will pay for the products the welfare state is concerned with one way or another—whether they buy them from private parties or finance them publicly.[3,4,5] Reflecting on one's own household budget makes this clear. The bulk of one's monthly earnings likely go to food, housing, health care, education, childcare, and saving for retirement, college for one's children, or a rainy day. Thus, the question is not whether funds should be spent on these products but how the state should be involved so as to guarantee, for everyone, the essential capabilities. Similarly, removing spending for these items from a state budget does not make spending on them go away; it merely shifts the source of the spending.

This chapter is guided by three overriding principles. The first is that normative goals are lexically prior to technical considerations about how to achieve them.* I distinguish between normative questions (what is right intrinsically or morally?) and technical questions** (what is the right thing to do in the sense that it instrumentally helps achieve goals?). Technical questions about the best way to achieve a goal, which economic theory can help answer, are only relevant when choosing among normatively justified options—options that all achieve the goal and achieve it in a normatively acceptable way.

Confusion on this point commonly arises when discussing economic efficiency (defined in more detail later). Though economic arguments sometimes imply that efficiency can be traded off with concepts like the duty of equal care, this perspective, which derives from consequentialist moral theory (e.g., utilitarianism), is not justified. The right is not traded off for the good. Instead, one seeks to maximize the good among the options that fulfill duties regarding what is right. There may be trade-offs between efficiency and particular patterns of distributive outcomes, such as income equality.*** But this is not a trade-off between efficiency and the normatively defensible concept of relational equality.

Second, the state is involved in all aspects of modern economies, whether the economic system is seen as capitalist or socialist. Property held, income earned, taxes owed, transfers paid, and in-kind benefits received are all interdependent parts of a system of social relations.[6] Market income or assets

---

* The exception would be if a goal simply cannot be achieved for technical reasons, because "ought" implies "can."

** These can also be considered questions of practical knowledge, or "know-how."

*** Such a trade-off might be permissible because equality of income is not a normative goal in its own right.

held do not represent a "natural" distribution external to this system. Thus, to be normatively justified, property rights regimes and other economic arrangements must be compatible with fulfilling the normative goals of social democracy. This also means that although people discuss minimizing government involvement in the economy, it is not clear that any particular policy (e.g., establishing markets) is more or less minimal than other policies (e.g., public production). Instead, the goal is to optimize what the state does.

The third principle is that, in many areas the welfare state is concerned with, state finance and production provides efficiency gains, compared with state delegation of finance and production to private parties. Frequently, economist Nicholas Barr notes, the welfare state does things that private markets do badly or not at all.[4] A potentially surprising conclusion that the topics of this chapter, along with chapters 9 and 10, lead to is that many of the policy tools often thought useful for achieving efficiency (e.g., private finance and provision, or means testing) are inefficient relative to alternatives like public provision and universalism. Thus, for guaranteeing many of the essential capabilities, public provision is the efficient option.

In applying economic theory, it is important to keep two caveats in mind. First, economic theory presents a model of the world. Just as with epidemiologic theory discussed in chapter 5, economic theory can help organize observations and build understanding. But any given theoretical perspective may not be useful in all cases, as it may oversimplify, focus on irrelevant aspects of the situation at hand, or simply be inapplicable to actually existing conditions. As the saying goes, the map is not the territory. Second, the results of many economic analyses depend heavily on specific normative underpinnings—often consequentialist (such as trying to maximize a utility or welfare function that does not distinguish between persons) or equality of welfare theories. Thus, if disagreements about those results, and the actions they suggest, arise, it can be helpful to ascertain whether there is agreement on the underlying normative framework. In some cases, the disagreement may be better understood as a disagreement about normative principles than technical approaches.

Economic Policies

This section introduces some basic ideas about economic policies that are useful for understanding their effects. These general concepts will be applied more specifically later in the book.

Policy Instruments

There are four main types of economic policy instruments or tools: regulation, public production, subsidy / specific tax, and general transfer / lump-sum tax.[4]

Regulations are laws and other rulemaking that set the conditions for people's behavior. Regulation can require actions or prohibit actions. For example, regulation may require an individual to purchase automobile insurance or prohibit untruthful advertising.

Public production refers to the creation of goods and services by the state. Common examples include national defense, police services, the legal system, and education.

A subsidy / specific tax refers to the state, *for a specific purpose*, distributing (subsidy) or taking in (specific tax) purchasing power. A subsidy can be viewed as a negative specific tax. By *specific purpose*, I mean that a subsidy / specific tax is tied to a particular product (e.g., a subsidy for food) or economic activity (e.g., an income tax on wages). For example, US Supplemental Nutrition Assistance Program (SNAP) benefits can only purchase specified food items. Subsidies can go to consumers (e.g., SNAP) or producers on consumers' behalf (e.g., Medicaid). Similarly, specific taxes can be paid by a producer (e.g., the employee share of FICA [Federal Insurance Contributions Act] tax that funds Medicare and Social Security benefits in the United States) or by a consumer (e.g., the employer share of FICA taxes).*

A general transfer refers to a payment made by the state, not tied to a specific product. Correspondingly, a lump-sum tax (sometimes called a "head tax") is a tax that is not related to any particular economic activity.**

Why distinguish between a subsidy / specific tax (tied to specific economic activity) and a general transfer / lump-sum tax (not tied to specific economic activity)? These policies may affect economic behavior differently.

---

* The concept of *tax incidence* will be discussed later.
** Confusingly, both a subsidy and a general transfer could be called "transfers"—a payment made without exchange of goods or services. Throughout, I use the unqualified term "transfer" when a distinction between a subsidy and a general transfer is not of primary importance.

Changing Economic Behavior

Because a subsidy/specific tax is tied to a particular economic activity or product, it differentially affects that activity or product, *relative* to other activities or products. For example, a food subsidy would tend to increase food purchases not only in an absolute sense but *relative* to other products as well. Imagine a person whose net income is $100, with $20 (20% of income) spent on food and $80 (80% of income) on housing. They then receive a $20 food subsidy. Now, their income is $120, and they might spend $30 (25% of income) on food (say, $20 from the subsidy and $10 from their other income) and $90 (75% of income) on housing ($80 as before plus $10 previously spent on food but freed up by the subsidy), because food is now relatively cheaper for them. Both their absolute and relative spending on food has increased. On the other hand, a general transfer, not tied to any particular economic activity, provides more purchasing power in an absolute sense but does not make any specific product relatively cheaper. Continuing the same example, a general transfer of $20 might lead to new expenditures of $24 (20%) on food and $96 (80%) on housing, increasing the absolute level of expenditure but not affecting the relative level, as both food and housing are relatively the same price as before. As specific taxes and lump-sum taxes are simply the inverse of subsidies and general transfers, respectively, they tend to have analogous effects. That is, specific taxes make the specified activity less desirable to engage in relative to alternatives, whereas lump-sum taxes typically do not differentially affect activities.

Income Effects and Substitution Effects

Two important ways that policies can change economic behavior are "income effects" and "substitution effects." An income effect of a policy refers to it prompting behaviors to maintain a given level of income under changing conditions. A substitution effect refers to a policy prompting reevaluation of the relative desirability of two options under changing conditions (as in the discussion of subsides/specific taxes, above). Often, a particular policy may have opposing income and substitution effects, and so the actual behavior change it causes will be a balance of these two forces.

To illustrate, consider a person paid $100 for an extra hour of work. At baseline, there is a 25 percent marginal tax rate, and that rate is raised to 50 percent. Previously, the person's net income would increase by $75 for an extra hour of work. Afterwards, the person would have to work 1.5 hours to increase their net income by $75. So, the "income effect" of the tax increase might push the person to work more, to maintain their income level. However, since the person now receives less net income for an extra hour of work, the relative desirability of working compared with leisure might change. Trading an additional hour of work for $75 more net income and one fewer hour of leisure may have been acceptable, but such a trade-off may not be worthwhile for $50; the "substitution effect" of the tax increase might push the person to work less, or to "substitute" leisure for labor. Analogous scenarios occur for subsidies or general transfers, rather than taxes. For example, the substitution effect of an earnings-related subsidy (i.e., a subsidy where the relative benefit increases with greater earnings), such as the US Earned Income Tax Credit, may incentivize working more, while the income effect may incentivize working less. The relative strength of income and substitution effects can be hard to predict and often vary across different situations.

Different Policies Can Achieve the Same Objective

In general, a normative argument for a particular objective does not, in and of itself, presuppose any particular policy to achieve it.[4] For example, though universal health care access may be normatively required, this does not entail public production (e.g., a national health service). The objective could, theoretically, also be achieved with a subsidy (such as the Medicare program in the United States), or a general transfer that people could use to purchase health insurance on the private market. Finally, although I have presented a distinct typology, policies can blend. For example, regulations that require the purchase of car insurance are effectively specific taxes.

Allocating Products: Market and Public Provision

A core function of the welfare state is to ensure that individuals have access to the products needed to guarantee the essential capabilities. Owing to scarcity and rivalrousness, there must be a normatively justifiable system to allocate those products. Thus, a common question in welfare state policy is whether products should be allocated by markets or in another way. This is a technical question with no general answer—only answers specific to particular times, places, and products. However, economic theory can offer general guidance as to when market versus public provision may be desirable.

Market provision typically involves multiple competing private producers, with consumers selecting products to purchase using prices—that is, relating what they have to pay for the product, under their budget constraint, to their judgment of some combination of the quality and quantity of the product on offer. Under market provision, prices are a regulatory force.

Public provision involves product distribution under a system of administrative rules, typically set through political processes. Allocation is not necessarily uniform—there may be choices across a menu of options or tailoring to circumstances. Further, public provision does not imply public production, as public finance for private producers using subsidies also represents public provision (e.g., Medicare health insurance in the United States). Moreover, public provision may incorporate user fees to some extent, meant to avoid overconsumption, which can look similar to prices. But fundamentally, under public provision, administration serves as the principal coordinating device, not prices.[1]

What advantages might market provision offer? The standard account is that markets help organize the production and distribution of products under conditions of scarcity by aggregating information, lowering production costs through competition, and matching the products producers produce to consumer preferences about what they want to consume.[4] In other words, markets can lead to *efficiency*.

There are at least two types of efficiency that market provision may help with. The first is *allocative efficiency*—distributing products to those who value them the most.* A related idea is that markets can help ensure that capital is being used most productively—that it is directed toward producing the product mix that consumers want. The theoretical ability of markets to yield allocative efficiency depends on the price mechanism. In an idealized market, competition will cause a price to equal the marginal cost of production, which will in turn reflect the opportunity cost—that is, the real cost of devoting the resources necessary to produce the product to that use, rather than the next best alternative. If markets are imperfect, the price

---

* More formally, a distribution is allocatively efficient in a Pareto sense if a change in that distribution to make someone better off cannot occur without making someone else worse off.

could reflect both the marginal cost of production and a "rent" (a payment in excess of the marginal cost of production). Eliminating rents is a primary rationale for markets. However, though competition can force down rents, it does not necessarily lower production costs, as, for example, advertising or administrative costs might increase with more competition and producers. Thus, market provision does not guarantee the lowest production costs, even in an idealized market.

Under market provision, the consumer can spend the amount of money for a given combination of product quality and quantity that is optimal to them (i.e., that maximizes their welfare or utility). The idea is that a consumer best understands their own trade-offs between product quality, quantity, and cost given their financial means (more formally, that a consumer can construct an "indifference map" for a given "budget constraint").[4] The price mechanism thus relates cost to an index of quality and quality.

The second type of efficiency markets can help with is *productive efficiency*—maximizing some combination of product quality and quantity for a given level of inputs. Here the idea is that competition between multiple producers seeking to maximize profit will drive improvements in production that lead to productive efficiency.

Because, under specific conditions, market provision can lead to allocative and productive efficiency, market allocation can be a useful tool for welfare state policy. However, if those conditions cannot be brought about, public provision may be more efficient.*

Conditions for Markets: Price Mechanisms and Profit Motives

Deciding whether market versus public provision is better for a particular product is complicated, and it depends on numerous specific factors. However, a useful, if perhaps oversimplified, heuristic is that market provision will not work well without functioning price mechanisms and if production cannot be organized around profitability.

As discussed in chapter 7, markets are not "natural" in the sense of existing outside the state—state policy is necessary to create and maintain the "free market."[7] As economist James Buchannan said, "some limits must be imposed on the working of pure self-interest. Individuals must abide by

---

*And, of course, efficiency is only one consideration of many regarding welfare state policy.

behavioral standards which dictate adherence to law, respect for personal rights, and fulfillment of contractual agreements—standards which may not, in specific instances, be consistent with objectively measurable economic self-interest. Absent such standards as these, markets will fail."[7]

A major policy area necessary for markets are property rights, which inevitably involves substantial government coercion.[8] Market provision typically requires other state regulation as well (e.g., contract law and currency), and perhaps specific producer-side regulation, typically around product quality (e.g., regulation of food additives). If markets are to include more than individual-based exchange, then regulations are needed to establish firms as forms of economic coordination. It also requires factor and transfer income policy that ensures individuals have sufficient purchasing power for the needed products, and possibly consumer-side regulation, typically around consumption quantity (e.g., a requirement to purchase health insurance). Further, market provision benefits from public infrastructure, education, and knowledge production. Thus, for markets to allocate products efficiently, a great many things must go right.

When Prices Do Not Work

An important field of study within economics involves understanding the conditions under which markets can allocate products efficiently.[4] This field is sometimes termed the study of *market failures*. However, I prefer the frame of "conditions needed for markets to work," as this emphasizes that markets require constant tending by the state to operate as intended. As noted above, a primary condition for markets to work well is a functioning price mechanism. Economics has identified a number of situations in which price mechanisms do not function well.[4]

EXTERNALITIES

Externalities (or "spillover effects") refer to situations where production or consumption of a product affects third parties *external* to those involved in the transaction. With externalities, the price may not fully capture its social effect. If the effect is a social harm, the price to a private party will be lower than optimal, resulting in overconsumption. If the effect is a social benefit, the price to a private party will be higher than optimal, resulting in underconsumption.

IMPERFECT COMPETITION

Imperfect competition occurs with barriers to market entry and exit, and high transaction costs. Imperfect competition also occurs when some parties to the transaction have greater market or bargaining power—they do not have to accept a relationship between prices and the marginal cost of production, and thus prices will contain rents. Contrastingly, in perfectly competitive markets, prices would reflect the marginal cost of production alone. High producer-side market power is termed monopoly or oligopoly.[4] High consumer-side market power is termed monopsony.[9] The concept of monopsony is particularly important for wage setting.[10,11] With monopsony, market power of employers (consumers of labor) can result in inefficiently low prices for labor (wages). Imperfect competition can also result from unequal power related to discrimination. For example, if consumers are excluded from transaction with some firms, through racist or sexist discrimination, they may face prices that include rents from remaining firms.

INCREASING RETURNS TO SCALE

Increasing returns to scale occur when an increase in inputs results in a disproportionately large increase in outputs.[4] For example, a 10 percent increase in inputs might increase output by 15 percent. This will tend to favor large producers, potentially culminating in a monopoly. These situations are sometimes called natural monopolies, because a monopoly is the productively efficient outcome. However, it is often not the allocatively efficient outcome, as productive efficiency occurs in parallel with increasing market power. Thus, prices may contain rents.

IMPERFECT INFORMATION

Imperfect information occurs when producers, consumers, or both do not have, or cannot make use of, the information needed for prices to reflect the marginal cost of production. On the consumer-side, this occurs when consumers are unable to judge product quality, or do not have accurate knowledge about their own preferences. For some products (education and health care, for example), judging quality at the time of purchase (or even after consuming the product) may be difficult or impossible. Such products are sometimes termed "credence goods."

Imperfect information can be an information provision problem (i.e., the relevant information is not available) or an information processing problem (i.e., the information is difficult to make use of, even if available). In these cases, people may not know what action would maximize their welfare (sometimes called "bounded rationality"), or they may know but not pursue it for various reasons (sometimes called "bounded will-power," although acting according to the motive of reasonableness rather than rationality could be understood in the same way). Imperfect information is common when time horizons are long, probabilities involved in the decision calculus are small, or the information is simply complex.

Beyond information about how consuming a product would affect them, the consumer must also have a well-defined budget constraint, information on prices, and be able to combine this information with judgments about quantity and quality. Without all of these factors in place, a consumer cannot make an informed choice, and the price mechanism will generally not function well.[4]

Further, information must be perfect on both sides. If one side is better informed than the other (e.g., lenders may understand the risks of loans better than borrowers, or borrowers may understand their risk of default better than lenders), then asymmetric information presents a barrier to the price mechanism functioning well.

INCOMPLETE CONTRACTS

A special type of incomplete information is an incomplete contract. A common form of incomplete contract occurs when one party, typically the state, contracts with a private producer to supply a product (often to a third party, such as an individual citizen), but the state cannot specify what is to be produced in explicit detail, and neither the state nor the third party can monitor product quality effectively. For example, it is very difficult to contract explicitly for "high quality health care." Further, it is difficult to monitor health care quality even after it has been produced, given that poor outcomes may result from either poor care or factors outside the control of those providing health care.[5] As low quality may be difficult to detect, the producer would have an incentive to reduce quality for a given level of cost, resulting in productive inefficiency (and likely social harm). This topic is highly relevant to decision-making about whether to publicly or privately produce products that are publicly financed, and I will return to it later in the book.

The Profit Motive

A second requirement for efficient market provision, after a well-functioning price mechanism, is that the profit motive can organize production. When that is not possible, missing or incomplete markets—markets that cannot supply the desirable quantity or quality of a product—occur. Missing markets can sometimes result from problems of coordination (e.g., collective action problems).

An important situation where production for profit fails is public goods. Public goods are non-rivalrous in consumption (meaning that one person's consumption does not prevent another person from consuming the product), non-excludable (meaning people cannot be easily prevented from consuming the product), and non-rejectable (meaning that the consumer cannot help but consume the product). A classic public good is national defense, as is much of public health (e.g., smallpox eradication). Because of non-excludability, production for profit (particularly profits made from user fees) is generally not feasible.

Policy Choices: Market versus Public Provision

A common welfare state policy choice is whether a particular product should be allocated through market versus public provision. Understanding the conditions needed for markets helps to understand whether market provision is likely to be efficient in particular circumstances. Of course, economic efficiency is not the only consideration when comparing normatively acceptable alternatives. Other factors include political feasibility and the likelihood of successful implementation (chapter 10). But a framework for deciding between market and public provision can help inform policy design.

A Framework for Market versus Public Provision

Table 8.1 presents a simplified framework with two dimensions: finance and production, which can each take two forms: public or private. Private finance implies that the funds for production come from private entities made as investments or from user fees remitted by private individuals and firms, whatever the underlying source of those funds (i.e., it would not matter if the funds originated as government transfers). Public finance implies that the funds for production come from the state expressly for that purpose. Private production implies that managerial authority over the pro-

Table 8.1. Market versus public provision

		Production for Profit	
		Yes	No
Price Mechanism	Yes	Private Finance, Private Production	Private Finance, Public Production
	No	Public Finance, Private Production	Public Finance, Public Production

Note: The gray box indicates market provision; the white boxes indicate public provision.

duction workforce is vested in private entities. Public production implies that managerial authority over the production workforce is vested in public entities.

To apply this framework, policymakers should think through two questions: "can price mechanisms be made to work?" and "is production for profit desirable?"

Making Price Mechanisms Work

A number of policies may be needed to make price mechanisms work. As noted above, the state needs to establish the necessary background legal and regulatory framework and infrastructure for markets to function. Also, critically, for markets to function, consumers need purchasing power. Market provision allocates products based on willingness to pay, which results from both preference intensity and purchasing power. Theoretically, under conditions of scarcity and resource equality, price mechanisms can allocate products efficiently, as presumably greater willingness to pay would stem from greater preference intensity, and thus indicates who would derive greater utility from the product. But in conditions of scarcity, inequality, and declining marginal utility of money—conditions we face presently—price mechanisms may lead to inefficient allocation. For example, a less well-off person's willingness to pay $40 may represent much greater preference intensity, and derived utility from the product, than a well-off person's willingness to pay $50. Inequality in purchasing power can therefore result in products going to those with greater willingness to pay but not necessarily stronger preferences, or greater derived utility. Thus, for markets to function well, factor and transfer income policy play a crucial role.

Beyond these general policies, required for all forms of market provision, market provision of specific products may require specific policies. When externalities are present, one way to address them is with a Pigouvian tax or subsidy, named after economist Arthur Cecil Pigou, an early investigator of externalities.[4,12] This applies a tax or subsidy to the transaction in order to better match the price paid to the social cost or benefit—increasing the price of harmful products and decreasing the price of beneficial ones.[4] This can change the level of consumption, but it does not set a minimum or maximum. Pigouvian approaches could be combined with regulation to set a minimum level (e.g., compulsory automobile insurance) or maximum level (e.g., capping the production of a pollutant) of some activity.

Policy can also help address information problems. Health and safety regulation to set a quality floor when quality would be difficult to judge (e.g., sanitary conditions for food preparation) is commonplace, as is requiring consumer information (e.g., ingredients) to be provided. Further, regulatory approaches that simplify the choices people have to make, or "nudge" them toward choices thought to be welfare-maximizing, may be useful.[4] For example, pension programs may include mandatory contributions to overcome issues with "bounded will-power."[4] However, regulation may be only partially effective, particularly for complex products or when information disclosure is difficult to enforce.

State involvement to increase competition among producers, such as antitrust regulation, is an indispensable part of market management. In some cases, however, especially when production is characterized by increasing returns to scale, it may be better to embrace a monopoly's productive efficiency. In these cases, the state may use subsidies to make prices faced by consumers more closely reflect marginal cost, or grant a license to run a monopoly under price regulation (as commonly occurs for utilities).[4] Antidiscrimination regulations can also help address "rents" within prices that may result from oppression (although their primary rationale is to help fulfill duties of recognition).

Finally, the price mechanism cannot be used when product differentiation by price, that is, variation in product quality based on price charged, is not normatively acceptable. With some products, like haircuts or televisions, budget options and luxury options at different price points present no normative concerns. But the products needed to guarantee the essential capabilities may be different. A society may decide that there are no good reasons for the quality of primary education or basic health care to vary across price points. In these cases, even if price mechanisms could function, allocation using the price mechanism would not be justified.

Is Production for Profit Desirable?

There are two common situations in which organizing production through the profit motive is not desirable. One is when essential products simply cannot be produced profitably. The other is when the quality of the product produced is difficult to monitor. For-profit firms operate under a profit-maximizing logic. If consumers, or state agents, can judge quality well, then profit maximization may coincide with value maximization, where value is understood to indicate some combination of quality and quantity for a given cost. But if quality is hard to judge, then the profit-maximizing strategy may be to reduce production costs by reducing difficult to detect aspects of quality.

Thinking through Market versus Public Provision

The above framework suggests general rules for policy design. This section illustrates how to apply this framework when considering whether to use market versus public provision to allocate a particular product. If price mechanisms function and production for profit is desirable, then both finance and production can be private (i.e., there can be market provision). Public provision is needed when price mechanisms do not function, production for profit is not desirable, or both. However, the specific reasons market provision will not work might influence the form public provision takes.

Market Provision: Private Finance and Private Production

When prices can be made to function with appropriate policies (including factor and transfer income policy to provide sufficient purchasing power) and production for profit is desirable, markets can be used to allocate products in ways that guarantee essential capabilities. Food, for example, is a product for which market provision often works well.

Public Provision: Private Finance and Public Production

Situations where price mechanisms function but production for profit does not call for private finance with public production. This can occur with increasing returns to scale—such as "natural monopolies" like some utility companies. Production can be financed privately (e.g., by user fees), but production is not organized for profit, which removes the incentives for prices to contain rents.

Public Provision: Public Finance, Public versus Private Production

If the price mechanism does not function well, public finance is needed. But with public finance, should production be private or public? This decision often turns on whether production for profit is likely to be helpful for achieving desired outcomes.

The general argument for private producers is that they offer consumer responsiveness, and that competition among them will reduce cost and improve quality. However, specific decisions are often more nuanced than this general argument suggests, and scholars have sought to elucidate when public finance with private production works best. Much of this literature emerged from debates about privatization—that is, when should the state outsource production to private firms?[13,14] However, the considerations are equally applicable for deciding when the state should take over production from private firms ("nationalization").

When trying to decide if competition among private producers is likely to be superior to public production, it is important to avoid the "nirvana fallacy." This is the mistake of comparing real problems of one system to hypothetical benefits of another. A more informed comparison understands the real benefits and drawbacks of both approaches. Avoiding this fallacy is important because many tasks public production is considered for are simply harder than those the private sector typically takes on. As an illustration of the point that the difficulty of the task is a key consideration, even though clients attending a gym's small group training session are likely healthier than patients in a hospital, it may not be salutary to have personal trainers take over from doctors.[15] In general, it cannot be assumed that private management of production will inevitably lead to better outcomes.

The question of private versus public production often revolves around (at least) one of four considerations: productive efficiency, consumer choice, incomplete contracts, and effective competition.[4,16]

For the consideration of productive efficiency, the idea is that competition among private producers operating under a profit motive could lead to innovation and refinements in production processes that reduce costs or in other ways increase productive efficiency. Public producers would not have profit as an incentive to innovate or control costs. Thus, all else equal, the greater the scope for innovation or cost reduction (without reducing quality), the stronger the argument for private production within public provision.

For the consideration of consumer choice, multiple private producers could allow for more consumer choice, which in turn could increase allocative efficiency. For this argument to hold, two things must be true. First, private producers must offer more choice than public producers, which is not always the case. Second, consumer choice must lead to allocative efficiency. This can be true, but it is highly situation dependent.

Consumer choice best promotes allocative efficiency when (a) consumer purchasing power is similar, (b) information is readily available and understood, (c) consumer tastes are diverse so that there is an advantage in having many options, and (d) costs for choosing badly are low and feedback occurs quickly, so that consumers can learn what they like from prior experiences.[4] These conditions might be met more readily by, say, a lunch order than primary education or health care. For products where these conditions are met, private production may be efficient. Otherwise, there may be little to gain, in efficiency terms, from expanding consumer choice.*

A third consideration relates to incomplete contracts. A major risk is that production for profit will drive down quality in order to increase profit. To avoid this, either the state must be able to specify exactly what private producers should produce, or consumers (or the state) must be able to monitor the quality of the product. Given imperfect information, consumers may

---

* For products needed to guarantee the essential capabilities, consumers are the constituents of the social democratic state—not customers but citizens.[16] This means that consumer preferences and choice are important concerns for both private and public producers regardless of allocative efficiency. Further, without information from prices, private and public producers must find other ways to incorporate information about consumer satisfaction. As political scientist Bo Rothstein says, "organizations which do not receive one sort of signal when they do something right, and another sort of signal when they do something wrong, will in the long run do more wrong things than right."[16(p201)]

not be able to do this. The state may be able to employ experts who could monitor quality in ways consumers cannot, but this requires sufficient state capacity, interest, and funding. And for many products, quality is simply difficult for anyone, even experts, to monitor. These problems suggest that the case for public production is stronger when it is difficult for the state to specify the contract precisely. It is also stronger the more difficult quality is to monitor (either by the state or consumers).[16] Conversely, the case for private production is stronger if the state can specify exactly what it wants; if the state (and/or consumers) have the resources, ability, and motivation to evaluate and discipline producers; if there are strong reputational incentives for private producers to maintain quality; and if consumer feedback can be incorporated via complaints ("voice") or choosing other producers ("exit").[4,16,17]

A common issue with quality monitoring is that a quantifiable outcome that reflects quality (a latent construct) is not necessarily a good metric for quality monitoring. This is because changes in the metric, once it becomes a target, do not necessarily imply changes to the latent construct—the changes could occur through channels different from the ones whereby the metric relates to the latent construct. For example, though better blood pressure control may indicate better medical care, changes in the mean level of systolic blood pressure within a health care system do not necessarily imply that care quality has improved—the changes could reflect instead that the health care system is now serving a healthier group of patients. In general, there are often opportunities to "game" quality evaluation by creating changes in whatever metric is used that do not reflect changes in quality.

The fourth consideration relates to competition between private producers.[16] For private production to yield the expected benefits, the state must create a functional competition between private producers. This competition could occur at the time of bidding for contracts or could be ongoing if there are multiple producers competing for consumers simultaneously. The second situation is more likely to improve productive efficiency. However, in many cases, the state is involved in production precisely because conditions needed for efficiency-producing competition are difficult to maintain.[16] Private production within public provision can effectively become a monopoly. This can enable rent-seeking that drives up spending. These situations can also be hard to reverse given the substantial costs (both financial and political) associated with transitioning from one private provider to another (or to public production). Thus, inefficient private production can become locked in. In general then, the case for private production is stronger the more the state can create and manage suitable competition between private producers.[16]

Replicating Price Functions

Regardless of whether public versus private production is chosen, without price mechanisms, public provision must replicate two functions that the price mechanism performs under market provision: price setting and quality monitoring. These functions can be performed publicly or privately.

With public finance and private production, the state is typically in a good position to negotiate prices, as it will be the largest, and possibly only, purchaser; it can thus benefit from economies of scale and monopsony power. As a result, there is little reason to outsource price setting.

Quality monitoring is challenging because for-profit producers have an incentive to reduce quality to increase profits. They may also have an incentive to over- or under-supply products, depending on the structure of the contract. This is a major problem if complex specialist products with serious consequences, uncertainty as to how to produce good outcomes, and long time-horizons—for example, health care and education—are to be produced privately. Substantial effort and resources would have to be devoted to quality monitoring in these cases. The state could outsource quality monitoring, but this could itself run into incomplete contracting issues, and the monitors themselves would have to be monitored, which may bring up the same issues recursively. It is therefore hard to make a general case for outsourcing quality monitoring.

With public finance and public production, price setting is typically handled internally, often through fixed budgets allocated politically. Quality monitoring can still be difficult, but there is no profit motive to reduce quality or mis-supply quantity. In situations with public production, it is generally desirable to separate producers from other aspects of the state, where quality monitoring will occur, to preserve some independence between producers and regulators.[16] For example, producers may be organized as a separate agency or service.

Actuarial and Social Insurance

Insurance exists primarily to solve the problem of imperfect information about the future. Without this problem—for example, if someone could know they would be out of work beginning on a certain date for a certain period of time—insurance would not be necessary.[18] The person could save enough money in advance to smooth consumption, or borrow against future earnings they would know are coming. Of course, real life does not work like this. One does not know when an event like sickness or unemployment will occur, or how long it will last, so it is difficult to save enough in advance. Conversely, in trying to be prepared for the worst, someone may save too much, inefficiently reducing consumption.

Insurance works by pooling risk. An event may be unpredictable for an individual but quite predictable on average. Thus, individually imperfect information about the future can be aggregated into (approximate) certainty. If someone is risk averse, that certainty has value above and beyond the loss insured against, so purchasing insurance can be rational. Another way to think about this is that self-insuring might require preparing for the worst-case scenario—the largest loss one might experience. But with insurance, one can prepare for the average loss, which may be much less.

Actuarial Insurance

Insurance exists in two forms: actuarial insurance under market provision, or social insurance under public provision. With actuarial insurance, the cost of insurance (including pay-outs for losses, administrative expenses such as claims verification, and profit) must be less than what people are willing to pay (i.e., the amount insured against plus the value of certainty gained). The typical formula for setting an actuarial insurance premium is[4(p87)]:

$$\pi_i = (1 + \alpha)p_i L$$

In this formula, π_i represents the premium paid by the i-th individual, α indicates the administrative costs (including profit), p_i indicates the individual's probability of incurring a loss, and L represents the value of the loss insured against (i.e., the amount paid if a loss occurs).

Actuarial insurance requires specific conditions. First, the insured event must be independent—one individual's loss should not affect the probability of another individual's loss. Common shocks, where event risk is connected systematically, are difficult to insure against actuarially. Common shocks include pandemics (where risk for a health outcome is linked) and recessions (overall macroeconomic conditions that affect unemployment risk). Next, only risk can be insured against—not uncertainty or certainty. To explain, consider risk to be an event probability between 0 and 1, and which can be estimated with confidence. Consider uncertainty to be an event probability between 0 and 1, but which cannot be estimated with confidence. And consider certainty to be an event probability of 0 or 1.*

Actuarial insurance is not feasible for cases of uncertainty—a premium cannot be set when the event probability cannot be calculated. Poorly defined uncertainty, rather than well-defined risk, is more common with small risk pools, and when time horizons are long (e.g., it is much harder to estimate the probability of an event 50, rather than 5, years from now). It is also a problem when probabilities are small (because small estimation errors will have a large impact), or when estimating the probability is simply difficult (this is one reason why insurance benefits typically cannot be indexed to inflation).[4]

Actuarial insurance is also not feasible when a loss is certain to occur in a given time period, as the premium would have to be equal to or greater than the loss insured against. This helps explain why preexisting conditions are typically not covered by health insurance policies unless regulations require them to be.

Actuarial insurance also does not function well for some kinds of risk. This is a particular problem when there is asymmetrical information between insurers and customers. Two common examples of this are hidden information ("adverse selection") and hidden action ("moral hazard").[4] Hidden information occurs when those more likely to experience a loss are more likely to purchase insurance. For example, those who are less healthy may be more inclined to buy health insurance than those who are healthier. To some extent, this can be factored into the premium (for example, by requiring a health questionnaire or physical examination prior to issuing insurance). However, if some health information can be hidden, then actual losses will tend to be greater than expected losses, and premiums will be set too low.

Hidden action occurs when the probability of a loss is, at least partially, determined by the person insured—especially if insurance coverage increases the risk of loss. For example, if automobile insurance leads to reckless driving, actual losses will be greater than expected. This is one reason

---

*I include 0 for completeness, but in practice it is irrelevant as there is no need to insure against events that cannot occur.

why pregnancy benefits are often not included in actuarial health insurance policies.[4] Actuarial insurance can be designed to help address hidden action, for example, by insuring for less than the full loss, raising premiums in the event of claims, or through cost-sharing, such as deductibles, co-pays, and co-insurance, but this may be only partially effective.

Other situations in which actuarial insurance does not function well are when administrative costs are high (this increases the premium without covering a larger loss), and when information is complex. This is particularly relevant for health care (where it may be difficult for consumers to make an informed decision about what health care coverage they need) and may also present a problem with defined contribution retirement plans, such as 401(k) accounts.

Finally, actuarial insurance is ill-suited to handle third-party payment problems. For example, in fee-for-service health care systems, losses are determined by individuals and their doctors. Neither has an incentive to keep health care utilization low. This could create overconsumption of health care services.

Social Insurance and the Welfare State

Many welfare state tasks can be framed as issues of social insurance—problems it would be useful to insure against, but where market provision of actuarial insurance fails.[4] Social insurance is insurance in the sense of protecting against risk. However, social insurance differs from actuarial insurance in three main ways. First, social insurance benefits do not need to be covered fully by premiums. This breaks the link between premium and risk—indeed, social insurance contributions are often flat fees or earnings related, rather than risk related. In other words, social insurance does not need a functioning price mechanism. Social insurance can have sources of finance beyond user premiums and can even operate at a loss when necessary. Second, social insurance contracts do not have to be fully specified in advance, so social insurance can adapt to changing circumstances in ways that actuarial insurance cannot. The legitimacy afforded by democratic government makes this possible. Third, social insurance is often obligatory, which helps overcome issues with adverse selection, and helps share risk across the largest possible pool.

These advantages mean that social insurance can not only protect against risk, but also uncertainty. For example, unemployment insurance can expand during recessions, and state pensions can be indexed to inflation. Social insurance also offers solutions to problems of imperfect consumer information (by incorporating expertise in program design that is not conflicted by a profit motive) and bounded rationality (through obligatory participation).[4] Administrative costs are typically low (as large risk pools with relatively uniform program design simplifies administration, benefits from economies of scale, and does not require marketing). Further, social insurance can overcome third-party payer problems by using budgets set through democratic political processes.

The social insurance functions of the welfare state help explain why criticisms that universalist welfare states policies seem to be captured by well-off interests, or simply move money around for those who are well-off, are misguided.[19-21] The universalist welfare state does, in effect, move money around for those who are well-off (along with everyone else)—but that is not a criticism. Shifting money from times when one does not need it to times when one does is the essence of insurance. The welfare state can perfect insurance in a way that actuarial insurance cannot, given its advantages in terms of scale and flexibility.

Fundamentally, protecting against uncertainty and risk are major tasks of the welfare state, and social insurance is a key tool for that.

Should We Care about Distortions?

Economists, particularly in the field of optimal taxation, call some policies, like subsidies / specific taxes, "distortionary" because they alter what is assumed to be an efficient allocation absent the subsidy / specific tax,[4] and cause people to value various activities, relative to other activities, differently than they might otherwise.* In contrast, a general transfer / lump-sum tax is not distortionary in the same way. Because it is non-specific, it gives a person no reason, in and of itself, to prefer one activity to another.**

Changes in economic behavior can be important considerations when

---

*When discussing distortions, it is critically important, though not always done, to specify the baseline that is being referred to.

**Although a general transfer may not change the behavior of the individual who receives it, if it is financed by a specific tax, that specific tax might change the behavior of the person who remits it. Thus, it is important to consider the entire tax-and-transfer system when analyzing the likely effects of particular policies. This topic is given more attention in chapters 9 and 10.

setting policy. However, I think calling those changes distortions (with the implication being an undesirable change) can be pejorative, as the status quo is not a natural baseline, there is no guarantee that the status quo distribution was efficient, and there is certainly no guarantee that it was just.[22] This means that the behavior change may be desirable. Indeed, behavior change could be the policy goal, rather than an unintended consequence, as with Pigouvian taxes and subsidies.

Moreover, though policy could change behavior, it may not. And if it does, the magnitude of behavior change may not be meaningful. Further, the policy may still be beneficial on net—the downsides may just be the cost of doing business if alternative approaches present even greater problems.[23] Thus, the specifics of each situation should be considered carefully.

How policy changes behavior is complex, and the incidence of a subsidy or tax (the benefit or cost) may not actually fall on the party that nominally receives the subsidy or remits the tax.[4] One reason for this is elasticity. Elasticity refers to how supply or demand changes when price changes. If supply rises greatly when prices rise and falls greatly when prices fall, then production is elastic; if it only changes a little, it is inelastic. The same goes for consumption—if demand rises greatly when prices fall and falls greatly when prices rise, consumption is elastic; otherwise, it is inelastic. The incidence of a subsidy / specific tax can depend on the relative elasticities of production and consumption.

To illustrate, imagine a consumer receives a subsidy to purchase some product. All else equal, the product will be cheaper for the consumer, and demand will increase. But this is only one side of the story. An increase in demand will encourage producers to increase supply, but how much they increase supply will depend on the elasticity of supply. If, for example, it is hard to increase production in the short run, perhaps because large capital investments are needed or inputs are scarce, then supply will not increase in step with demand. This provides an opportunity for rent-seeking, as producers will be able to charge more than their marginal cost, owing to relative scarcity. This is sometimes called short-side power.[24] In this case, though the subsidy was paid to the consumer, the producer may receive most of the benefits. Alternatively, if demand is relatively less elastic than supply (as may be the case for lower-wage workers), the benefits of a producer-side subsidy (such as the Earned Income Tax Credit) may accrue disproportionately to consumers (i.e., employers).[25]

Policies can use relative elasticities advantageously. For example, policy-makers may introduce public options to compete with private producers.[26] In the example above, a consumer-side subsidy was intended to increase consumption of some product, but supply was relatively less elastic than demand. This can lead to rent-seeking by incumbent producers, and the subsidy may not increase consumption as much as intended. Were there, in this market, a competing public producer operating without a profit motive, they may not rent-seek. Their prices may more closely reflect marginal cost, which would pressure other producers to do the same—and thus the subsidy may be more effective in increasing consumption. One case where this approach may be useful is public universities as producers of higher education. Increasing government funding for public universities could prevent exorbitant increases in tuition or incentives for for-profit "diploma mills" to siphon off student loan and grant money without producing value in return.[26]

The final point to make about changes in behavior related to subsidies / specific taxes is that they may simply be not all that concerning. Efficiency is relevant for comparing options that all achieve normative goals. If a goal cannot be achieved without an "inefficient" change in behavior, discussions of inefficiency are not justified. Viewing efficiency as something to be traded off with other normative goals implicitly (or explicitly) adopts a consequentialist normative framework (such as utility maximization). As an extreme example, whether slavery is more efficient than free labor is irrelevant, as slavery is simply not normatively acceptable. Similarly, a system of taxes, transfers, and property rights that meets duties of distribution and recognition can only be compared to other systems that do the same, as a political economic system that does not meet these duties is not normatively justified.

The Economic Style of Reasoning

I have emphasized throughout this book that a key goal of social policy is to achieve the normative goals of democratic equality. The tools of economics can be useful when designing policies to achieve these goals. However, as sociologist Elizabeth Popp Berman has traced out, there is a school of thought that she calls the "economic style of reasoning," which applies the tools of economics differently.[27] This school of thought views the pursuit of efficiency, rather than relational equality, as the primary policy goal. As

Berman put it, "The commitments to universality, rights, and equality had been sidelined by an emphasis on efficiency, incentives, and choice."[27] The policy recommendations this school of thought provides often view market provision as the "first-best" method for allocating products, make a virtue of consumer choice and competition, and choose economic incentives as the primary tool for managing people's behavior.

The economic style of reasoning has had widespread influence. Examples of this influence include the use of cost-effectiveness as a tool for policy analysis, emphasizing progressivity in public finance (discussed in chapter 9), and promoting targeting and means testing in public benefits (discussed in chapter 10). Another example, in the realm of market governance, is valuing allocative efficiency over ensuring that people receive the products they need to guarantee the essential capabilities.

The economic style of reasoning has both normative and technical problems. The major normative problem is that it treats efficiency as a normative goal rather than one of several technical considerations.* Emphasizing efficiency over equality, or viewing them as commensurate, would be an example of prioritizing the good over the right. This is not normatively defensible, for reasons discussed in chapters 3 and 4. The pursuit of efficiency is only acceptable within bounds set by normative considerations, which the economic style of reasoning often does not respect.

The technical problems typically relate to the simplifications needed to use the tools of economic theory (e.g., operationalization of latent or otherwise difficult to quantify concepts). These simplifications can distort the meaning of what is being pursued, and can ignore important, but hard to measure, constructs. An analysis in this school of thought might be premised on the idea that policymakers should choose the policy option that produces the best aggregate outcome, considering all the benefits and burdens of each option. While seemingly sensible, in practice knowledge of policy proposals' likely effects is often quite imprecise, and some important effects may not be quantifiable. Further, different effects may not all be commensurate. In other words, the "information base" for the analysis actually conducted can fall quite short, compared with what is meant to be

---

*Proponents may not acknowledge that their emphasis on efficiency is normative, but the value placed on efficiency is clearly connected to consequentialist theories of justice, like utilitarianism.

included. Though often justified as useful approximations, the results obtained from analyses using the assumptions and simplifications needed to make the methods tractable may not actually offer much guidance for real-world decision-making. By analogy, if the fastest route across town, a major highway, is blocked due to construction, taking the small surface roads that most closely approximates the highway's path may not be the next fastest route—instead, the next fastest route may go in a completely different direction.

Even worse, the information base that the analyst selects, and the weights the analyst applies to trade off various effects thought to be commensurate, can have a decisive influence on the outcome of the analysis. This presents an opportunity for the analyst to put their thumb on the scale—hiding the interests of the analyst or their sponsors within supposedly impartial analysis. Such analyses purport to determine what is rational for society overall, but instead they may simply reflect the interests of those producing the analysis.

Summary

This chapter has discussed elements of economic theory useful for understanding how the welfare state can achieve its normative goals. However, it is important to keep in mind that economic theory is only one of several perspectives needed for policy design. This chapter also discussed that, because the state is involved in all aspects of economic activity, there is no real choice between big or small government. Instead, the key question is often whether market versus public provision best enables the state to fulfill its duty of equal care. Markets are not naturally occurring phenomena—they are state programs that need constant tending and active management. Market provision works well when prices can be made to reflect societal opportunity costs and when the prevailing property rights regime guarantees sufficient purchasing power to all. In other cases, public provision is more appropriate—often because market provision cannot meet normative goals, or public provision is simply more efficient.

A common policymaking mistake is applying economic theory at the stage of normative goal setting, rather than for helping to achieve goals already set. Economic theory can guide people in making use of their available resources, but it is fundamentally indifferent to the acceptability of the bargaining positions in which they are located. If those positions are not normatively acceptable, economic theory cannot provide an objection to chang-ing them. Similarly, knowledge about how to maximize a particular outcome for a fixed cost in a given period can be helpful for policymakers. But choos-ing to make that the only policy consideration is a difficult normative posi-tion to justify.

A technical barrier in using economic theory is that such theory may not reflect reality. Many standard results in economics assume households and firms in perfectly competitive markets, with prices equating supply and de-mand. But in the real world, firms have market power to set prices and bar-gaining power to set wages. Further, supply and demand represents only one set of influences on economic outcomes, along with institutions and norms.[22] Real-world economies are characterized by unequal power, imperfect infor-mation, and the failure of many markets to form—there is no a priori rea-son to think they are efficient or that additional intervention would inher-ently decrease efficiency.[22] Often, economic analysis gives the "right" answer for an economy that does not exist.

Ultimately, the goal of social democracy is to guarantee the capabilities needed to stand as an equal in society. The welfare state can translate these normative goals into material conditions. Moreover, for reasons discussed in this chapter, the welfare state can help achieve these goals efficiently. As Barr says, "Even if all poverty and social exclusion could be eliminated, so that the entire population were middle class, there would still be a need for institutions to enable people to insure themselves and to redistribute over the life cycle. Though private institutions are often effective, they face pre-dictable problems, and attempts to address those problems inescapably in-volve state intervention."[18(p1)] Thus, the welfare state is ultimately indispens-able for making best use of scarce resources, to improve everyone's health.

9

Financing the Welfare State

How to finance the policies needed to achieve the goals of social democracy is a crucial question. Taxes are central to the answer. Although there are other important sources of public finance, taxation plays an outsized role in achieving many social democratic goals, and therefore in achieving health equity. People think of taxes pejoratively, but they should be viewed more positively. Taxes are an elegant and moral solution to an otherwise intractable collective action problem. Paying taxes is a way for individuals to work collectively for justice and express principles of reasonableness that underlie society as a system of cooperation between free and equal citizens.

Further, the products the welfare state concerns itself with are ones that consume a large part of household budgets, whether financed publicly or privately. People will pay for food, housing, health care, and education one way or another.[1] If taxes do not finance the essential capabilities, user fees paid to private firms will instead. Focusing only on state spending for particular products is an example of the "public cost" fallacy—the idea that only public outlays for an activity count when considering its cost. The concern should not be whether money is paid to the state versus private firms but what that money buys. Given strong efficiency arguments for state involvement in the finance and production of many essential products (chapter 8), it would likely cost more to get the same quantity and quality of those products using market provision.[1] Thus, public provision can actually increase the net income people have to pursue activities they value after the essential capabilities are guaranteed.[2]

This chapter will discuss important public finance considerations. Public finance is needed to fulfill the duties of distribution and recognition that permit a just system of social relations and result in health equity. In this chapter, it is important to keep in mind the discussion of efficiency in chapter 8. Efficiency is an instrumentally valuable, technical consideration useful for helping to choose among options that meet normative goals. Too often, economic arguments about efficiency conflate effectively normative (often in the utilitarian or welfarist tradition) claims about aggregate well-being with descriptive or technical concerns about how to achieve normatively justified goals given available resources. But unless a policy can achieve normative goals, concerns about its efficiency are not relevant. In other words, it is difficult to see why productive or allocative efficiency would be desirable without reference to the context in which production and distribution occur.

Taxation Is Not Expropriation

People sometimes view taxes as "taking" property that is theirs. But as discussed in chapter 7, taxation is part of an interdependent economic system that also includes income earned, transfers paid, and in-kind benefits received, which creates a normatively justifiable property rights regime.[3] Property is not encroached upon by taxation—taxation helps create property rights.[3] As philosophers Liam Murphy and Thomas Nagel note:

> The conviction that determines our approach to all more specific questions is that there are no property rights antecedent to the tax structure. Property rights are the product of a set of laws and conventions, of which the tax system forms a part. Pre-tax income, in particular, has no independent moral significance. It does not define something to which the taxpayer has a pre-political or natural right, and which the government expropriates from the individual in levying taxes on it. All the normative questions about what taxes are justified and what taxes are unjustified should be interpreted instead as questions about how the system should define those property rights that arise though the various transactions—employment, bequest, contract, investment, buying and selling—that are subject to taxation."[3(p74)]

This means that factor income is not a baseline to measure government expropriation against. As Murphy notes, "pre-tax income can't be used as a baseline because it is, in fact, an output of the very system (taxation and all the rest) we are trying to make just."[4]

Another way to think about this point is that particular tax laws or property rights regimes cannot be justified on their own. Instead, they are justified institutionally, as part of an entire system of social relations. The relevant question is whether that system is just. Fundamentally, taxes are justifiable when they form part of a just system—one that shows equal care for each individual, and situates everyone in a relationship of equality.[5,6]

Costs of Public Programs

There are different concepts of costs that are relevant to public finance. *Fiscal costs* are public outlays—the money the state spends on a particular policy or program. Fiscal costs are what appear in program budgets or national accounts.

Another cost concept is *real costs*—that is, resources in the form of inputs used to produce specific goods and services. Real costs indicate resources used for one activity that cannot be used for another—more production somewhere means less production somewhere else. Distinguishing between fiscal and real costs is important because policies can have different fiscal costs while having the same real costs, and vice versa.

For example, consider two scenarios. In the first, the state provides health insurance to everyone, and in the second, the state requires everyone to purchase private health insurance (the amount of health care used and prices charged by providers are the same in both scenarios). The first scenario would have large fiscal health care costs, while the second would not. But in both cases, the real cost, in terms of resources used for health care, would be the same. Regardless of whether spending is attributed to the state or private parties, the resources used for health care cannot be used for roads or education. Thus, policies with different fiscal costs may have equivalent real costs. Thinking in terms of fiscal and not real costs is what gives rise to the public cost fallacy noted above.

Alternatively, policies with equivalent fiscal costs may have different real costs. This is particularly relevant when discussing general transfers as types of state expenditures. When the state spends money on, for example, providing health care, it commands resources that cannot then be put to another use. But if the state spends an equivalent amount of money on general transfers, for example, pensions or child allowances, it is not committing real resources to a particular use in the same way. Instead, the state is merely changing who the transferred resources are said to belong to.*

---

* A general transfer program typically does have administrative costs, and those do represent committing real resources to a particular purpose.

A third cost concept is *macroeconomic costs*. Macroeconomic costs relate to changes in economic activity that result from a policy. Macroeconomic costs can result from the income and substitution effects discussed in chapter 8 and can occur on both the tax side (i.e., they can affect the economic activity of those remitting taxes) and on the transfer side (i.e., they can affect the economic activity of those who receive benefits).

A fourth cost concept is *opportunity costs*. Opportunity costs can be thought of as the next best alternative use of the resources, which must be foregone in order to devote resources to a chosen course of action. Opportunity costs occur because of the rivalrousness of real resources. Though opportunity costs are not included in budget figures, they are important to consider, because they make clear the constraints under which policy is made.

Goals of Taxation

Often, the most salient goal of taxation is to raise revenue. A body of economic scholarship, sometimes termed optimal taxation, focuses on understanding the configuration of tax rates and regulations that best does this.[2,7,8] But discussions of raising revenue should not be separated from discussions of how that revenue will be used. Instead, the desirability of a tax and the policies it finances should be evaluated together, comparing the outcomes produced with those of alternative approaches. In other words, when speaking of taxation and revenue, the goal is not simply to raise revenue but to raise revenue *for a purpose*, and so the benefits a tax enables should be considered alongside any costs.

A second goal of taxation is to help establish the conditions under which markets allocate products efficiently. One way this can occur is by equalizing the distribution of wealth and income, as discussed in chapter 8.[9,10] Another way taxation can make markets more allocatively efficient is by internalizing externalities.[2] For example, taxes on the production of certain pollutants could help ensure that markets are pricing their societal cost. Pigouvian taxes are taxes applied to address a negative externality (i.e., when societal costs are not fully incorporated into market prices).[2,11] Similarly, a Pigouvian subsidy addresses a positive externality (when societal benefits are not fully incorporated into market prices). Misunderstanding the goal of this taxation (behavior change rather than raising revenue) can lead to bad analysis. For example, suppose a Pigouvian tax is used to discourage consumption of cigarettes, because they harm health.[12-14] Such a tax may not raise much revenue if it successfully discourages smoking, but that would not be an argument against the tax. Moreover, concerns about the tax falling primarily on people who are less well-off could be misplaced, since the benefits of behavior change could also accrue primarily to the same individuals.

A third goal of taxation relates to its role within society's distributive institutions. A justification commonly given for an economic system with a principal role for market earnings is that such a system can generate more production, and thus greater national income, than alternatives. This could work to everyone's advantage by allowing greater standards of living than would otherwise be possible. However, unjustly high income and unjust accumulation of wealth provide power that can undermine equal social standing.[6,15,16] As part of the system that creates the conditions under which the national income is earned and distributed, taxes can play a key role in ensuring that income is distributed justly. Thus, another goal of taxation is to establish and maintain a relationship of equality throughout society.

A fourth goal of taxation is the democratization of capital and systems of capital reproduction. Decisions about how to invest capital raised by taxation can be made democratically, rather than privately. This can help fulfill duties of recognition by giving people more say in how capital, which results from joint efforts, should be employed.[5,17]

In summary, the goal of taxation is not to raise revenue for unspecified purposes. When thinking about taxation, not considering the goals it is meant to achieve can lead to mistaken conclusions about the appropriate course of action.

Concepts in Taxation

Given the importance of taxation to the egalitarian state, understanding different technical aspects of taxation is helpful for understanding egalitarian state policy design.

Tax Base

The tax base is defined by the taxable unit and what is taxed—it is what a tax rate (or other taxation scheme) is applied to. The taxable unit could be an individual, a household, or a particular type of transaction. What is taxed is typically some economic activity—either related to production or consumption.* Exclusions or deductions may further define the tax base. For example, an income tax scheme may define an individual as the taxable unit and their annual wages as what is taxed, exclude the first $10,000 in earnings from the tax base, and allow health care spending to be deducted from the tax base.

Tax Incidence

Tax incidence relates to the fact that a tax's remitter may not bear the real cost of that tax (chapter 8). For example, half of the FICA (Federal Insurance Contributions Act) payroll taxes that finance Social Security and Medicare in the United States are paid by employers, and half are paid by employees. However, the incidence falls fully on employees—the money paid by the employer would go to the employee in the absence of the tax.[18] Tax incidence may not be straightforward, so for any specific policy proposal it is important to investigate where the incidence may fall.

Taxes Are Paid by People

All taxes are ultimately paid by people. This is obvious for income taxes. It is also readily apparent for taxes based on transactions, like sales tax. Although the tax is *on* a transaction (the purchase of a particular product), it is the person buying who pays. This is also true, though perhaps less obvious, for corporate taxes, or other taxes on assets—asset owners, like corporation shareholders, effectively pay the tax.

Progressivity

The concept of progressivity relates to an evaluation of whether a quantity of interest (e.g., a tax payment or transfer benefit) varies on the basis of income (either factor income or net income). If discussing a tax or other payment made by an individual, "progressive" typically means that the quantity of interest is lower for an individual with lower income than an individual with higher income, "flat" or "proportional" means that the quantity of interest does not vary by income, and "regressive" typically means that the quantity of interest is greater for an individual with a lower income than an individual with higher income. If talking about a benefit received,

---

*An exception is a lump-sum tax, which is not tied to specific economic activity.

progressive means that the quantity of interest is greater for an individual with lower income than an individual with higher income, flat or proportional means the quantity of interest does not vary by income, and regressive means that the quantity of interest is lower for an individual with lower income than an individual with higher income. When talking about a benefit received, terms related to "targeting" are sometimes used similarly to terms related to progressivity. This will be discussed in more detail in chapter 10.

Confusingly, when assessing progressivity, the quantity of interest can be either a relative measure or an absolute measure. A relative measure is typically expressed as a percentage of income—it is constructed by dividing the payment or benefit amount by the person's income (e.g., 5% of income). An absolute measure is typically expressed as a dollar amount, irrespective of income (e.g., $5,000).

On the relative scale, if someone who made $10,000 paid 10 percent of their earnings in taxes and someone who made $20,000 paid 20 percent of their earnings in taxes, that would be progressive. If someone who made $10,000 and someone who made $20,000 each paid 10 percent of their earnings in taxes, that would be proportional. If someone who made $10,000 paid 20 percent of their earnings in taxes and someone who made $20,000 paid 10 percent of their earnings in taxes, that would be regressive. Progressivity on the relative scale can also be discussed in terms of *marginal* rates rather than *average* rates. For example, on the relative scale, if one paid 10 percent on the first $10,000 in earnings and 20 percent on all earnings above $10,000, that would be a progressive tax. If one paid 10 percent on all earnings, regardless of amount, that would be a proportional tax. If one paid 10 percent on the first $10,000 and then 5 percent on all earnings above $10,000, that would be a regressive tax.

On the absolute scale, if someone with $50,000 in income paid $5,000 in tax and someone with $100,000 in income paid $10,000 in tax, that would be progressive. If someone with $50,000 in income paid $5,000 and someone with $100,000 in income paid $5,000, that would be flat. And if someone with $50,000 in income paid $5,000 and someone with $100,000 in income paid $1,000, that would be regressive.

The assessment of progressivity can vary based on the scale used. For example, if a person with an income of $50,000 made a payment of $5,000 and a person with an income of $100,000 made a payment of $5,000, the payments would be flat on the absolute scale and regressive on the relative scale. A quantity cannot be flat on both the absolute and relative scale, unless the quantity is $0. Depending on the situation, it may make sense to use either the absolute or relative scale, so when evaluating an argument it is helpful to ascertain which scale the person making the argument is using. Progressivity with regard to taxation is most commonly, but not always, discussed on the relative scale.

To make matters even more confusing, terms regarding progressivity can be used descriptively (whether and how the quantity varies by income) or normatively ("regressive bad, progressive good"). I only use terms regarding progressivity descriptively in this book.

Types of Taxation

Most taxes relate to either production or consumption, the two aspects of economic exchange. On the production side, taxes can apply to labor or capital. Thus, broadly, there are three main types of taxation: taxes on labor, paid (nominally) by workers; taxes on capital, paid (nominally) by asset owners; and taxes on consumption, paid (nominally) by consumers.

Taxing Labor Income

Production-side taxes on labor income form the heart of the US federal tax system, along with that of many other countries. Labor income taxes often have two components. The first is sometimes called a payroll tax and is typically related to social insurance contributions—such as FICA taxes in the United States. Payroll taxes often have a proportional rate structure and may even cap the tax base, making the overall structure regressive on the relative scale. For example, in 2022 FICA taxed the first $147,000 earnings at 12.4 percent for Social Security's Old-Age, Survivors, and Disability Insurance (OASDI) program contributions, with $0 contribution thereafter (the Medicare portion of FICA has no maximum wage base and so is proportional, rather than regressive, on the relative scale).[19]

The other major component of labor taxation in the United States is the progressive income tax. A progressive income tax is typically progressive on the relative scale and structured with increasing *marginal* tax rates—for example, 0 percent on the first $10,000 in income, 10 percent on the next $10,000, 20 percent on the next $10,000, and so on.

Reasons for Progressive Income Taxes

There are good reasons for income taxes to have a structure that is progressive on the relative scale. A theoretical argument for progressivity relates to the declining marginal utility of income.[2] A dollar generally means less to someone who has more money than it does to someone who has less. Thus, progressive marginal rates help correct for the differential impact that proportional taxation would have. For example, a 25 percent tax on earnings between $0 and $20,000 for someone who earns only $20,000 would likely have much greater impact on their standard of living than a 25 percent tax on earnings between $0 and $200,000 for someone who earns $200,000. Structuring the income tax as, for example, a 5 percent tax on the first $50,000 in earnings and 25 percent for earnings above $50,000 helps avoid this problem. A second argument for progressivity relates to a potential macroeconomic cost of taxes—reduced labor supply owing to substitution effects. Some argue that high marginal rates will have substantial macroeconomic costs, as people are put off working. However, even very high marginal rates have not, historically, been associated with meaningful macroeconomic costs.[18,20–24] For example, from 1936 to 1981, a time of substantial economic growth in the United States, the top marginal labor income tax rate was 70 percent or above.[18,20,25] Indeed, recent work has suggested that top marginal tax rates around 70 percent may be optimal from the perspective of raising revenue, with little danger of economic harm.[21,26] Moreover, there is reason to think that progressive income taxes have lower macroeconomic costs than flat or regressive alternatives. Empirically, the substitution effect reduces labor supply more among those with low, rather than high, earnings prospects.[27,28] That is, labor supply is more elastic for lower, versus higher, earners. Thus, to raise the same amount of revenue, a progressive tax, by disproportionately affecting those with lower labor supply elasticity, typically has lower macroeconomic costs than alternatives.[27]

Third, a progressive structure is good for raising revenue, as it goes where the money is. Fourth, high marginal rates can discourage very high wage seeking, which can improve efficiency as very high wages often represent rents rather than value-added.[25,29] Fifth, high marginal rates can help prevent positional externalities. Positional externalities are situations where spending on "positional" products (products whose value lies primarily in comparison to what others have, such as the square footage of mansions) misallocates spending away from more socially useful products.[30] Sixth, high marginal rates help to compress the income distribution and prevent accumulation of extreme wealth. As noted above, this helps to achieve social democratic goals, such as fair equality of opportunity[31] and equal social standing.[6] Seventh, as will be discussed in more detail in chapter 10, progressive income taxation can serve a global "targeting" function in that it helps ensure that those with lower incomes receive proportionately more benefit from the tax-and-transfer system than those with higher incomes.

Altogether, progressive income taxation can be useful for administering the egalitarian state. However, as will be discussed later in this chapter, arguments for progressivity can be overdone.

Taxing Capital Income

Taxing capital income is another important form of production-side taxation. Some forms of capital income are relatively straightforward to tax, such as interest from investments. However, taxing other types can be more complicated than taxing labor income.[18,26] For example, in the case of capital gains (income in the form of appreciation in an asset's value), it can be challenging to value (a prerequisite to taxation) gains in "illiquid" assets (assets for which there is not a ready market), or when gains are deferred (i.e., if an asset has not been sold, any gains in its value are unrealized).[26]

Despite the difficulties, there are solutions. For example, mark-to-market programs require asset owners to periodically value their assets and pay tax on gains made (or deduct losses).[26] For assets with clear values, like mutual funds, this is straightforward. But for illiquid assets, a solution is to couple mark-to-market programs with a retrospective accrual tax. This taxes gains made at time of the sale, along with a deferral charge that offsets any tax advantage to deferring gains.[26]

Treating Capital and Labor Income Similarly

Unless capital and labor income are treated similarly by the tax system (forming a "comprehensive income tax"[18]), there will be opportunities for tax avoidance by reclassifying capital as labor income (or vice versa).[18] This would undermine the fairness of the tax system overall, and it would increase the share of taxation that has to fall on labor income.[26] Though some argue that capital should be given special treatment to encourage growth, or because the incidence of capital taxation falls on labor anyway, these arguments have little empirical support.[18,26] Indeed, arguments for giving capital special treatment may be motivated more by material interest and ideology than sound economics.

A key example of the need to treat capital and labor income similarly occurs with corporate income taxation. Corporate profits can be distributed as dividends or kept within firms as unrealized income in the form of higher share prices. If profits are taxed more lightly than labor income, this creates a powerful incentive for asset owners to reclassify income as capital rather than labor as a form of tax avoidance.[18] Further, though some argue that corporate taxes inhibit economic growth, there seems to be little evidence for this idea.[32] Thus, corporate income taxation is an important part of an overall tax system, and economically sound proposals for taxing corporate profits and mitigating tax avoidance are available.[18,26]

Inheritance and Interpersonal Transfers

Another important aspect of capital taxation is inheritances and other interpersonal transfers or gifts made outside the household. In general, these should be taxed as income for the person they are transferred to.[3,33] Though such taxes may not raise substantial revenue, they prevent the accumulation of dynastic wealth, which undermines relational equality.[33] Inheritance taxes are often derided as "death taxes,"* or supposedly unfair "double" taxation—taxing income as it is earned and then again as it is transferred. But it is not clear why this is objectionable. For instance, paying income taxes when income is earned and sales taxes when income is spent does not seem to raise similar concerns. Further, the tax should be understood as being paid by the beneficiary of the transfer, not the donor. Finally, taxing unearned income from interpersonal transfers is certainly not more unfair than taxing earned income.

Taxing Wealth

Beyond taxing flows of income from capital, what about taxing stocks of wealth? Wealth holdings are very unequal in the United States.[34,35] Because extreme wealth is inimical to equal social standing, reducing these extremes

---

* As economists emphasize that taxation discourages the taxed behavior, a "death tax" may in fact be salutary.

is an important policy goal. Wealth taxes can help unwind ill-gotten gains, accrued under unjust systems of social relations.[36] Given currently unequal holdings, a wealth tax is likely to raise substantial revenue. Over time, as holdings become more equal, revenue would likely decline. But a wealth tax would still serve to discourage accumulation of extreme wealth, working in conjunction with high marginal income tax rates.[18] In taxing wealth, sometimes a distinction is made between capital (wealth used to finance production) and other types of wealth (such as one's primary residence, used for consumption of housing services). However, such a distinction can present opportunities for tax dodging.

Wealth tax proposals have a long history. A prominent 19th-century example is the land value tax, sometimes called "geoism," "single-tax," or "Georgism" after political economist Henry George, who advocated it.[37] The idea is that a tax on the value of land (not improvements on it such as buildings) can capture the economic rents associated with natural resources that cannot be attributed to the effort of any person, without otherwise affecting economic behavior.[37]

Property tax is probably the most familiar wealth tax in the United States. Property tax illustrates both the difficulties of implementing wealth taxation and that these difficulties are surmountable. Chiefly, the difficulties of wealth taxes relate to valuation and liquidity.[26] When there is a market for assets, valuation is straightforward, even if the asset itself is not sold. For example, in the case of property tax, appraisers can assess the value of property by comparing it to similar properties recently sold. For assets where value is harder to determine, however, retrospective systems that assess value once sold may need to be implemented.[26]

Wealth taxation also requires that the asset holder have sufficient liquidity to pay the tax. For wealth that is held as liquid assets, for example, stocks and bonds, this presents little difficulty. But for property taxes, a person who does not wish to sell all or part of their property needs some other source of liquidity. Thus, workable wealth taxes must make some consideration for liquidity. Such consideration should not, however, make holding illiquid assets financially advantageous, as that would incentivize transforming liquid assets into illiquid ones. Moreover, wealth taxes should work harmoniously with income taxes to avoid incentives to convert income into wealth as a tax dodge. Despite these challenges, feasible, economically sound wealth tax policy exists, and wealth taxes can be an important part of the egalitarian state.[18,26]

Taxing Consumption

Consumption-side taxes are remitted by those purchasing a particular product. They include sales taxes, tariffs, duties, excise taxes, and value-added taxes (VAT). User fees and, in some circumstances, fines can also be thought of as consumption taxes.[38]

Consumption taxes can theoretically be progressive, proportional, or regressive.[39] However, because there is typically no consumption tax on savings, consumption taxes tend to be more regressive, on the relative scale, than production-side taxes. This is because a greater share of a well-off person's income goes to savings than a less well-off person's. For example, a person with $20,000 in net income may well spend all of it in a given year, and thus pay consumption tax on 100 percent of their net income. A person with $200,000 in net income may spend $150,000 and save $50,000, paying consumption tax on only 75 percent of their net income.

Some tax reform proposals suggest moving away from production-side taxes and toward consumption taxes, possibly combined with wealth taxes (to tax what is saved).[3] However, the advantage of this approach over an income tax is unclear.[3]

Though not a replacement, consumption taxes do have important roles in conjunction with income and wealth taxes as part of an overall tax system. When income and wealth are more equal in a society, progressive income taxes and wealth taxes raise less revenue.[18] Consumption taxes can fill in this gap. For example, a type of consumption tax called a VAT was implemented in many European countries after the Second World War, a time when capital supplies were low and income distributions were compressed. They were then, and continue to be, important sources of revenue to support the welfare state.

VATs deserve more consideration in the United States.[39,40] Indeed, the United States is somewhat atypical in that most US consumption taxes take the form of sales taxes, where tax payments are remitted only by the end consumer, rather than VATs, where payments are made at each stage of production, distribution, and sale.[18] To illustrate the difference, a sales tax might be paid only by the person who purchases a bag of potato chips. However, a

VAT might be paid by the manufacturer when purchasing potatoes, the supermarket chain when buying potato chips wholesale, and the consumer. Although the incidence of both sales taxes and VATs typically falls on the end consumer, VATs are often more efficient to administer and difficult to dodge, particularly when using the credit-invoice method.[18]

There are a number of VAT proposals worth considering as ways to finance welfare state programs.[18,39] Currently, given extreme concentrations of wealth in the United States, a VAT may not be a priority—revenue might be better raised from those with extreme wealth, for example. But as a society becomes more equal, a VAT is likely to be an important component of a tax system that supports social democratic goals.

Implementing Taxation

Tax implementation strongly influences how well a tax system functions. This section discusses three aspects of tax implementation: trade-offs between tax base and tax rates, designing the tax system to promote tax paying norms, and tax salience.

Broaden the Base, Lower the Rate

To raise a given amount of revenue, there is an inherent trade-off between the tax base (what the tax rate is applied to) and the tax rate (what percentage of the tax base is paid as tax). An aphorism in public finance is "broaden the base, lower the rate." Specifically, the broader or more encompassing the tax base, the lower the tax rate needed to raise a given amount of revenue. For efficiency reasons, it is typically desirable to make the tax base as wide as possible, which keeps the rate as low as possible.[20,41] In particular, some argue that the macroeconomic costs* of taxation (the economic activity forgone under greater taxation related to economic behavior change) may increase nonlinearly with increasing tax rates. One argument is that macroeconomic costs increase with the square of the marginal tax rate.[42] To illustrate, consider a baseline scenario in which two people, each earning the same amount, are each taxed at 20 percent. If the tax base was halved such that only one of the two people were to be taxed, then, if nothing else changed, the rate would need to double to raise the same revenue. Further, because the person taxed might choose to work less given the higher

---

*Also called the "deadweight loss" or "effective burden."

tax rate, such base narrowing may require even higher rates to raise the same revenue. At some point, raising the same revenue may not even be possible. Thus, changing from a broad-base, lower rate to a seemingly equivalent narrow-base, higher rate may decrease revenue. Of course, such theoretical concerns might not be borne out in the real world, but they provide a general argument for keeping the tax base broad in order to keep the tax rates low as low as possible.

Problems with "User Pays"

One case where base narrowing causes problems is employing user fees for public finance. Some argue that a principle of "user pays" improves allocative efficiency by better matching expenditures with consumption preferences.[38] However, a "user pays" policy substantially narrows the base used to finance a particular product. This results in high prices at the point of consumption (effectively, a larger tax for consumers of the product) and tends to decrease consumption of the product more than other methods of financing production. Decreasing consumption may be appropriate when there would otherwise be overconsumption. However, user fees typically decrease consumption bluntly, which can be harmful. For example, in the Rand Health Care Experiment, user fees reduced consumption of both beneficial and less beneficial health care, as it was difficult for consumers to distinguish.[43]

Finance via user fees can also create a spiral where high prices owing to the narrow base reduce consumption and thus producer revenue, which incentivizes cost cutting. This reduces quality, which lowers demand and further increases prices as economies of scale are lost. Moreover, emphasizing user fees for finance can make revenue dependent on the business cycle and can hollow out state capacity through underfunding. This contributes to the idea that the state provides poor services, and it can incentivize stratification where those who are well-off seek private alternatives.[38] Far from being an unintended consequence, these outcomes are consistent with one reason that some advocate user fees for public finance—an ideological preference for inegalitarian property rights regimes.[38] Indeed, the "user pays" principle is often intended to undermine public provision.

For products almost everyone will need at some point, a "user pays" system inefficiently forgoes the ability to smooth costs over time. Further, when positive externalities exist, "user pays" misses an opportunity to internalize them. For example, relying primarily on user fees to finance higher education, which may have social benefits through increased productivity, is likely inefficient.[44]

Finally, if user fees are to be employed at all for products needed to guarantee essential capabilities, everyone must have sufficient purchasing power. This is a case where taxation and other forms of public finance intersects with factor and transfer income policy.

Avoiding Tax Avoidance

A second aspect of tax implementation is that everyone should pay their fair share.[3] A social norm of paying taxes as civic duty is vital for a well-functioning state. That norm is corroded when tax dodging, whether through legal maneuvers or illegal tax evasion, is seen as something smart, rather than unreasonable.[18] Well-off individuals dodging taxes and bragging about it has effects that go beyond revenue loss.[18,45] This is all the more true if less well-off individuals are taxed more heavily to make up the shortfall.

Three principles that support tax paying norms are to make taxation understandable, to treat different sources of income similarly, and to have well-funded and equitably implemented enforcement.[3,34,45,46]

A complicated, opaque tax code creates opportunities for tax dodging and makes it harder to have faith in public institutions. Second, as noted above, treating different sources of income (e.g., from wages versus capital) differently creates opportunities for tax dodging, with few corresponding benefits.[26,34]

Finally, enforcement must be given appropriate emphasis (and funding). Those with high factor incomes and wealth have the most to gain from tax dodging, so sophisticated tax dodging attempts must be anticipated.[18,45] Preventing opportunities for tax dodging through tax system design is important. Also critical are audits and other compliance checks, recognizing that substantial resources may be deployed in an effort to avoid paying taxes.[18] As noted above, the benefits of fair enforcement go beyond revenue, as they help establish norms rooted in reciprocity and reasonableness that underlie the idea of a just society.[4,18,38,46]

Tax Salience

A third aspect of tax implementation is tax salience—how noticeable paying a particular tax is. Tax salience has an important effect on a tax's perceived burden, and thus it is relevant for considerations of political feasibility and perceived legitimacy. There is also evidence that lower tax salience results in smaller substitution effects.[47-50]

In general, taxes are less salient when there are several low-rate taxes rather than fewer high-rate taxes; when there are smaller, more frequent payments rather than larger, less frequent payments; when payments are made on an individual's behalf; and when the process is automated and/or integrated with the activity being taxed. Some taxes use these principles well. The VAT is one, which is typically paid seamlessly with each purchase. Another is income tax withholding. A third is payroll taxes, where some portion of the tax is remitted by the employer. Although the tax incidence ultimately falls on the worker, the structure reduces salience. A major advantage of these approaches is that they substantially reducing gaming and avoidance opportunities, which both increases revenue through greater compliance and lowers enforcement costs.[18]

Taxes that involve large, infrequent payments or substantial processes of reconciliation increase salience. One example of this in the United States is property taxes, which are typically assessed as a large annual payment. The income tax system in the United States, which involves complicated reconciliation of withholdings, sources of income not subject to withholding, and a complex system of deductions and tax expenditures, is a high-salience system that likely contributes to taxpayer dissatisfaction.

An important part of reducing tax salience is keeping the tax base broad. This tends to reduce complexity (e.g., administration is easier when there are few exceptions to what should be taxed) and permits lower rates.

Tax salience can also be used against social democratic goals. For instance, mandated expenditure (e.g., being required to purchase private health insurance) essentially functions as taxation. However, that effective taxation does not appear on the books, which can provide a political talking point against programs that may better achieve normative goals through public finance. As an example, consider a 10 percent payroll tax that allows for publicly financed health insurance versus being mandated to purchase health insurance from a private firm. The former could be depicted as a high-tax system of health care finance, while the latter could be depicted as low tax. However, owing to inefficiency, private insurance might require 15 percent of one's income to yield similar services. Relatedly, this is one reason that comparing taxes paid across countries or between different policy proposals can be misleading, as it might depend on arbitrary definitions about what is considered a tax.

With all aspects of the welfare state, implementation is crucial for achieving normative objectives, and taxation is no exception. Because designing taxation with a broad base, to keep rates low, is an important principle, efforts by special interests to achieve carve-outs or other special treatment to narrow the tax base should be carefully evaluated. Further, encouraging (and enforcing) tax paying norms, and reducing salience in a way that helps, rather than hinders, the state in creating a just society are important considerations for tax policy.

Overemphasizing Progressivity

As noted above, there are good arguments for a tax system to be progressive overall. However, progressivity is valuable instrumentally—that is, as a technical matter about achieving goals—not intrinsically, and can easily become overemphasized. Considering financing alone, without also considering the effects of the policy or program being financed, is misguided, and this mistake commonly occurs in discussions of progressivity.

To recap, progressivity on the relative scale relates to tax rates, or the proportion of the tax base one pays in taxes, that vary with income or wealth. Rates or proportions that increase with income or wealth are progressive, rates or proportions that do not vary are proportional (or "flat"), and rates or proportions that decrease are regressive. As noted above, I use progressive, proportional, and regressive purely descriptively—progressive does not mean inherently good nor does regressive mean inherently bad.*

Fundamentally, the goal of raising revenue is to put resources toward particular normative objectives. To achieve those objectives, both the method of raising revenue and the amount of revenue raised are important to consider. In some cases, owing to economic, political, or implementation considerations, a less progressive (or even regressive) approach may raise more revenue than a more progressive one. Further, the net effect of that larger amount of revenue may be superior to a more progressive approach, with

---

* As noted earlier in the chapter, progressivity can be applied to transfers as well, but, confusingly, progressivity of transfers is often discussed on the absolute scale (e.g., a larger absolute transfer amount for those with lower income). The arguments made in this section apply regardless of whether one is thinking in absolute or relative terms. However, inconsistently mixing the absolute and relative scale can be confusing.[51]

regard to achieving policy objectives. Moreover, because status quo income distributions are often very unequal,[52] the net effect of a program could easily be beneficial for those less well-off, even if financed regressively, because the combination of taxes and transfers results in a more equal net income distribution.

Mathematically, the distributive effect of a tax-and-transfer policy depends on factor income (both in absolute terms and the degree of factor income inequality present), the tax rate applied to various levels of factor income (progressivity on the relative scale), and how the transfers (whether as cash, subsidies, or in-kind services) financed by tax revenue are distributed. Thus, progressivity is only one of several variables that determine the final distributive outcomes.

The Importance of Revenue Raised

To illustrate, consider a series of examples proposed by policy analyst David Sligar (table 9.1).[53] In scenario A, the factor income distribution, as represented by two categories with a mean factor income of $200,000 and $20,000, respectively, is highly unequal. The tax system is progressive on the relative scale (those in the lower-income category pay nothing in taxes), but the rates are low and raise little revenue in absolute terms. The transfer distribution is strongly in favor of those in the lower-income category, who receive 80 percent of revenue raised. This approach minimally affects the higher-income category's net income, but it improves net income for those in the lower-income category. However, compare this with scenario B, which has the same factor income distribution but imposes a proportional tax of 20 percent and distributes only half of revenue raised to those in the lower-income category. Despite being less progressive, the net income for those in the lower-income category in scenario B is higher in both absolute and relative terms than in scenario A. Now consider scenario C. This has the same factor income distribution but a regressive tax structure—a 30 percent tax rate for the higher-income category and a 40 percent rate for the lower-income category. The transfer distribution is split equally between categories, yet the net income for those in the lower-income category is now higher than in both scenarios A and B. Next, consider scenario D, which starts with the same factor income distribution. In this scenario, not only is the taxation structure regressive on the relative scale (50% for the higher income group, 60% for the lower income group), but the transfer distribution is re-

Table 9.1. Illustration of progressivity

Factor income (in $)	Tax rate (%)	Tax payment (in $)	Transfer distribution (%)	Transfer payment (in $)	Net income (in $)	Difference in factor and net income (%)
			Scenario A			
200,000	10	20,000	20	4,000	184,000	−8.00
20,000	0	0	80	16,000	36,000	80.00
			Scenario B			
200,000	20	40,000	50	22,000	182,000	−9.00
20,000	20	4,000	50	22,000	38,000	90.00
			Scenario C			
200,000	30	60,000	50	34,000	174,000	−13.00
20,000	40	8,000	50	34,000	46,000	130.00
			Scenario D			
200,000	50	100,000	60	67,200	167,200	−16.40
20,000	60	12,000	40	44,800	52,800	164.00
			Scenario E			
120,000	40	48,000	45	44,100	116,100	−3.25
100,000	50	50,000	55	53,900	103,900	3.90

gressive as well—60 percent of transfers go to the higher-income group, and 40 percent go to the lower-income group. Despite this regressive structure, the net income of those in the lower-income category is higher than in scenarios A, B, and C. Finally, for completeness, consider scenario E. In scenario E, factor income inequality is much lower. The tax structure is regressive, but the transfer distribution structure is slightly progressive. Here, the net income of those in the lower-income category is the highest of any of the scenarios—and, despite the regressive tax structure, the net income distribution is almost equal between categories.

This simplistic example shows that the progressivity of the tax structure is only one of several relevant factors. The amount of revenue raised is crucial, as is the factor income distribution and how the revenue raised is distributed. Regressivity is often undesirable, but charges of regressivity should not be used to derail a plan that would have important benefits for those with lower factor income. One should instead compare all the elements, including the expected outcomes, of any two proposals rather than favoring a more progressive proposal by default.

Progressivity and Factor Income Distributions

The underlying factor income distribution is very important in questions of progressivity. To raise revenue for a given purpose, the state needs to go where the money is. If a society's distributive institutions distribute factor income unequally, revenue must be raised primarily from those with high factor incomes, regardless of the progressivity of the approach used. The more unequal factor income is, the greater the share of total revenue that appears to come *from* the well-off. But this does not indicate that such a "progressive" system is normatively desirable.

With more egalitarian distributive institutions for factor income, however, it becomes impossible to raise substantial revenue from individuals with higher factor income. There will be few such individuals, and their factor incomes will not be very high. In these cases, less progressive strategies are necessary, and indeed a more progressive strategy could be counterproductive from the perspective of raising revenue.

Why Is Progressivity Overemphasized?

Given that progressivity is only one of many considerations for achieving the policy objectives of social democracy, why does public debate put so much value on it? I believe there are at least five common reasons.

First, I think the primary reason progressivity is emphasized is its connection to the belief in efficiency as a virtue. Some arguing for progressivity are, explicitly or implicitly, adopting a utilitarian or similar consequentialist normative framework that views maximizing the impact of a given pool of resources as normatively good. On this view, a progressive program is inherently preferable because the well-off lose less utility through taxes. As discussed in chapter 8, however, concerns about utility maximization are relevant only among normatively acceptable options. This argues for progressivity being instrumentally valuable in some cases, rather than intrinsically valuable.

Second, it may be related to the idea that income equality itself is the normative goal (as opposed to relational equality). If income equality is the goal, regressive public finance could seem, superficially, counterproductive, even though, as the above example shows, regressive public finance does not inherently lead to unequal net income distributions.

Third, overemphasis on progressivity may stem from a misinterpretation of the Rawlsian difference principle. This would arise if one interpreted the difference principle as suggesting that particular policies should be selected based on maximally benefiting the least well-off, with progressivity as an index of benefit to the least well-off. In other words, the idea is that a progressively financed policy inherently benefits the least well-off more than a regressively financed one, because less money to finance it would "come from" less well-off individuals. I think this is mistaken for two reasons. First, I disagree with this interpretation of the difference principle. I think the difference principle is applicable to the basic structure of society, suggesting that society should be arranged in such a way that the least well-off are as well off as they could be, overall. It does not follow that every policy should be evaluated with reference to the difference principle. Second, even if one accepted this interpretation of the difference principle, as previously discussed, progressivity as a mechanism of finance is only one factor that determines a policy's outcomes. Since a progressive finance arrangement may not have any close connection to the relative benefits of the policy, fixating on the mechanism of finance alone is unfounded.

Fourth, an overemphasis on progressivity may relate to a residualist vision of the welfare state. If the goal of the welfare state were for the well-off to help those "in need," progressivity in financing welfare state programs would seem to fit naturally with that goal.

Fifth, it is worth mentioning that arguments about progressivity can be used in bad faith, to push toward more progressive, but less effective, or smaller, or politically fraught, approaches, as a way of dividing support among those with egalitarian impulses.

Progressivity and Cross-Country Comparisons

It can be very hard to make comparisons about progressivity across countries. Countries differ dramatically in factor income distribution, what is financed via taxation, whether transfer payments are taxed, and how revenue raised by taxation is distributed, all of which affect judgments about progressivity. Further, differences in the use of tax expenditures (or more generally what counts as a tax and what counts as a transfer) can greatly complicate assessments of progressivity. For example, imagine a refundable child tax credit that gives $2,000 to those with income less than $20,000, in a system with a 10 percent tax rate for everyone. In such a system, a person with a factor income of $20,000 and a qualifying child would have a tax payment of $0 (because the credit wipes out the tax payment), an effective tax rate of 0 percent, and a net income of $20,000. Now consider structuring this as a transfer instead of a tax credit. In such a system, a person with a factor income of $20,000 and a qualifying child would have a tax payment of $2,000, an effective tax rate of 10 percent, and a net income of $20,000 (because they received a $2,000 transfer in addition to their remaining $18,000 in factor income after their tax payment). The second system would be viewed as less progressive with regard to taxation, but there is no difference in the person's net income in either system. Moreover, when countries vary in whether a particular product is financed via taxation or other means, comparisons can be hard to make. Above, I discussed an example of one country that levied a tax to finance health care publicly, and another that compelled individuals to purchase health insurance privately, with regard to tax salience. This difference in approach would also complicate comparisons of progressivity of the two tax systems. Because the costs of health insurance, a major expense in both countries, are not included in the taxation scheme of one country, comparing the two regarding progressivity could be very misleading. Finally, as a recurring theme, comparing progressivity without comparing outcomes, such as net income or standard of living, is incomplete.

Ultimately, progressivity is only one consideration of many for public finance. The key focus, as always, should be on how well a tax-and-transfer system achieves its normative goals.

Public Finance beyond Taxation

Aside from taxation, other important forms of public finance include debt finance, income from state assets, and social wealth funds.

Debt Finance

A state can borrow, or issue debt, to finance public spending. Debt finance is frequently considered in three situations. The first is as counter-cyclical stimulus—that is, to boost demand during economic downturns. Such stimulus proved successful, for example, during the Great Depression and the COVID-19-related financial crisis.[54-59] Insufficient public stimulus is also blamed for the slow and uneven recovery of the Great Recession after the 2007 banking crisis.[60] Debt finance during business cycle downturns is particularly important because financing spending with taxation would blunt the stimulus effect of the spending.[59]

The second situation relates to maintaining demand even during normal economic times. Schools of economic thought associated with John Maynard Keynes and Michał Kalecki see a role for ongoing state involvement, including debt finance as one tool, to stimulate demand. The goal of such an approach is full employment (discussed in more detail in chapter 13).[56–59]

A third situation relates to outlays for physical capital and infrastructure, like building social housing, bridges, schools, and hospitals. These projects typically have high but temporary outlays, rather than imposing ongoing spending obligations. Issuing debt in the form of bonds is a common way governments finance such projects.

For public debt, the key consideration is typically not the absolute level of debt but the ratio of debt to gross domestic product (GDP). Problems can emerge when this ratio increases relative to the status quo.[61] Factors that determine whether the ratio increases include current spending and public revenue, but also interest on existing debt and growth in GDP.[62] Thus, if current spending and public revenue remain constant, interest rates that are lower than GDP growth rates can cause the debt-to-GDP ratio to decrease on its own. During those times, a temporary increase in debt-financed public spending may have little impact on the debt-to-GDP ratio. In other words, when interest rates are lower than GDP growth rates, the real cost of borrowing is low. When the real cost of borrowing is low, debt finance may help meet policy objectives more efficiently than other forms of finance.

Although debt finance is a useful tool in the right circumstances, it is not well suited for many welfare state programs. In particular, debt finance is not good policy for ongoing outlays like health care and education. This is because these programs guarantee capabilities that are needed at all times. Finance for these programs is necessary regardless of whether borrowing is relatively cheap or expensive. Thus, it is typically preferable to have a less volatile source of finance for many welfare state programs.

State Assets

State assets can be used for public finance in several ways. Leasing public land and physical assets, such as buildings, for commercial use (such as ranching or mining) has a long history. Further, given that the state is a major funder of scientific and technological research, there is substantial scope for using intellectual property rights as state assets. Such rights could be, for example, licensed to raise revenue or employed so as to hold down the costs of products that use state intellectual property (e.g., medications), thereby reducing the costs of certain services (e.g., health care).

Social Wealth Funds

Finally, a method of public finance that deserves extended discussion is social wealth funds. Social wealth funds publicly hold assets, such as stocks or real estate, in a fund to be used for social benefit.[63] They are an old idea, but interest in them has grown considerably in the last 40 years, leading to a number of recent proposals.[17,64–67] A particularly well-developed proposal comes from policy analyst Matt Bruenig.[63] The capital income from social wealth funds can be used to pay dividends to people directly. For example, a social wealth fund could pay a monthly dividend equal to a percentage of asset growth over a rolling 60-month average (to smooth payments), setting aside some proceeds for inflation-proofing and reinvestment.[63] Such a fund would importantly improve the distribution of wealth in the United States.[63] Alternatively (or in addition), proceeds could be used to finance essential services, such as health care.

Social wealth funds are feasible. In the United States, Alaska has operated, for four decades, a social wealth fund that pays an annual dividend to residents.[68] Globally, Norway is the preeminent example.[63] At present, the majority of Norway's national wealth is publicly owned, through a suite of funds.

Social wealth funds are logical finance mechanisms for social insurance or universal basic income programs (discussed in more detail in chapter 12). A common argument against such programs is that by financing them with taxes on labor income, they take money from those who earn it and provide it to others who did not. That understanding of taxation is incorrect, but it is politically salient. Social wealth funds help avoid this issue, as all individuals have similar claims on unearned capital income, particularly income that derives from society's common resources.[63] Thus, social wealth funds embody an understanding of society as a system of fair cooperation.

Social wealth funds offer several other advantages. First, as economist Thomas Piketty has documented, returns to capital often exceed economic growth, resulting in feedback loops that promote wealth accumulation for capital owners.[69] That is not an immutable law of nature, but rather it is the product of decisions that establish distributive institutions.[56,70] It does, however, speak to the difficulty of establishing lasting political controls on private wealth accumulation. While those must be pursued, a social wealth fund can also hedge against failure of those strategies, capturing excessive returns to capital that can be used to fulfill the state's duty of equal care. Social wealth funds can also hedge against economic changes such as automation that may reduce labor demand, and protect against capital flight. Finally, they may be particularly useful as investments in industries whose profits primarily come from extracting public resources, such as logging and mining.[63] Since those profits largely depend on public resources, social wealth funds provide a way for the public to receive its share.

Social wealth funds represent an important democratization of capital and a way to distribute wealth fairly. Further, they have few downsides. Thus, they should play an important role in financing the egalitarian state.

Summary

Public finance is critical for achieving the normative goals of social democracy, and thus health equity. However, public finance must be considered in conjunction with the policies it finances. As Murphy says, "justice in taxation is not a matter of some fair distribution of tax burdens as measured against pre-tax income. It is about how well or badly the tax system, together with the other elements of the economic and welfare system, secures just results."[4] Further, he notes that we should recognize "the proper place of taxes as just one instrument in the total set of economic institutions that can bring about a just society."[4] For this reason, any particular tax or other aspect of public finance should not be evaluated on its own but as part of an overall regime, with the judgment based on the regime's ability to achieve normative goals.

It is worth reiterating that factor income is the product of a system of social relations—it is not an independent construct that can be used to assess burdens imposed by the state. In the terminology of economists, it is endogenous. That means that taxation is emphatically not theft—indeed, taxation is a key component of the system that makes property rights possible.

While many systems of public finance might achieve social democratic goals, there are some principles that have worked well in practice. A progressive comprehensive income tax (one that treats capital and labor income similarly), with relatively high top marginal tax rates (around 70%), typically serves as the heart.[21] There is little evidence that such rates have substantial negative economic effects, and much evidence that they have social bene-fits.[18,20-24] These income taxes are supplemented with a mix of wealth and consumption taxes. That mix should be more heavily slanted toward wealth taxes when wealth inequality is greater and transition toward consumption taxes as wealth becomes more equal. Finally, the system of public finance should use social wealth funds to democratize a nation's assets.

Achieving the goals of social democracy, and health equity, requires tak-ing public finance seriously. Taxation and other forms of public finance are not necessary evils or expropriation but are instead important innovations that allow everyone to work collectively in the pursuit of justice.

Practice of the Welfare State

The previous three chapters examined the theoretical underpinnings of welfare state policies, the economics of those policies, and their financing. This chapter discusses implementing those policies.

Implementation is a vital step in translating the principles of social democracy into concrete policies that can transform the material conditions in which people live. Successful policy implementation requires a coherent strategy; a wide, deep, and enduring political coalition; and effective administration.[1] Key topics include how the state develops and maintains legitimacy, and how implementation can fail. Further, this chapter returns to the discussion of universalism versus residualism, here focusing on why the universalist approach is frequently easier to implement successfully. This provides a technical justification for universalism to go alongside its normative justification. Implementation is where questions of what the state *should* do collide with questions about what the state *can* do.[2] Ultimately, successful implementation of just policies generates and sustains support for the egalitarian state.

Legitimacy

Legitimacy relates to citizens' belief in a state's right to govern and citizens' acceptance of any particular policy. Political scientist Bo Rothstein delineates three aspects of state legitimacy, regarding how citizens tolerate state intervention, accept state decisions, and cooperate as part of the state.[2] Institutions and policies that are, and are seen to be, just can generate their own support and legitimacy.[2,3] This makes successful implementation more likely, further enhancing legitimacy.

Government-Level Legitimacy

Social norms strongly affect the legitimacy of a government and that government's ability to achieve its goals. Specifically, the commitment to reasonableness (chapter 3) underlies norms of reciprocity, collective action, and solidarity that are necessary for social democratic governance.[4] Rather than expecting these norms to come from a society's background culture, however, they can be shaped by political institutions.[2,5] Rothstein argues that social norms "can be explained by the manner in which political institutions structure the decision-making situation faced by actors and influence trust."[2(p134)] Democratic institutions like legislatures, free speech, and public debate do not simply aggregate a society's preferences—they discover and change them, hopefully for the better.[2] Choices about the structure of institutions and the democratic process not only reflect but also shape the norms that prevail. Thus, the design of social democratic political institutions helps determine both legitimacy and social outcomes.

Policy-Level Legitimacy

The theory of contingent consent helps explain why particular policies are seen as legitimate.[2,6] Policies are perceived as legitimate when their goals are seen as just, their burdens are fairly distributed, and they are administered fairly. Correspondingly, a policy needs three types of arguments to establish its legitimacy. The first relates to issues of substantive justice—why a particular policy is the right thing to do. The second explains why a policy's burdens are distributed fairly. Everyone's burden need not be the same, but some should not shoulder heavy burdens while others shirk theirs. Feeling taken advantage of works against legitimacy. The third relates to procedural justice—the policy must treat people fairly. Corruption or discrimination will tend to delegitimize a policy. Ultimately, consent for a particular policy is contingent upon making those arguments convincingly.[6]

What Can the State Do?

Implementing a policy successfully depends on both policy design choices and the background conditions in which the policy is enacted.[2] Design choices can make a policy easier or harder to administer, and existing knowledge and technology can make some policy goals easier or harder to achieve.

Table 10.1. Policy dimensions

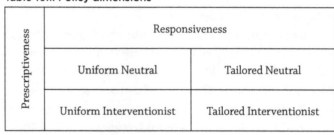

	Responsiveness	
	Uniform Neutral	Tailored Neutral
	Uniform Interventionist	Tailored Interventionist

(Prescriptiveness, shown vertically on the left side)

Easy and Hard Policy Design

One way to think about the likelihood of successful policy administration is along two dimensions (table 10.1).[2] The first is responsiveness to individual circumstances. A uniform policy treats everyone similarly, while a tailored policy takes into account specifics of the individual's situation. In general, a tailored policy will be more difficult to administer than a uniform policy. The second dimension relates to prescriptiveness. A neutral policy leaves a beneficiary free to use benefits as they see fit. An interventionist policy has a perfectionist vision and guides beneficiaries toward favored uses of the benefit. In general, an interventionist policy will be more difficult to administer than a neutral policy.

Four hypothetical policies to address food insecurity illustrate these ideas. A uniform neutral policy provides a flat (equal for everyone) cash transfer. Beneficiaries can use the money as they choose, and the state trusts that food will be among the purchases. A tailored neutral policy provides a cash transfer scaled to household size and factor income, excluding those with income above a threshold. This is harder to administer than the uniform neutral policy, needing more information at enrollment and periodic monitoring to adjust transfer amounts.

A uniform interventionist policy provides a flat voucher that can only be used for certain healthy foods. This is harder to administer than the uniform neutral policy, as it requires defining "healthy foods," implementing a purpose-built system for issuing the vouchers, ensuring the vouchers are widely accepted, and monitoring redemption of vouchers for appropriate products. Finally, a tailored interventionist approach issues vouchers for healthy foods, scaled to household size and income, and is conditional on attending nutrition education classes meant to encourage healthy eating.

Such a program will be more difficult to administer than the others, given its multiple components.

This typology is not an argument for or against any approach—each might be appropriate in a specific context. The added complexity of tailored and/or interventionist programs may produce better outcomes than other options. However, policy design should consider ease or difficulty of administration. In general, it is very hard to beat a cash transfer for administrative ease.

Easy and Hard Policy Problems

Another consideration about what the state can do relates to existing knowledge and technology.[2] In some cases, how to achieve particular outcomes is clear. In others, there may be substantial uncertainty. The state may need to act regardless, but existing knowledge and technology serve as background constraints, and some problems are simply harder to solve than others under prevailing conditions.

As an analogy, imagine that there are two patients, each suffering from a different illness. The first patient's illness is well studied. Although treatment is complex and the outcome depends on many factors, these factors are known, measurable, and there are good treatment options for every combination of factors. The second patient has an illness that is not well studied. Outcomes depend on factors not well understood and other factors that are known but difficult to measure. In both cases, some action is needed—the patients are suffering. However, the treatment approach will be very different. In the first case, care can be standardized, and a successful outcome is likely. In an analogous public policy context, the policy could be implemented by a simple bureaucracy with clear rules. Monitoring would largely consist of assessing whether the rules have been followed, with confidence that if they are, good outcomes will result.

In the second case, a priori specification of the correct approach will be difficult. Expert practitioners must use their judgment, and finding the best course of treatment may take trial and error. Even then, success may be unlikely. For policies, this would be analogous to delegating authority to professionals who exercise judgment and discretion, and who are empowered with wide latitude to achieve the best outcomes they can. Monitoring would have to focus on outcomes, rather than processes, but those outcomes will be highly variable, and at least partially outside of practitioners' control. Owing both to the broad leeway practitioners must have, and the unclear connection between actions and outcomes, monitoring will be challenging, and the legitimacy of the policy can readily come under threat. In general, the difficulty of the situation should be appreciated when evaluating the policy that tries to address it.

Finally, the state cannot do everything and must be strategic in the tasks it takes on.[2] For normatively required goals, a state must try to fulfill its duty, even if difficult to accomplish. But the likelihood of success is always an important consideration, as the failure of one policy may undermine others. Perceived competence supports legitimacy.

Implementation Failure

Besides the topics just discussed, policy implementation has other common failure modes.

Lack of Information

In public provision scenarios without price signals, producers—public or private—may not receive the feedback needed to monitor quality and respond to consumer demand. Thus, other signals must be built so producers know how well they are performing.[2] Such signals could include ways for consumers to use "voice" power (e.g., registering complaints, involvement in oversight or regulatory boards, consumer representatives on committees that make production decisions) and "exit" power (e.g., fostering competition between producers so consumers can choose one they prefer).[7]

State Capacity

Another way implementation can fail is lack of state capacity. State capacity is the technical ability of the state to achieve its goals. State capacity is a heterogeneous concept, with no single measure. Any state likely has varying capacity in different domains. Nevertheless, state capacity is very important. Because state capacity is publicly financed, there is often substantial pressure to economize, which is a mistake. The products the welfare state needs to provide are essential. Therefore, whatever state involvement is warranted should be financed appropriately. The alternative is not "saving money" but finding second-best ways to guarantee essential capabilities.

Building state capacity is an important goal in its own right—it could be seen as a positive externality with social benefits that go beyond any particular policy or program. Adequate state capacity means that there can be a true choice between public versus private production, rather than having to default into private production for lack of an alternative. This is especially important when it is difficult to establish the conditions needed for efficient private production. Because state capacity is so important, those who prefer private production for ideological (or material) reasons often focus on undermining it.[8] A common tactic is to starve the state of capacity, and then point to the results of insufficient capacity as evidence of the private sector's superiority.

Differential Implementation

A national-scale program in the United States will inevitably present myriad opportunities for local implementation to vary. Monitoring and evaluation are vital for limiting unjustified variation. Of special concern is that racial and other forms of oppression may coincide with differential implementation. The state must ensure that formally universalist programs are substantively universalist and that oppression and other forms of injustice do not undercut their benefits.

Administrative Burdens

Administrative burdens (and related concepts such as ordeal mechanisms and red tape) are another important implementation consideration.[9,10] Administrative burdens are onerous experiences for individuals interacting with a policy or program.[9,10] Administrative burdens may stem from programmatic aspects that serve a useful purpose, and could be unavoidable. However, they should be minimized. Sociologist Pamela Herd and political scientist Donald Moynihan categorize administrative burdens as: (1) *learning burdens* (related to learning about the program, such as what the eligibility requirements are), (2) *compliance burdens* (related to adhering to program rules, such as submitting needed documentation or frequent recertification), and (3) *psychological burdens* (e.g., stress and stigma resulting from presenting benefits as "charity" rather than rights of citizenship).[9,10] The "ordeal mechanisms" literature views these burdens as having a socially beneficial effect, by helping to target services to those who need them the most. Supposedly only those most in need will submit to the ordeal.[9,11] But an ordeal mechanism approach is not compatible with duties of recognition. Further, to the extent that inability to navigate a complicated system correlates with need, ordeals may paradoxically direct benefits *away from* those most in need.[10,12] Thus, ordeals typically undermine, rather than enhance, the effectiveness of the program.[9,13]

Ordeal mechanisms and administrative burdens are conceptualized from the perspective of a policy beneficiary (or their advocate). Red tape is conceptualized from the perspective of a policy administrator. Red tape refers to rules and procedures that make public administrators' jobs more difficult, without a clear benefit. Red tape can lead to implementation failure by making administrators less able to carry out their duties.[9]

Residualism and Risk of Implementation Failure

Residualist policies often have greater administrative burdens, ordeals, and red tape than universalist ones. This is because making a policy more tailored and/or interventionist typically increases its administrative complexity. An emphasis on tailoring is inherent to residualist logic—the benefit should be reserved for those in need. Further, residualism often argues for interventionist policies to set right the lives of those who have "mismanaged" them—the mismanagement being implied by being in need.[2] Moreover, compared with universalist policies, residualist policies may be less intelligible given their greater complexity, and they are more likely to be stigmatizing. Both of these factors further increase the risk of implementation failure.

How Should Policy Fail?

Part of policy design is considering what happens if implementation fails. Implementation failure can result in those who should have access to a product not having access, or those who should not have access to a product having access. Though neither scenario is desirable, imperfect implementation may be inevitable. Therefore, it is important to consider the expected consequences of implementation failure, and what direction it might be preferable to fail "toward."

Managing Competition

A common approach for policy implementation is to have multiple publicly financed private producers of products necessary for the essential capabilities, with or without public producers (a "public option").[14] For such an approach to result in acceptable outcomes, several conditions must be met.[2] First, any product variation must be above some minimum standard. Private producers may wish to offer "extras" to attract consumers, but if quality falls below acceptable standards in search of profit, the duty of equal care will be violated.

Next, when there are public producers, publicly financed private producers should not be allowed to charge user fees greater than public producers. Allowing this creates two-tiered systems.

Third, private producers must not be able to cherry-pick by differentially selecting those who are likely to have better outcomes or needs that are easier to address. This creates two-tiered systems where difficult cases are handled by some (often public) producers, with other producers benefitting from arbitrage between what they are paid and the easier to meet needs of better-off consumers.

Finally, services must be available to everyone on equal terms. There cannot be discrimination in who can access the services of particular producers, as this would violate the duty of equal care.

Regulation, monitoring, and evaluation are vital for the success of managed competition. If neither the state nor consumers can adequately monitor quality and access along the lines described above, this is a strong argument against allowing competition. Waste, fraud, and abuse can come from private contractors as readily as public producers. Guarding against this requires adequate state capacity and appropriate funding. There should also be clear structural protections and ethical codes to avoid entanglement between producers and monitors. This is applicable whether producers are public or private. In the case of public production, public producers should essentially be semiautonomous or otherwise walled off from the core functions of the state, so that the monitors employed by the state retain independence.[2]

Mandated Expenditures

Mandated expenditures are policy instruments that require individuals to purchase a privately produced product, such as car insurance or health care coverage. Such regulations can have their place—they may be more politically feasible than explicitly financing and/or producing products. However, they have substantial drawbacks as well. The same situations that motivate the use of mandated expenditures may also preclude effective monitoring of implementation. Further, abdication of explicit public finance means that mechanisms to finance policies broadly, such as taxation, may be off the table. Instead, finance may inefficiently occur through user fees. And of course, mandated expenditures for products needed for the essential capabilities are only acceptable when factor and transfer policy assures necessary purchasing power for everyone. Finally, private implementation could be advantageous (e.g., the state may not suffer blame for poor implementation), but it could also increase the scope for differential implementation that may not fulfill the duty of equal care.

Tax Expenditures

Tax expenditures implement policy through the tax code. Tax expenditures often take one of two forms—tax credits, which can be applied against a tax liability, and tax deductions, which shrink the tax base. As examples, a child tax credit may remove $2,000 per qualifying child from one's income tax liability, and, in the United States, employer spending on health insurance for an individual is not included in the taxable wage base, even though it is part of an employee's overall compensation. Tax expenditures can function as subsidies or general transfers (chapter 8).

If a tax credit is *refundable*, the beneficiary is entitled to the full amount even if their tax liability is less than the credit. For example, with a refundable credit of $2,000, a person whose tax liability is $1,000 would pay $0 in tax *and* receive a $1,000 tax refund (half of the credit covering their tax liability and the balance paid to the individual). With a *nonrefundable* credit, the credit can cover tax liability, but the balance is not paid as a benefit. For example, with a nonrefundable credit of $2,000, a person whose tax liability is $1,000 would pay $0 in tax but would not receive a tax refund. A nonrefundable credit is effectively an earnings-related benefit in that it offers greater benefit to those who earn more (and thus would otherwise have greater income tax liability). For instance, with a $2,000 nonrefundable credit, a person who earns $10,000 in income and owes $1,000 in taxes would receive only a $1,000 credit, while a person who earns $20,000 in income and owes $2,000 in taxes would receive a $2,000 credit. A refundable credit is neutral toward earnings.

Tax Expenditures Reinforce Stratification

Tax expenditures can reinforce social stratification in several ways. One way is by offering differential benefits. For example, making home mortgage interest tax deductible only benefits those who can afford to purchase a home. Many tax expenditures in the United States differentially benefit well-off individuals, owing to nonrefundability or the specific economic activity they apply to.

A second way tax expenditures reinforce stratification is by hiding the extent to which well-off individuals benefit from state programs. By administering some benefits through the tax code and others as stand-alone programs, tax expenditures stealthily benefit those with higher incomes. This helps create the illusion that well-off individuals do not receive government assistance, unlike less well-off individuals using other programs. For example, those receiving tax expenditures for employer-sponsored health insurance may not see the similarities between their subsidized health insurance and the subsidized health insurance of Medicaid beneficiaries. Similarly, those helped by the mortgage interest tax deduction may not see themselves as receiving housing assistance in the same way as those using the housing choice voucher program ("Section 8"). Although potentially administratively efficient or important for political feasibility, the downsides of structuring policy as tax expenditures should be taken seriously.

A third way tax expenditures reinforce stratification is that tax expenditures frequently miss those who do not file taxes—typically less well-off individuals who have no tax liability. This means that implementing a program as a tax credit could differentially benefit those who are better off, relative, for example, to an otherwise similar program that proactively sends benefit checks to everyone. Missing non-filers has proven stubbornly difficult to rectify and may be insurmountable.[15,16]

Targeting and Means Testing

Targeting is a confusing and commonly misunderstood topic, often emphasized due to its supposed relationship to efficiency. Like progressivity (chapter 9), targeting refers to disproportionality of benefits from a policy or regime across categories of individuals.[17-19] Categories are often defined by factor income,* and programs can be targeted toward those with lower incomes ("pro-poor" targeting), untargeted (benefits do not vary by income), or targeted to those with higher incomes ("pro-rich" targeting).** Also like

---

* Targeting could also occur on other dimensions, such as age or racial and ethnic categories.
** Unless otherwise specified, I use the term *targeting* to mean "pro-poor targeting."

terms related to progressivity, targeting is frequently expressed on the relative scale (e.g., program benefits as a percentage of factor income), but it can be expressed on the absolute scale (e.g., dollar amounts), as well. One way to measure targeting formally is with a concentration coefficient.[17,19]

Targeting is different from a policy's design logic: universalism versus residualism. Universalism and residualism refer to the intentions of a policy— whether the policy is meant to be the first-line approach used by everyone or only as a last resort.[17] Targeting refers to the distributive mechanics of the policy. Both residualist and universalist policies can be pro-poor targeted, untargeted, or pro-rich targeted. However, universalism and residualism implement targeting very differently.

Residualist versus Universalist Targeting

Archetypically, a targeted residualist program is means-tested (meaning those with income or assets above a certain threshold are ineligible for benefits), and benefits phase out, or decrease, at some rate as income or assets increase before going to $0 at the means-testing threshold.* Such a program is targeted *prospectively* (i.e., eligibility and benefit amount is based on factor income prior to issuance of benefits), at the *program level*, and *explicitly* (program rules set different benefit levels for different individuals).

An archetypical universalist regime offers relatively equal benefits to everyone and finances those benefits with a tax system that results in targeting on net—those with lower factor incomes benefit disproportionately. In other words, when assessing the degree of targeting in a universalist system, it is important to examine net incomes in total, rather than benefit amounts from any one particular program. Such universalist regimes can be thought of as being targeted *retrospectively* (i.e., based on income at the end of a particular period, such as the tax year), at the *regime level*, and *implicitly* (tax liabilities provide the targeting, rather than explicit modification of benefits). Thus, both residualist and universalist approaches can distribute resources disproportionately to those with lower factor income, but they use different mechanisms to do so. As I will discuss, these different mechanisms provide administrative, economic, and political advantages for the universalist approach.

---

*The absence of a benefits phaseout is sometimes called a "benefits cliff."

Targeting Is Technical, Not Normative

Some view the question of targeting as having normative implications, even claiming that a program is not really "for the poor" unless there is a substantial degree of targeting.[18] This is mistaken. I view the question of targeting as a technical one, in many ways parallel to that of progressivity (chapter 9). A pro-poor targeted program is not inherently better than an untargeted or a pro-rich targeted program. Targeting is, at most, instrumentally valuable, not a policy goal in itself.

Problems with Residualist Targeting

Residualist targeting has a number of administrative, economic, and political downsides.[20,21] First, the need to assess income or assets to determine eligibility and/or benefit amount imposes greater administrative burdens than universalist programs. If eligibility determination occurs on a program-by-program basis, these burdens can be multiplied across many programs. Further, targeted residualist programs often require frequent recertification to maintain eligibility and adjust benefit amounts as income fluctuates. These administrative burdens greatly limit the reach of targeted residualist programs.[16] Such programs rarely reach more than 80 percent of eligible individuals, and they sometimes reach fewer than 20 percent.[16] Moreover, greater burdens mean that targeted residualist programs typically have greater overhead costs than universalist regimes.

Another administrative problem with residualist targeting is that having to establish need can create an adversarial dynamic between program administrators and beneficiaries. Would-be beneficiaries are incentivized to overstate their need, and administrators are inclined to disbelieve those they are meant to help. When cases of fraud occur, even if rare, the oppositional structure tends magnify them.[2] Finally, targeted residualist policies inherently create two-tiered systems because they are meant to benefit only some, leaving others to use different approaches to meet their needs.

In contrast to residualist targeting, a major benefit of universalist targeting—targeting at the level of the overall tax-and-transfer system—is administrative simplicity.[22] Eligibility is typically categorical (e.g., all children are eligible for a universalist child benefit), which eases initial enrollment and may obviate recertification. Further, adjustment of benefit amounts occurs through the tax code, is made retrospectively (e.g., as part of tax filing), and is implemented by the tax agency alone, rather than by many separate agencies. Thus, progressive income and wealth taxation can produce the same targeting effect as means testing, while solving much of the administrative difficulty of program-level targeting. Finally, since universalist programs are used by everyone, they work against social stratification and stigma.[22]

Residualist targeting has important economic implications as well. First, withdrawal of benefits as factor income increases represents an implicit tax.[21,23] With an explicit income tax, as factor income increases, so do tax liabilities, and thus net income does not increase as quickly as factor income. With the implicit tax of benefit withdrawal, as factor income increases, benefits decline, and thus net income does not increase as quickly as factor income.

The correspondence between explicit and implicit taxation can be combined with knowledge of economic behavior change (chapter 8) to produce general expectations about how residualist targeting may affect labor supply. Considering substitution effects, benefits that have a factor income related phaseout will tend to disincentivize labor supply (since earning more factor income reduces the benefit), flat benefits should be neutral (because the benefit is the same regardless of factor income), and earnings-related (or pro-rich targeted) benefits will incentivize labor supply (work is worth more). Income effects would tend to work in the opposite direction as substitution effects.*

To make the expected effects of targeted residualist programs on labor supply concrete, imagine a child benefit that pays $500 per month per child if monthly income is $0. However, this benefit decreases by $0.25 per $1 of income. If monthly income were $1,000, the benefit would be $250 per child per month, and if monthly income were $2,000 or above, there would be no benefit. Thus, there is an *effective marginal tax rate* of 25 percent. Even if tax is not collected explicitly, each additional $1 of factor income only leads to $0.75 of net income, just as with a 25 percent income tax rate.[23,24] The economic effect of benefit withdrawal is analogous to the effect of tax remit-

---

*Expected impacts related to financing a program are the converse of those related to receiving benefits. That is, substitution effects of a regressive tax might incentivize greater labor supply, substitution effects of a proportional tax may have little impact, and substitution effects of a progressive tax might incentivize reduced labor supply. Income effects would be expected to follow the opposite pattern. Of course, in practice the magnitude of either or both of these effects may be negligible.

tance.[25] As policy analyst David Sligar notes: "Means testing reduces the economic reward associated with a particular activity, usually by withdrawing a benefit based on a percentage of each dollar earned. In economic substance it is thus identical to a tax."[26] Residualist targeting can lead to a "poverty trap," because the withdrawal of benefits represents a counterincentive for individuals to increase factor income. Moreover, across several targeted residualist programs, effective marginal tax rates above 100 percent are possible, meaning people can be worse off, in absolute terms, for earning more factor income. The benefits withdrawn can be greater than the extra income earned.

A second economic problem with residualist targeting is that the tax base that finances such a program is typically narrower than a similar universalist one. Compare the targeted residualist program described above to a universalist program that provides a $500 per child per month benefit regardless of parental income, both of which finance benefits paid with a progressive income tax. Relative to the universalist program, the targeted residualist program can be thought of as being partially financed by an income tax (for the benefits paid out), and partially financed by a means-testing tax, which covers the difference between what would be spent for the universalist program and the targeted residualist program.[27] The means-testing tax, however, can only be "paid" by people otherwise eligible for the program (here, people with children) but whose income is too high to receive the full benefit. Thus, the base for the means-testing tax (parents whose income is greater than the threshold for full benefits) is narrower than the base for an income tax (anyone with earned income). This means that the implicit tax rate is higher than would be needed to raise the same revenue if applied to a broader base. For this reason, although any tax incidence achieved through means testing and phaseouts can be achieved through explicit taxation, the converse is not true.[28]

A third economic problem with residualist targeting is that the total means-testing tax that can be "paid" is capped at the maximum benefit amount.[25] For example, since the maximum benefit is $500 per child per month, the most a person with one child can pay in implicit tax is $500, regardless of income. This means that the tax rate is regressive, on the relative scale, in that those with higher incomes pay a lower percentage of their income in means-testing tax than those with midrange incomes.

Consider three individuals, each with one child, and monthly incomes of

$1,000, $4,000, and $8,000. Using the same example of a child benefit as above, and ignoring other taxes, the first person has an effective average tax rate (the tax rate over their entire income) of 25 percent for the child benefit program (25% on their $1,000 of income). The second person's rate is 12.5 percent (25% of their first $2,000 in income, and then 0% on the next $2,000, for a tax "bill" of $500 on $4,000 of income). The third person's rate is 6.25 percent (25% of their first $2,000 in income, and then 0% on the next $6,000, for a tax "bill" of $500 on $8,000 of income). For incomes above the threshold at which no benefit is received in targeted residualist programs, the effective *marginal* tax rate goes to 0, and the contribution of the forgone benefit to the effective *average* tax rate is declining. Thus, those with midrange incomes (where benefits are phased out) could face a higher effective average tax rate than those with higher incomes (above the phaseout).* Although regressivity is not inherently bad, the regressivity, on the relative scale, common with targeted residualist programs should at least be recognized. Further, these features can contribute to those with midrange incomes feeling like the state is not treating them fairly—taxing them heavily for the benefit of those less well-off, while those with greater incomes get off lightly.

A fourth economic problem with targeted residualist programs relates to the amount of benefits they distribute—their distributive budget. The net income of those with lower income depends on the absolute amount transferred. This amount is the product of the percentage of the distributive budget transferred to a given person (related to targeting) and the absolute amount of the distributive budget. The size of this distributive budget is not fixed—it is set through political processes.[29] Because residualist approaches inherently single out a portion of the population to be helped by everyone else, they may be less effective in marshalling political support for large distributive budgets than programs that benefit more people. As Rothstein notes, when transfers are presented as an issue of taking from the rich to give to the poor, the rich are unlikely to part with large sums.[2] Empirically, there is substantial support for the idea that universalism can transfer greater absolute amounts of resources to those with lower incomes than targeted residualist approaches. In a classic cross-country comparison study, sociologist Walter Korpi and political scientist Joakim Palme discussed what

---

*Depending on what other taxes are assessed.

they called the "paradox of redistribution."[29] They found strong evidence that more universalist states had larger distributive budgets, and ultimately better outcomes for the less well-off, than residualist states. This spawned a large body of follow-up research, which has substantiated the finding that universalist tax-and-transfer regimes produce better outcomes than residualist states that target at the level of individual programs.[17,19,30,31]

Residualist Targeting Does Not "Save Money"

Proponents argue that targeted residualist programs "save money" because they "cost less" than a similar universalist program for which more people would be eligible and benefits would not be scaled. In other words, residualist targeting directs scarce resources to where they can do the most good.

The intuition seems clear. With a given amount of tax payments to distribute, the per-person amount you distribute will be larger if you only distribute to a subset of the population (e.g., those with low factor income), rather than the entire population. However, as discussed above, this targeted residualist structure adds an additional, implicit, tax that the universalist program does not have. The trick is that national accounting rules, used to formally track state income and outlays ("fiscal costs"), do not count the implicit tax. If they did, it would be clear that targeted residualist programs can offer larger benefits to those less well-off than similar universalist programs only by financing them with additional (implicit) taxes. Thus, the fiscal "superiority" of targeted residualist programs stems only from accounting rules, not economic substance.

Table 10.2 illustrates how accounting rules create illusory savings for means testing. In this example, imagine a population of 1,000 people; 200 of them earn $0 factor income, and 800 of them earn $100,000. In scenario A, a targeted residualist benefit offers $10,000 to those with no factor income and $0 to those with factor income. To finance this benefit, an explicit tax of 2.5 percent is levied on those earning factor income. The net income of those without factor income is now $10,000 per person and the net income of those with factor income is now $97,500 per person. In scenario B, a universal benefit of $10,000 is offered to everyone. To finance this, a tax of 12.5 percent is levied on those with factor income. As a result, the net income of those without factor income is now $10,000 per person and the net

Table 10.2. The illusory savings of residualist targeting

Scenario A: Targeted residualist. Total "on the books" spending (fiscal cost) = $2,000,000

Number	Factor income (in $)	Benefit per person (in $)	Total benefit paid (in $)	Explicit tax collected (in $)	Implicit tax collected (in $)	Explicit tax rate	Implicit tax rate	Effective tax rate	Net income
200	0	10,000	2,000,000	0	0	0	0	0	10,000
800	100,000	0	0	2,000,000	8,000,000	0.025	0.1	0.125	97,500

Scenario B: Universal. Total "on the books" spending (fiscal cost) = $10,000,000

Number	Factor income (in $)	Benefit per person (in $)	Total benefit paid (in $)	Explicit tax collected (in $)	Implicit tax collected (in $)	Explicit tax rate	Implicit tax rate	Effective tax rate	Net income
200	0	10,000	2,000,000	0	0	0	0	0	10,000
800	100,000	10,000	8,000,000	10,000,000	0	0.125	0	0.125	97,500

income of those with factor income is now $97,500 per person. This is exactly the same as scenario A, despite the different benefit structure and tax rate. How did this happen?

In targeted residualist scenario A, the explicit tax was 2.5 percent. But the people who earned $100,000 in factor income also implicitly "paid" $10,000 in taxes, through their forgone benefit. Combining that with the $2,500 they paid in explicit taxes (.025 × $100,000), they "paid" $12,500 in combined implicit and explicit taxes, for an effective tax rate of 12.5 percent on the $100,000 in factor income that they earned ($12,500 / $100,000). Thus, although the spending that appears on the state budget (fiscal costs) is lower for the means-tested program, as is the explicit tax rate needed to finance it, the economic situations of all parties are identical. The "savings" are just an accounting sleight of hand.*

Illusory Savings, Real Costs

If everyone's economic situation is the same, is the targeted residualist program preferable for other reasons, such as efficiency or macroeconomic costs?** Some would argue yes, because the fiscal costs are typically financed by taxes. Those taxes, through substitution effects, could lead people taxed to work less than they otherwise would. This forgone production creates a macroeconomic cost ("deadweight loss"). Therefore, if a targeted program can achieve the same outcomes with lower fiscal costs, it would be more efficient. In the famous analogy of economist Arthur Okun, attempt-

---

* With targeted residualist programs, everyone who receives less than the full benefit (including no benefit) makes an implicit tax payment that offsets the amount they do not receive. The implicit average tax rate is equivalent to the amount they do not receive divided by their factor income (or whatever base of income or assets is used to adjust benefit levels). In this example, since the base used was factor income and everyone with factor income had the same factor income, the implicit tax rate in scenario A was the same for everyone with factor income: 10 percent ($10,000 in foregone benefits over $100,000 in factor income). In reality, the implicit average tax rate could vary by factor income (or other base). Because the amount of the tax payment is capped at the maximum benefit, this rate will decline as factor income (or other base) increases. For example, an individual with a factor income of $200,000 in scenario A would have had an implicit average tax rate of 5 percent.

** Two other relevant points against this argument are that, first, tradeoffs between the right and the good are not acceptable, and so macroeconomic costs needed to achieve normatively required objectives are not necessarily a concern. Second, given currently low rates, greater income taxation is not likely to have meaningful macroeconomic costs in the United States right now.[32-34]

ing to distribute income through tax-and-transfer programs is like carrying water in a leaky bucket—some money leaks away before it can be transferred.[35]

What this argument neglects, however, is that the difference in fiscal cost between the targeted residualist benefit and the universalist benefit is financed by an implicit tax—as people earn more, their benefit declines, just as if it were taxed away. The implicit tax has its own macroeconomic costs that should be considered. First, some evidence suggests that the work disincentives from benefit phaseouts may be even greater than those from explicit taxation.[36] Second, labor supply is typically more elastic for those with midrange incomes than higher incomes (that is, that those with midrange incomes reduce labor supply to a greater extent, in response to greater marginal tax rates, than those with higher incomes).[37] This means that the macroeconomic costs of raising the same amount of revenue through a means-testing tax, which more heavily affects middle-income individuals relative to a progressive income tax, are likely greater. Third, as noted above, the implicit tax falls on a narrow base and thus requires a higher tax rate than an explicit tax on a larger base. This is also likely to increase the macroeconomic costs of the targeted residualist program relative to a universalist regime.[24] Finally, as noted above, the administrative costs of targeted residualist programs are typically higher than universalist ones, which reduces, for a given amount of funds, the amount available for transfers. So overall, not only are the supposed cost savings of the targeted residualist program illusory, the illusory savings themselves have a cost—meaning that a residualist program typically costs more, in real terms, than a similar universalist program.

Overall, it is generally not true that targeted residualist programs are more efficient than universalist regimes. As always, there may be reasons aside from efficiency to choose a targeted residualist program (e.g., perhaps a targeted residualist program can garner more political support than a universalist one), but it is generally a mistake to argue for targeting on efficiency grounds.

Targeting and the Public Cost Fallacy

There is another sense in which targeted residualist programs do not save money, relative to universalist regimes, in real resources terms. This relates to the public cost fallacy, in which only public spending used to guarantee essential capabilities is counted, instead of counting both public and private spending used to guarantee essential capabilities. One argument for residualist targeting is that those with lower incomes have no alternative resources without a state transfer, and so would forgo spending for a particular capability, whereas better-off individuals would still have the capability without the transfer.

For example, say essential health care costs $5,000, and there is a program to offer a universalist $3,000 health care benefit. Perhaps a person with lower factor income, in the absence of the program, could only spend $2,000. In that case, the health care benefit of $3,000 will have gone to someone who "really needs it," in the sense that they would have forgone needed care without the transfer. In contrast, say that a well-off person would be able to spend $5,000 in the absence of a state transfer. With a $3,000 universalist health care benefit, a well-off person would spend $3,000 from the benefit plus $2,000 of factor income, for a total of $5,000. Now say that the universalist benefit were changed to a targeted residualist one, such that the lower income individual still received a $3,000 benefit but the well-off individual no longer did. In this case, both will still obtain essential health care—the lower income individual through the benefit, and the well-off individual by drawing on other funds. Therefore, the argument goes, the means test has saved $3,000 in fiscal costs.

But in real resources terms, the means test saved nothing. It simply changed the source of the funds—from transfer income to factor income. Thus, the difference in fiscal costs between a targeted residualist benefit and a universal one is just a shift in real costs from those who would have financed the universalist benefit onto those who do not receive the residualist benefit (i.e., those who pay more in implicit tax than they would have paid in explicit tax in a universalist regime).[24]

Residualist Targeting and Distributional Conflict

The above example helps make clear how the choice between residualism and universalism can be seen as a distributional issue, but perhaps not in the way it first appears. On the benefits side, it might seem like the distributional conflict is between those with lower income who would receive benefits under either program and those with middle incomes who would receive benefits under universalist but not targeted residualist programs. But looking at the entire tax-and-transfer system clarifies that the distributional conflict is between those with middle incomes and those with higher incomes. Partially financing programs with a residualist means-testing tax implies that relatively more of the burden of program financing is borne by those with middle incomes, compared with financing the program entirely though progressive income taxation. The "savings" from benefits clawed back represent distribution from those with middle incomes to those with higher incomes. In contrast, universalist distributive institutions are arranged so that those with higher incomes bear relatively more of the financing burden. Therefore, those with middle incomes might be net beneficiaries under universalism but not under residualism. Arguments for residualist targeting can thus be seen as a form of misdirection, meant to obfuscate the fact that financing universalist programs via explicit progressive income taxation would likely be advantageous for those with middle incomes, relative to the implicit taxes that finance targeted residualist programs.

Universalist Targeting

The key to understanding pro-poor targeting under universalism is to recognize that the targeting occurs at the level of the regime, that is, when considering the entire tax-and-transfer system—not at the level of an individual policy or program. This administrative mechanism offers both better outcomes and administrative, economic, and political advantages.

Universalist targeting is accomplished by providing transfer income relatively equally, in absolute terms, across factor income strata (sometimes even increasing as factor income increases owing to earnings-related benefits), while also collecting greater absolute amounts of taxes from strata with higher factor income. Such a regime can, on net, offer greater benefit to those with lower factor incomes, even if individual policies or programs do not.

To illustrate, consider an example proposed by Rothstein (table 10.3).[2] There are 10 people, who each remit 45 percent of their factor income in taxes, and receive an equal transfer—one-tenth of the total revenue raised. This transfer is not only completely untargeted, but it is also financed by a proportional tax. Despite this, in absolute terms, the net income of the least well-off person is $30,250, from a factor income of $10,000. In relative terms, the ratio of incomes between the top and bottom decile, one measure of income inequality, declines from 10 ($100,000 / $10,000) to 2.6 ($79,750 / $30,250).

Table 10.3. Illustration of untargeted distribution

Person	Factor income ($)	Tax rate (%)	Tax payment ($)	Transfer ($)	Net income ($)
1	10,000	45.00	4,500	24,750	30,250
2	20,000	45.00	9,000	24,750	35,750
3	30,000	45.00	13,500	24,750	41,250
4	40,000	45.00	18,000	24,750	46,750
5	50,000	45.00	22,500	24,750	52,250
6	60,000	45.00	27,000	24,750	57,750
7	70,000	45.00	31,500	24,750	63,250
8	80,000	45.00	36,000	24,750	68,750
9	90,000	45.00	40,500	24,750	74,250
10	100,000	45.00	45,000	24,750	79,750

Earnings-Related Benefits

Paradoxically, universalist regimes can be pro-poor targeted in effect even when individual programs within them seem to be pro-rich targeted. This is relevant when considering benefits that increase with earnings. Why have earnings-related benefits? One role of the welfare state is consumption smoothing—the piggy bank function.[1] For example, pensions and unemployment insurance help people preserve their standard of living after retirement or unexpected job loss. If such programs were not earnings related, they would not do this for well-off individuals. This would risk creating a two-tiered system where those who are less well-off rely on state benefits, but those who are better off seek out supplementary benefits from the private sector. A two-tiered system could weaken political support for the state program, as the well-off would have little to gain from maintaining it. Further, the well-off could come to view themselves as supporting a system they do not benefit from. This would undermine norms of reciprocity and could be counterproductive to the goals of the egalitarian state. Overall, the goal of the egalitarian state is not to produce strict income equality—it is to produce equality of social standing. Depending on the circumstances, policies that result in less equal net income distributions may be justifiable in pursuit of that goal.

Programs with earnings-related benefits to retain support from those with higher factor income can still differentially benefit those with lower factor incomes, however. One approach is to structure programs with a relatively large basic benefit available for everyone (which would replace a greater percentage of factor income for those with lower factor income), supplemented with an earnings-related component that has an upper cap but is still sufficient to stave off the development of private alternatives. For example, imagine an unemployment insurance benefit that provides a $500 per week minimum benefit, with an earnings-related component that caps at $1,000. A person who previously earned $500 per week and loses their job would receive $500 (replacing 100% their income), while a person who previously earned $1,250 per week would receive $1,000 (replacing 80% of their income)—likely still enough for consumption smoothing over a short period of time.

Given the efficiency gains social insurance makes possible, such a structure could still be a good deal for those who are well-off—they could receive greater benefits for a given contribution (tax payment or premium) than private alternatives.[1] Assuming the basic benefit is sufficient to guarantee needed capabilities, and the earnings-related component does not undermine the relationship of equality, such a policy is not normatively objectionable. If a deviation from strict income equality was normatively justifiable in the first place (i.e., some individuals, justifiably, earn more than others), then follow-on programs that incorporate this difference in income, like earnings-related benefits, should not be objectionable either.

Earnings-related benefits also help provide work incentives,* which is important as everyone in society can benefit from greater productivity, if the proceeds are distributed justly. Finally, earnings-related benefits may increase a policy's political support, which could in turn increase the distributive budget available, benefiting those with lower factor income.

Despite their usefulness, earnings-related benefits can be overdone. Balancing basic and earnings-related components of benefits can be difficult and result in overdistribution to well-off individuals if done wrong. This can undermine the normative goals of the program.[17,39] Earnings-related components also add administrative complexity.

Finally, earnings-related components make more sense in some instances than others. For example, earnings-related pensions can be justified on the basis of consumption smoothing. However, earnings-related health care ben-

---

*Economic theory suggests that the substitution effects of an earnings-related benefit are analogous to those of a tax cut, although whether that effect is meaningful in practice likely varies across situations.[38]

efits do not make sense, as well-off individuals do not need a different standard of health care than those who are less well-off.

Targeting as Creating Capabilities

Another way universalist programs can be considered targeted is by differentially creating capabilities for less well-off individuals. For instance, without public provision, less well-off individuals may forgo education or health care, while well-off individuals simply purchase education and health care on the market (they may be "inframarginal" consumers). Universalist education and health care programs would then have the effect of preferentially benefiting less well-off individuals. Similarly, minimum wage laws affect both those who are single parents trying to support their children, and teenagers from wealthy households working summer jobs for pocket money. Such laws may not seem targeted (there may even be more well-off teenagers working minimum wage jobs), but in their absence the capabilities of the single parent might be reduced, while those of the teenagers might be unaffected. Thus, such a law works to the disproportionate advantage of less well-off individuals.

Proportionate Universalism

Universalist programs can be structured as a basic benefit with an additional means-tested component that phases out. This has been called "targeting within universalism" by sociologist Theda Skocpol[40] or "proportionate universalism" by social epidemiologist Michael Marmot,[41] and it has attracted considerable interest.[17,29,31] As the means-tested component phases out, the total benefit equals the basic benefit alone. This differs from residualist programs where an individual receives no benefit above the means-test threshold. The universalist aspects of this approach may help with political support and avoiding stigma (everyone uses the program in some way). However, it has many of the same disadvantages, in terms of administrative complexity and effective marginal tax rates, as residualist approaches. Further, it will always be possible to create, through the tax-and-transfer system, a universalist program that has the same effect without needing to target at the program level, by simply adjusting the basic benefit level and system of finance. Thus, I see no particular advantage for this approach, although it may not be objectionable when politically advantageous.

Targeting and the Prevention Paradox

Targeting may sometimes be undesirable. One example of this relates to what epidemiologist Geoffrey Rose called the "prevention paradox."[42] When trying to prevent a bad outcome, it would seem sensible to focus on individuals at highest risk for that outcome. But if those individuals are a relatively small proportion of the total population at risk, such a program may have less overall impact than a more inclusive strategy that affects more people. For example, table 10.4 depicts groups at high, medium, and low risk of death from an income-related health condition. There are three intervention scenarios: one targeted to high-risk individuals, one targeted to high- and medium-risk individuals, and one untargeted. The intervention for high-risk individuals reduces deaths very effectively but is costly. The interventions that serve more people are less expensive per person, but they are less effective. The total cost of all three interventions is the same. The overall effect, in terms of deaths averted, is largest for the least targeted intervention, even though it is least effective per person.

This is a simplistic example, and variation in factors like the actual risk distribution, the risk reduction achievable with various interventions, and their cost could yield different conclusions. Further, there may be other normative or political considerations—scenario C saw fewer deaths averted among high-risk individuals than scenario A. Nevertheless, this example illustrates problems that can result from emphasizing targeting rather than outcomes. Ratcheting down eligibility until only the highest risk individuals are included will make an intervention more targeted, but it is ultimately a race to the bottom that may not help achieve the goals of social democracy.[12]

Final Points on Targeting

There is an inherent interrelationship between factor income policy and transfer income policy in that one role of transfer income policy is to manage the factor income distribution that factor income policy creates. In other words, different transfer income policy is needed when factor income policy creates relatively equal, compared with unequal, distributions of factor income. These issues are discussed in more detail in chapters 11–13. Further, as with progressivity in taxation, targeting in transfer income policy will be less relevant the more equally distributed factor income in a society is.

In sum, my view of the empirical evidence in aggregate is that universal-

Table 10.4. Illustration of the prevention paradox

			Scenario A: Most targeted			
Category	Risk	Size of population	Status quo deaths	Intervention relative risk reduction	Deaths under intervention	Deaths averted
High	0.4	1,000	400	0.50	200	200
Medium	0.2	4,000	800	0.00	800	0
Low	0.1	5,000	500	0.00	500	0
Entire population	0.17	10,000	1,700	0.12	1,500	200
			Scenario B: Somewhat targeted			
Category	Risk	Size of population	Status quo deaths	Intervention relative risk reduction	Deaths under intervention	Deaths averted
High	0.4	1,000	400	0.25	300	100
Medium	0.2	4,000	800	0.25	600	200
Low	0.1	5,000	500	0.00	500	0
Entire population	0.17	10,000	1,700	0.18	1,400	300
			Scenario C: Least targeted			
Category	Risk	Size of population	Status quo deaths	Intervention relative risk reduction	Deaths under intervention	Deaths averted
High	0.4	1,000	400	0.20	320	80
Medium	0.2	4,000	800	0.20	640	160
Low	0.1	5,000	500	0.20	400	100
Entire population	0.17	10,000	1,700	0.20	1,360	340

ist regimes have been more successful in improving the situation of those less well-off than targeted residualist programs.[17,29,31] Thus, both normatively and technically, the better way to implement egalitarian state policies is through universalist regimes with categorical eligibility, transfers that are relatively equal, in absolute terms (supplemented by earnings-related benefits where necessary), and a tax system that collects more, in absolute terms, from those with greater factor incomes.[43]

The Politics of Universalism

Once established, universalist policies are rarely removed by democratic means.[2,5,29,44] This path dependence suggests that universalism offers political stability. But what are the political dynamics involved? Why might people support, or oppose, a universalist welfare state?

To answer this question, the concepts of legitimacy and competence discussed above are helpful. The theory of contingent consent[6] helps make sense of policy legitimacy—policies are likely to be seen as legitimate when they are seen as just, their burdens are shared, and they are procedurally fair. But legitimacy must be constantly tended. Further, the state must be seen as competent—people must expect that it can achieve its goals. In this section, I highlight aspects of universalism that facilitate these political considerations.

Coalitions for Universalist Policy

A particular policy or program must be justified normatively. As discussed in chapter 7, both universalist and residualist welfare states may have justifiable goals, but the methods of universalism, for example, framing policies as rights of citizenship rather than charity, have strong normative arguments in their favor.[45]

Further, those a policy materially benefits may be more apt to view it as just out of self-interest and thus form a natural constituency for it. Because more people are eligible for universalist policies than similar residualist policies, the base of support is typically greater. Some have suggested that universalist policies may also increase solidarity across income stratra[29] (i.e., those with midrange factor incomes may become more attuned to issues that affect those with lower factor incomes and support policies that benefit others for that reason) or class, although other studies have contested this idea.[46-49] Such coalitions would further strengthen support for universalism. But cross-class coalitions are not necessary—a policy that benefits many different individuals can be supported by those individuals for their own reasons. If political processes inherently court the group that "breaks even" (i.e., has tax liabilities equal to benefits received, or has net income equal to factor income), then increasing the factor income level at which one breaks even can broaden the base of support.*

Moreover, individuals know that their situation could change.[2] A person who presently does not break even might still support universalism because under residualism, if they become disabled or unemployed, they would have to reach destitution before receiving benefits—benefits that moreover would preserve little of their prior standard of living.

---

*This is related to the median voter model.

A historical example illustrates how moving away from universalism can undermine political support. In the 1960s, the United States deemphasized more universalist, New Deal–era policy, and emphasized more residualist, Great Society–era policy.[8] Referring to this change, economists James Buchanan and Marilyn Flowers wrote: "By a dramatic shift in the prevailing mythology, the willing taxpayer may become part of the taxpayer revolution. Whereas he may have previously considered himself to be receiving a flow of benefits as valuable at the margin as his dollar of tax, he may come to feel the flow of benefits has diminished below expectations."[50]

Shared Burdens

A second part of contingent consent is that policy burdens need to be shared fairly (even if not equally). As anyone who has done a group project remembers, others not pulling their weight corrodes morale. Universalism takes seriously the idea of shared burdens. For example, even those with lower income are not exempt from the payroll taxes used to fund Social Security pensions and Medicare in the United States—everyone contributes. Further, because universalist programs are more inclusive, those who contribute less comprise a relatively small proportion of users. Universalist programs are not *for* those in need per se. As Rothstein notes, sometimes "the best way to help the poor is not to talk about them."[2(p160)] In contrast, residualism undermines the idea of shared burdens. By creating policies only for "the poor," the clear implication is a separation between those who benefit from a policy and those burdened by it.

Procedural Fairness

The final aspect of contingent consent is procedural fairness. Because universalist programs are first-line approaches, with categorical eligibility criteria, they typically have intelligible rules and straightforward administrative procedures.[2] In contrast, the administrative needs of residualist programs frequently create complex rules and require a large bureaucracy, which can be alienating and impenetrable for citizens. Further, taking on more administrative tasks increases opportunities for administrative variation, which can make policies feel arbitrary and unfair, and increase the scope for discrimination. Thus, residualism makes perceptions of procedural fairness harder to maintain.

Competence

It is difficult to support a policy that is not administered compe-tently. Universalist principles facilitate competent administration. First, uni-versalism helps increase uptake of programs among those who are eligible by lowering administrative burdens. Categorical eligibility makes eligibility determination easier and can avoid the need for complicated certification, recertification, and eligibility monitoring.[2] Universalism also increases up-take by having the same program for everyone, which works against stigma. This helps even those who would be eligible for a similar residualist program.[2] For example, community eligibility for free school meals is a universalist approach in which all students at a particular school are eligible. The resid-ualist alternative is to make students prove low household income to receive free school meals. The stigma this creates worsens uptake—community el-igibility leads to greater program use even for those eligible under the resid-ualist approach.[51] Further, the simplicity of universalist programs tends to reduce administrative costs, which further enhances perceived competence.[2]

With residualist programs, more complicated eligibility rules makes suc-cessful administration harder, and increase administrative costs. Adminis-trative burdens are greater, which reduces uptake.[10] Thus, though a goal of residualist policies is to target benefits to the least well-off, the inherent administrative burdens of residualism often mean that the least well-off may not actually receive benefits. From a fundamental cause perspective, administrative burdens represent a pathway whereby the same factors a pro-gram seeks to remedy prevent the program from doing so.[52] Further, because residualist programs are more difficult to implement fairly and effectively, suboptimal results can undermine support for social policy in general. Even for those who may have been sympathetic to the policy goals in principle, constant reports of fraud, cheating, and inept administration can lead to thinking that nothing works.

A final political consideration relates to maintaining state services. Under universalism, there is little role for private duplication. When most people, including the well-off, use a public product, there is a powerful constituency who can advocate for high quality and responsiveness to consumer prefer-ences. However, if better-off individuals cannot use state services, the con-stituency to maintain high quality in public products may be less powerful.

Summary

Policies translate normative goals into material conditions. They should be normatively justified, technically sound, and designed for successful implementation under prevailing conditions.

Legitimacy and competence are key factors in successful policy implementation. Legitimacy is won by making a clear normative case for a given policy, designing it so that its burdens are shared, and administering it fairly. Competence is enhanced by design choices that realistically consider what a state can do. Sometimes policies that are more difficult to implement (e.g., tailored and/or interventionist approaches) are worthwhile, but the difficulty of implementation needs to be considered carefully. Often, a simple cash transfer is hard to beat.

Targeted residualist programs do not typically offer cost savings or efficiency gains over universalist alternatives. Further, a key finding in the body of work that examines the relationship between targeting and net income is that the size of the distributive budget trumps the degree of targeting.[17,29,31] A more targeted program does not necessarily help those in need if the amount of resources it has to distribute is small. Moreover, it seems to be very difficult, in practice, for targeted residualist programs to realize the budget necessary to achieve the outcomes that universalist programs can.

Universalist policies offer advantages over residualist policies regarding political support, legitimacy, and ease of administration. Nevertheless, policies that are universalist in design must also be universalist in practice. Programs must have an ethos of service and responsiveness to concerns of users, or support will erode. Further, discrimination and other forms of oppression can create barriers to receiving the full benefits of policies even if formal access is equal.

The state's duty of equal care cannot be fulfilled unless policy implementation succeeds. Paying attention to policy implementation in both design and practice is a vital part of achieving the goals of social democracy, and thus health equity.

Transfer Income Policy I

In-Kind Services

Ensuring individuals have consumption power for the products needed to guarantee the essential capabilities is one of the primary goals of the egalitarian state. Transfer income policy, which distributes both monetary and nonmonetary transfer income, is a key part of providing that power for all individuals, across the life course.[1,2]

Transfer income policy matters not only for those who are not receiving factor income but for those who are too. For those not receiving factor income (and recall that only around half of the US population at a given point in time receives factor income from paid labor[3,4]), transfer income policy reduces dependence on support from family members and guarantees essential capabilities for those without others to depend on. For those currently receiving factor income, transfer income policy affects worker bargaining power. When essential capabilities are guaranteed for everyone, workers have a stronger negotiating position, which helps ensure that workers' factor income is sufficient to guarantee the essential capabilities.[5] This is one example of how transfer income policy and factor income policy are complementary aspects of the egalitarian state. Further, transfer income policy helps equivalize living standards across households of varying composition. Without transfer income policy, two households with the same factor income, but with different numbers of individuals who do not receive factor income, would have different standards of living. Finally, as discussed in chapters 7, 8, and 10, there are good reasons, both normative and technical, for public provision of certain products for everyone.[6]

In this chapter and the next, I discuss some important considerations related to transfer income policy design. I do not seek to review comprehensively evidence for the effectiveness of any given policy instrument. Instead, I aim to highlight approaches that are normatively justified (or point out ones that are not). Further, when multiple approaches might be justified, I discuss relevant considerations for choosing between them. As always, it is important to remember that transfer income policy forms a part of an over-all tax-and-transfer system. I discuss the components separately for explica-tion, but in practice transfer income policy and public finance are best con-sidered together (e.g., the impact of a new transfer income program should be evaluated together with the impact of changes in the tax code that will finance it).

Goals of Transfer Income Policy

The fundamental goal of transfer income policy is to guarantee es-sential capabilities. This goal is fundamental in the sense that a transfer income policy regime, whatever its other merits, should be rejected if does not achieve this goal.

However, transfer income policy often has additional goals. One is con-sumption smoothing.[7] As discussed in chapter 7, the factor income one earns over a lifetime is distributed unequally: typically nonexistent in child-hood and older age, peaking in midlife, and perhaps punctuated by interrup-tions for sickness, unemployment, studies, and caregiving. However, people usually find maintaining a similar standard of living across those periods desirable—who wants their standard of living to fall during retirement? Transfer income policy can efficiently provide consumption smoothing.[7]

A second goal of transfer income policy is to prevent unjust concentra-tions of power resulting from extreme wealth. As discussed in chapter 7, al-though strict income equality is not necessarily the goal of social democracy, extreme income inequality has a corrosive effect on a system of social rela-tions, allowing some individuals to accumulate wealth and power that can undermine relational equality.[8,9] Factor income policy that leads to a more equal income "pre-distribution" (discussed in chapter 13) can address in-come inequality, but transfer income policy can as well. In practice, factor income policy and transfer income policy, along with civil and political rights, work together to ensure income is distributed justly.

Third, as discussed in chapter 8, public provision can supply many prod-ucts to individuals at lower real cost than market provision.[6,10] For example, while those in the paid labor force may be able to purchase health insurance on the private market, a public health insurer, or public production of health care, may be more efficient—allowing for similar health care at lower real cost. Thus, beyond its necessity for achieving normative goals, transfer income policy can contribute to achieving those goals efficiently.

Finally, principles of universalism argue for simplified administration and avoiding two-tiered, stratified, or segregated systems. These principles see application in transfer income policy that supplies products to all individuals for whom they are needed, rather than restricting eligibility to those without factor income.

Rational Transfer Income Policy

Because the fundamental goal of transfer income policy is to guarantee essential capabilities, rational transfer income policy starts with defining those capabilities. Chapter 4 gave examples, but ultimately these must be determined through a democratic process, within allowable normative constraints. Then, a society must decide how the essential capabilities are to be guaranteed.

Cash Benefits and In-Kind Services

In considering how to guarantee the essential capabilities, it can be helpful to distinguish two forms of transfer income policy: in-kind services and "cash benefits." With in-kind services, consumption power is transferred to individuals through administrative rules. In-kind services make available, under a public provision framework (e.g., with public finance through producer-side subsidies, or public production), products for which price mechanisms and/or production for profit do not work well. In-kind services are often free at point of service, or at least price exerts little influence on selecting a specific producer—product differentiation by price is usually not intended. Further, although there can be user fees meant to avoid overconsumption, user fees are not the primary method of finance.

For the products to be allocated under a market provision framework (chapter 8), consumption power requires purchasing power. Transfer income policy can provide this through policy instruments of general transfers and consumer-side subsidies.

I characterize both general transfers and consumer-side subsidies as cash benefits. A general transfer is an unrestricted transfer of purchasing power. Consumer-side subsidies are restricted transfers of purchasing power—they can only be used for a specific purpose. I still call consumer-side subsidies "cash benefits," even though they are not really cash, because such subsidies are meant to be used within a market provision framework, and they function analogously to cash. That is, with consumer-side subsidies, consumers are meant to trade off price, quantity, and quality, reflecting their preferences, under a budget constraint, just as they would with cash. The subsidy provided by the Supplemental Nutrition Assistance Program in the United States is an example.

To make clear the distinction between in-kind services and cash benefits (both consumer-side subsides and general transfers), consider the following. An in-kind service would be state provision of a university education without tuition or fees. A consumer-side subsidy would be a $10,000 tuition voucher that can be used at any accredited university, either public where it would cover the full cost, or private where it might only partially cover the cost, but it cannot be used for anything other than tuition. A general transfer would be state provision of $10,000 in cash upon graduating high school, which one might use to pay university tuition, or to start a business, or to invest in the stock market.

Two Aspects of Quality

One can distinguish two aspects of product quality, "essential quality" and "experiential quality" (I sometimes abbreviate these to "quality" and "experience"). Essential quality relates to how well consuming the product produces the intended effect of its consumption. Experiential quality relates to the experience of consuming the product. Consumers' ability to judge the essential quality and the experiential quality of the same product can differ. In particular, although consumers can typically judge experiential quality well for all products, the ability to judge essential quality varies across products. There are some products where consumers can judge essential quality well. For other products, however, judging quality requires expertise that few have, or it is simply difficult for everyone. To illustrate, a restaurant may have lousy service (experience) and serve good food (quality)—and a typical consumer can judge each aspect well. However, a doctor may provide care with a good bedside manner (experience), which a consumer can judge well, but make poor treatment recommendations (quality), and that may be much harder to judge. Products where essential quality is difficult to judge are sometimes called "credence goods."

As I will discuss later in this chapter, differing consumer ability to judge quality across product types turns out to be an important factor in transfer income policy design.

Public or Private Production of In-Kind Services

With publicly provided in-kind services, a common decision point is between public finance with private production (i.e., the state contracts for private production) and public finance with public production (i.e., the state produces the product itself). The general case for public finance with private production is that private producers may be more responsive to consumer preferences and could compete to drive down rents, possibly lowering the real resources spent on the product. The primary risks of private production are reduced quality owing to profit seeking and discrimination against consumers.

To recap the discussion from chapter 8 regarding these issues, responding to consumer preferences is more likely to produce better outcomes when consumer preferences for versions of a product vary substantially, when information to make an informed choice can be easily provided and understood, when consumers can readily judge all aspects of the product's quality, and when a poor-quality product is not very harmful.[6] If the state can establish effective competition between for-profit producers, private production may improve quality, consumer responsiveness, and productive efficiency.[6] But in some cases, the state cannot generate effective competition, and private production becomes a state-granted monopoly, with little to be gained over public production.[11] Moreover, particularly in fields with strong norms of altruism, empathy, caring, or peer recognition, production for profit may not be the best way to assure quality or spur quality improvement.[12]

When contracting, the state must be able to specify what it wants to be produced and have the capacity and willingness to monitor compliance with contract terms. Alternatively, if terms cannot be specified very completely such that quality can be monitored during production (or otherwise before consumption), quality must be monitored after consumption, either by the state or consumers (if that is possible). Without such monitoring, private producers are likely to reduce quality to increase profit.[11] This is a particular concern in situations that involve information imperfections, such as complex information, substantial uncertainty, or harms that manifest only in the long run.[6]

Multiple private producers will also have an inherently smaller consumer base and may have to forgo economies of scale that a single public producer could achieve.

Finally, the state must be able to ensure that private producers serve all potential consumers on fair terms. Private producers may have incentives to cherry-pick (disproportionately serve those thought to be more desirable consumers), which could undermine access for some, facilitate oppression, violate the state's duty of equal care, and create two-tiered systems.[11]

Even when some private production is desirable,* it can be advantageous to maintain a public producer as a "public option," which can pressure private producers to maintain quality and control prices, especially when monitoring quality is difficult.[13]

Cash Benefits and Market Provision

For products that will be allocated under market provision, cash benefits provide purchasing power to help ensure that consumers are substantively free to choose. Further, they help product choices better reflect preference intensity, rather than ability to pay.

Cash benefits are often used alongside product regulation to set a quality floor. For example, food safety or building codes can set a minimum standard for food and housing quality, and beyond that individuals can choose budget or luxury products, allocating their resources as they prefer.

Determining the value of cash benefits to provide is complicated. Conceptually, one can think of the amount needed as that required to purchase all products necessary to guarantee the essential capabilities, minus the value of those products provided as in-kind services. In discussing concepts about cash benefit policy, I will assume that an amount has been determined through a democratic process and refer to "income sufficient for essential capabilities." This is shorthand for "monetary income sufficient to buy on the market those products needed to guarantee the essential capabilities that a society has decided should be supplied through market provision."

Thinking about a sufficient cash benefit level invites the question—sufficient for whom? An important insight of the capabilities approach dis-

---

* Even though a uniform, high-quality version of a necessary product should be available to everyone, private finance and production of alternate versions (e.g., private health care separate from a state system) may still be normatively justifiable (e.g., based on principles of state neutrality).

cussed in chapters 3 and 4 is that individuals vary in their ability to convert income into capabilities.[14,15] Thus, determining a broadly applicable benefit level is difficult, and I do not attempt to do so here. Instead, I assume that an amount appropriate for most individuals can be determined, which will define a "basic benefit."* However, transfer income policy must supplement the basic benefit for individuals who require more resources than typical to have the same capabilities. For example, people who cannot prepare food for themselves could require more resources to have similar nutritional capabilities, relative to people who can prepare food for themselves. In the discussion below, I will illustrate how personal care policy could be used to supplement a basic benefit by providing additional resources (either as cash or in-kind services). Analogous approaches could be used in other situations that require additional resources to achieve the same capabilities.**

Throughout the discussion of transfer income policy, I assume policy implementation along universalist principles, as discussed in chapters 7 and 10.

In-Kind Services

In this section, I discuss three products with strong cases for public provision as in-kind services: basic education, health care, and personal care. All should be publicly financed, and I discuss considerations about public versus private production. These products cannot be transferred or resold, and they are generally only useful when needed, which lessens concerns about overconsumption. However, if overconsumption is a concern, user fees are sometimes useful, as long as such user fees are considered when setting cash benefit levels—so that consumption choices truly reflect preferences rather than ability to pay.

Basic Education

Basic education helps prepare children to be adult members of society. In the United States, basic education typically corresponds to kindergarten through 12th grade (primary and secondary school), but it could include prekindergarten educational programs, and is often compulsory, at

---

* In practice, the level of basic benefit may be lower for children than adults, given household economies of scale and that children are not in single-person households.

** Though it is conceptually possible that some individuals may require less than the basic benefit to guarantee particular capabilities, this is likely to be ignored in practice, so the primary practical concern will be adding resources.

least until later grades.* In basic education policy, the distinction between quality of education (e.g., the outcomes produced) and the experience of education (e.g., parent and child preferences about education delivery) is important.

There is a strong case for public finance of basic education, as children cannot make consumption decisions for themselves. Further, not only does trading off price for quality not make sense for basic education that everyone should have, but trading off the quality of a child's education based on a parent's choice about price would invite substantive concerns about fair equality of opportunity. Moreover, given positive externalities from social benefits that basic education provides, there would likely be underinvestment in the absence of public finance.

There is also a strong case for public production of basic education. Private production presents major issues around selection of students, which can easily lead to two-tiered systems. Additionally, there are important incomplete contracting issues. Available quality metrics, like standardized test scores, may only be loosely correlated with the true goals of education.[6,16] Combined with issues related to selection of students into schools, this can make it difficult to differentiate between the provision of better quality education from the selection of students more likely to score highly. For-profit production introduces risk of reduced quality in search of profits, which can have irreversible harms and be hard to detect, especially in the short term, because quality is difficult to judge. On a small scale, some private producers can produce better outcomes than some public producers, just as some public producers can produce better outcomes than other public producers. This is especially true when private production is introduced specifically owing to performance problems of particular public producers. But whether a system of private production can create better educational outcomes than a system of public production is unclear. Indeed, there is important evidence that switching, at scale, from public to private producers has important harms.[17] Quality-improving competition among producers of basic education is difficult to establish, and it is not clear that for-profit production is the best way to drive quality improvement in education.[17] The field of education has deeply held norms of professionalism and

---

*I discuss advanced or tertiary education, such as college or vocational training, in chapter 12.

caring, and harnessing those values may be better ways to improve quality than financial incentives.

Taken together, these considerations argue for public finance and production of education. Of course, there should be formal mechanisms to incorporate preferences of parents and students into basic education. These include procedures to give voice (e.g., school boards and parent associations) and exit power (e.g., the ability to change schools). In practice, public production of basic education has been a successful model worldwide.

Regardless of public versus private production, the principal goal of basic education is to help children to have substantive freedom in their adult lives. This is an integral part of the state meeting its obligation to provide fair equality of opportunity. Moreover, individuals must develop their capacity for moral reasoning, so society can sustain democratic and egalitarian government. This aspect of education can be considered *civics*.

Because a goal of basic education is to provide a consistent and high level of quality for all children, financing mechanisms should pool sources of funds broadly. Though there may be local variation in aspects of student experience, there should not be local variation in quality. Basic education finance that relies too heavily on local mechanisms, such as district-level property taxes, risks such variation and should be avoided.

Health Care

As discussed in chapters 5 and 6, three central aspects of health care policy relate to access, quality, and equity.* Health care is a vast topic, and in this chapter on transfer income I focus on issues related to access—in particular issues of health care finance and production.** Though much more than health care determines health, health care certainly is important for health and health-related capabilities. As such, ensuring the capability to receive needed health care ("access") is an essential task of the egalitarian state.

Health care access could be allocated under market provision, with the state providing general transfers or subsidies to ensure everyone can purchase it. However, the price mechanism does not function well for health

---

* In the sense that care should not be influenced by racism or other inegalitarian ideologies, although it should vary by clinical situation and adapt to the social circumstances individuals are in.

** One topic I do not discuss is public health services, which, as public goods, typically command relatively broad agreement on the necessity of public finance and production.

care, which makes market provision unappealing on technical grounds. A key reason the price mechanism does not function is that health care quality is very difficult to judge. As above, I distinguish between quality, the clinical outcomes produced by health care, and experience, like responsiveness to consumer preferences in the delivery of health care.

Those consuming health care can judge experience well. When quality and experience are correlated, this can help with judging quality. Moreover, quality and experience are sometimes interdependent. For example, a long wait to access care for time-sensitive conditions is both a quality and an experience issue. However, a substantial body of evidence suggests that distinguishing high-quality from low-quality care is in general difficult, and that consumers respond to higher prices by reducing consumption of both high- and low-quality health care.[18-27]

Rational choice as a consumer requires both knowledge of prices and the ability to judge quality.[6] Without both, individuals cannot make rational trade-offs between price and quality.[6] As an example, even though an individual might know that going to ophthalmologist 1 for cataract surgery will cost less than ophthalmologist 2, understanding the implications of that choice, in terms of surgical outcomes, is difficult. How much worse could the cataract surgery outcome be to make a $500 difference in cost worthwhile? How likely is the outcome to be that much worse?

Further, in many cases shopping around is not possible, as people may not know when they will need care (e.g., in emergency situations), what care they need (e.g., the appropriate cancer treatment regimen may be unknown at the time of diagnosis), or for how long they will need it. Finally, even if all of this were solvable, it is not clear that having budget versus luxury options for issues of care quality (as opposed to experience) is normatively defensible.

Since the price mechanism does not function, health care requires public provision, and in particular public finance.* Public finance helps ensure that

---

*Though the US health care system is often said to be primarily private, virtually all US health care is publicly financed, at least partially. Public finance occurs for public insurers like Medicare, Medicaid, or Tricare; public producers like the Veterans Affairs health care system and the Indian Health Service; and through subsidies—either in the form of tax expenditures for employer-sponsored health insurance (e.g., exclusion from the income tax base), or made pursuant to the Affordable Care Act for insurance purchased on health insurance exchanges.

health care is allocated by clinical need and not ability to pay. The policy choice, then, is between public and private production. In health care, public production typically means public ownership of hospitals and clinics, with physicians, nurses, and other health care workers as state employees. The UK National Health Service uses this approach. Private production could involve either private facility ownership and employment of personnel involved in producing care, with the state handling administrative oversight of payments and quality monitoring (e.g., traditional Medicare in the United States), or there could be additional entities (i.e., private health insurers) to which the state delegates some administrative functions (e.g., Medicare Advantage in the United States). Either public or private production can be normatively acceptable, and both approaches are in use across the world. Each approach has its own benefits and drawbacks. In discussing these options, I want to be clear that universal access is a fundamental requirement, and so versions of these approaches that do not guarantee universal access are not worth discussing.

There are four interrelated dimensions any health care system with universal access must optimize over: quality, experience, utilization, and spending.

The need to optimize over these dimensions plus structural constraints inherent to either public or private production lead to predictable issues. As quality is foundational, neither approach typically intends to reduce quality, so explicit trade-offs usually occur on other dimensions. However, unintended reductions in quality can occur. Overall, the combination of quality, utilization (e.g., volume, range of services available, versions of care that are more versus less expensive to produce), and experience (e.g., waiting times, locations, operating hours) tends to trade off with spending. Greater quality, more utilization, and better experience each typically require greater spending. Lower spending often means lower levels of at least one of those other dimensions of health care.

PUBLIC PRODUCTION

Perhaps the primary strength of public production is cost containment. Total spending is typically controlled through global budgets, set politically. Public producers benefit from economies of scale and monopsony power. They also do not have a profit motive for greater than indicated utilization, or for prices to contain rents. With global budgets, public production can avoid "third-party payor" problems, which occur when neither the producer nor consumer, who together determine utilization, directly face a budget constraint. Further, with public production there is no motive to increase profits by reducing quality.

However, public production also has disadvantages. In the absence of competition, consumer experience could suffer, especially if consumers do not have exit and voice power.[11] Despite this theoretical possibility, however, the finding that introducing "internal markets" in some public production systems did not produce better experience suggests that producer competition may not be of primary importance for experience.[28] Similarly, some argue that lack of profit motive will lead to lower quality of care. However, there is little evidence to support this, as quality for adequately funded public producers is typically comparable or superior to that of private producers.[29-33]

More concerning, however, is the potential for underfunding. If budgets are set too low, public producers typically try to maintain quality by reducing elective utilization and economizing aspects of health care that contribute to consumer experience, which can lead to longer waits for nonurgent care, a lower variety of available services, and less responsive staff. In these cases, experience will suffer. With extreme underfunding, quality can suffer as well.

The price mechanism relates the cost incurred by the purchaser to the quality and quantity of the product purchased. In the absence of a functioning price mechanism, there must be alternative mechanisms to determine how much will be paid for a given unit of health care production ("rate setting"), monitor quality, and manage utilization. In systems with public production, those tasks are usually retained by the entity that organizes production. Rate setting effectively occurs administratively, in the context of global budgeting, and rates likely reflect actual production costs. Quality monitoring also typically occurs internally, and there is no profit motive to reduce quality. Both financial and nonfinancial (e.g., norms of caring and professionalism) means of managerial oversight and quality assurance can be harnessed to maintain health care quality.[34-38] Finally, utilization management tends to occur through standardization (e.g., guidelines, care pathways, and formularies) from which little deviation is permitted. This has both advantages (e.g., procedural fairness and cost containment) and disadvantages (e.g., less scope for individualization of care).

PRIVATE PRODUCTION

The potential advantages of a system with public finance and private production principally relate to experience. Individuals can judge well their experience of health care delivery, such as waiting times, being treated courteously and with respect, having convenient hours and locations, and responding to after-hours concerns. Returning to the ophthalmologist example above, a person could readily judge whether they prefer the hours, location, or bedside manner of one ophthalmologist to another. Thus, at least theoretically, a system in which private producers compete over potential consumers could do well on the dimension of experience by responding to consumer preferences.

The primary disadvantages of public finance and private production relate to cost containment. If little emphasis is placed on cost containment (e.g., in a fee-for-service system), then third-party payor problems will exert continuous upward pressure on spending, as neither producers nor consumers face a budget constraint. Producers may also have financial incentives to oversupply care, and/or recommended unnecessary but more profitable forms of care.

However, attempts to contain costs can also create problems in these systems. Capitation and risk contracting bring an incentive for private producers to increase profits by providing less or less expensive care. It can be difficult to detect whether this is also lower quality care, as "quality metrics" typically used for this purpose may reflect preferential selection of patients who are healthier or in other ways better off, rather than care quality.[36-51] The ability to exploit the limitations of quality monitoring means that private producers may also have incentives to exclude individuals who need more care, exaggerate the needs of those they care for, or both. Of particular concern is that financial incentives to select against individuals in (or at heightened risk of) poor health could intersect with oppression. Since oppression predictably produces poor health, such incentives could lead to discrimination within health care against individuals who already experience oppression in other settings.

Because of these incomplete contracting issues—health care must be individualized, so the state cannot specify exactly what care someone should get in every circumstance, and judging quality and appropriateness of utilization after the fact is difficult—oversight of private producers is often challenging. It requires substantial state capacity and political will, and even then it may not be successful.

As with public production, the absence of a functioning price mechanism means that rate setting, quality monitoring, and utilization management need to occur in other ways. These functions can occur publicly (as with traditional Medicare in the United States), or they can be outsourced to private entities—health insurers or "payors"—that are often, but not always, separate from health care producers.

There is little reason to think private entities would be better at negotiating rates than public entities, given they inevitably have less market power than a single public payor.[6,52] Indeed, empirically, private entities are typically unable to negotiate better unit prices from producers than public entities.[53,54]

With regard to quality monitoring, there is an argument that profit may motivate private entities to perform this task better than public entities. However, the major problems of quality monitoring relate to the nature of health care, so it is not clear that private entities have much scope to perform better than public ones.

User fees for consumers are common forms of utilization management. However, as noted above, these reduce both needed and less needed care, and thus are rarely desirable.[18-27] Other utilization management strategies include administrative review (such as prior-authorizations and peer-to-peer approvals) to limit care. Although they may reduce utilization, and theoretically could guide clinicians to appropriate care, these strategies also impose important, but frequently unmeasured, costs in terms of consumer and producer time and consumer experience. Further, in practice they frequently worsen quality by denying care that is appropriate.[55] Another form of utilization management is refusal to insure certain categories of individuals or to cover certain types of health care, which then must be addressed through regulation.

Using private insurers can also create externalities because many benefits of health care are realized over relatively long time frames. Since individuals frequently change insurers ("churn"), insurer spending may be lower than desirable on care that results in long-term benefits.

The profit motive for insurers also presents problems related to risk-adjusted payments. Risk adjustment relates to individuals' risk of incurring health care costs. Risk adjusting payments incentivizes "gaming" to imply higher risk, and thus receive greater payments. Such gaming can substantially increase costs, with little improvement in quality.[40,56]

Ultimately, the potential benefits of private insurance are premised on its ability to better manage the costs and quality of private producers than public entities. However, it is important to think through how that might occur. The elements of health care spending are the unit cost of each health care product and the quantity consumed of each product. Private insurers generally cannot do better than a single public purchaser for negotiating unit costs, owing to the single public purchaser's monopsony power. Therefore, the only way private insurers can lower production costs is utilization management—some combination of decreasing utilization of care and shifting the care that is delivered from more expensive to less expensive versions. As noted above, such utilization management activities have important implications for health outcomes—implications that may be hard to detect given the difficulty of monitoring health care quality and the long time frames over which some health care effects manifest.

Further, even when done legitimately, utilization management typically creates important administrative burdens for both health care producers and consumers. Navigating the imposed burdens (e.g., the time spent obtaining prior authorization) may not be fully counted as fiscal costs, but it does impose opportunity costs (e.g., they take time away from caring for other patients). This can make it difficult to assess whether such utilization management activities actually produce "savings" in terms of real resources, even if they appear to decrease reported types of spending.

Overall, there is little reason to think, and little empirical evidence, that private entities offer advantages over public entities for managing private health care producers. Instead, using private entities to monitor private producers introduces additional complexities and risks, and they require their own regulation and oversight. In the end, this regulation and oversight is such that a system of private insurance capable of meeting normative goals becomes, effectively, an offshoot of the state, surrendering many of the hypothetical advantages of private entities.[5,52]

To sum up this section, public finance of health care is unavoidable for a normatively justified system. The choice then is between public and private production. Public production can typically control spending well, but possibly at the expense of patient experience owing to underfunding. Private production may enhance experience, but typically at the risk of higher spending, lower quality, unequal access, or all of the above. Despite these predictable problems, either approach can be, and has been, made to work, so the decision about which approach to use should be made democratically.

Personal Care

Activities of daily living include dressing, bathing, grooming, personal hygiene, eating, toileting, mobility, and transferring from lying to sitting to standing positions. Instrumental activities of daily living include food preparation, housekeeping, doing laundry, shopping, managing medications, managing finances, using communication devices, and using transportation. When healthy, people may take activities of daily living and instrumental activities of daily living for granted. But when individuals cannot perform some of these activities themselves owing to illness or injury, others must assist them. This assistance is personal care.* Personal care is often needed by older adults, and for individuals with disabilities.[57] An important conceptual distinction is between the specific aspects of personal care one needs owing to impairment in activities of daily living and/or instrumental activities of daily living, and basic needs that everyone has. For example, to meet nutritional needs, one may shop for food, purchase food, prepare food, and eat the food. The cost of purchasing food (a basic need) is distinct from costs related to needing assistance with shopping for, preparing, and consuming food (personal care).

Personal care has three main aspects: residential (or institutional) care, in-home care, and "extra expenses" (e.g., needing certain products owing to disability, like an automobile equipped for wheelchair users). Though distinct, personal care is often intertwined with health care, and many of the dynamics discussed in the health care section are applicable to personal care.

Personal care faces many of the same issues, in relation to judging the quality of care and the risks of for-profit production, that health care faces, but perhaps to a lesser extent given generally less complex services and less uncertainty about the outcomes of personal care.** Given the nature of personal care, consumers can generally judge the experience of personal care

---

*Analogous terms are "long-term services and supports" and "social care." I discuss child-care separately from other types of personal care, in chapter 12.

** For example, it may be easier to judge whether a personal care attendant is providing appropriate bathing assistance than whether an ophthalmologist is providing appropriate cataract surgery.

well (or, depending on the reason care is needed, such as cognitive deficits, someone may be able to judge on their behalf), and likely vary in their preferences. Together, these factors suggest that public finance with private production may work well for personal care. However, as individuals may vary substantially in how easy or difficult it is to provide care for them, careful monitoring of access to private producers is necessary to avoid cherry-picking. Alternatively, public production of personal care, with appropriate exit and voice mechanisms, is common and can work well too. Therefore, deciding between public versus private production should occur democratically. Finally, there are some aspects of personal care, particularly related to extra expenses, which might fit under a market provision framework. Thus, personal care could be structured as a mix of in-kind services and cash benefits.

When possible, in-home, rather than residential, care is typically desirable. To support in-home care, cash benefits can provide for extra expenses, such as home renovations to install shower bars or wheelchair ramps. However, residential care is sometimes needed, and so high-quality residential care options must be available.

Personal care should be conceptualized separately from income support policies that relate to one's ability to participate in the labor market (chapter 12). The need for personal care and income support may or may not coexist. For example, an individual with a disability related to a spinal cord injury may have a full-time paid job (and thus not require disability income), but they might need assistance with toileting or bathing (and thus require personal care).

The distinction between personal care needs and basic needs provides one way to operationalize the insight that individuals vary in their ability to convert resources into capabilities—with benefits for extra expenses providing the needed supplement.[15] Personal care policy can thus be a model for other cases where this variation exists.

Summary

This chapter has discussed the role of transfer income policy within the egalitarian state, the key forms of transfer income policy, and considerations regarding which form to use. Finally, it discussed three important areas of transfer income policy best structured as publicly provided in-kind services: basic education, health care, and personal care. The following chapter continues the discussion of transfer income policy, covering cash benefits to be used for products best allocated by markets.

12

Transfer Income Policy II

Cash Benefits

Having discussed products best publicly provided as in-kind services in the prior chapter, this chapter discusses cash benefits, meant to provide purchasing power for those products needed to guarantee the essential capabilities that are best allocated by the market. There are three main approaches to cash benefits policy: social assistance, social insurance, and basic income.[1] *Social assistance* policies condition transfers on financial need. What I am terming *social insurance* policies condition transfers on risk of destitution that arises for "categorical" or "role-related" reasons (chapter 7) that can preclude earning adequate factor income. *Basic income* policies condition transfers only on citizenship or membership in a society. Of course, any real-world system will not fit an ideal type, and there are often practical reasons to mix and match among approaches. But contrasting the approaches is instructive.

Social assistance policies are common—two US examples are TANF (Temporary Aid to Needy Families) and SNAP (the Supplemental Nutrition Assistance Program). Because social assistance is conditioned on financial need, means testing is typically involved. Social assistance policies are major programs in residualist welfare states. But in universalist welfare states, social assistance policies have limited, if any, role. Therefore, I do not discuss social assistance policies in depth (see chapters 4, 7, and 10 for more on the shortcomings of residualism and means testing).

Social insurance policies are meant to protect against the risk of being unable to earn factor income sufficient to guarantee the essential capabilities. This risk stems from inhabiting a particular category or role (chapter 7). Social insurance policies do not require people to reach destitution before providing benefits; rather, they seek to prevent destitution by providing benefits once people enter a situation where the risk of it is high. Examples of such situations include older age, disability, and unemployment. In common usage, a hallmark of social insurance policies is that they are "contributory" in the sense that individuals should pay into the system before receiving benefits. Further, in common usage, social insurance is funded primarily by hypothecated* contributions rather than general taxation.[2] Together, this typically means that people need to be connected to the system for some period of time before receiving benefits (e.g., a pension might only vest after a certain number of contributing quarters), and that only risks occurring after entering the paid labor force are insured against.

In this book, I use the term *social insurance* in a more expansive (perhaps idiosyncratic) way. The contributory principle is important politically, but it can be relaxed somewhat to better advance the objectives of social democracy. Hewing too closely to the contributory principle misses an opportunity to pool risk more broadly, and efficiently, through taxation. Moreover, the concept of social insurance should be expanded to include protections against risk that occurs before one enters the paid labor force, or that may prevent one from entering it. Thus, we can view child benefits and support during advanced education (such as university or vocational programs) as prospective, rather than retrospective, social insurance. Or, by analogy to the contrast between actuarial versus social insurance, these types of pre-contributory risks could be viewed as social, as opposed to actuarial, loans. In any event, the central idea is that the concept of pooling risk can be applied to policies that protect against risk both before and after individuals enter the paid labor force. In this expanded view of social insurance,** the contributory principle may be modified such that contributions are expected when feasible (e.g., paying taxes after entering the paid labor force) but are not required prior to benefit issuance.

Basic income provides, conditioned on citizenship alone (citizen or membership requirements are also typical for social assistance and social insurance, along with other eligibility criteria), cash benefits that guarantee the

---

* Contributions at least notionally meant for a specific purpose.

** An alternative term for this expanded vision of social insurance might be "social security," which is consistent with how that term was meant when introduced by social reformers in the early 20th century. In the United States, however, the term social security is closely connected in everyday discourse with the public pension system, so that could be confusing.

essential capabilities.* This could be combined with additional approaches—for example, a basic income supplemented with social insurance against specific risks. Basic income presents a straightforward approach to cash benefits but also a number of complications discussed later in this chapter.

Fundamentally, either a social insurance or basic income approach to cash benefits can be normatively acceptable. Thus, the choice becomes a political one regarding which approach can garner sufficient democratic support, and a technical one about which one can be implemented effectively and efficiently. These decisions are inherently "local" in the sense that there is not a single best approach for all places and times. In the following sections, I will discuss a social insurance approach to cash benefits in more detail and contrast it with a basic income approach.

A final point for cash benefits policy relates to policy costs (chapter 9). Unlike for in-kind services, state outlays for cash benefits mostly represent changing ownership claims rather than committing real resources to particular uses. In other words, fiscal and real costs are not equivalent. Cash benefits do have real costs from tax-and-transfer policy administration, but these are typically low. They may also have macroeconomic costs from income and substitution effects, which are important to consider when selecting among normatively justifiable approaches to cash benefit policy.

A Social Insurance Approach to Cash Benefits

As I am using the term, the goal of social insurance is to protect against the risk of an income insufficient for the essential capabilities, related to specific roles individuals may inhabit. Social insurance policies form part of a regime, in combination with other transfer income policy (e.g., in-kind services such as health care), and other egalitarian state policies, such as those that affect labor market earnings and the opportunities one has available.

A common benefit design structure across social insurance policies is a

---

* It is helpful to view basic income (an income sufficient to guarantee the essential capabilities) as a subset of guaranteed income (providing income conditioned only on citizenship or membership in a society). Guaranteed income that is not sufficient to be a basic income must be supplemented by other programs. However, guaranteed income not sufficient to be a basic income could have the important real-world benefit of serving as a backup for situations that may fall through the cracks of other programs owing to failures of administration or implementation.

"basic benefit" (chapter 11) that provides purchasing power for products needed to guarantee essential capabilities that are best allocated by markets. For some social insurance policies, an additional earnings-related benefit may be useful both to provide consumption smoothing and to position the benefit as the primary insurance mechanism, consistent with the principles of universalism.

The six key role-based risks that social insurance policies seek to protect against relate to being an older adult, a child, disabled, unemployed, a student, and/or a caregiver. Inherent to the idea of social insurance is a judgment about what types of risk warrant social protection. Each of these risks, in their own way, relate to major categories, or roles, that people may inhabit during their lives that inhibit participation in the paid labor force, and thus carry risk of being unable to earn sufficient factor income to guarantee the essential capabilities. I refer to these situations as "roles" because it emphasizes their relational nature and helps make clear that these are not inherent traits but rather "states" that occur at different times in one's life. Protecting those in each role through social insurance implies social recognition that inhabiting the protected role provides a good reason* for not being able to earn sufficient factor income. By offering protection for those inhabiting particular roles, it is important to acknowledge that this invites the concern that the state is, strongly, no longer being neutral toward people's conception of the good, or, perhaps more weakly, being unduly intrusive, in violation of relational equality, in determining which risks are to be insured against. Though I recognize these concerns, I believe that a social insurance system can still be compatible with the normative demands of democratic equality. I discuss this issue in more detail below.

In the following sections, I discuss relevant considerations for specific social insurance policies. I do not discuss policy implementation in any detail but simply highlight some important points in each case.

Older-Age Pensions

Older-age pensions are a social insurance archetype and a leading welfare state fiscal expenditure.[3] Pensions successfully support income for

---

* One that can be justified as reasonable. In other words, people can understand why telling someone inhabiting one of these roles to get a job to support themselves is not an appropriate response.

older adults and are associated with important health benefits.[4,5] Pensions can be financed in two main ways: pay as you go (PAYG), where benefits are paid from current tax revenue, or fully funded, where funds are accumulated by an age cohort while working and then distributed after retirement.[6,7] Pension benefits also come in two main types. A defined benefit system provides a specified benefit amount, often indexed to inflation. A defined contribution system has individuals contribute into a (typically tax advantaged) account while working, with the resulting sum made available during retirement. This approach places risk on the individual—the individual could outlive their savings, or inflation could leave them with insufficient income. However, assuming there are mechanisms to insure against these risks, either approach can be effective.

Whatever financing mechanism is chosen, pensions represent a claim on future output.[6,7] Thus, future productivity is centrally important to pension feasibility. This is obvious with PAYG systems funded by taxes on production, but it pertains to fully funded systems just the same. If future output declines, perhaps owing to fewer workers or decreased productivity, demand will outstrip supply, inflating prices and lowering the purchasing power of accumulated funds. Therefore, fully funded systems are not inherently more economically sound than PAYG systems. For any pension system to work, future productivity must be sufficient to support pensioners who, almost by definition, are no longer engaging in production but still have consumption needs. Factors that affect future levels of production include the domestic birth rate, immigration, technological advances, and the ability to harness international production through trade and capital investment. Despite debate in the economics literature, fully funded systems do not seem to offer clear advantages over PAYG systems, and the costs of transitioning from a PAYG system to a fully funded system can be substantial enough to wipe out any benefits that do exist.[2,6,7]

No matter how designed, the goal of older-age pensions is to provide sufficient income to, in combination with other policies, guarantee the essential capabilities. A typical approach is to set a basic benefit level available to all older individuals. This can be augmented with a publicly financed earnings-related benefit, along with options for private pensions either as enterprise* benefits or individually. Private options are often subsidized through tax ex-

---

* Job-related.

penditures, but the distributional implications of this should be considered carefully.

An important pension design element is the age at which benefits begin. Both a society's mean and distribution of life expectancy are relevant considerations. Further, because pensions represent a claim on future output, they are bound up with questions of political power between generations.[3] As a society's healthy life expectancy changes, the age at which pensions begin may need to change as well, but this should not become an excuse for unnecessary benefit cuts meant to disadvantage those who rely more heavily on public, rather than private, pensions.[6]

Child Benefits

Rates of childhood poverty typically exceed those of the population overall,[8] as children cannot (and should not, if they could) work to earn factor income. The same level of factor income will not produce the same standard of living if that income needs to support children in addition to those who earn it.[9] Material deprivation during childhood worsens health throughout one's life, along with educational attainment and life outcomes more broadly.[10,11] For these reasons, child benefits are a crucial part of the egalitarian state.

Three elements of child benefits are child allowances, childcare benefits, and parental benefits. I discuss child allowances and childcare benefits here, and parental benefits in the caregiving section below.

Child allowances are cash benefits meant to ensure that parents have sufficient purchasing power for products children need that are best allocated under market provision (e.g., food, clothes, diapers). A child allowance should be structured as a basic benefit, with no earnings-related component (children do not work). A monthly cash payment, paid on the child's behalf to the primary caregiver, is likely the most effective way to get benefits to children.[12] Any concerns about children from well-off families not needing the benefit are best addressed through progressive taxation, rather than implementing means testing or phaseouts.[13]

Childcare benefits are provided as in-kind services, with either public or private production, in many countries. However, childcare could also be provided under market provision, coupled with consumer-side subsidies or general transfers. The decision about providing childcare as an in-kind service or subsidy, versus providing a general transfer, has important implications regarding paid labor for parents of young children. In-kind childcare, or childcare subsidies, would incentivize engaging in paid labor. General transfers would be more neutral regarding the choice between paid labor and caregiving, as such transfers could either pay for childcare outside the home or serve as income for parents providing care.*

As one final point, child benefits help align people's desires (and to some extent, biological capacity) to have children (often earlier in adulthood) with the financial security needed to provide for children.[9] Otherwise, there can be a mismatch as factor income tends to be lower earlier in adulthood than later in one's working years. Thus, child benefits not only help guarantee essential capabilities for children but provide substantive freedoms for (potential) parents.

Disability Benefits

Disability benefits provide purchasing power for working-age adults who have impaired ability to participate in paid labor. The current system of disability benefits in the United States is a patchwork of enterprise benefits, local, state, federal, and private insurance programs. It would be better to have a simpler and more consistent approach, with a national-level program to pool risk more efficiently.[2] Disability benefits should be coordinated with personal care policies, given overlap in eligible populations.

It can be administratively helpful to divide disability benefits into short- versus long-term benefits. The first situation includes illness, injury, or physiologic incapacity (e.g., late in pregnancy) where a return to full earning capacity is expected relatively quickly (say, one year or less). The second situation includes long-term and permanent disability, which could either begin in adulthood (or otherwise after commencement of earning factor income) or prior to earning factor income (e.g., lifelong or in childhood). Of course, disability occurs in children and older adults as well, but since there is no expectation that these individuals support themselves with factor income, disability benefits are not needed (although personal care may be).

Short-term disability benefits should encompass medical leave from work but should not be contingent on a work history, as one may experience

---

*For young children, there can be overlap between out-of-home childcare and the beginning of basic education (e.g., preschool). To the extent that a program represents basic education, every child should receive it. To the extent that a program represents out-of-home childcare, the state should be indifferent to receipt.

short-term disability that prevents working even if not working at onset. The short-term program should be structured as a basic benefit with an earnings-related component (to provide consumption smoothing and buy-in). To encourage safe working conditions, there should be a workers' compensation component to the program, where the employer bears a greater financing burden in appropriate cases.[14]

The long-term program should be structured similarly to the short-term program. It should not be contingent on a work history, and it should have both a basic benefit and an earnings-related component and include workers' compensation. The basic benefit would apply to everyone (including those with a lifelong or childhood-onset disability). The main difference between short- and long-term programs is that the earnings-related benefit for long-term disability would likely be smaller than for short-term disability (e.g., replacing a lower percentage of previous earnings), and the long-term program may include more stringent eligibility determination.

A difficult aspect of longer-term disability income policy is balancing support with enabling people to be as productive as they can. Some disabilities preclude all paid labor, but other disabilities only lessen the capacity. Individuals with such disabilities may want to work, and society would benefit from them doing so. If disability benefits are withdrawn based on people's earnings, perhaps because greater earnings are taken to reflect inherently less severe disability, it could disincentivize paid labor just as means testing does. Disability benefits that rely on an initial determination of disability but do not change based on subsequent earnings would avoid this problem.[15] However, they could be perceived as illegitimate. The difficulty of striking the right balance argues for political solutions.

Unemployment Benefits

Spells of unemployment are common across working age.[16] Existing unemployment insurance benefits in the United States have important shortcomings: they are available only for certain job types, offer low levels of benefits, and have brief durations.[17-19] To address these problems, a basic unemployment benefit should be available for all working-age adults who are looking for work. This should not depend on work history, and it should not have limits on benefit duration. To smooth consumption and promote buy-in, the basic benefit should be supplemented with an earnings-related component. This will typically not represent full wage replacement (given "moral hazard")[6,17] and could have a time limit, after which a person still looking for work would receive the basic benefit. Unemployment benefits are usually, at least partially, financed by a combination of employer and employee contributions, which is reasonable. However, as the benefits should be available to all working-age adults, this should be supplemented by general taxation.

Conditioning unemployment benefits on seeking a job can introduce administrative difficulties. Ascertaining job-seeking in a way that expresses the appropriate respect to individuals without stigmatizing them, and does not incentivize applying for jobs one has no interest in, must be an overriding consideration for program administration.[20]

One final aspect of unemployment benefits is that the state can augment cash benefits with policies to increase the chance of reemployment (active labor market policies). Active labor market policy instruments include job search assistance, job training programs, and job creation (for example, through subsidies paid to employers to create hiring demand or public works projects).[21]

Student Benefits

Being able to pursue advanced, noncompulsory, tertiary education such as college, professional, and/or vocational training after one has completed basic education is an important capability. Beyond the importance of this capability for many individuals, society has an interest in more productive members, as their output can affect the standard of living for everyone.

There are several important considerations for financing advanced education. First, advanced education typically precludes earning factor income (at least full time), so students need income support for both tuition and living expenses. A system that expects such support to come from family transfers works against fair equality of opportunity, by favoring those from well-off families. Further, having to take on debt with uncertain repayment prospects, as is common with mortgage-type student loans where repayment is based on the amount loaned rather than returns to education (i.e., future earnings), also works against fair equality of opportunity.[2,6,22] Finally, there is an opportunity cost in forgoing work, which could provide income to support other family members. This also disproportionately affects those from less well-off families, who may defer their own education to support loved ones.

The issue of forgone factor income is best addressed by egalitarian state policies that support other individuals directly, which leaves living expenses and tuition for student benefits policy.

Living expenses are likely best offered as cash benefits, as they mostly relate to products well-supplied through markets (e.g., food). This can be a basic benefit as, even if a student does have an earnings history, they are pursuing advanced education voluntarily, and thus can factor temporarily lower consumption into their decision-making. One way to structure this benefit that may be more neutral between advanced education and paid employment is a "youth benefit," which could be a basic benefit offered for, say, six years after the end of basic education. For those who pursue advanced education, this could cover living expenses, while for those who start working, it would help make up for low earnings most individuals experience at the beginning of their career.[23]

Tuition is a user fee for advanced education. The degree to which tuition should be used to finance advanced education depends on policy goals.[24,25] One goal for advanced education may be to develop "human capital." Proponents view the skills and credentials that advanced education provides as a stock of human capital,[22,25,26] which can later become a flow of income.[2,25,26] A second goal is to provide the capability to pursue advanced education as a valuable freedom.[24,27] A third goal could be to promote advanced education as a positive externality.[6,22] Advanced education imparts skills that can raise society's overall level of production and helps develop faculties that could make people better citizens. Without student benefits, pursuit of advanced education may be less than socially optimal.

The emphasis placed on each of these goals has implications for the form student benefits should take. Proponents of the human capital view tend to emphasize the returns to education that accrue to individuals.[24,25] They would favor policy that emphasizes individuals bearing a larger share of costs (call this approach "learner pays"). Under learner pays, student benefits would be structured as a loan. Given the problems with mortgage-type loans noted above,[2] student benefit loans should be repayable contingent on future earnings (income-based repayment), with an expiration period (e.g., any unpaid balance is forgiven after, say, 25 years). Interest on the loan should reflect the real cost of borrowing.[2] As an expression of state neutrality, such loans should be available for as wide a range of educational programs as possible.

If, instead of emphasizing human capital, one emphasizes advanced education as an important freedom, and/or as a positive externality, policy should de-emphasize the student's share of the costs (call this "public pays"). Public pays has been on the decline in the United States, in favor of learner pays, since the 1970s.[2,24,28,29]

Public pays would make less use of tuition. It would argue for greater state support of advanced education, perhaps including a mix of consumer-side advanced education subsidies, public finance of private educational institutions, and public production via public educational institutions. This would represent a distributional choice in favor of those pursuing advanced education, which argues for a wide variety of publicly financed advanced education options, including not only university and professional education but also vocational training and retraining opportunities for individuals. To the extent that higher education improves productivity, one could view subsidies for it as a form of industrial policy.

Because individuals from well-off backgrounds are overrepresented among those who pursue advanced education, public pays can be seen as a giveaway to well-off individuals. However, those with advanced education are also more likely to be high earners. This means that public pays, if financed by progressive income taxation, could be seen as a form of income-based repayment—one that may be easier to administer than individual-level income-based repayment programs. So, if combined with other approaches to address the reasons why individuals from less well-off backgrounds are less likely to go to college, public pays could be justified.

In reality, a combination of income-based repayment loans and public finance is likely needed. However, it is important to remember that although income-based repayment makes sense in principle, some versions implemented in the United States and other countries have undermined its promise. Thus, as in all areas of policy, implementation needs careful attention.

A final point is that, despite advanced (and basic) education's importance for fair equality of opportunity, essential capabilities should not depend on educational attainment. Given everyone's fundamental moral equality, the essential capabilities should be guaranteed to everyone, regardless of education level.

Caregiving Benefits

Caregiving, such as raising children or caring for family and friends incapacitated by illness or injury, instead of engaging in paid labor, is sometimes viewed as an optional choice people can make if they can be supported by others (e.g., family transfers). It should not be seen this way. Caregiving is vital for social reproduction, and everyone needs care at points in their life. As philosopher Elizabeth S. Anderson notes, viewing caregiving as optional rather than a vital social function reflects an androcentric, atomistic, and sexist norm.[20] Given the necessary role that caregiving serves in the division of labor that makes society possible, and not least for gender equity, caregiving benefits should be part of social insurance.[20]

There are two key dimensions of caregiving benefits: duration (short, say one year or less, versus long), and who the care is for (children or adults).

Situations involving short-term care for children, such as parental benefits after a child joins the family, are likely best addressed with policies structured similarly to unemployment and short-term disability benefits. A basic benefit should be available regardless of whether one was in the paid labor force when caregiving begins, as caregiving precludes the ability to seek paid employment. The basic benefit should be sufficient to guarantee essential capabilities for the caregiver, and it should be supplemented with an earnings-related benefit.* Parental benefits should be available for and flexibly divisible between both parents. The duration of benefits should be set through a political process, but a one-year period may be reasonable.

For short-term caregiving for adults, the approach should be similar, but the duration of earnings-related benefits may be shorter. Some financing of the costs of adult caregiving, particularly at a basic benefit level, could come through personal care policy for the person receiving care.

Long-term caregiving for adults would typically imply a transition from a potentially earnings-related benefit to a basic benefit. Financing for this should be related to personal care policy, an example being personal care attendant programs.[21]

Cash benefits policy regarding long-term caregiving for children entails choices about whether to emphasize caregiving or paid labor. A choice that emphasizes caregiving would be to provide a basic benefit for full-time caregivers. Logistically, one way to accomplish this would be to count caregiving as a qualifying reason for a basic unemployment benefit, perhaps up to a certain age for the child, or to classify full-time caregivers as employees of a government childcare organization. Another approach, discussed in the

---

*The child's needs should be addressed through separate child benefits.

child benefits section above, would be to provide a general transfer that could be spent on childcare for those who choose paid labor over caregiving and serve as income for those who choose caregiving over paid labor. This would effectively be neutral between encouraging paid labor and caregiving. A third approach, also discussed above, would be to offer childcare subsidies or in-kind childcare. This would encourage paid labor.

An important aspect of valuing caregiving is its intersection with other programs. For example, older-age pensions often use time spent in the workforce in the calculation of benefits. Counting caregiving as a qualifying activity for purposes of other programs appropriately recognizes caregiving as a vital social function.

Basic Income

Basic income is a normatively justifiable alternative to social insurance-based cash benefits policy. Basic income provides, conditional on citizenship or membership in a society alone, a periodic cash payment sufficient to guarantee the essential capabilities.[1,30] Basic income policies are a subset of guaranteed income policies, which can provide any amount of income. Not all guaranteed income programs are normatively justifiable on their own. Unless sufficient to guarantee the essential capabilities, guaranteed income must be supplemented with other cash benefits.

Basic income could be implemented in many ways. To my mind, the most straightforward would be a monthly or fortnightly payment. Another option is a negative income tax, proposed by British politician Juliet Rhys-Williams as part of the Beveridge Committee in the United Kingdom, and popularized in the United States by economist Milton Friedman.[1,30-34] The negative income tax is administered through the income tax system. When people file their taxes, those whose factor income is below some threshold receive a transfer payment. The size of the transfer payment decreases as factor income increases, eventually going to $0, and individuals begin to pay ("positive") income tax. A negative income tax can be thought of as turning a nonrefundable standard income tax deduction into a refundable one. Given issues of consumption smoothing over the course of the year, implementations of negative income taxes may need to include advance payments, reconciled during tax filing.

There were several large-scale experiments evaluating effects of guaranteed income (some of them large enough to be considered basic income) beginning in the 1960s, and since 2010 there has been renewed experimental interest, with a number of demonstration and pilot programs of basic (or guaranteed) income ongoing at the time of writing.[32,34] To my knowledge, no society has implemented a basic income program large enough to replace fully social insurance and/or social assistance programs, but there are established guaranteed income programs such as the Alaska Permanent Fund Dividend.[30,35] The Earned Income Tax Credit and Child Tax Credit in the United States are similar to a negative income tax in some ways, but they are currently conditional on earned factor income, and so they are better thought of as wage subsidies (chapter 13).

While hardly definitive, evidence to date does suggest positive effects of basic (or guaranteed) income programs, particularly for mental health and quality of life. However, the comparison has typically been to a status quo condition in a residualist welfare state, rather than universalist social insurance.[15,32,36]

A common concern about basic income programs is the macroeconomic costs that could arise by affecting labor supply, through income and substitution effects (chapter 8).[33] Empirically, however, income effects (i.e., an individual choosing to work less because income is now available without work) seem to be rather small.[37–41] And although substitution effects may be relevant depending on how basic income is financed (e.g., via progressive income taxation), evidence suggests that even high marginal income tax rates may not lead to meaningful substitution effects.[42] Overall, macroeconomic costs of basic income are uncertain,[33] but there seems to be little reason to expect them to be large.

Further, as normative goals cannot be met without transfer income policy, macroeconomic costs are of concern only among the set of policies that can meet normative goals. In this regard, effects of basic income may be similar to social insurance, and in any event would need to be considered in combination with other outcomes including effects on health and well-being.

Proponents of basic income note several potential benefits over social insurance. First, basic income could simplify cash benefit policy by obviating the need for social insurance programs (although basic income should not replace in-kind services). Further, administrative burdens for basic income would likely be lower than for social insurance.

Second, because basic income does not condition benefits on any particular role, distorting influence is minimized. For example, a social insurance disability benefit may incentivize an individual to overemphasize the extent of their disability and lessen labor force participation, but basic income does not create that dynamic.

Third, and perhaps most to the heart of the difference between social insurance and basic income, by not conditioning transfer payments on seeking work, basic income would make paid labor more voluntary. Basic income proponents may see this as "decommodifying" in the sense that engaging in paid labor, even when one is able to and opportunities for paid labor are available, is not required to support one's self.[43]

Comparing Social Insurance and Basic Income

There are some versions of both social insurance and basic income approaches that can be normatively justified. Thus, decisions between them should be made on technical grounds, considering economics, implementation, and political aspects.

Describing the Regimes

First, to fix ideas, I would like to describe a normatively justified version of both social insurance and basic income. As discussed before, a life span can be roughly divided into child, working-age adult, and older adult periods. Within working-age adults, relevant roles are being disabled, being unemployed, being a student, being a caregiver, earning factor income (e.g., as a worker engaging in paid labor, as someone who is self-employed, or as someone who owns assets used in production and receives capital income), and not earning factor income without inhabiting any of those other roles. This last role would include people who are engaging in unpaid household production (but not caregiving), "early" retirees (i.e., before the age at which one could collect an older-age pension), and people who otherwise choose not to work.

Social insurance would protect against the risk of destitution in six of those roles: older-age, childhood, being disabled, being unemployed, being a student, and being a caregiver. Factor income policy (chapter 13) would protect those earning factor income. A person not earning factor income without inhabiting any of those other roles would not receive cash benefits but would still receive in-kind services. The social insurance programs would provide a basic benefit sufficient to guarantee essential capabilities, along with an earnings-related benefit in some situations (e.g., older-age pensions, disability benefits, unemployment benefits). There would be some citizenship or residency eligibility requirement. Financing would come from a mix of employer and employee contributions, along with general state revenues (e.g., income, wealth, and consumption taxation).

A basic income regime would provide basic income to individuals who meet the citizenship or residency requirement. There would be no other eligibility requirements. Basic income for adults would be the same as the basic benefit offered for unemployment or disability in the social insurance approach. Basic income for children would be the same as the social insurance child allowance. There would be little justification for specific employer or employee contributions, so financing would come from general state revenues alone.

How do these regimes compare? First, the two approaches are more similar than they might appear. For children, there is no practical difference between social insurance and basic income. For older adults, the main difference would be the presence of an earnings-related benefit under social insurance (and a basic benefit alone with basic income). For working-age adults in the roles protected by social insurance, the support provided by either regime would be very similar (again mainly differing on earnings-related benefits). Thus, the fundamental difference between social insurance and basic income comes down to whether cash benefits would be provided to those who are working and to those who could work but choose not to.

Justifying the Regimes

The first, and most important, question is whether each regime is normatively justifiable. The justification for basic income is simple. As everyone receives a basic income sufficient to guarantee the essential capabilities, the state meets its duty of equal care (at least with respect to capabilities meant to be guaranteed through cash benefits). However, there is a possible objection. By offering cash benefits even for people who could earn factor income but choose not to, people could opt out of contributing to the system when able. This violates norms of reciprocity and undermines the idea of society as a system of fair cooperation.

But there are counterarguments. First, since in-kind services, such as health care, would not be withheld under the social insurance regime for those who are not working, there is acceptance that some benefits should be offered to everyone at all times. Cash benefits should not be treated differently than in-kind services, especially because the rationale for supplying products as in-kind services is a technical one (i.e., these are products for which market provision does not work well), rather than there being something normatively distinctive about products provided in that way. Thus, if the state is to take seriously both its obligation to show equal care and to be neutral toward conceptions of the good, it must accept that some individuals will choose not to earn factor income but nevertheless deserve to have the essential capabilities guaranteed. If cash benefits are part of how the state fulfills its duty of equal care, then transfer payments must be made to people who do not earn factor income even though they could.

Second, as articulated by sociologist David Calnitsky, part of the reason that modern economic activity is so productive, and thus could be taxed to finance basic income, comes down to contributions made by others.[43] The modern level of productive ability is not determined solely by the effort of those producing now but also by knowledge produced and technological advances made by those who came before us ("total factor productivity"). Thus, current productivity represents a patrimony, of which everyone is entitled to a share. The current property rights regime allows idle rich individuals to be exempted from work and live off of inheritances from their forebears. Perhaps an alternative property rights regime that includes basic income would be acceptable on the same grounds. Taken together, I think these arguments are persuasive enough that a basic income approach could be normatively justified, although I am not sure that the matter is fully settled.

What about social insurance? The social insurance regime does not protect people who could earn factor income but choose not to, when they are also not inhabiting one of the protected roles. That is in keeping with the underlying logic of the approach—to protect against situations that would keep one from being able to earn sufficient factor income. In this interpretation, the state fulfills its duty of equal care by creating, through a system of civil and political rights, and factor income policy, conditions under which one might engage in paid labor on fair terms. Further, it protects against risks that would prevent someone from being able to earn a living. Such a regime guarantees a person's essential capabilities in the sense that they could turn to the state for support if needed. From the social insurance perspective, choosing not to be in the labor force when also not inhabiting any of the other roles is simply not a risk that needs to be insured against. I find this argument persuasive.

Macroeconomic Costs

Assuming then that either regime can be normatively justified, what are other important considerations? One consideration relates to the macroeconomic costs of the regimes, which stem from possible income effects for those who receive benefits and substitution effects related to financing the regimes. Since basic income offers benefits regardless of whether one is seeking work, the expectation would be that basic income has larger income effects than social insurance. Since social insurance primarily offers benefits to those who would not be able to work in the absence of benefits, its effect on labor supply is likely to be smaller. Social insurance may have some income effects at the margins for caregivers, unemployed individuals, and students, but these would be the same as for basic income.

Either regime will incur fiscal costs related to program administration and benefits paid. How these are financed can create macroeconomic costs related to substitution effects. The administrative fiscal costs of basic income are likely to be lower, but administrative costs are likely to be a very small component of either regime—perhaps a few percentage points of total outlays at most. For example, the administrative cost of the US Old-Age, Survivors, and Disability Insurance (OASDI; the primary Social Security Administration social insurance pension) is under 1 percent of total benefits.[44]

The fiscal costs of benefits paid is likely to be substantially greater for basic income since benefits are offered to everyone. Using the breakdown of roles presented in chapter 7, if approximately half of the US population fills a role that would be protected by social insurance, then about twice as many people would receive cash benefits under basic income, compared with social insurance. These greater outlays may create greater macroeconomic costs through substitution effects (e.g., basic income may require higher marginal income tax rates than social insurance). Of course, the magnitude of any differential substitution effect may not be meaningful, and even if it is, it may be worthwhile.

Overall, then, macroeconomic costs for basic income are likely to be greater than social insurance. Basic income should have, compared with social insurance, similar or larger income effects on labor supply. Further, because for any benefit level basic income is likely to have greater fiscal costs than social insurance, whatever substitution effects financing would have are likely to be greater for basic income, compared with social insurance.

Implementation

The next set of concerns involves program administration. Basic income clearly has an advantage here. Given only minimal eligibility criteria, basic income is likely to be much simpler to administer than social insurance. This makes for lower administrative costs and likely greater take-up than social insurance programs where eligibility must be determined. Further, though social insurance eligibility could and should be made objective and straightforward, in practice, especially in the presence of inegalitarian ideologies such as racism, social insurance may present greater scope for biased program administration. On the other hand, experience has shown that universalist social insurance programs can be run with very low overhead costs[44] and reach virtually all who would be eligible. Thus, the extent of administrative differences in practice between the two regimes is unclear. Overall, however, there is little reason to think social insurance would be superior to basic income in this regard.

The next set of considerations relate to adjusting benefit levels. Cash benefits may need to be adjusted for earnings-related reasons (to smooth consumption and promote buy-in among higher earners) or capabilities-related reasons (e.g., to ensure similar capabilities when people vary in their ability to convert resources into capabilities). With social insurance, it is straightforward to add an earnings- or need-related component to the benefit structure. With basic income, how to proceed is less clear. The first option would be to layer separate social insurance programs on top of basic income. This could effectively adjust benefit levels but would be an important change in the basic income approach. It would introduce the same concerns about distortions as social insurance programs, along with increasing administrative overhead and burdens. However, these issues may occur on a smaller scale than with a full social insurance regime, as they would only be relevant for a subset of cases. Another option would be only offering basic income, leaving individuals to organize benefit adjustments through private markets. Historically, there has been partial success in forming markets for earnings-related pensions and disability benefits (less so for unemployment benefits).[6] However, this option risks creating a two-tiered system where the well-off come to rely on private benefits. This could, paradoxically, undermine the universality that basic income is meant to foster. For adjustments related to differences in individual ability to convert resources into capabilities, there is likely no market alternative. Thus, some system of social insurance may be unavoidable.

Worker Bargaining Power

The next consideration relates to how cash benefits affect those who are working. Proponents of basic income argue that by effectively making work optional, basic income substantially increases the bargaining power that workers have.[43] This could translate to important benefits for workers, such as improved working conditions, shorter hours, and better wages, and serve as a counter-cyclical stabilizer during economic downturns. Socially, it would direct capital to those businesses that can succeed while treating workers as equals, weeding out more exploitative firms. Thus, basic income would go a long way toward improving equality in the sphere of economic relations. These are all important benefits, but unemployment insurance policy along the lines described above would achieve the same benefits. Therefore, basic income and social insurance are likely similar in this regard.

Political Considerations

Basic income and social insurance have different political implications. Political winds can change quickly, and it is important to help shape the understanding of these issues instead of simply working with the "conventional wisdom." However, basic income does face a number of political obstacles. Though this does not rule out its feasibility, to my knowledge basic income of the kind described here has not been enacted at scale in any country. But the social insurance programs discussed here are common worldwide (some even in the United States). Second, for financing, some evidence suggests that hypothecated finance (nominally dedicating sums raised for particular purposes), along with combining several small taxes to replace one larger tax, may be politically advantageous.[45] Quasi-contributions reduce tax salience, and thus could raise similar sums with less psychic cost.[45] This approach fits well with social insurance but not with basic income. Third, generating political support for basic income could be an uphill climb. Social insurance protects against risks that could befall anyone, providing a leverage point for political organizing. But for basic income benefits that would go to those currently earning sufficient factor income, the justification may be less clear. Why tax individuals only to give them transfer income that makes no material difference to their life? This objection is not insurmountable. The same objection is posed in favor of means testing, and it might be met in the same way—by appealing to administrative simplicity. But whether universalist basic income has the same advantages over universalist social insurance as universalist social insurance has over residualist, means-tested social assistance, is unclear. Moreover, the inclusion of those who are not working invites political attacks. A clear theme in US politics is using racism to divide those who have similar material interests, so it seems almost inevitable that there would be racialized attacks on basic income. Such attacks would seek to undermine support by painting White individuals as contributors to the system and non-White individuals as takers, despite any facts to the contrary.[46] Similar attacks could, of course, be made against a social insurance system, particularly the unemployment insurance system I have described, but the design of such a system provides, at least, an inherent defense—it protects those not working for what is recognized to be a "good" reason.

Even if not racialized, political attacks pitting makers against takers are almost certain to occur. Forestalling such attacks is one reason economist Anthony Atkinson proposed a "participation income" approach that conditioned basic income on a set of socially sanctioned activities beyond paid labor (e.g., volunteering).[1,47] While potentially effective in forestalling this problem, it does so only by making basic income more like social insurance.

Social Wealth Funds to the Rescue?

It may be possible obviate some of these political attacks by financing basic income with dividends from a social wealth fund.[35] Since transfer payments would be financed, not through taxes on production but through unearned income from asset holding, this would undermine the argument about benefits for those not in the paid labor force. All income from assets is unearned, so there would be no reason to treat income from assets held by a social wealth fund any differently from private assets. Indeed, many guaranteed income policies use such a model—for example, the Alaska Permanent Fund.[35] Further, because this would lessen the need for finance through taxation, it could lower the macroeconomic costs of basic income as well. Of course, a social insurance regime could be financed in the same way, with the same advantages.

It would take some time for a social wealth fund to accumulate assets sufficient to generate a dividend large enough to be a meaningful source of finance. Thus, a practical path forward would be to establish a social insurance-based system, along with a social wealth fund that distributes an equal dividend to all individuals. When the dividend of the social wealth fund is small, it could provide an appreciated windfall but would not be sufficient to guarantee the essential capabilities. Over time, however, it may grow to the point where it can provide a basic income. At that point, redundant aspects of social insurance could be deprecated, leaving smaller-scale social insurance programs to address earnings-related benefits and issues with converting resources to capabilities. However, because dividends from a social wealth fund could fluctuate, it would be important to retain sufficient capacity in social insurance programs to ensure essential capabilities could be guaranteed in the event of a downturn.

Summing Up

The differences between a normatively justifiable social insurance and basic income approach to cash benefits are less than meets the eye. Both would offer benefits to large segments of the population. The fundamental difference is about whether to offer cash benefits to workers and to those who choose not to be in the labor force. The main advantages of basic income are universality and simplicity. The main downsides relate to finance and political vulnerability. Further, because basic income is not a complete solution, some social insurance would still be needed. This could negate some hypothetical advantages of basic income. Since there are good arguments for both basic income and social insurance regimes, the approach that can garner more political support should prevail. There is probably not a single best regime for all places and times. However, whichever approach is taken, a social wealth fund, which could make implementing either regime more tractable, should be considered.

Housing

Overall, housing mostly falls into a market provision framework, and thus essential capabilities related to housing can largely be guaranteed through cash benefits. However, I discuss it separately because there are some complicating factors that call for elements of public provision.

One complicating factor is that housing construction requires large capital outlays and long lead times, and maintaining surplus units incurs substantial costs. Therefore, it can be difficult to match housing supply to demand. Further, people often wish to own their home, because they view owner-occupied housing as not only providing them housing services but also serving as a stock of wealth, and as a form of insurance against high future housing costs (analogous to rent control). However, having wealth bound up in home values affects homeowners' material interests. Specifically, it can incentivize homeowners to try to limit housing supply and exert control over who occupies nearby units. This is not only to increase scarcity rents on home values but also because increases in home values mainly occur through appreciation of land value (determined by neighborhood desirability), rather than appreciation in the value of the structure (which in fact tends to depreciate).[48] Further, housing markets also have substantial frictions given the importance people place on physical proximity to family and social ties, along with work, which means a simple supply-and-demand model often does not fit housing market behavior well. Finally, to an extent greater than for many other products like food or clothing, housing prices exhibit considerable local variation, which can make it hard to match cash benefit levels to local prices.

These factors all represent coordination problems that argue for relatively more state management than is typically needed for products allocated under market provision. First, adequate cash benefit and factor income policy should be the foundation of housing policy—more equal income flows and wealth holdings will tend to make housing markets work better as differential preferences become more important than differential ability to pay. Second, state-led planning for housing development is needed. Leaving housing development to private developers with short time horizons, and risking interruption of already lengthy development timelines by business cycle issues, is a recipe for undersupply. Third, social housing (e.g., state-owned housing units, rented at either market or subsidized rates) is an important public option given supply-side constraints in many areas.[49] Social housing also has the advantage of divorcing receipt of housing services from asset holding, which has practical advantages for ongoing housing policy.[50] Fourth, given the inherent power imbalance, strong protections of tenants from landlords are necessary. These include not only protections against evictions but also, especially given the relationship between housing conditions and health,[51-54] protections related to housing quality and maintenance. Further, strong, and enforced, antidiscrimination regulations are needed, given pervasive racial discrimination in housing markets.[55] Fifth, policies need to adapt to local housing conditions. In the right setting, rent control and housing subsidies can help prevent forced moves, evictions, and homelessness. The importance of these policies as stopgaps, however, should not distract from longer-term goals of addressing housing needs through adequate income on the demand side and adequate housing stock on the supply side.

Summary

Transfer income policy is an indispensable part of the egalitarian state. By using a combination of in-kind services (when public provision is needed) and cash benefits (when market provision is feasible), transfer income policy, as part of a tax-and-transfer system, works with factor income policy, and civil and political rights, to meet the state's duty of equal care.

13

Factor Income Policy

Factor income can result from wages or asset holding, and factor income policy affects the conditions under which wages are earned and productive assets are put to use. Factor income, principally from wages, is the primary source of income for most working-age individuals. In a market economy, factor income policy has wide-ranging effects as it shapes much of society's economic activity. Thus, along with tax-and-transfer policy and civil and political rights, factor income policy is an important part of the egalitarian state.

A goal of factor income policy within the egalitarian state is to enable individuals who are working to earn income that provides for the essential capabilities, when combined with the transfer income received by the individual and other members of the household (e.g., health care and child benefits). A second goal is to help ensure that individuals are treated as equals within their economic relationships.[1] These relationships may not necessarily be equal in terms of skills or abilities, but everyone should, for example, have the power to strike a fair bargain and not be compelled to accept any employment terms offered, on pain of starvation.[2] Within these normative constraints, it is also desirable that factor income policy contributes to a high level of economic productivity, and growth in economic production, as the national income relates directly to the material standard of living a society can achieve.

This chapter aims to discuss key aspects of factor income policy, while recognizing that factor income policy is intrinsically interrelated with transfer income policy and civil and political rights. It starts by discussing overarching goals of factor income policy, followed by a discussion of labor market institutions. It then covers the topic of full employment and ends with a discussion of factor income policy as it relates to asset holding.

Goals of Factor Income Policy

The overarching goals of factor income policy relate to justice in the economic sphere.[1-3] Cooperating with others to produce goods and services forms a major part of many individuals' lives, and doing so results not only in the material outputs necessary for survival but also, in many cases, a sense of pride and purpose. Fulfilling the state's duty of equal care in the economic sphere involves assuring that people are situated in a relationship of equality in their economic relations.[1] Factor income policy is part of establishing a normatively justified system of property and other economic rights. This relates not only to duties of distribution but also to duties of recognition, such as ensuring that working conditions treat people as equals.[1]

Addressing Power Imbalances

A fundamental problem factor income policy must face is the power imbalance between employers and employees that emerges in capitalist economic systems, where the state delegates ownership of productive assets to private individuals. There may be tremendous economic advantages to such arrangements. However, these arrangements also predictably put asset holders in an advantageous position relative to those who must work.[2,4,5] For such a system to be normatively defensible, strong policies that counteract this fundamental inequality are needed. In chapter 7, I argued that the welfare state can be viewed as a normatively justifiable system of property and other economic rights related to the distribution of the national income. Similarly, factor income policy can be viewed as establishing a normatively justifiable system of property and other economic rights related to the ownership of productive assets—specifically about the way productive assets can be put to use in a society that is a system of fair cooperation among equals.[6]

Modern economic production is complex and may require elements of hierarchy to organize it.[7] However, whatever a person's position within a production process, their treatment must be consistent with their fundamental moral equality. This includes not only their ability to strike a bargain regarding distribution of the proceeds of joint production but also being treated with respect and having their interests given a fair hearing during the process of production. It also means being in a position of substantive freedom to choose, or reject, a particular job.[7] Factor income policy helps ensure that any hierarchy that does occur in productive arrangements does not undermine equality of social standing.

One metric of the balance of power between asset owners and workers is the extent to which earnings received by employees, as a group, are linked to productivity.[8,9] When employer power is greater, a greater share of a firm's proceeds are assigned to the owners of the productive assets, rather than workers, and that share can grow as productivity increases.[8,10-12] This can be an important indication of power imbalance.

Substantive Freedom, Not Perfect Competition

The fundamental power imbalance between those who own productive assets and those who do not, created by a property rights regime that allows for private ownership of productive assets, means that real-world labor markets often do not function like the idealized representation of markets in economic models. Features of such models include assumptions of equal power, perfect competition, and workers being paid their marginal product.[13,14] One concept relevant to understanding the deviation from idealized economic models that this structural power imbalance creates is the idea of monopsony. The term was coined by economist Joan Robinson, and the concept builds on the work of institutional economists in the first half of the 20th century.[15,16] Monopsony in this context refers to a power imbalance that favors employers as the purchasers of labor.[17-20] This power imbalance, along with "frictions" in the job search process, the relatively small pool of job openings with specific combinations of features (e.g., working conditions and commuting distance), the social meaning people attach to their work, and norms around wage setting, means that idealized "perfectly competitive" models often do not model real-world labor markets well.[14,16,18]

Because simple supply-and-demand accounts are not accurate depictions of real-world labor markets, they are often of limited utility in predicting the impact of factor income policy. Minimum wage laws provide an important example. Idealized models predict that minimum wage laws should increase unemployment.[16,21] However, recent findings suggest that in existing economic conditions, which are characterized by monopsony, many minimum wage increases do not meaningfully reduce employment.[22,23]

Despite the deviation of actual labor markets from idealized representations, the goal of factor income policy is not necessarily to implement policy fixes that make markets work more like the models. Instead, the aim is to construct labor markets that function as part of the overall project of the egalitarian state.[19,24] Even if technical problems in making labor markets perfectly competitive were surmountable, making labor markets function in this way would not necessarily be desirable. At most, it could be instrumentally valuable if it helped fulfill the state's duty of equal care.[1,19] But rather than seeking to make life imitate art, the true goal is to create economic freedom, which requires policy that balances power between owners of productive assets and workers—between employers and employees.

Pre-Distribution

Factor income policy can help ensure a more equal initial distribution of factor income (sometimes called "pre-distribution").[25] When pursuing a just distribution of net income, factor income policy and transfer income policy will be interrelated. For example, a more egalitarian distribution of factor income requires different tax-and-transfer policy than a more unequal distribution of factor income. While any distribution of factor income could be modified by tax-and-transfer policy so as to guarantee the essential capabilities to all, there are some arguments that favor a more egalitarian distribution of factor income. The most compelling one is that unequal distributions of factor income typically result from power imbalances in relations of production. Therefore, what is at issue is not simply duties of distribution but duties of recognition. In other words, though the tax-and-transfer system may be able to distribute sufficient income to everyone, tax-and-transfer policy may not address working conditions that do not recognize individuals' equality.[2,26] An economic system that produces a very unequal factor income distribution is likely to be one that excludes many individuals from good jobs. In addition to violating duties of recognition, this could also create social stratification and a "makers versus takers" mentality corrosive to solidarity and reciprocity.

Macroeconomic Considerations

Another goal of factor income policy relates to how it fits into a society's macroeconomic policy. Macroeconomic policy is of course broad, and not all of it is a matter for the egalitarian state. However, there are areas that strongly intersect. For example, although avoiding high inflation (a general rise in prices) and economic growth may not be direct goals of the egalitarian state, these can be important policy goals for society overall. Economic growth, if it can be achieved justly, could raise the material standard of living for everyone. Moreover, the egalitarian state relies in part on maintaining, or expanding, future productivity (chapter 12).[27,28] This needs to be achieved within normative constraints, but the goals of the egalitarian state are certainly not in conflict with goals of economic growth—indeed, they can reinforce each other.[29,30]

The Impossibility of Just Deserts

I end this section with a discussion of something that is not a goal of factor income policy but is commonly assumed to be. The "just deserts"[31] view is that workers should be paid their marginal product. However, this idea is not only normatively indefensible (for reasons discussed in chapter 7) but also infeasible, as labor markets are unable to allocate to individuals their marginal product. With complex modern production, it is not possible to uniquely identify any particular worker's marginal product.[32] Marginal product accounting can be useful for determining how to achieve some output goal given choices about the arrangement of available inputs, but it does not establish what inputs, such as a person's labor, have produced a given amount or share of the output.[32,33] In short, the idea that an individual participating in joint production has a uniquely identifiable marginal product is mistaken. Thus, viewing factor income policy as being about ensuring each individual is assigned their marginal product is both unjustified and quixotic.[32,34]

Labor Market Institutions

A major aim of factor income policy is to shape labor markets in ways consistent with the normative goals of social democracy. Labor markets do not function as perfectly competitive markets, and the goal of factor income policy is not necessarily to fix these market failures. Instead, a goal is to balance power between employers and workers so that individuals can earn factor income that provides the essential capabilities, while also working under conditions that recognize their fundamental equality. Societally, a goal is to maintain (and grow) high levels of productivity within normative constraints.

There are a number of ways to achieve these goals, and it may be that no particular labor market institution is required. For example, in the United States, minimum wage laws have been an important worker protection.[16]

But in some countries (e.g., Norway) with high union membership, there are no national minimum wage laws. A wage floor is set through union negotiations. Ultimately, the concern is with achieving the goals of social democracy, not necessarily with the approach to doing so.

The state's role in setting labor market conditions is central to achieving normatively justifiable outcomes. The rationale for markets is that they optimize production and allocation within given constraints. If the state does not establish appropriate constraints, there is no guarantee market outcomes will be normatively justifiable—not least because the fact that market processes produced an outcome does not justify that outcome. Without state action to establish and maintain normatively justifiable labor market institutions, any voluntary action taken by a firm, even if socially desirable (e.g., making working conditions less miserable), becomes a cost that their competitors may not have to pay.[5] If such action does not improve profitability, the firm will be driven out of business. Thus, setting appropriate labor market conditions is part of the state's duty of equal care. Doing otherwise makes just working conditions contingent on their profitability—prioritizing the good over the right or the rational over the reasonable. Instead, when state action sets the conditions for everyone, market mechanisms can deliver efficiency within normatively justifiable constraints.

Egalitarian labor market institutions must situate employers and employees in a relationship of equality. Given the inherent power imbalance that asset ownership represents, the major task of these institutions is to counterbalance that power differential. There are many ways to accomplish this, and these policies may empower employees individually or collectively (or both, as greater individual power may feed greater collective power).

Transfer Income Policy

First, background transfer income policy is important as it helps set the conditions under which individuals seek employment and consider their alternatives. In particular, this includes unemployment insurance; policies around sick, family, and disability benefits; and policies around childcare (chapter 12).

Regulating Employment Conditions

Next, one can think of a set of policies that regulate wages, employment security, and working conditions. These include minimum wage laws, occupational health and safety regulations, and regulations regarding terminations, working hours, overtime, and vacations.

A major source of unequal power in favor of employers is at-will employment, which allows employees to be fired for any reason. Working toward just cause policies that offer workers greater protections against arbitrary employment termination is an important policy goal. With just cause policies, employees have more power to advocate for better conditions within the workplace, as, under at-will employment, such advocacy often leads to termination. Moreover, the threat of at-will termination deepens power imbalances between employees and employers.

Another important set of regulations relate to the employment relationship, including classification of workers as employees. Given changes to employment that emphasize casualization of the employment relationship, anti-precarity regulations are increasingly important.[14] These includes regulations around predictability of work scheduling[35] and limits on the use of noncompete clauses and nondisclosure agreements to prevent individuals from seeking other employment. Often, independent contractor classification is used to dodge labor laws.[36] In cases where workers are clearly employees, this requires enforcement of laws regarding classification. But as economic activity changes, there may be good reasons for increasing use of independent contractor roles. In this case, rethinking the link between worker classification and protections offered (i.e., making protections offered for independent contractors similar to those for employees) makes sense. In general, moving away from enterprise benefits—systems where, for example, health insurance, short-term disability benefits, and pensions are provided by employers rather than publicly, would not only help makes the employee versus independent contractor distinction less important but also help reduce the power imbalance between employers and employees. Further, legal frameworks that make it easier to organize businesses as worker cooperatives may be particularly useful in cases where disputes over worker classification are common—such as sectors that are relatively labor intensive, have modest capital requirements, and are highly decentralized (e.g., home cleaning and transportation services).

Antidiscrimination

Discrimination in the labor market is all too common. Racism, sexism, and other inegalitarian ideologies lead to situations where some individuals (in the United States, particularly women and individuals racialized as Black, Hispanic, and/or Indigenous) are not hired, and receive less income for their work when hired, than they otherwise would.[37–39] Policies that address this discrimination include passing and enforcing antidiscrimination laws related to hiring, promotion, and compensation; affirmative action programs; and enforcement of rules and regulations regarding workplace hostility that may be directed toward individuals because of inegalitarian ideologies.

Collective Bargaining

Collective bargaining is an area of factor income policy that deserves extended attention, because it can help institutionalize employee power. Labor unions have been a powerful force for promoting equality in the economic sphere.[40–44] Strong evidence links them to higher wages and better working conditions, which help advance normative goals and improve health directly.[45,46] Further, declines in labor unions are associated with increasing inequality of factor income and worsening working conditions.[40,41,47]

Labor unions represent collective action by workers to advocate for their interests. Such collective action faces three main problems.[5,48] The first is worker vulnerability—attempts by workers to organize can easily lead to being fired, which, in the absence of alternative means of support, would imperil their well-being. Second, collective action must aggregate the interests of many people, which may differ (e.g., one person may be willing to trade off fewer working hours for lower pay, and another may prefer the opposite). Third, collective action can suffer from "free-riding," where individuals try to receive the benefits of collective action without contributing. Policy can affect each of these issues, and thus affects union formation, maintaining union membership, and the effectiveness of unions in representing members' interests. US policy makes it harder to form and maintain a union and substantially limits union power, relative to many other countries.[26,49] Worker vulnerability can be addressed through transfer income policy, moving away from enterprise benefits, and regulatory reforms such as ending at-will employment. The problem of interest aggregation is made harder when employers pit employees against each other, and enforcement of laws designed to prevent employer interference with union formation can help address this. One way to deal with free-riding is reform of regulations like right-to-work laws. Further, collective bargaining law relating to the process of union recognition, how bargaining units are determined, bargaining unit level (e.g., specific firms [or specific jobsites within firms] versus sector-wide), and the use of strikes all affect union formation and effectiveness. Of course, oversight is needed to ensure unions represent the interests of their members well, but there is no avoiding the importance of unions in working toward social democracy. Unions are not optional institutions appropriate only on a case-by-case basis at the firm level. They are a fundamental institution, ideally at the sector level, for factor income policy that balances power between employers and workers in order to realize equality of standing in the economic sphere.

One example of how collective bargaining arrangements at the sector level ("sectoral bargaining") can work is as part of boards that set wages and working conditions throughout an entire industrial sector.[50,51] For instance, rather than having negotiations occur within a single automobile manufacturing firm, negotiations occur between worker and owner representatives of all automobile manufacturers. An advantage of sectoral bargaining is that by setting terms of employment sector-wide, it puts pressure on less productive firms to improve productivity.[52,53] Thus, sectoral bargaining not only helps achieve normative goals related to wages and working conditions, but it can push toward more productive allocations of capital within a society. Sectoral bargaining can be one element of what is sometimes called the "coordinated market economy."[54] In the coordinated market economy,* the state creates formal structures where various non-state bodies representing stakeholders within the economy (e.g., unions and trade organizations) negotiate agreements that govern the conditions of production and employment. These organizations are sometimes given roles in administering social insurance programs like unemployment insurance—sometimes called the Ghent system.[55,56] However, if this is done, care must be taken to ensure individuals are not left out or treated unfairly by these bodies, which would violate the state's duty of equal care.

Aside from labor unions, there are additional ways to formalize employee representation in the economic sphere. Worker cooperative businesses are one approach,[57] as is "co-determination," in which employee representatives

---

*Also sometimes called "corporatism," under the analogy of the representative organizations functioning like vital organs working together to promote the health of the state (the body politic).

serve on corporate boards.[58,59] Finally, corporate governance structure regulations and norms that support corporate social responsibility, rather than shareholder primacy, can motivate a balance of power between workers and employers.

Full Employment and Job Guarantees

Full employment is a policy goal that plays an important role in balancing power between employers and employees.[4] When unemployment is low, employees are in a more favorable bargaining position with employers, relative to when unemployment is high. Moreover, full employment as a policy goal also helps with economic growth, drawing people into the workforce and providing an incentive for firms to utilize workers as productively as possible. Technically, full employment occurs when there is no "deficient-demand" unemployment—or in other words when there is sufficient aggregate demand to provide jobs for all who are willing and able to hold them.*

States can take a number of actions to pursue full employment, which are sometimes collectively referred to as government stimulus. These include public production (e.g., building roads or schools) and issuing general transfers and/or subsidies to individuals, in order to stimulate consumer demand. The goal of full employment is often coupled with the goal of moderate inflation. Economic theory suggests that government stimulus to reach full employment should not be inflationary, as being below full employment implies that unused resources are available.[60] At or above full employment, government stimulus can lead to inflation, as this implies limitations in real resources, leading to supply constraints that result in price rises. Central banks are often tasked with striking this balance.

Deficit spending to create full employment is controversial.[4,61] As discussed in chapter 9, deficit spending is desirable during economic downturns as the stimulus is needed and other methods of public finance, such as increasing taxes, would be counterproductive.[4] Alternatively, in situations where full employment has been achieved and inflation is occurring, deficit spending would be undesirable. In any event, spending sufficient to guarantee the essential capabilities is normatively required. The way in which that

---

*This does not necessarily mean unemployment will be zero—there could be "frictional unemployment" as people seek new jobs, and/or "structural unemployment," where there is a mismatch between workers' abilities and available jobs.

spending should be financed (e.g., through taxation versus deficit spending), however, depends on specific context.

An important focus of full employment policy relates to the state's role in job creation. One form this could take is active labor market policies, discussed in chapter 12. Active labor market policies include job search assistance, retraining, offering employer subsidies for hiring long-term unemployed workers, and public employment.

A more controversial version of full employment policy is the job guarantee.[62-64] Under a job guarantee, the state serves as an employer of last resort, meaning everyone (under certain conditions) who seeks a job can receive one. Although there are some attractive features of this idea, there are several downsides as well. First, it is hard for job guarantee work to be anything other than "make-work" employment. Certainly, if there are, say, infrastructure projects worth doing, then public employment can be worthwhile. But those jobs should result from the desirability of the particular project, not from a job guarantee. Further, the jobs may require specific skills that not every individual has. The job guarantee seems most applicable for jobs that do not really need doing—that is, ones without another sufficient rationale. The benefits of a policy that slots people into make-work jobs seems unclear. Further, social insurance benefits needed to guarantee the essential capabilities should not be conditioned on participation in a job guarantee program. Such "workfare" systems would not meet the state's duty of equal care.[1] Overall, I think the goals proponents say a job guarantee would achieve are better pursued through other policy approaches, including unemployment insurance, active labor market policies, and factor income policy to make the conditions under which individuals earn factor income more just.

Another common policy that relates to full employment goals are working tax credits.[13] In the United States, the Earned Income Tax Credit (EITC) is a prominent example.[65] Working tax credits are meant to incentivize wage labor, often by increasing the benefit level as earnings increase, before plateauing and eventually phasing out. This has the effect of subsidizing low wages. The idea of making work more remunerative certainly fits well within the overall goals of factor income policy, and such credits have been empirically successful at poverty alleviation within residualist welfare states (often because they are explicitly designed to push people just across poverty thresholds).[66,67] However, their rationale does present some conceptual challenges. By subsidizing low wage work, working tax credits make it possible for employers to pay lower wages than they might otherwise.[65] This implicitly presumes that there are advantages to enabling employers to pay low wages and have the state make up the difference between what employers pay and what workers need for their essential capabilities. However, what those advantages are is unclear. Other forms of factor income policy, such as minimum wage laws or facilitation of unionization, might better address goals of both encouraging labor force participation and helping workers earn sufficient factor income. Further, given monopsony power of employers (effectively, a demand constraint on the purchase of labor), employers inevitably capture some of the value of working tax credits.[65,68] Moreover, working tax credits may suppress wages not only for workers "made whole" by the credit, but also for workers who do not qualify for the credit. Finally, because working tax credits are tied to the tax system, claiming the benefit is often complicated,[69] benefits are typically issued only annually, and the connection between the benefit and work performed may not be obvious. Overall, the design of such credits may work against universal uptake, consumption smoothing, and motivating labor force participation.[67,70]

Asset Holding

This chapter has primarily focused on factor income from labor, but individuals can receive factor income from asset holding as well. An important decision within factor income policy is the extent to which asset holding should be encouraged. One consideration regarding such policy is that income from assets could decrease labor supply through income effects. Another consideration is the form of asset holding that is encouraged. The two primary options are to hold assets collectively (e.g., through a social wealth fund), or to encourage individual ownership of private assets. Two nonfactor income policy examples of where public policy has encouraged individual ownership of private assets are housing and pension policy, which have taken that approach in the later 20th and early 21st centuries.[71]

I do not think policy efforts to encourage private asset holding are normatively objectionable, but there are important downsides worth considering. The first is that private asset holding essentially shifts risk from the state and onto individuals. For example, private pension schemes and home-ownership have been beset by bubbles and market collapses, resulting in substantial economic harms to individuals, with little recourse to government assistance.[71] Second, even if an initial stock of assets could be equally distributed, differential appreciation would likely lead to substantial variation in asset values after a period of time. This could work against equal social standing and toward social stratification between those whose holdings have appreciated more than others. It could also create intergenerational conflict (as older individuals may have had more time for assets to appreciate) and dynastic wealth. Of course, public intervention could address the problem for those who lose out. But in that case, it would be hard to see what the point of private asset holding would be, if ultimately the state simply makes up any losses.

Another consideration relates to differing views of consumer price inflation. Monetary policy that focuses on taming inflation by creating unemployment and decreasing worker bargaining power favors asset ownership, while allowing some inflation if necessary to permit wage growth and full employment favors wage earners.[60,71] Thus, public policy that seeks to expand asset ownership could exacerbate conflict between those whose incomes derive primarily from labor versus asset holding. Finally, private asset holding may work against norms of reciprocity by encouraging individuals to mobilize against socially desirable policies that lessen asset value. For example, those who currently own homes might oppose new housing development, to encourage scarcity rents on their home value.

Unlike encouraging private asset holding, which can have important downsides, I think a social wealth fund, as discussed in chapters 9 and 12, has many benefits and few drawbacks. Therefore, establishing social wealth funds is an important goal for social democratic policy.[72]

Summary

The key goals of factor income policy are to balance power between asset owners and workers, and to ensure that the conditions under which production takes place are just. Much of current employment law, and the laws that structure the use of firms as units of economic coordination, derive from "master and servant" relations, and create legally imposed hierarchy.[73] If it is thought that there are efficiency benefits to organizing productive activity in this way, there must also be countervailing laws and policies to counteract the anti-egalitarian effects of these laws. Without such efforts, formal (and substantive) economic inequality quickly leads to substantive political and civil inequality, and over time it may even allow some actors to accrue enough power to threaten formal political and civil equality.

Achieving the goals of social democracy requires public policy that works against the inherent power imbalance created by private ownership of productive assets. Such policy creates just labor market institutions, rather than simply aiming to make labor markets work like idealized economic models. Labor unions are likely to play a crucial role in such efforts.

Just factor income policy not only helps to fulfill the state's duty of equal care to those in the paid labor force, but it helps ensure a high level of productivity in society overall. This in turn makes the project of the egalitarian state feasible and sustainable.

14

Civil and Political Rights

Many of the policies necessary for economic democracy—a system of property and other economic rights that situate individuals in relationships of equality with others—are controversial. Indeed, even the idea of economic democracy may be controversial. But the idea of civil and political democracy is not.* Civil rights (like equal protection under the law, due process, and freedom of speech, religion, and conscience) and political rights (like universal adult suffrage and the freedom to run for office) are codified in law and command broad popular support. The United States has a large measure of formal civil and political equality—yet is deeply unequal.

Why? This chapter argues that the interrelationship between the spheres of social relations—civil, political, and economic—helps explain why social inequality exists despite formal civil and political equality. Further, it provides examples of how lack of economic rights both undermines civil and political rights and helps thwart the changes needed to address injustice.[1-4]

Social Inequality

Unequal social standing in the United States partly stems from ongoing violations of existing rights, owing to inegalitarian ideologies such as racism and sexism. But another important cause is the failure to achieve economic democracy. Indeed, a central thesis of social democracy is that without democracy in all spheres, democracy in any sphere is incomplete and tenuous.

---

* Given the assault on political and civil rights, particularly at the state level, that has accelerated since 2020, this may come to be seen as a naïve statement.

When formal inequality exists, it is not surprising that it generates substantive inequality, which can be used to justify the formal inequality. But formal equality that is incomplete—that is, when it does not extend through all spheres of social relations—can serve a similar role. Indeed, incomplete formal equality is perhaps more insidious in legitimating the results caused by remaining inequality.[5] Because many modes of political contestation advantage those with greater economic resources, equality of civil and political rights can be used to hide the role of unequal economic rights in making the interests of those advantaged by inequality more likely to prevail.

When I say that economic rights are unequal, I do not mean simply that one individual has a right to, say, their house and income, and nobody has a right to the same house and income.[6] Such rivalrousness is true but trivial. Instead, economic rights are unequal because some individuals have a right to a particular house and a particular income, and others have no right to any house or any income. Thus, the present economic, and in particular property, rights regime does not provide equality in economic relations—it creates inequality: haves and have-nots. The potential to accumulate extreme wealth, and the power that that wealth provides, gives a motive to curtail others' civil and political rights, as doing so can work to one's pecuniary advantage. At the same time, lack of economic rights not only leaves those who are oppressed with few resources to fight back, but it can also motivate them to tolerate civil and political oppression for fear of destitution.

Thus, the lack of economic democracy risks undermining civil and political rights. As historian R. H. Tawney said, "Arbitrary economic power, exercised for purposes of personal profit is as incompatible with democracy as arbitrary political power."[7]

Undermining Civil and Political Rights

In the United States at present, lack of economic rights undermines civil and political rights in several ways. One example is residential segregation (chapter 6).[8-10] Another is restrictions on public discussion of issues related to racial justice and sexual orientation, on penalty of unemployment.[11-14]

Perhaps the clearest example, however, relates to law enforcement. The United States is the world leader in incarceration.[15-21] Criminal justice involvement is heavily concentrated among those with lower incomes.[17-20,22,23] It is also a clear expression of racist oppression, targeting individuals not racialized as White at every level, from traffic patrols and stop-and-frisk policies to prosecutions, sentencing, and probation and parole.[16,17,19,20] Criminal justice system involvement not only results in harsh penalties when incarcerated, but it contributes to economic marginalization and exclusion throughout one's life.[16–18,22]

The US carceral state can be viewed as a mixture of two elements—a necessary response to crime and inappropriate, oppressive state action. Enforcement of criminal laws provides a clear example of how inegalitarian ideologies can lead to oppression. The criminal justice system inherently involves case-by-case decision-making, which presents occasions for bias and discrimination. These includes decisions about who is questioned by police, use of force,[24] whether prosecutors should bring charges, sentencing, and the conditions of probation and parole. Discretion combined with inegalitarian ideologies, which lead to viewing Black individuals, and other individuals not racialized as White, as inherently dangerous, is a recipe for oppression.

But while these forms of oppression violate civil rights directly, lack of economic rights contributes to hyper-incarceration as well. Poverty, material deprivation, and crime are all closely connected.[16–18,20,22] And in the United States, increases in crime that initially spurred the development of contemporary carceral policy were rooted in deteriorating economic conditions and an inadequate welfare state.[17,20] Hyper-incarceration is both a reactive response to the problems injustice causes and a mechanism for keeping an unjust system of social relations in place.[17,18,23,25,26] Whether law enforcement is responding to actual crime or overreacting as a form of oppression, the root is injustice, and the solution is to work for justice throughout the entire system of social relations.

Pursuing Economic Democracy

As noted above, formal equality in some areas can be used to justify the results of inequality in other areas. This occurs repeatedly in political contestation in the United States and is a key strategy to prevent the establishment of economic democracy. One example is the use of burdensome voter registration requirements that result in differential exclusion of those with lower income. Similarly, when casting ballots, restricting voting hours and times, not providing leave from work, or inadequate polling location staffing serves the same purpose and clearly violates the state's duty of equal care.

Another example is gerrymandering—splitting those thought likely to vote similarly across multiple voting districts or concentrating them in a small number of districts. This works against the principle of one person one vote by diluting the political standing of some and enhancing the standing of others. In the United States, gerrymandering as a form of racist oppression has a long history. This is currently illegal[27] but still happens frequently. Moreover, some other forms of gerrymandering, particularly with regard to how individuals are expected to vote, are legal.[28] Clearly, lesser political standing based on how someone might vote violates the duty of equal care. Possible solutions include only considering factors uncorrelated with voting preferences when drawing districts, or moving away from majoritarian, winner-take-all systems to systems of proportional representation. Increasing the use of proportional representation in local, state, and federal elections may be an important way to help achieve the goals of social democracy.[2-4]

A third example relates to filling elected offices. Private finance of elections substantially limits who may run and gives undue influence, both during campaigns and while governing, to those who provide campaign funds. This makes elected officials more likely to favor the interests of their donors and less responsive to those who do not contribute to election financing.[29-31]

Balancing individuals' ability to support their causes with the state's duty of equal care is difficult. However, if individual wealth can translate into political power, then either the scope of private finance in politics must be substantially limited (e.g., through publicly financed elections), or the distribution of income and wealth must be equalized.[32] Allowing a very unequal distribution of income and wealth while placing few restrictions on the role of private finance in politics is not compatible with the state's duty of equal care.

Summary

One theme of this book has been the incompleteness of US democracy. This incompleteness helps explain why some formal equality has not meant substantive equality throughout the system of social relations, and it helps explain health inequity. What democracy requires then are economic rights that work in concert with civil and political rights. This is in part because civil and political democracy requires the capabilities for substantive participation in civil and political life, which economic rights help provide. But it is also because lack of economic rights undermines civil and political rights. This brief chapter provided a few key examples of how that can happen.

15

Conclusions

My aim with this book has been to present the argument that health equity is a product of a just system of social relations and that the way to achieve it is by implementing a policy regime that democratizes the civil, political, and economic spheres of people's lives: social democracy.

It is important to acknowledge some of this book's limitations. I have omitted important topics, such the relationship between climate change, environmental justice, and health, owing to space limitations. I have also chosen approaches that some will fairly object to, such as sketching out an ideal[1] benchmark of justice to compare against (although in doing so I do not think I have abstracted away from issues of oppression or subordination), and viewing society as a relatively self-contained unit, which is never completely true.[2]

This last chapter provides a brief restatement of the central argument, a reiteration of some important points, and a discussion of five areas where progress can be made toward social democracy.

Health Equity and Social Democracy: A Restatement

The central argument of this book is founded on two ideas: (1) health is an emergent embodied phenotype produced by the system of social relations one is enmeshed in,[3] and (2) health inequity is injustice that harms health. Thus, the way to achieve health equity is to achieve justice throughout a system of social relations, across the life course.

This invites the question of how to think about just social relations. Just social relations are systems of fair cooperation among free and equal citizens who possess the twin moral powers of rationality and reasonableness.[4]

The role of the state is to set the conditions under which social relations occur, and the fundamental moral equality of its citizens imposes on the state the duty that in doing so it must show equal care for the life of each citizen.[5,6] The important sense of equality is relational—that is, the state seeks equal social standing, as opposed to hierarchy, for its citizens.[7-9] Practically, the state fulfills its duty of equal care by implementing policies that recognize all citizens as equals and that distribute the resources necessary to stand in a relationship of equality with others. The essential capabilities, those capabilities that allow individuals to have substantive equality of social standing within a political democracy, serve as the metric with which to assess whether the state has met its duty of equal care.[7,10]

The egalitarian state consists of the aspects of the state used to meet the duty of equal care. The egalitarian state translates values into material conditions through policy, making technical choices about how best to do so that are informed by economics, epidemiology, medicine, political science, public administration, public health, sociology, and other bodies of empirical knowledge. The egalitarian state concerns itself not only with civil and political rights but also cash benefits and in-kind services necessary to guarantee the essential capabilities for all individuals (the "welfare state"), setting the conditions for fair cooperation in systems of joint production, and taxation both for finance and as an egalitarian tool in its own right.

The political movements of the 19th and 20th centuries made important progress in achieving, at least formally, civil and political democracy, but they did not achieve economic democracy, and the United States does not currently meet its duty of equal care. This produces injustice that harms health, or health inequity. Further, the failure to achieve economic democracy threatens to undermine past democratic achievements, as economic power congeals into undemocratic institutions that shape civil and political, along with economic, rights. To achieve health equity there must be democracy throughout the entire system of social relations—the civil, political, and economic spheres. This is the goal of social democracy as a political project.[11-16]

Policies that have aimed to improve health equity over the last two decades have been complex and technocratic, focused on specific problems created by inequality rather than inequality itself.[17] They have often aimed at multiagency and multi-sector collaboration that is prone to implementation failure. The supposed advantage of these policies was feasibility under political conditions hostile to equality, but they have had little effect. Ulti-mately, the policies that can bring about health equity will require extensive political contestation. I hope that this book is useful in understanding what to pursue in that contestation.

Equality of What?

One point to reiterate is the central importance of identifying the appropriate type of equality to seek.[7,18] I have argued, in the tradition of re-lational egalitarians, that the important type of equality has to do with so-cial standing.[5,7,19] Not recognizing the importance of relational equality leads to a number of problems. These include mistaking proportionality of certain outcomes for justice, focusing on particular patterns of resource distribu-tion rather than the capabilities those resources facilitate, and overempha-sizing particular policy approaches, such as progressive taxation or program targeting, to the detriment of achieving the goals of relational equality.

Disparity as a metric of health equity is one example of these problems. To be clear, differences in health outcomes across categories defined by as-criptive identity very frequently stem from injustice. But disparity is an im-perfect metric. Not only are differences in health outcomes across categories of individuals not necessarily unjust, but an equal distribution of those out-comes is not necessarily just. Using disparity as metric provides at best a limited and incomplete picture of health equity, and at worst, a misleading one. Health equity should not be thought of as a lack of difference in health outcomes across categories of individuals, but instead as the health state that occurs under just conditions.

A second example of emphasizing the wrong type of equality occurs with income inequality. Extreme income inequality often stems from injustice. It is a symptom of relational inequality and can worsen relational inequality in a vicious cycle. However, achieving income equality per se is not the norma-tive goal, and some income inequality may be not only unobjectionable but helpful for creating relational equality. For example, since individuals differ in their ability to convert income into capabilities, for reasons including dis-ability or the experience of oppression, unequal income may be necessary to produce equal essential capabilities.[20] Judging the justice of income inequal-ity requires examining how it came to be and its effects. As with health out-comes, knowing that an income distribution is unequal does not imply that it is unjust, and knowing that it is equal does not imply that it is just. Of course, there is a dynamic relationship between power and resources. Resources typically flow from power, and unjustly unequal power often leads to unequal resources. Conversely, when unjustly unequal power exists, distributing resources to those who are treated unjustly is a key form of redress. However, doing so is in service of achieving relational equality, and a pattern of resource distribution is important only instrumentally—to the extent it reflects, or helps achieve, relational equality.

An overemphasis on income equality can also lead to overemphasizing certain aspects of a policy—such as the progressivity of taxation or how targeted a transfer program is—because such aspects would seem to be essential for reducing income inequality. There can be good reasons for favoring such approaches, but in service of relational equality. A more progressive taxation schedule that raises an insufficient amount of revenue is not more desirable than a regressive schedule that raises the revenue needed. Similarly, any benefits of targeting can be readily offset by the administrative burdens, small distributive budgets, and stratification and stigma that targeting can engender. Justifiable policy must fulfill duties of both distribution and recognition. The targeted policies of the residualist welfare state are often unable to meet duties of distribution.[21] But even if they could, the residualist welfare state does not meet duties of recognition, because it creates hierarchy by distributing resources as charity from superiors to inferiors, rather than as rights owed to equals.[7,11,14,22]

The Economy Is a Government Program

Another point to reiterate is that all aspects of the economy involve socially constructed rules about how to distribute the product of joint production, such as property rights.[23] A central barrier to the distributive institutions necessary to guarantee essential capabilities and achieve health equity is the belief that people are entitled to their factor income and thus tax-and-transfer policy represents taking from individuals what is theirs. But the economy is a social institution that serves as a mechanism for social organization, and factor income is endogenous to the economic institutions a state establishes.[14,24] Factor income earned, property held (and its market value), taxes owed, and transfers and in-kind services received are all part of the same system of social relations and their determination is interrelated.[25] None of them exist outside of this system, and the justification for, or critique of, any of these elements must refer to whether the system they are part of produces just outcomes—that is, whether it works to fulfill the state's duty of equal care and position people in a relationship of equality.

Property rights are not fundamentally about how people relate to objects, but, like all institutions, they are about how people relate to each other.[26] Understanding property rights as institutions means that there is no redistribution, just distribution. Taxation is not state expropriation, but one part of a society's regime of economic institutions that make property holding normatively justifiable in the first place. Moreover, there is no trade-off between equality and efficiency—the right has priority over the good. Questions about productive or allocative efficiency have to be answered in the setting of particular background conditions. If those background conditions are unjust, they must be changed. Questions about efficiency are only relevant when choosing between normatively justified options that all reflect relational equality.

Long-Term Goals and Practical Progress

In the long-term, social democracy seeks to achieve (1) a system of rights across civil, political, and economic spheres that recognizes individuals' fundamental equality; (2) a universalist welfare state providing in-kind services and cash benefits to form the material basis for substantive freedom across the life course, measured in terms of essential capabilities; (3) labor market institutions that balance power between workers and employers; and (4) a system of public finance, including taxation and a social wealth fund, that both finances the egalitarian state and works against accumulations of resources that would undermine relational equality.

The United States is far from achieving these goals. In countries where major elements of a well-functioning egalitarian state have been enacted, such work has been the project of decades, if not generations. But practical progress toward social democracy can be made in the short-term, even if no single policy will achieve it. Such progress not only yields benefits from the policies themselves, but it can create reinforcing loops that help to achieve long-term goals.[11,27]

There are many ways to achieve the normative goals of social democracy, and so I have tended not to emphasize particular versions of policies. Instead, I have highlighted, in general terms, goals various policies should achieve and considerations for choosing among normatively acceptable options. Further, political and social movements need to seize windows of opportunity and respond to pressing needs as they develop. For these reasons, there is little value in setting down a perfectionist list of policy next steps. However, some examples to work toward in key areas, with the caveat that these are local to the United States at the time I am writing, may be helpful.

The first area is a publicly financed universal capability to receive comprehensive health care. Though health care is only one part of achieving health equity, it is an important part. Lack of universal access to comprehensive health care in the United States is a major injustice. A system that provides the capability to receive health care for everyone should be publicly financed, but it can be either publicly or privately produced. I see little advantage to private production, but it may be more politically feasible in the United States given entrenched interests. There is also little argument in favor of private health care administration on either normative or efficiency grounds, but it may be politically necessary. However it is arranged, there should be a single system of universal health care access that covers individuals for their entire lives—not tied to employment, age, or other eligibility criteria. It should be based on a strong foundation of primary care, with access to specialty and acute care; it should include coverage not only for health care facility use and provider visits but also for treatments (e.g., medications) and medical equipment, and make limited if any use of user fees.

The second area is a child allowance. The conditions under which children grow up profoundly affect all aspects of their lives, including their health.[28] The principles of life course epidemiology make clear why interventions for children often have lifelong benefits. Child allowances should be structured as universal, flat, cash benefits. Children should be treated as individuals by the state, and thus benefits should not be tied to parental earnings or expectations about parental behavior. Practically, the allowance should be paid monthly to the primary caretaker. Child allowances are good not only for children as individuals but are socially beneficial as children grow up to be healthier and more productive.

A third area is a system of fair taxation. General principles of such a system include prioritizing raising the revenue necessary to achieve normative policy goals, comprehensive income taxation (treating income from capital and labor similarly), having a broad tax base, interdicting tax dodging, and recognizing goals of taxation beyond raising revenue, such as reducing (or ideally, preventing) concentrations of power.[25,29,30] Specific details, however, must be responsive to local conditions, and they may change as the system of taxation itself changes those conditions. For example, in a society with very unevenly distributed wealth, wealth taxation is helpful for raising revenue. But as wealth becomes more equally distributed, it may be less helpful. Similarly, if factor income is very unevenly distributed, then steeply progressive income taxation will both raise revenue and help to avoid unjust accumulations of wealth. But the more evenly factor income is distributed, the less progressivity helps to raise revenue. Given extremely unequal distributions of wealth and factor income in United States at present, some useful policies include wealth taxation, a more progressive federal income tax system (which can also help serve a global targeting function for welfare state programs), reform of state and local taxation to be more progressive, treating income from capital and labor similarly, decreasing the opportunities for tax avoidance, and increasing enforcement of tax paying.[25,29-31]

A fourth area is the establishment of a social wealth fund.[32] Such a fund would not only help with public finance, but it would serve as a material indication of everyone's equality. A social wealth fund is also a hedge against an economy that is better at producing wealth than jobs, and it helps to democratize control of capital. The value of a social wealth fund compounds over time, so starting to build one now, even on a small scale, could have an important impact.

A final area for progress is to move toward a system of centralized and coordinated collective bargaining with an emphasis on unionization. Strong unions and other forms of collective bargaining work against the structural imbalance of power between workers and employers. Key ways to strengthen collective bargaining include interdiction of employer interference in union organizing, especially unjustified termination of workers who organize; reform of solidarity undermining regulations; a more streamlined process of union recognition; and greater use of sectoral bargaining. As with any type of organization, examples of unions that did not represent the interests of their members well can be found. But those examples do not undermine the fundamental need for institutions that can represent worker interests collectively. Weak or nonexistent unions exacerbate the structural imbalance of power in favor of employers, with unjust consequences.

The Conclusion of the Conclusions

When I started my career in research, I viewed health equity work as primarily a technical concern of health care delivery. That is, the questions were about how to deliver health care that could mitigate the injustice people had faced and how to stop the discriminatory and otherwise oppressive actions that happen within health care. These are, I still think, important questions. When people experience health-harming injustice, we must treat its consequences. And when oppression exists within health care, as it commonly does, it should be rooted out. But I no longer think that those questions are the primary questions of health equity. At the beginning of this book, I said that health inequity is social failure embodied. The work of health equity then is the work of egalitarian social transformation. No person's individual action will bring about health equity. No single policy or program will either. Health equity can only be achieved as a political project with a clear goal: to establish a state in which people's fundamental equality is recognized across all sites of human cooperation: civil, political, and economic. This is the project of social democracy.

As I write this in 2023, human health is not fully under human control. Lives are cut short without explanation, treatments fail, and good health often comes down to good luck. Someday, perhaps that will no longer be true. But in 2023, health equity *is* under human control. It is fully, completely, and solely under our control. The burden of that fact is that the existence of health inequity indicts us in collective failure. The emancipatory promise of it is that, if we want, we can build a world of equal care.

References

1. Introduction

1. Krieger N. *Epidemiology and the People's Health: Theory and Context*. Oxford University Press; 2013.

2. Marmot M, Bell R. Fair society, healthy lives. *Public Health*. 2012;126 Suppl 1:S4–S10. doi:10.1016/j.puhe.2012.05.014.

3. World Health Organization. *Social Determinants of Health*. Accessed May 10, 2021. https://www.who.int/westernpacific/health-topics/social-determinants-of-health.

4. McMahon NE. Framing action to reduce health inequalities: what is argued for through use of the "upstream-downstream" metaphor? *J Public Health Oxf Engl*. Published online May 27, 2021. doi:10.1093/pubmed/fdab157.

5. Coleman-Jensen A, Rabbitt MP, Gregory CA, Singh A. *Household Food Security in the United States in 2019*. US Department of Agriculture; September 2020. Economic Research Report No. 275. Accessed November 3, 2020. http://www.ers.usda.gov/publications/pub -details/?pubid=99281.

6. Lynch J. *Regimes of Inequality*. Cambridge University Press; 2021.

7. Reed A Jr. *Django Unchained*, or, *The Help*: How "Cultural Politics" Is Worse Than No Politics at All, and Why. Nonsite.org. Published February 25, 2013. Accessed May 6, 2022. https://nonsite.org/django-unchained-or-the-help-how-cultural-politics-is-worse-than -no-politics-at-all-and-why/.

8. Anderson ES. What is the point of equality? *Ethics*. 1999;109(2):287–337. doi:10 .1086/233897.

9. Dow G, Higgins W. *Politics against Pessimism: Social Democratic Possibilities since Ernst Wigforss*. New ed. Peter Lang AG, Internationaler Verlag der Wissenschaften; 2013.

10. Marshall TH. *Citizenship and Social Class: And Other Essays*. University Press; 1950.

11. Tawney RH. *Equality*. 5th ed. HarperCollins Publishers; 1964.

12. Anderson E. *Private Government: How Employers Rule Our Lives*. Reprint ed. Princeton University Press; 2019.

13. Anderson E. The fundamental disagreement between luck egalitarians and relational egalitarians. *Can J Philos*. 2010;40(suppl 1):1–23. doi:10.1080/00455091.2010 .10717652.

14. Dworkin R. *Sovereign Virtue: The Theory and Practice of Equality*. Trade Paperback ed. Harvard University Press; 2002.

15. Barr N. *Economics of the Welfare State*. Annotated ed. Oxford University Press; 2020.

16. Ruger JP. *Health and Social Justice*. Oxford University Press; 2010.

17. Centers for Disease Control and Prevention. *Minority Health and Health Equity*. Centers for Disease Control and Prevention. Published April 27, 2021. Accessed May 10, 2021. https://www.cdc.gov/healthequity/index.html.

18. Agency for Healthcare Research and Quality. National Healthcare Quality & Disparities Reports. Accessed May 10, 2021. http://www.ahrq.gov/research/findings /nhqrdr/index.html.

19. Murphy L, Nagel T. *The Myth of Ownership: Taxes and Justice*. Oxford University Press; 2004.

20. Bruenig M. Toward a new liberalism. *The Policy Shop* blog. December 16, 2013. Accessed April 14, 2022. https://drive.google.com/file/d/1q_IqYXFNJ8yDGSPmU -or8BpmAEeZ6SNm/view.

21. Fried BH. *The Progressive Assault on Laissez Faire: Robert Hale and the First Law and Economics Movement*. Harvard University Press; 2001.

22. Krieger N. *Ecosocial Theory, Embodied Truths, and the People's Health*. Oxford University Press; 2021.

23. Krieger N. Measures of racism, sexism, heterosexism, and gender binarism for health equity research: From structural injustice to embodied harm—An ecosocial analysis. *Annu Rev Public Health*. 2020;41:37–62. doi:10.1146/annurev-publhealth-040119 -094017.

24. Fields KE, Fields BJ. *Racecraft: The Soul of Inequality in American Life*. Reprint ed. Verso; 2014.

25. Jones CP. Levels of racism: a theoretic framework and a gardener's tale. *Am J Public Health*. 2000;90(8):1212–1215. doi:10.2105/ajph.90.8.1212.

26. Dawes DE. *The Political Determinants of Health*. Johns Hopkins University Press; 2020.

27. Williams DR, Lawrence JA, Davis BA. Racism and health: Evidence and needed research. *Annu Rev Public Health*. 2019;40:105–125. doi:10.1146/annurev-publhealth -040218-043750.

28. Berkowitz SA. The logic of policies to address income-related health inequity: A problem-oriented approach. *Milbank Q*. Published online March 22, 2022. doi:10.1111 /1468-0009.12558.

29. Esping-Andersen G. *The Three Worlds of Welfare Capitalism*. Princeton University Press; 1990.

30. Jacques O, Noël A. Targeting within universalism. *J Eur Soc Policy*. 2021;31(1):15–29. doi:10.1177/0958928720918973.

31. Rothstein B. *Just Institutions Matter: The Moral and Political Logic of the Universal Welfare State*. Illustrated ed. Cambridge University Press; 1998.

32. Anttonen A, Sipilä J. Universalism in the British and Scandinavian social policy debates. *Welf State Universalism Divers*. Published online January 1, 2012:16–41. doi:10 .4337/9781849803830.00007.

33. Jacques O, Noël A. Targeting within universalism. *J Eur Soc Policy*. 2021;31(1):15–29. doi:10.1177/0958928720918973.

34. Anttonen A, Häikiö L, Stefánsson K, eds. *Welfare State, Universalism and Diversity*. Edward Elger Publishing; 2014. Accessed March 22, 2022. https://www.e-elgar.com/shop /usd/welfare-state-universalism-and-diversity-9781781951873.html.

35. Keynes JM. *The General Theory of Employment, Interest, and Money*. Harcourt, Brace & World; 2016.

2. What Is Health Equity?

1. World Health Organization. *Social Determinants of Health.* Accessed May 10, 2021. https://www.who.int/westernpacific/health-topics/social-determinants-of-health.

2. Office of Disease Prevention and Health Promotion. *Healthy People 2020 – Disparities.* Accessed May 10, 2021. https://www.healthypeople.gov/2020/about/foundation-health -measures/Disparities.

3. Centers for Disease Control and Prevention. *Minority Health and Health Equity.* Centers for Disease Control and Prevention. Published April 27, 2021. Accessed May 10, 2021. https://www.cdc.gov/healthequity/index.html.

4. Whitehead M. The concepts and principles of equity and health. *Int J Health Serv Plan Adm Eval.* 1992;22(3):429–445. doi:10.2190/986L-LHQ6-2VTE-YRRN.

5. Carter-Pokras O, Baquet C. What is a "health disparity"? *Public Health Rep.* 2002; 117(5):426–434.

6. Reed A, Chowkwanyun M. Race, class, crisis: the discourse of racial disparity and its analytical discontents. *Social Regist.* 2012;48. Accessed May 10, 2021. https://socialist register.com/index.php/srv/article/view/15650.

7. Aspholm RR, Johnson C. Betting on "The Greek": How the NFL is banking on biological racism. Nonsite.org. Published February 1, 2021. Accessed May 10, 2021. https://nonsite.org/betting-on-the-greek-how-the-nfl-is-banking-on-biological-racism/.

8. Institute of Medicine (US) Committee on Understanding and Eliminating Racial and Ethnic Disparities in Health Care. *Unequal Treatment: Confronting Racial and Ethnic Disparities in Health Care.* (Smedley BD, Stith AY, Nelson AR, eds.). National Academies Press (US); 2003. Accessed May 10, 2021. http://www.ncbi.nlm.nih.gov/books/NBK220358/.

9. Agency for Healthcare Research and Quality. *National Healthcare Quality & Disparities Reports.* Accessed May 10, 2021. http://www.ahrq.gov/research/findings/nhqrdr /index.html.

10. Braveman P. What are health disparities and health equity? We need to be clear. *Public Health Rep.* 2014;129(Suppl 2):5–8.

11. *Healthy People 2030.* health.gov. Accessed May 6, 2022. https://health.gov/healthy people.

12. Robert Wood Johnson Foundation. *What Is Health Equity?* RWJF. Published May 1, 2017. Accessed May 11, 2021. https://www.rwjf.org/en/library/research/2017/05/what -is-health-equity-.html.

13. American Medical Association. *Advancing Health Equity: A Guide to Language, Narrative and Concepts.* Accessed December 2, 2021. https://www.ama-assn.org/about /ama-center-health-equity/advancing-health-equity-guide-language-narrative-and -concepts-0.

14. Michaels WB, Reed A. The trouble with disparity. Nonsite.org. Published September 10, 2020. Accessed May 11, 2021. https://nonsite.org/the-trouble-with-disparity/.

15. APM Research Lab. Color of Coronavirus: COVID-19 deaths analyzed by race and ethnicity. APM Research Lab. Accessed May 10, 2021. https://www.apmresearchlab.org /covid/deaths-by-race.

16. Johns Hopkins Coronavirus Resource Center. *Mortality Analyses.* Johns Hopkins

Coronavirus Resource Center. Accessed May 10, 2021. https://coronavirus.jhu.edu/data/mortality.

17. Bor J, Stokes AC, Raifman J, et al. *Missing Americans: Early Death in the United States, 1933–2021.* Published online June 30, 2022. doi:10.1101/2022.06.29.22277065.

18. Centers for Disease Control and Prevention. *Health Equity Considerations and Racial and Ethnic Minority Groups.* Centers for Disease Control and Prevention. Published February 11, 2020. Accessed May 10, 2021. https://www.cdc.gov/coronavirus/2019-ncov/community/health-equity/race-ethnicity.html.

19. Centers for Disease Control and Prevention. *Mortality Trends by Race and Ethnicity Among Adults Aged 25 and over: United States, 2000–2017.* Centers for Disease Control and Prevention. Published July 24, 2019. Accessed May 10, 2021. https://www.cdc.gov/nchs/products/databriefs/db342.htm

20. Fontenot K, Semega J, Kollar M. *Income and Poverty in the United States: 2017.* US Census Bureau. Accessed May 10, 2021. https://www.census.gov/library/publications/2018/demo/p60-263.html.

21. Wagstaff A, van Doorslaer E. Income inequality and health: what does the literature tell us? *Annu Rev Public Health.* 2000;21(1):543–567. doi:10.1146/annurev.publhealth.21.1.543.

22. Schulman KA, Berlin JA, Harless W, et al. The effect of race and sex on physicians' recommendations for cardiac catheterization. *N Engl J Med.* 1999;340(8):618–626. doi:10.1056/NEJM199902253400806.

23. Mocanu V, Kuper TM, Marini W, et al. Intersectionality of gender and visible minority status among general surgery residents in Canada. *JAMA Surg.* 2020;155(10):e202828. doi:10.1001/jamasurg.2020.2828.

24. McClain AC, Gallo LC, Mattei J. Subjective social status and cardiometabolic risk markers by intersectionality of race/ethnicity and sex among U.S. young adults. *Ann Behav Med Publ Soc Behav Med.* Published online May 4, 2021. doi:10.1093/abm/kaab025.

25. McCall L. The complexity of intersectionality. *Signs.* 2005;30(3):1771–1800. doi:10.1086/426800.

26. Harari L, Lee C. Intersectionality in quantitative health disparities research: A systematic review of challenges and limitations in empirical studies. *Soc Sci Med 1982.* 2021;277:113876. doi:10.1016/j.socscimed.2021.113876.

27. Graetz N, Boen CE, Esposito MH. Structural racism and quantitative causal inference: A life course mediation framework for decomposing racial health disparities. *J Health Soc Behav.* Published online January 8, 2022:221465211066108. doi:10.1177/00221465211066108.

28. Governor Whitmer and Lt. Governor Gilchrist Highlight Significant Reduction in Racial Disparities of COVID-19 Cases and Deaths. Accessed May 10, 2021. https://www.michigan.gov/whitmer/0,9309,7-387-90499_90640-540768--,00.html.

29. Michigan: Race & ethnicity historical data. The COVID Tracking Project. Accessed May 10, 2021. https://covidtracking.com/data/state/michigan/race-ethnicity/historical.

30. Mehta Laxmi S., Beckie Theresa M., DeVon Holli A., et al. Acute myocardial infarction in women. *Circulation.* 2016;133(9):916–947. doi:10.1161/CIR.0000000000000351.

31. Bairey Merz C. Noel, Andersen Holly, Sprague Emily, et al. Knowledge, attitudes,

and beliefs regarding cardiovascular disease in women. *J Am Coll Cardiol*. 2017;70(2): 123–132. doi:10.1016/j.jacc.2017.05.024.

32. Robinson Jennifer G. What women (and clinicians) don't know hurts them. *J Am Coll Cardiol*. 2017;70(2):133–135. doi:10.1016/j.jacc.2017.05.037.

33. Stock EO, Redberg R. Cardiovascular disease in women. *Curr Probl Cardiol*. 2012; 37(11):450–526. doi:10.1016/j.cpcardiol.2012.07.001.

34. Johnson HM, Gorre CE, Friedrich-Karnik A, Gulati M. Addressing the bias in cardiovascular care: Missed & delayed diagnosis of cardiovascular disease in women. *Am J Prev Cardiol*. 2021;8:100299. doi:10.1016/j.ajpc.2021.100299.

35. Heron M. Deaths: leading causes for 2017. *Natl Vital Stat Rep Cent Dis Control Prev Natl Cent Health Stat Natl Vital Stat Syst*. 2019;68(6):1–77.

36. Kauh TJ, Read JG, Scheitler AJ. The critical role of racial/ethnic data disaggregation for health equity. *Popul Res Policy Rev*. Published online January 8, 2021:1–7. doi:10 .1007/s11113-020-09631-6.

37. United States Department of Justice. *Section VII: Proving Discrimination – Disparate Impact*. Published January 12, 2017. Accessed March 3, 2022. https://www.justice.gov/crt /fcs/t6manual7.

38. Boyd R. On racism: a new standard for publishing on racial health inequities. *Health Affairs* blog. Accessed January 22, 2021. https://www.healthaffairs.org/do/10.1377 /hblog20200630.939347/full/.

39. Cunningham S. *Causal Inference: The Mixtape*. Yale University Press; 2021.

40. Pearl J, Glymour M, Jewell NP. *Causal Inference in Statistics: A Primer*. Wiley; 2016.

41. Angrist JD, Pischke JS. *Mostly Harmless Econometrics: An Empiricist's Companion*. Princeton University Press; 2009.

42. Westreich D. *Epidemiology by Design*. Oxford University Press; 2019.

43. Hernán MA, Robins JM. *Causal Inference: What If*. Chapman & Hall/CRC; 2020.

3. Equality of What?

1. Sen A. Equality of what? In: McMurrin S, ed. *Tanner Lectures on Human Values*. Vol. 1. Cambridge University Press; 1980:195–220.

2. Dworkin R. *Sovereign Virtue: The Theory and Practice of Equality*. Trade Paperback ed. Harvard University Press; 2002.

3. Anderson ES. What is the point of equality? *Ethics*. 1999;109(2):287–337. doi:10 .1086/233897.

4. Wilson J. Nietzsche and equality. In: von Tevenar G, ed. *Nietzsche and Ethics*. Peter Lang; 2007.

5. Aristotle. *Aristotle: Nicomachean Ethics*; Cambridge University Press; 2014.

6. Nietzsche F. *Beyond Good and Evil*. Penguin Classics; 2003.

7. Wilhoit F. The travesty of liberalism. Crooked Timber. Published March 21, 2018. Accessed March 7, 2022. https://crookedtimber.org/2018/03/21/liberals-against -progressives/.

8. Rawls J. *Justice as Fairness: A Restatement*. 2nd ed. (Kelly EI, ed.). Harvard University Press; 2001.

9. Anderson E. The fundamental disagreement between luck egalitarians and

relational egalitarians. *Can J Philos*. 2010;40(suppl 1):1–23. doi:10.1080/00455091.2010
.10717652.

10. Darwall S. *The Second-Person Standpoint: Morality, Respect, and Accountability*.
Harvard University Press; 2009.

11. Sibley WM. The rational versus the reasonable. *Philos Rev*. 1953;62(4):554–560.
doi:10.2307/2182461.

12. Rawls J. *A Theory of Justice*. 2nd ed. Belknap Press of Harvard University Press;
1999.

13. Scanlon TM. Contractualism and utilitarianism. In: Sen A, Williams B, eds.
Utilitarianism and Beyond. Cambridge University Press; 1982:103–128. doi:10.1017
/CBO9780511611964.007.

14. Rothstein B. *Just Institutions Matter: The Moral and Political Logic of the Universal
Welfare State*. Illustrated ed. Cambridge University Press; 1998.

15. Ashford E, Mulgan T. Contractualism. In: Zalta EN, ed. *The Stanford Encyclopedia
of Philosophy*. Metaphysics Research Lab, Stanford University; Summer 2018. Accessed
March 7, 2022. https://plato.stanford.edu/archives/sum2018/entries/contractualism/.

16. Tawney RH. *Equality*. 5th ed. HarperCollins Publishers; 1964.

17. Anderson E. *Private Government: How Employers Rule Our Lives*. Reprint ed.
Princeton University Press; 2019.

18. Crick B. *In Defense of Politics*. 2nd ed. University of Chicago Press; 1972.

19. Polanyi K. *The Great Transformation: The Political and Economic Origins of Our Time*.
2nd ed. Beacon Press; 2001.

20. Rawls J. *Lectures on the History of Moral Philosophy*. (Herman B, ed.). Harvard
University Press; 2000.

21. Burke E. *Reflections on the Revolution in France*. Cambridge University Press; 2014.

22. Harris I. Edmund Burke. In: Zalta EN, ed. *The Stanford Encyclopedia of Philosophy*.
Metaphysics Research Lab, Stanford University; Summer 2020. Accessed June 24, 2021.
https://plato.stanford.edu/archives/sum2020/entries/burke/.

23. Esping-Andersen G. *The Three Worlds of Welfare Capitalism*. Princeton University
Press; 1990.

24. Mills CW. *The Racial Contract*. Cornell University Press; 1999.

25. Locke J. *Locke: Two Treatises of Government*. Cambridge University Press; 1988.

26. Uzgalis W. John Locke. In: Zalta EN, ed. *The Stanford Encyclopedia of Philosophy*.
Metaphysics Research Lab, Stanford University; Spring 2020. Accessed June 24, 2021.
https://plato.stanford.edu/archives/spr2020/entries/locke/.

27. Berlin I. *Liberty: Incorporating Four Essays on Liberty*. 2nd ed. (Hardy H, ed.). Oxford University Press; 2002.

28. Nozick R. *Anarchy, State, and Utopia*. Basic Books; 2013.

29. Mack E. Robert Nozick's political philosophy. In: Zalta EN, ed. *The Stanford Encyclopedia of Philosophy*. Metaphysics Research Lab, Stanford University; Summer 2018.
Accessed June 24, 2021. https://plato.stanford.edu/archives/sum2018/entries/nozick
-political/.

30. Fried BH. *The Progressive Assault on Laissez Faire: Robert Hale and the First Law and
Economics Movement*. Harvard University Press; 2001.

31. Konczal M. *Freedom from the Market: America's Fight to Liberate Itself from the Grip of the Invisible Hand*. New Press; 2021.

32. Arrow KJ. The organization of economic activity: Issues pertinent to the choice of market versus non-market allocation. In: *The Analysis and Evaluation of Public Expenditures: The PBB-System, Joint Economic Committee, 91st Cong., 1st Sess.*; 1969.

33. Bruenig M. *The Policy Shop* blog. Accessed April 14, 2022. https://drive.google .com/file/d/1q_IqYXFNJ8yDGSPmU-or8BpmAEeZ6SNm/view.

34. Hale RL. Coercion and distribution in a supposedly non-coercive state. *Polit Sci Q*. 1923;38(3):470–494. doi:10.2307/2142367.

35. *Shelley v Kraemer*, 334 US 1 (1948). Legal Information Institute. Accessed May 19, 2022. https://www.law.cornell.edu/wex/shelley_v_kraemer_(1948).

36. Mill JS. *Principles of Political Economy: The Complete 5 Books*. CreateSpace Independent Publishing Platform; 2018.

37. Murphy L, Nagel T. *The Myth of Ownership: Taxes and Justice*. Oxford University Press; 2004.

38. Cohen GA. Freedom and money. In: Otsuka M, ed. *On the Currency of Egalitarian Justice, and Other Essays in Political Philosophy*. Princeton University Press; 2011:166–192. Accessed June 24, 2021. http://www.jstor.org/stable/j.ctt7rp56.13.

39. Sen A. *Development as Freedom*. Reprint ed. Anchor; 2000.

40. Sen A. Just deserts: Amartya Sen. The New York Review of Books. Published online March 4, 1982. Accessed April 20, 2022. https://www.nybooks.com/articles/1982 /03/04/just-deserts/.

41. Shackleton R. Total factor productivity growth in historical perspective. *Congr Budg Off Work Pap 2013–01*. https://www.cbo.gov/sites/default/files/113th-congress-2013 -2014/workingpaper/44002_TFP_Growth_03-18-2013_1.pdf.

42. Weekend reading: Matt Bruenig: What is wealth? *Equitable Growth*. Published May 1, 2016. Accessed March 22, 2022. http://www.equitablegrowth.org/weekend-reading-matt -bruenig-wealth/.

43. James EJ, Taussig FW, James EJ. The state as an economic factor. *Science*. 1886; ns-7(173S):485. doi:10.1126/science.ns-7.173S.485.

44. Offe C, Wiesenthal H. Two logics of collective action: Theoretical notes on social class and organizational form. *Polit Power Soc Theory*. 1980;1:67–115.

45. Arneson R. Equality of opportunity. In: Zalta EN, ed. *The Stanford Encyclopedia of Philosophy*. Metaphysics Research Lab, Stanford University; Summer 2015. Accessed June 24, 2021. https://plato.stanford.edu/archives/sum2015/entries/equal-opportunity/.

46. Bruenig M. Meritocrats and egalitarians. Accessed January 17, 2023. https:// mattbruenig.com/2016/02/21/meritocrats-and-egalitarians/.

47. Marshall TH. *Citizenship and Social Class: And Other Essays*. University Press; 1950.

48. Driver J. The history of utilitarianism. In: Zalta EN, ed. *The Stanford Encyclopedia of Philosophy*. Metaphysics Research Lab, Stanford University; Winter 2014. Accessed June 24, 2021. https://plato.stanford.edu/archives/win2014/entries/utilitarianism-history/.

49. French EB, McCauley J, Aragon M, et al. End-of-life medical spending in last twelve months of life is lower than previously reported. *Health Aff (Millwood)*. 2017;36(7): 1211–1217. doi:10.1377/hlthaff.2017.0174.

50. Marvasti FF, Stafford RS. From "sick care" to health care: Reengineering prevention into the U.S. system. *N Engl J Med*. 2012;367(10):889–891. doi:10.1056/NEJMp1206230.

51. Briggs R. Normative theories of rational choice: Expected utility. *The Stanford Encyclopedia of Philosophy*. Published August 8, 2014. Accessed June 24, 2021. https://plato.stanford.edu/archives/spr2017/entries/rationality-normative-utility/#OutUti.

52. Sen AK. Rational fools: A critique of the behavioral foundations of economic theory. *Philos Public Aff*. 1977;6(4):317–344.

53. Hausman DM. The impossibility of interpersonal utility comparisons. *Mind*. 1995;104(415):473–490.

54. Mill JS. *On Liberty*. 8th ed. (Rapaport E, ed.). Hackett Publishing; 1978.

55. Cohen GA. On the currency of egalitarian justice. *Ethics*. 1989;99(4):906–944.

56. Arneson RJ. Equality and equal opportunity for welfare. *Philos Stud Int J Philos Anal Tradit*. 1989;56(1):77–93.

57. Roemer JE. *Theories of Distributive Justice*. Harvard University Press; 1998.

58. Young IM. *Responsibility for Justice*. Oxford University Press; 2013.

59. Scanlon TM. *Why Does Inequality Matter?* Reprint ed. Oxford University Press; 2020.

60. Rawls J. The basic structure as subject. *Am Philos Q*. 1977;14(2):159–165.

61. Nussbaum MC. *Frontiers of Justice: Disability, Nationality, Species Membership*. Harvard University Press; 2007.

62. Robeyns I, Byskov MF. The capability approach. In: Zalta EN, ed. *The Stanford Encyclopedia of Philosophy*. Winter 2020. Metaphysics Research Lab, Stanford University; 2020. Accessed June 24, 2021. https://plato.stanford.edu/archives/win2020/entries/capability-approach/.

63. Sen A. *Inequality Reexamined*. Harvard University Press; 1995.

64. Reynolds MM. Health power resources theory: A relational approach to the study of health inequalities. *J Health Soc Behav*. 2021;62(4):493–511. doi:10.1177/00221465211025963.

65. Nussbaum MC. *Creating Capabilities: The Human Development Approach*. Reprint ed. Harvard University Press; 2013.

66. Ruger JP. *Health and Social Justice*. Oxford University Press; 2010.

4. Democratic Equality

1. Anderson ES. What is the point of equality? *Ethics*. 1999;109(2):287–337. doi:10.1086/233897.

2. Anderson E. The fundamental disagreement between luck egalitarians and relational egalitarians. *Can J Philos*. 2010;40(suppl 1):1–23. doi:10.1080/00455091.2010.10717652.

3. Scanlon TM. Contractualism and utilitarianism. In: Sen A, Williams B, eds. *Utilitarianism and Beyond*. Cambridge University Press; 1982:103–128. doi:10.1017/CBO9780511611964.007.

4. Darwall S. *The Second-Person Standpoint: Morality, Respect, and Accountability*. Harvard University Press; 2009.

5. Rawls J. *Justice as Fairness: A Restatement*. 2nd ed. (Kelly EI, ed.). Harvard University Press; 2001.

6. Berlin I. *Liberty: Incorporating Four Essays on Liberty*. 2nd ed. (Hardy H, ed.). Oxford University Press; 2002.

7. Marshall TH. *Citizenship and Social Class: And Other Essays*. University Press; 1950.

8. Rawls J. *A Theory of Justice*. 2nd ed. Belknap Press of Harvard University Press; 1999.

9. Tawney RH. *Equality*. 5th ed. HarperCollins Publishers; 1964.

10. Korsgaard CM. Commentary on G. A. Cohen and Amartya Sen. In: *The Quality of Life*. Oxford University Press; 1993. doi:10.1093/0198287976.003.0004.

11. Dworkin R. *Sovereign Virtue: The Theory and Practice of Equality*. Trade Paperback ed. Harvard University Press; 2002.

12. Cohen GA. On the currency of egalitarian justice. *Ethics*. 1989;99(4):906–944.

13. Roemer JE. *Theories of Distributive Justice*. Harvard University Press; 1998.

14. Sen A. Equality of what? In: McMurrin S, ed. *Tanner Lectures on Human Values*. Vol. 1. Cambridge University Press; 1980.

15. Riley AR. Advancing the study of health inequality: Fundamental causes as systems of exposure. *SSM - Popul Health*. 2020;10:100555. doi:10.1016/j.ssmph.2020.100555.

16. Young IM. Five faces of oppression. *Philos Forum*. 1988;19(4):270.

17. Vrousalis N. Exploitation, vulnerability, and social domination. *Philos Public Aff*. 2013;41(2):131–157. doi:10.1111/papa.12013.

18. Michaels WB, Reed A. The Trouble with Disparity. Nonsite.org. Published September 10, 2020. Accessed May 11, 2021. https://nonsite.org/the-trouble-with-disparity/.

19. Reed A. Marx, race, and neoliberalism. *New Labor Forum*. 2013;22(1):49–57. doi:10.1177/1095796012471637.

20. Fields KE, Fields BJ. *Racecraft: The Soul of Inequality in American Life*. Reprint ed. Verso; 2014.

21. Michaels WB. Race into culture: A critical genealogy of cultural identity. *Crit Inq*. 1992;18(4):655–685.

22. Courtwright AM. Justice, stigma, and the new epidemiology of health disparities. *Bioethics*. 2009;23(2):90–96. doi:10.1111/j.1467-8519.2008.00717.x.

23. Link BG, Phelan JC. Conceptualizing stigma. *Annu Rev Sociol*. 2001;27(1):363–385. doi:10.1146/annurev.soc.27.1.363.

24. Young IM. *Responsibility for Justice*. Oxford University Press; 2013.

25. Marcus RY. *Pirkei Avot: Ethics of the Fathers*. Holtzberg Memorial ed. Kehot Publication Society; 2009.

26. Scanlon TM. *Why Does Inequality Matter?* Reprint ed. Oxford University Press; 2020.

27. Dow G, Higgins W. *Politics against Pessimism: Social Democratic Possibilities since Ernst Wigforss*. New ed. Peter Lang AG, Internationaler Verlag der Wissenschaften; 2013.

28. Link BG, Phelan J. Social conditions as fundamental causes of disease. *J Health Soc Behav*. 1995;Spec No:80–94.

29. Krieger N. *Epidemiology and the People's Health: Theory and Context*. Oxford University Press; 2013.

5. How Injustice Harms Health

1. Young IM. *Responsibility for Justice*. Oxford University Press; 2013.

2. Krieger N. Embodiment: a conceptual glossary for epidemiology. *J Epidemiol Community Health*. 2005;59(5):350–355. doi:10.1136/jech.2004.024562.

3. Krieger N. Measures of racism, sexism, heterosexism, and gender binarism for health equity research: from structural injustice to embodied harm—an ecosocial analysis. *Annu Rev Public Health*. 2020;41:37–62. doi:10.1146/annurev-publhealth -040119-094017.

4. Krieger N. *Ecosocial Theory, Embodied Truths, and the People's Health*. Oxford University Press; 2021.

5. Krieger N. *Epidemiology and the People's Health: Theory and Context*. Oxford University Press; 2013.

6. Wright EO. *Class Counts: Comparative Studies in Class Analysis*. Cambridge University Press; 1996.

7. Brady D, Blome A, Kleider H. How politics and institutions shape poverty and inequality. In: *The Oxford Handbook of the Social Science of Poverty*; Oxford University Press; 2016:117–140. doi:10.1093/oxfordhb/9780199914050.013.7.

8. Jepperson RL. Institutions, institutional effects and institutionalism. In: *The New Institutionalism in Organizational Analysis*. University of Chicago Press; 1991:143–163.

9. Western B. *Between Class and Market*. Princeton University Press; 1997.

10. National Research Council (US) Committee on New and Emerging Models in Biomedical and Behavioral Research. *Biomedical Models and Resources: Current Needs and Future Opportunities*. National Academies Press (US); 1998. Accessed October 26, 2021. http://www.ncbi.nlm.nih.gov/books/NBK230285/.

11. Susser M, Stein Z. *Eras in Epidemiology: The Evolution of Ideas*. Oxford University Press; 2009.

12. McMichael AJ. The health of persons, populations, and planets: epidemiology comes full circle. *Epidemiol Camb Mass*. 1995;6(6):633–636.

13. Rothman KJ. *Epidemiology: An Introduction*. 2nd ed. Oxford University Press; 2012.

14. World Health Organization. *Social Determinants of Health*. Accessed May 10, 2021. https://www.who.int/westernpacific/health-topics/social-determinants-of-health.

15. Marmot M, Friel S, Bell R, Houweling TAJ, Taylor S; Commission on Social Determinants of Health. Closing the gap in a generation: health equity through action on the social determinants of health. *Lancet* 2008;372(9650):1661–1669. doi:10.1016/S0140 -6736(08)61690-6.

16. Fair Society Healthy Lives (The Marmot Review). Institute of Health Equity. Accessed October 26, 2021. https://www.instituteofhealthequity.org/resources-reports /fair-society-healthy-lives-the-marmot-review.

17. Adler NE, Newman K. Socioeconomic disparities in health: pathways and policies. *Health Aff Proj Hope*. 2002;21(2):60–76. doi:10.1377/hlthaff.21.2.60.

18. Adler NE, Rehkopf DH. U.S. disparities in health: descriptions, causes, and mechanisms. *Annu Rev Public Health*. 2008;29:235–252. doi:10.1146/annurev.publhealth .29.020907.090852.

19. Braveman P, Gottlieb L. The social determinants of health: it's time to consider the causes of the causes. *Public Health Rep.* 2014;129(Suppl 2):19–31.

20. Braveman PA, Cubbin C, Egerter S, Williams DR, Pamuk E. Socioeconomic disparities in health in the United States: what the patterns tell us. *Am J Public Health.* 2010;100 Suppl 1:S186–196. doi:10.2105/AJPH.2009.166082.

21. Centers for Disease Control and Prevention. *Social Determinants of Health.* Centers for Disease Control and Prevention. Published September 30, 2021. Accessed October 26, 2021. https://www.cdc.gov/socialdeterminants/index.htm.

22. Dawes DE. *The Political Determinants of Health.* Johns Hopkins University Press; 2020.

23. Maani Hessari N, Ruskin G, McKee M, Stuckler D. Public meets private: conversations between Coca-Cola and the CDC. *Milbank Q.* 2019;97(1):74–90. doi:10.1111/1468-0009.12368.

24. de Lacy-Vawdon C, Livingstone C. Defining the commercial determinants of health: a systematic review. *BMC Public Health.* 2020;20(1):1022. doi:10.1186/s12889-020-09126-1.

25. Mialon M. An overview of the commercial determinants of health. *Glob Health.* 2020;16(1):74. doi:10.1186/s12992-020-00607-x.

26. Bennett B. Law, global health, and sustainable development: the Lancet Commission on the Legal Determinants of Health. *J Law Med.* 2020;27(3):505–512.

27. Napier AD, Ancarno C, Butler B, et al. Culture and health. *Lancet.* 2014;384(9954):1607–1639. doi:10.1016/S0140-6736(14)61603-2.

28. Seligman HK, Schillinger D. Hunger and socioeconomic disparities in chronic disease. *N Engl J Med.* 2010;363(1):6–9. doi:10.1056/NEJMp1000072.

29. Housing and health: an overview of the literature. *Health Affairs.* Accessed June 3, 2020. https://www.healthaffairs.org/do/10.1377/hpb20180313.396577/full/.

30. Gundersen C, Ziliak JP. Food insecurity and health outcomes. *Health Affairs.* 2015; 34(11):1830–1839. doi:10.1377/hlthaff.2015.0645.

31. Sapolsky RM. The influence of social hierarchy on primate health. *Science.* 2005; 308(5722):648–652. doi:10.1126/science.1106477.

32. Pickett KE, Wilkinson RG. Income inequality and health: a causal review. *Soc Sci Med 1982.* 2015;128:316–326. doi:10.1016/j.socscimed.2014.12.031.

33. McEwen BS. Protective and damaging effects of stress mediators. *N Engl J Med.* 1998;338(3):171–179. doi:10.1056/NEJM199801153380307.

34. Guidi J, Lucente M, Sonino N, Fava GA. Allostatic load and its impact on health: a systematic review. *Psychother Psychosom.* 2021;90(1):11–27. doi:10.1159/000510696.

35. Geronimus AT. The weathering hypothesis and the health of African-American women and infants: evidence and speculations. *Ethn Dis.* 1992;2(3):207–221.

36. Lynch J. *Regimes of Inequality.* Cambridge University Press; 2021.

37. Link BG, Phelan J. Social conditions as fundamental causes of disease. *J Health Soc Behav.* 1995;Spec No:80–94.

38. Phelan JC, Link BG, Tehranifar P. Social conditions as fundamental causes of health inequalities: theory, evidence, and policy implications. *J Health Soc Behav.* 2010; 51(Suppl):S28–40. doi:10.1177/0022146510383498.

39. Boyd J, Bambra C, Purshouse RC, Holmes J. Beyond behaviour: how health inequality theory can enhance our understanding of the "alcohol-harm paradox." *Int J Environ Res Public Health*. 2021;18(11):6025. doi:10.3390/ijerph18116025.

40. Williams DR, Lawrence JA, Davis BA. Racism and health: evidence and needed research. *Annu Rev Public Health*. 2019;40:105–125. doi:10.1146/annurev-publhealth -040218-043750.

41. Armstrong GL, Conn LA, Pinner RW. Trends in infectious disease mortality in the United States during the 20th century. *JAMA*. 1999;281(1):61–66. doi:10.1001/jama .281.1.61.

42. Berkowitz SA. The logic of policies to address income-related health inequity: a problem-oriented approach. *Milbank Q*. Published online March 22, 2022. doi:10.1111 /1468-0009.12558.

43. Doyal L. *The Political Economy of Health*. Pluto Press; 1979.

44. Waitzkin H, Iriart C, Estrada A, Lamadrid S. Social medicine then and now: lessons from Latin America. *Am J Public Health*. 2001;91(10):1592–1601. doi:10.2105 /AJPH.91.10.1592.

45. Jones NL, Gilman SE, Cheng TL, Drury SS, Hill CV, Geronimus AT. Life course approaches to the causes of health disparities. *Am J Public Health*. 2019;109(S1):S48-S55. doi:10.2105/AJPH.2018.304738.

46. Kawachi I, Subramanian SV, Almeida-Filho N. A glossary for health inequalities. *J Epidemiol Community Health*. 2002;56(9):647–652. doi:10.1136/jech.56.9.647.

47. Bailey ZD, Krieger N, Agénor M, Graves J, Linos N, Bassett MT. Structural racism and health inequities in the USA: evidence and interventions. *Lancet Lond Engl*. 2017; 389(10077):1453–1463. doi:10.1016/S0140-6736(17)30569-X.

48. Boyd R. On racism: a new standard for publishing on racial health inequities. *Health Affairs*. Accessed January 22, 2021. https://www.healthaffairs.org/do/10.1377 /hblog20200630.939347/full/.

49. Courtwright AM. Justice, stigma, and the new epidemiology of health disparities. *Bioethics*. 2009;23(2):90–96. doi:10.1111/j.1467-8519.2008.00717.x.

50. Link BG, Phelan JC. Conceptualizing stigma. *Annu Rev Sociol*. 2001;27(1):363–385. doi:10.1146/annurev.soc.27.1.363.

51. Prins SJ, McKetta S, Platt J, Muntaner C, Keyes KM, Bates LM. The serpent of their agonies: exploitation as structural determinant of mental illness. *Epidemiology*. 2021;32(2):303–309. doi:10.1097/EDE.0000000000001304.

52. Muntaner C, Ng E, Prins SJ, Bones-Rocha K, Espelt A, Chung H. Social class and mental health: testing exploitation as a relational determinant of depression. *Int J Health Serv Plan Adm Eval*. 2015;45(2):265–284. doi:10.1177/0020731414568508.

53. Barr N. *Economics of the Welfare State*. Annotated ed. Oxford University Press; 2020.

54. Mason JW. Wealth distribution and the puzzle of Germany. Accessed December 20, 2022. https://jwmason.org/slackwire/wealth-distribution-and-puzzle-of/.

55. Khullar D, Chokshi DA. Health, income, & poverty: where we are & what could help. *Health Affairs* Brief. Accessed March 12, 2021. https://www.healthaffairs.org/do /10.1377/hpb20180817.901935/full/.

56. Levesque AR, MacDonald S, Berg SA, Reka R. Assessing the impact of changes in household socioeconomic status on the health of children and adolescents: a systematic review. *Adolesc Res Rev*. Published online February 2, 2021:1–33. doi:10.1007/s40894 -021-00151-8.

57. Courtin E, Kim S, Song S, Yu W, Muennig P. Can social policies improve health? A systematic review and meta-analysis of 38 randomized trials. *Milbank Q*. 2020;98(2): 297–371. doi:10.1111/1468-0009.12451.

58. Muennig P, Franks P, Jia H, Lubetkin E, Gold MR. The income-associated burden of disease in the United States. *Soc Sci Med 1982*. 2005;61(9):2018–2026. doi:10.1016 /j.socscimed.2005.04.005.

59. Brady D, Guerra C, Kohler U, Link B. The long arm of prospective childhood income for mature adult health in the United States. *J Health Soc Behav*. Published online March 6, 2022:00221465221081094. doi:10.1177/00221465221081094.

60. Brady D, Giesselmann M, Kohler U, Radenacker A. How to measure and proxy permanent income: evidence from Germany and the U.S. *J Econ Inequal*. 2018;16(3): 321–345. doi:10.1007/s10888-017-9363-9.

61. Kinge JM, Modalsli JH, Øverland S, et al. Association of household income with life expectancy and cause-specific mortality in Norway, 2005–2015. *JAMA*. 2019;321(19): 1916–1925. doi:10.1001/jama.2019.4329.

62. Wagstaff A, van Doorslaer E. Income inequality and health: what does the literature tell us? *Annu Rev Public Health*. 2000;21(1):543–567. doi:10.1146/annurev.publhealth .21.1.543.

63. Truesdale BC, Jencks C. The health effects of income inequality: averages and disparities. *Annu Rev Public Health*. 2016;37:413–430. doi:10.1146/annurev-publhealth -032315-021606.

64. Adeline A, Delattre E. Some microeconometric evidence on the relationship between health and income. *Health Econ Rev*. 2017;7(1):27. doi:10.1186/s13561-017-0163-5.

65. Sreenivasan G. Ethics and epidemiology: the income debate. *Public Health Ethics*. 2009;2(1):45–52. doi:10.1093/phe/php004.

66. Lynch J, Smith GD, Harper S, et al. Is income inequality a determinant of population health? Part 1. A systematic review. *Milbank Q*. 2004;82(1):5–99. doi:10.1111/j.0887 -378x.2004.00302.x.

67. Tan JJX, Kraus MW, Carpenter NC, Adler NE. The association between objective and subjective socioeconomic status and subjective well-being: a meta-analytic review. *Psychol Bull*. 2020;146(11):970–1020. doi:10.1037/bul0000258.

68. Beckfield J, Bambra C, Eikemo TA, Huijts T, McNamara C, Wendt C. An institutional theory of welfare state effects on the distribution of population health. *Soc Theory Health*. 2015;13(3):227–244. doi:10.1057/sth.2015.19.

69. Feinstein L, Sabates R, Anderson TM, Sorhaindo A, Hammond C. What are the effects of education on health? *OECD*. Published online 2006. Accessed October 27, 2021. https://www.oecd.org/education/innovation-education/37425753.pdf.

70. Zajacova A, Lawrence EM. The relationship between education and health: reducing disparities through a contextual approach. *Annu Rev Public Health*. 2018;39:273–289. doi:10.1146/annurev-publhealth-031816-044628.

71. Zimmerman E, Woolf SH. Understanding the relationship between education and health. *NAM Perspect*. Published online June 5, 2014. doi:10.31478/201406a.

72. Sommers BD, Baicker K, Epstein AM. Mortality and access to care among adults after state Medicaid expansions. *N Engl J Med*. 2012;367(11):1025–1034. doi:10.1056/NEJMsa1202099.

73. Baicker K, Taubman SL, Allen HL, et al. The Oregon experiment—effects of Medicaid on clinical outcomes. *N Engl J Med*. 2013;368(18):1713–1722. doi:10.1056/NEJMsa1212321.

74. Miller S, Johnson N, Wherry LR. Medicaid and mortality: new evidence from linked survey and administrative data. *Q J Econ*. 2021;136(3):1783–1829. doi:10.1093/qje/qjab004.

75. Goldin J, Lurie IZ, McCubbin J. Health insurance and mortality: experimental evidence from taxpayer outreach. *Q J Econ*. 2021;136(1):1–49. doi:10.1093/qje/qjaa029.

76. Card D, Dobkin C, Maestas N. Does Medicare save lives?. *Q J Econ*. 2009;124(2):597–636. doi:10.1162/qjec.2009.124.2.597.

77. Goodman-Bacon A. The long-run effects of childhood insurance coverage: Medicaid implementation, adult health, and labor market outcomes. *Am Econ Rev*. 2021;111(8):2550–2593. doi:10.1257/aer.20171671.

78. Elements of access to health care. Agency for Healthcare Research and Quality. Accessed October 27, 2021. https://www.ahrq.gov/research/findings/nhqrdr/chartbooks/access/elements.html.

79. Starfield B, Shi L, Macinko J. Contribution of primary care to health systems and health. *Milbank Q*. 2005;83(3):457–502. doi:10.1111/j.1468-0009.2005.00409.x.

80. Friedberg MW, Hussey PS, Schneider EC. Primary care: a critical review of the evidence on quality and costs of health care. *Health Aff (Millwood)*. 2010;29(5):766–772. doi:10.1377/hlthaff.2010.0025.

81. National Academies of Sciences, Engineering, and Medicine; Health and Medicine Division; Board on Health Care Services; Committee on Implementing High-Quality Primary Care. *Implementing High-Quality Primary Care: Rebuilding the Foundation of Health Care*. (Robinson SK, Meisnere M, Phillips RL, McCauley L, eds.). National Academies Press (US); 2021. Accessed October 27, 2021. http://www.ncbi.nlm.nih.gov/books/NBK571810/.

82. Basu S, Berkowitz SA, Phillips RL, Bitton A, Landon BE, Phillips RS. Association of primary care physician supply with population mortality in the United States, 2005–2015. *JAMA Intern Med*. 2019;179(4):506–514. doi:10.1001/jamainternmed.2018.7624.

83. Silver D, Zhang J. Impacts of basic income on health and economic well-being: evidence from the VA's disability compensation program. National Bureau of Economic Research. https://www.nber.org/papers/w29877. Published March 28, 2022.

84. Ruger JP. *Health and Social Justice*. Oxford University Press; 2010.

85. Health care quality and outcomes. OECD. Accessed October 27, 2021. https://www.oecd.org/els/health-systems/health-care-quality-and-outcomes.htm.

86. Hong CS, Atlas SJ, Chang Y, et al. Relationship between patient panel characteristics and primary care physician clinical performance rankings. *JAMA*. 2010;304(10):1107–1113. doi:10.1001/jama.2010.1287.

87. MacLean CH, Kerr EA, Qaseem A. Time out—charting a path for improving performance measurement. *N Engl J Med*. Published online April 18, 2018. doi:10.1056/NEJMp1802595.

88. Wilensky G. The need to simplify measuring quality in health care. *JAMA*. 2018;319(23):2369–2370. doi:10.1001/jama.2018.6858.

89. Stange KC, Etz RS, Gullett H, et al. Metrics for assessing improvements in primary health care. *Annu Rev Public Health*. 2014;35:423–442. doi:10.1146/annurev-publhealth-032013-182438.

90. Berwick DM. Era 3 for medicine and health care. *JAMA*. 2016;315(13):1329–1330. doi:10.1001/jama.2016.1509.

91. McWilliams JM. Pay for performance: when slogans overtake science in health policy. *JAMA*. 2022;328(21):2114–2116. doi:10.1001/jama.2022.20945.

92. Hill-Briggs F, Adler NE, Berkowitz SA, et al. Social determinants of health and diabetes: a scientific review. *Diabetes Care*. Published online November 2, 2020:dci200053. doi:10.2337/dci20-0053.

93. Golden SH, Joseph JJ, Hill-Briggs F. Casting a health equity lens on endocrinology and diabetes. *J Clin Endocrinol Metab*. 2021;106(4):e1909-e1916. doi:10.1210/clinem/dgaa938.

94. Eberly LA, Yang L, Eneanya ND, et al. Association of race/ethnicity, gender, and socioeconomic status with sodium-glucose cotransporter 2 inhibitor use among patients with diabetes in the US. *JAMA Netw Open*. 2021;4(4):e216139. doi:10.1001/jamanetworkopen.2021.6139.

95. Williams DR, Lawrence JA, Davis BA, Vu C. Understanding how discrimination can affect health. *Health Serv Res*. 2019;54 Suppl 2:1374–1388. doi:10.1111/1475-6773.13222.

96. Govender V, Penn-Kekana L. Gender biases and discrimination: a review of health care interpersonal interactions. *Glob Public Health*. 2008;3 Suppl 1:90–103. doi:10.1080/17441690801892208.

97. Centola D, Guilbeault D, Sarkar U, Khoong E, Zhang J. The reduction of race and gender bias in clinical treatment recommendations using clinician peer networks in an experimental setting. *Nat Commun*. 2021;12(1):6585. doi:10.1038/s41467-021-26905-5.

98. Solomon EM, Wing H, Steiner JF, Gottlieb LM. Impact of transportation interventions on health care outcomes: a systematic review. *Med Care*. 2020;58(4):384–391. doi:10.1097/MLR.0000000000001292.

99. Gottlieb LM, Wing H, Adler NE. A systematic review of interventions on patients' social and economic needs. *Am J Prev Med*. 2017;53(5):719–729. doi:10.1016/j.amepre.2017.05.011.

100. Sieck CJ, Sheon A, Ancker JS, Castek J, Callahan B, Siefer A. Digital inclusion as a social determinant of health. *Npj Digit Med*. 2021;4(1):1–3. doi:10.1038/s41746-021-00413-8.

101. Progress on drinking-water, sanitation and hygiene: 2017 update and SDG baselines. Accessed October 27, 2021. https://www.who.int/publications-detail-redirect/9789241512893.

102. Smith KR, Frumkin H, Balakrishnan K, et al. Energy and human health. *Annu Rev Public Health*. 2013;34:159–188. doi:10.1146/annurev-publhealth-031912-114404.

103. Te Vazquez J, Feng SN, Orr CJ, Berkowitz SA. Food insecurity and cardiometabolic conditions: a review of recent research. *Curr Nutr Rep*. Published online June 21, 2021. doi:10.1007/s13668-021-00364-2.

104. Palakshappa D, Ip EH, Berkowitz SA, et al. Pathways by which food insecurity is associated with atherosclerotic cardiovascular disease risk. *J Am Heart Assoc*. 2021;10(22): e021901. doi:10.1161/JAHA.121.021901.

105. Berkowitz SA, Seligman HK, Choudhry NK. Treat or eat: food insecurity, cost-related medication underuse, and unmet needs. *Am J Med*. 2014;127(4):303–310.e3. doi:10.1016/j.amjmed.2014.01.002.

106. Frank DA, Neault NB, Skalicky A, et al. Heat or eat: the Low Income Home Energy Assistance Program and nutritional and health risks among children less than 3 years of age. *Pediatrics*. 2006;118(5):e1293–1302. doi:10.1542/peds.2005-2943.

107. Berkowitz SA, Meigs JB, DeWalt D, et al. Material need insecurities, control of diabetes mellitus, and use of health care resources: results of the Measuring Economic Insecurity in Diabetes study. *JAMA Intern Med*. 2015;175(2):257–265. doi:10.1001/jama internmed.2014.6888.

108. Berkowitz SA, Hulberg AC, Placzek H, et al. Mechanisms associated with clinical improvement in interventions that address health-related social needs: a mixed-methods analysis. *Popul Health Manag*. Published online December 18, 2018. doi:10.1089/pop.2018 .0162.

109. O'Connor DB, Thayer JF, Vedhara K. Stress and health: a review of psychobiological processes. *Annu Rev Psychol*. 2021;72:663–688. doi:10.1146/annurev-psych-062520 -122331.

110. Slavich GM. Life stress and health: a review of conceptual issues and recent findings. *Teach Psychol Columbia Mo*. 2016;43(4):346–355. doi:10.1177/0098628316662768.

111. Powell-Wiley TM, Baumer Y, Baah FO, et al. Social determinants of cardiovascular disease. *Circ Res*. 2022;130(5):782–799. doi:10.1161/CIRCRESAHA.121.319811.

112. Geronimus AT, Bound J, Waidmann TA, Rodriguez JM, Timpe B. Weathering, drugs, and whack-a-mole: fundamental and proximate causes of widening educational inequity in U.S. life expectancy by sex and race, 1990–2015. *J Health Soc Behav*. 2019;60(2): 222–239. doi:10.1177/0022146519849932.

113. Geronimus AT, Hicken M, Keene D, Bound J. "Weathering" and age patterns of allostatic load scores among Blacks and whites in the United States. *Am J Public Health*. 2006;96(5):826–833. doi:10.2105/AJPH.2004.060749.

114. Geronimus AT, Pearson JA, Linnenbringer E, et al. Weathering in Detroit: place, race, ethnicity, and poverty as conceptually fluctuating social constructs shaping variation in allostatic load. *Milbank Q*. 2020;98(4):1171–1218. doi:10.1111/1468-0009 .12484.

115. Baicker K, Allen HL, Wright BJ, Taubman SL, Finkelstein AN. The effect of Medicaid on management of depression: evidence from the Oregon Health Insurance Experiment. *Milbank Q*. 2018;96(1):29–56. doi:10.1111/1468-0009.12311.

116. Ridley M, Rao G, Schilbach F, Patel V. Poverty, depression, and anxiety: causal evidence and mechanisms. *Science*. 2020;370(6522). doi:10.1126/science.aay0214.

117. Li M, Kennedy EB, Byrne N, et al. Systematic review and meta-analysis of

collaborative care interventions for depression in patients with cancer. *Psychooncology*. 2017;26(5):573–587. doi:10.1002/pon.4286.

118. Momen NC, Plana-Ripoll O, Agerbo E, et al. Association between mental disorders and subsequent medical conditions. *N Engl J Med*. 2020;382(18):1721–1731. doi:10.1056/NEJMoa1915784.

119. Heart disease and mental health disorders. Centers for Disease Control and Prevention. Published May 5, 2021. Accessed October 27, 2021. https://www.cdc.gov/heartdisease/mentalhealth.htm.

120. Mani A, Mullainathan S, Shafir E, Zhao J. Poverty impedes cognitive function. *Science*. 2013;341(6149):976–980. doi:10.1126/science.1238041.

121. Schilbach F, Schofield H, Mullainathan S. The psychological lives of the poor. *Am Econ Rev*. 2016;106(5):435–440. doi:10.1257/aer.p20161101.

122. Schofield H, Venkataramani AS. Poverty-related bandwidth constraints reduce the value of consumption. *Proc Natl Acad Sci U S A*. 2021;118(35):e2102794118. doi:10.1073/pnas.2102794118.

123. Baird HM, Webb TL, Sirois FM, Gibson-Miller J. Understanding the effects of time perspective: a meta-analysis testing a self-regulatory framework. *Psychol Bull*. 2021;147(3):233–267. doi:10.1037/bul0000313.

124. Zhao J, Tomm BM. Psychological responses to scarcity. Oxford Research Encyclopedia of Psychology. doi:10.1093/acrefore/9780190236557.013.41.

125. Fieulaine N. Poor temporality or temporal poverty? The social roots and correlates of time perspective. *Personal Individ Differ*. 2014;60:S12. doi:10.1016/j.paid.2013.07.349.

126. Leigh JP, Chakalov B. Labor unions and health: a literature review of pathways and outcomes in the workplace. *Prev Med Rep*. 2021;24:101502. doi:10.1016/j.pmedr.2021.101502.

127. Schnall PL, Dobson M, Rosskam E, eds. *Unhealthy Work: Causes, Consequences, Cures*. Routledge; 2009.

128. Krieger N, Waterman PD, Hartman C, et al. Social hazards on the job: workplace abuse, sexual harassment, and racial discrimination—a study of Black, Latino, and white low-income women and men workers in the United States. *Int J Health Serv Plan Adm Eval*. 2006;36(1):51–85. doi:10.2190/3EMB-YKRH-EDJ2-0H19.

129. Rivera AS, Akanbi M, O'Dwyer LC, McHugh M. Shift work and long work hours and their association with chronic health conditions: a systematic review of systematic reviews with meta-analyses. *PloS One*. 2020;15(4):e0231037. doi:10.1371/journal.pone.0231037.

130. Marmot MG, Smith GD, Stansfeld S, et al. Health inequalities among British civil servants: the Whitehall II study. *Lancet*. 1991;337(8754):1387–1393. doi:10.1016/0140-6736(91)93068-k.

131. McKee M, Reeves A, Clair A, Stuckler D. Living on the edge: precariousness and why it matters for health. *Arch Public Health*. 2017;75(1):13. doi:10.1186/s13690-017-0183-y.

132. Wacquant L. Class, race & hyperincarceration in revanchist America. *Daedalus*. 2010;139(3):74–90.

133. Boyd RW. Police violence and the built harm of structural racism. *Lancet Lond Engl*. 2018;392(10144):258–259. doi:10.1016/S0140-6736(18)31374-6.

134. Bor J, Venkataramani AS, Williams DR, Tsai AC. Police killings and their spillover effects on the mental health of black Americans: a population-based, quasi-experimental study. *Lancet Lond Engl.* 2018;392(10144):302–310. doi:10.1016/S0140-6736(18)31130-9.

135. Incarceration and health: a family medicine perspective (position paper). Published December 12, 2019. Accessed October 27, 2021. https://www.aafp.org/about/policies/all/incarceration.html.

136. Brennan Center for Justice. Conviction, imprisonment, and lost earnings: how involvement with the criminal justice system deepens inequality. Accessed September 8, 2021. https://www.brennancenter.org/our-work/research-reports/conviction-imprisonment-and-lost-earnings-how-involvement-criminal.

137. Amaro H, Sanchez M, Bautista T, Cox R. Social vulnerabilities for substance use: stressors, socially toxic environments, and discrimination and racism. *Neuropharmacology.* 2021;188:108518. doi:10.1016/j.neuropharm.2021.108518.

138. Lewis M. Brain change in addiction as learning, not disease. *N Engl J Med.* 2018; 379(16):1551–1560. doi:10.1056/NEJMra1602872.

139. Golden SD, Earp JAL. Social ecological approaches to individuals and their contexts: twenty years of health education & behavior health promotion interventions. *Health Educ Behav Off Publ Soc Public Health Educ.* 2012;39(3):364–372. doi:10.1177/1090198111418634.

140. Bronfenbrenner U. Toward an experimental ecology of human development. *Am Psychol.* 1977;32(7):513–531. doi:10.1037/0003-066X.32.7.513.

141. Henderson S, Wells R. Environmental racism and the contamination of Black lives: a literature review. *J Afr Am Stud.* 2021;25(1):134–151. doi:10.1007/s12111-020-09511-5.

142. Climate change, health and equity. Accessed October 27, 2021. https://www.apha.org/topics-and-issues/climate-change/guide.

143. Perdue WC, Stone LA, Gostin LO. The built environment and its relationship to the public's health: the legal framework. *Am J Public Health.* 2003;93(9):1390–1394.

144. Williams DR, Collins C. Racial residential segregation: a fundamental cause of racial disparities in health. *Public Health Rep.* 2001;116(5):404–416.

145. Massey DS, Denton NA. *American Apartheid: Segregation and the Making of the Underclass.* Later Printing ed. Harvard University Press; 1993.

146. Wacquant L. Urban Outcasts: A Comparative Sociology of Advanced Marginality. Polity; 2007.

147. Boyd RW. The case for desegregation. *Lancet Lond Engl.* 2019;393(10190):2484–2485. doi:10.1016/S0140-6736(19)31353-4.

148. Brubaker R. *Grounds for Difference.* Reprint ed. Harvard University Press; 2017.

149. Taylor KY. Race for Profit: How Banks and the Real Estate Industry Undermined Black Homeownership. Illustrated ed. University of North Carolina Press; 2019.

150. Reed A. The trouble with uplift. *The Baffler.* Published September 4, 2018. Accessed December 2, 2021. https://thebaffler.com/salvos/the-trouble-with-uplift-reed.

151. Riley AR. Advancing the study of health inequality: Fundamental causes as systems of exposure. *SSM - Popul Health.* 2020;10:100555. doi:10.1016/j.ssmph.2020.100555.

152. Yong E. How public health took part in its own downfall. *The Atlantic*. Published October 23, 2021. Accessed October 27, 2021. https://www.theatlantic.com/health/archive/2021/10/how-public-health-took-part-its-own-downfall/620457/.

6. Inegalitarian Ideologies and Health

1. Krieger N. Measures of racism, sexism, heterosexism, and gender binarism for health equity research: from structural injustice to embodied harm—an ecosocial analysis. *Annu Rev Public Health*. 2020;41:37–62. doi:10.1146/annurev-publhealth-040119-094017.

2. Krieger N. *Ecosocial Theory, Embodied Truths, and the People's Health*. Oxford University Press; 2021.

3. Williams DR, Lawrence JA, Davis BA. Racism and health: evidence and needed research. *Annu Rev Public Health*. 2019;40:105–125. doi:10.1146/annurev-publhealth-040218-043750.

4. Bailey ZD, Krieger N, Agénor M, Graves J, Linos N, Bassett MT. Structural racism and health inequities in the USA: evidence and interventions. *Lancet Lond Engl*. 2017;389(10077):1453–1463. doi:10.1016/S0140-6736(17)30569-X.

5. Reed A. "Let me go get my big white man": the clientelist foundation of contemporary antiracist politics. Nonsite.org. Published May 12, 2022. Accessed May 16, 2022. https://nonsite.org/let-me-go-get-my-big-white-man/.

6. Therborn G. *Ideology of Power and the Power of Ideology*. Verso Books; 1982.

7. Roberts D. *Fatal Invention: How Science, Politics, and Big Business Re-Create Race in the Twenty-First Century*. 2nd ed. New Press; 2012.

8. Homan P. Structural sexism and health in the United States: a new perspective on health inequality and the gender system. *Am Sociol Rev*. 2019;84(3):486–516. doi:10.1177/0003122419848723.

9. Fields KE, Fields BJ. *Racecraft: The Soul of Inequality in American Life*. Reprint ed. Verso; 2014.

10. Reed A, Chowkwanyun M. Race, class, crisis: the discourse of racial disparity and its analytical discontents. *Social Regist*. 2012;48. Accessed May 10, 2021. https://socialistregister.com/index.php/srv/article/view/15650.

11. Jones CP. Levels of racism: a theoretic framework and a gardener's tale. *Am J Public Health*. 2000;90(8):1212–1215. doi:10.2105/ajph.90.8.1212.

12. Hammonds EM, Herzig RM, eds. *The Nature of Difference: Sciences of Race in the United States from Jefferson to Genomics*. Illustrated ed. MIT Press; 2009.

13. Washington HA. *Medical Apartheid: The Dark History of Medical Experimentation on Black Americans from Colonial Times to the Present*. Illustrated ed. Anchor; 2008.

14. Krieger N. *Epidemiology and the People's Health: Theory and Context*. Oxford University Press; 2013.

15. Gravlee CC. How race becomes biology: Embodiment of social inequality. *Am J Phys Anthropol*. 2009;139(1):47–57. doi:10.1002/ajpa.20983.

16. Lewontin RC. The apportionment of human diversity. In: Dobzhansky T, Hecht MK, Steere WC, eds. *Evolutionary Biology*. Vol. 6. Springer US; 1972:381–398. doi:10.1007/978-1-4684-9063-3_14.

17. Jorde LB, Wooding SP. Genetic variation, classification and "race." *Nat Genet*. 2004;36(11):S28–S33. doi:10.1038/ng1435.

18. How science and genetics are reshaping the race debate of the 21st century. Science in the News. Published April 18, 2017. Accessed October 27, 2021. https://sitn .hms.harvard.edu/flash/2017/science-genetics-reshaping-race-debate-21st-century/.

19. Rosenberg NA, Pritchard JK, Weber JL, et al. Genetic structure of human populations. *Science*. 2002;298(5602):2381–2385. doi:10.1126/science.1078311.

20. Lewis ACF, Molina SJ, Appelbaum PS, et al. Getting genetic ancestry right for science and society. *Science*. 2022;376(6590):250–252. doi:10.1126/science.abm7530.

21. Brubaker R. *Grounds for Difference*. Reprint ed. Harvard University Press; 2017.

22. Michaels WB. Race into culture: a critical genealogy of cultural identity. *Crit Inq*. 1992;18(4):655–685.

23. Mead L. Poverty and culture. *Society*. Published online July 21, 2020. doi:10.1007 /s12115-020-00496-1.

24. Omi M, Winant H. *Racial Formation in the United States*. 3rd ed. Routledge; 2014.

25. Loveman M. Making "race" and nation in the United States, South Africa, and Brazil: taking making seriously. *Theory Soc*. 1999;28(6):903–927. doi:10.1023/A:1007 054226164.

26. *Shelley v Kraemer*, 334 US 1 (1948). Legal Information Institute. Accessed May 19, 2022. https://www.law.cornell.edu/wex/shelley_v_kraemer_(1948).

27. Baker RS, Brady D, Parolin Z, Williams DT. The enduring significance of ethno-racial inequalities in poverty in the U.S., 1993–2017. *Popul Res Policy Rev*. Published online September 2, 2021. doi:10.1007/s11113-021-09679-y.

28. Jones CP. Confronting institutionalized racism. *Phylon 1960–*. 2002;50(1/2):7–22. doi:10.2307/4149999.

29. Spencer SJ, Logel C, Davies PG. Stereotype threat. *Annu Rev Psychol*. 2016;67: 415–437. doi:10.1146/annurev-psych-073115-103235.

30. Williams DR, Lawrence JA, Davis BA, Vu C. Understanding how discrimination can affect health. *Health Serv Res*. 2019;54 Suppl 2:1374–1388. doi:10.1111/1475-6773.13222.

31. Krieger N. Discrimination and health inequities. *Int J Health Serv Plan Adm Eval*. 2014;44(4):643–710. doi:10.2190/HS.44.4.b.

32. Lynch SN. U.S. House passes bill to end disparities in crack cocaine sentences. Reuters. Accessed October 27, 2021. https://www.reuters.com/world/us/us-house-passes -bill-end-disparities-crack-cocaine-sentences-2021-09-28/.

33. Kline PM, Rose EK, Walters CR. *Systemic Discrimination Among Large U.S. Employers*. National Bureau of Economic Research; 2021. doi:10.3386/w29053.

34. De Blasio Stop Frisk Reform. Stop and Frisk and the Urgent Need for Meaningful Reforms. Scribd. Published May 2013. Accessed October 27, 2021. https://www.scribd .com/document/142769203/De-Blasio-Stop-Frisk-Reform.

35. Lin JS, Hoffman L, Bean SI, et al. Addressing racism in preventive services: methods report to support the US Preventive Services Task Force. *JAMA*. Published online November 8, 2021. doi:10.1001/jama.2021.17579.

36. Mohottige D, Boulware LE, Ford C, Jones C, Norris K. Use of race in kidney

research and medicine. *Clin J Am Soc Nephrol CJASN*. Published online November 17, 2021:CJN.04890421. doi:10.2215/CJN.04890421.

37. Jones CP. Toward the science and practice of anti-racism: launching a national campaign against racism. *Ethn Dis*. 28(Suppl 1):231–234. doi:10.18865/ed.28.S1.231.

38. Beech BM, Ford C, Thorpe RJ, Bruce MA, Norris KC. Poverty, racism, and the public health crisis in America. *Front Public Health*. 2021;9:699049. doi:10.3389/fpubh .2021.699049.

39. Brubaker R, Cooper F. Beyond "identity." *Theory Soc*. 2000;29(1):1–47.

40. McCall L. The complexity of intersectionality. *Signs*. 2005;30(3):1771–1800. doi:10 .1086/426800.

41. Combahee River Collective. The Combahee River Collective Statement (1977). BlackPast.org. Published November 16, 2012. Accessed October 27, 2021. https://www .blackpast.org/african-american-history/combahee-river-collective-statement-1977/.

42. Crenshaw K. Demarginalizing the intersection of race and sex: a Black feminist critique of antidiscrimination doctrine, feminist theory and antiracist politics. *Univ Chic Leg Forum*. 1989;140:139–167.

43. Compare the Speeches. The Sojourner Truth Project. Accessed October 27, 2021. https://www.thesojournertruthproject.com/compare-the-speeches.

44. Harari L, Lee C. Intersectionality in quantitative health disparities research: a systematic review of challenges and limitations in empirical studies. *Soc Sci Med 1982*. 2021;277:113876. doi:10.1016/j.socscimed.2021.113876.

45. Kauh TJ, Read JG, Scheitler AJ. The critical role of racial/ethnic data disaggregation for health equity. *Popul Res Policy Rev*. Published online January 8, 2021:1–7. doi:10 .1007/s11113-020-09631-6.

46. Wemrell M, Karlsson N, Perez Vicente R, Merlo J. An intersectional analysis providing more precise information on inequities in self-rated health. *Int J Equity Health*. 2021;20(1):54. doi:10.1186/s12939-020-01368-0.

47. Merlo J. Multilevel analysis of individual heterogeneity and discriminatory accuracy (MAIHDA) within an intersectional framework. *Soc Sci Med 1982*. 2018;203: 74–80. doi:10.1016/j.socscimed.2017.12.026.

48. Evans CR, Leckie G, Merlo J. Multilevel versus single-level regression for the analysis of multilevel information: the case of quantitative intersectional analysis. *Soc Sci Med 1982*. 2020;245:112499. doi:10.1016/j.socscimed.2019.112499.

49. Wright EO. *Class Counts: Comparative Studies in Class Analysis*. Cambridge University Press; 1996.

50. Graetz N, Boen CE, Esposito MH. Structural racism and quantitative causal inference: a life course mediation framework for decomposing racial health disparities. *J Health Soc Behav*. Published online January 8, 2022:221465211066108. doi:10.1177 /00221465211066108.

51. Táíwò OO. Being-in-the-room privilege: elite capture and epistemic deference. The Philosopher. Accessed October 27, 2021. https://www.thephilosopher1923.org/essay -taiwo.

52. Bright LK. Empiricism is a standpoint epistemology. The Sooty Empiric. Published

June 3, 2018. Accessed March 11, 2022. http://sootyempiric.blogspot.com/2018/06
/empiricism-is-standpoint-epistemology.html.

53. MacDorman MF, Thoma M, Declcerq E, Howell EA. Racial and ethnic disparities
in maternal mortality in the United States using enhanced vital records, 2016–2017. *Am J
Public Health*. 2021;111(9):1673–1681. doi:10.2105/AJPH.2021.306375.

54. Essien UR, Kim N, Hausmann LRM, et al. Disparities in anticoagulant therapy
initiation for incident atrial fibrillation by race/ethnicity among patients in the Veterans
Health Administration system. *JAMA Netw Open*. 2021;4(7):e2114234. doi:10.1001/jama
networkopen.2021.14234.

55. Phelan JC, Link BG. Is racism a fundamental cause of inequalities in health? *Annu
Rev Sociol*. 2015;41(1):311–330. doi:10.1146/annurev-soc-073014-112305.

56. Bright LK. White psychodrama. *J Polit Philos*. Published March 15, 2023. https://
doi.org/10.1111/jopp.12290.

57. Advancing health equity: A guide to language, narrative and concepts. American
Medical Association. Accessed December 2, 2021. https://www.ama-assn.org/about/ama
-center-health-equity/advancing-health-equity-guide-language-narrative-and-concepts-0.

58. Singh NP. Racial metaphors. *Dissent Mag*. Accessed May 19, 2022. https://www
.dissentmagazine.org/article/racial-metaphors.

59. Chibber V. *The Class Matrix: Social Theory after the Cultural Turn*. Harvard University Press; 2022.

60. Reed T. *Toward Freedom: The Case Against Race Reductionism*. Verso; 2020.

61. Smith PH. The quest for racial democracy: Black civic ideology and housing
interests in postwar Chicago. *J Urban Hist*. 2000;26(2):131–157. doi:10.1177/0096
14420002600201.

7. The Theory of the Welfare State

1. Brady D. *Rich Democracies, Poor People: How Politics Explain Poverty*. Illustrated ed.
Oxford University Press; 2009.

2. Berkowitz SA. The logic of policies to address income-related health inequity: a
problem-oriented approach. *Milbank Q*. Published online March 22, 2022. doi:10.1111
/1468-0009.12558.

3. Rolph ER. The concept of transfers in national income estimates. *Q J Econ*. 1948;
62(3):327–361. doi:10.2307/1882835.

4. Fried BH. *The Progressive Assault on Laissez Faire: Robert Hale and the First Law and
Economics Movement*. Harvard Univesity Press; 2001.

5. Polanyi K. *The Great Transformation: The Political and Economic Origins of Our Time*.
2nd ed. Beacon Press; 2001.

6. Bruenig M. Why discussions of government benefits are so wrong. Accessed
December 5, 2022. https://mattbruenig.com/2013/05/09/why-discussions-of-government
-benefits-are-so-wrong/.

7. Glennerster H. *Understanding the Cost of Welfare*. 3rd ed. Policy Press; 2017.

8. Annual Social and Economic Supplements. United States Census Bureau. Accessed
March 11, 2021. https://www.census.gov/data/datasets/time-series/demo/cps/cps-asec
.html.

9. Barr N, Diamond P. The economics of pensions. *Oxf Rev Econ Policy*. 2006;22(1): 15–39.

10. Barr N. *Economics of the Welfare State*. Annotated ed. Oxford University Press; 2020.

11. Anderson ES. What is the point of equality? *Ethics*. 1999;109(2):287–337. doi:10 .1086/233897.

12. Berg J, Gibson A. Why the world should not follow the failed United States model of fighting domestic hunger. *Int J Environ Res Public Health*. 2022;19(2):814. doi:10.3390 /ijerph19020814.

13. Young IM. *Responsibility for Justice*. Oxford University Press; 2013.

14. Brubaker R. *Grounds for Difference*. Reprint ed. Harvard University Press; 2017.

15. Sligar D. Egalitarianism requires child benefits. Western Sydney Wonk. Published January 23, 2022. Accessed December 5, 2022. https://westernsydneywonk.wordpress .com/2022/01/23/egalitarianism-requires-child-benefits/.

16. Apps P. *Family Taxation: An Unfair and Inefficient System*. Centre for Economic Policy Research, Research School of Economics, Australian National University; 2006. Accessed November 16, 2022. https://econpapers.repec.org/paper/auudpaper/524.htm.

17. Murphy L, Nagel T. *The Myth of Ownership: Taxes and Justice*. Oxford University Press; 2004.

18. Murphy L. How not to argue for tax justice. *Boston Review*. Accessed March 22, 2022. https://bostonreview.net/articles/liam-murphy-how-not-argue-tax-justice/.

19. Weekend reading: Matt Bruenig: What is wealth? *Equitable Growth*. Published May 1, 2016. Accessed March 22, 2022. http://www.equitablegrowth.org/weekend-reading-matt -bruenig-wealth/.

20. Bruenig M. The other move on property. Accessed March 22, 2022. https://matt bruenig.com/2014/01/12/the-other-move-on-property/.

21. Scanlon TM. *Why Does Inequality Matter?* Reprint ed. Oxford University Press; 2020.

22. Bruenig M. Desert theory, rehashed. Published May 9, 2014. Accessed December 5, 2022. https://mattbruenig.com/2014/05/09/desert-theory-rehashed/.

23. Shackleton R. Total factor productivity growth in historical perspective. *Congr Budg Off Work Pap 2013–01*. https://www.cbo.gov/sites/default/files/113th-congress-2013 -2014/workingpaper/44002_TFP_Growth_03-18-2013_1.pdf.

24. Sen A. Just deserts: Amartya Sen. Published online March 4, 1982. Accessed April 20, 2022. https://www.nybooks.com/articles/1982/03/04/just-deserts/.

25. Nozick R. *Anarchy, State, and Utopia*. Basic Books; 2013.

26. Locke J. *Locke: Two Treatises of Government*. Cambridge University Press; 1988.

27. Barr N. *The Welfare State as Piggy Bank: Information, Risk, Uncertainty, and the Role of the State*. Oxford University Press; 2001.

28. Vanhuysse P, Medgyesi M, Gal RI. Welfare states as lifecycle redistribution machines: decomposing the roles of age and socio-economic status shows that European tax-and-benefit systems primarily redistribute across age groups. *PLoS ONE*. 2021;16(8): e0255760. doi:10.1371/journal.pone.0255760.

29. Bruenig M. Socialism and the welfare state. Accessed January 10, 2022. https:// mattbruenig.com/2021/05/12/socialism-and-the-welfare-state/.

30. Bruenig M. The private property and personal property distinction. Accessed March 22, 2022. https://mattbruenig.com/2021/05/12/the-private-property-and-personal-property-distinction/.

31. Esping-Andersen G. *The Three Worlds of Welfare Capitalism*. Princeton University Press; 1990.

32. Muller J, Raphael D. Does unionization and working under collective agreements promote health? *Health Promot Int*. Published online December 13, 2021:daab181. doi:10.1093/heapro/daab181.

33. Rothstein B. *Just Institutions Matter: The Moral and Political Logic of the Universal Welfare State*. Illustrated ed. Cambridge University Press; 1998.

34. Jacques O, Noël A. Targeting within universalism. *J Eur Soc Policy*. 2021;31(1):15–29. doi:10.1177/0958928720918973.

35. Anttonen A, Sipilä J. Universalism in the British and Scandinavian social policy debates. *Welf State Universalism Divers*. Published online January 1, 2012:16–41. doi:10.4337/9781849803830.00007.

36. Anttonen A, Häikiö L, Stefánsson K, eds. *Welfare State, Universalism and Diversity*. Edward Elger Publishing; 2014. Accessed March 22, 2022. https://www.e-elgar.com/shop/usd/welfare-state-universalism-and-diversity-9781781951873.html.

37. Sen A. *Development as Freedom*. Reprint ed. Anchor; 2000.

38. Marshall TH. *Citizenship and Social Class: And Other Essays*. University Press; 1950.

39. Bleich SN, Rimm EB, Brownell KD. U.S. Nutrition assistance, 2018: modifying SNAP to promote population health. *N Engl J Med*. 2017;376(13):1205–1207. doi:10.1056/NEJMp1613222.

40. Mozaffarian D, Fleischhacker S, Andrés JR. Prioritizing nutrition security in the US. *JAMA*. 2021;325(16):1605–1606. doi:10.1001/jama.2021.1915.

41. Rawls J. *Justice as Fairness: A Restatement*. 2nd ed. (Kelly EI, ed.). Harvard University Press; 2001.

42. Joint Committee on Taxation, Congress of United States. Estimates of Federal Tax Expenditures for Fiscal Years 2019–2023. Accessed May 13, 2021. https://www.jct.gov/publications/2019/jcx-55-19/.

43. Atkinson AB. *Inequality: What Can Be Done?* Harvard University Press; 2015.

44. Quadagno J. *The Color of Welfare: How Racism Undermined the War on Poverty*. Rev ed. Oxford University Press; 1996.

45. Reed T. *Toward Freedom: The Case Against Race Reductionism*. Verso; 2020.

46. Calnitsky D. Structural and individualistic theories of poverty. *Sociol Compass*. 2018;12(12):e12640. doi:10.1111/soc4.12640.

47. Bruenig M. *The Policy Shop* blog. Accessed April 14, 2022. https://drive.google.com/file/d/1q_IqYXFNJ8yDGSPmU-or8BpmAEeZ6SNm/view.

8. Economics of the Welfare State

1. Kaufman BE. Institutional economics and the minimum wage: broadening the theoretical and policy debate. *Ind Labor Relat Rev*. 2010;63(3):427–453.

2. Smith A. *The Wealth of Nations: Books 1–3*. Penguin Classics; 1982.

3. Glennerster H. *Understanding the Cost of Welfare*. 3rd ed. Policy Press; 2017.

4. Barr N. *Economics of the Welfare State*. Annotated ed. Oxford University Press; 2020.

5. Arrow KJ. (1963). Uncertainty and the Welfare Economics of Medical Care. The American Economic Review. 1963;53(5):941–973.

6. Murphy L, Nagel T. *The Myth of Ownership: Taxes and Justice*. Oxford University Press; 2004.

7. Cooper M. Infinite regress: Virginia school neoliberalism and the tax revolt. *Capital J Hist Econ*. 2021;2(1):41–87. doi:10.1353/cap.2021.0002.

8. Hale RL. Coercion and distribution in a supposedly non-coercive state. *Polit Sci Q*. 1923;38(3):470–494. doi:10.2307/2142367.

9. Robinson J. *The Economics of Imperfect Competition*. Palgrave Macmillan UK; 1969. doi:10.1007/978-1-349-15320-6.

10. Dube A. Impacts of minimum wages: review of the international evidence. GOV. UK. Accessed March 28, 2022. https://www.gov.uk/government/publications/impacts-of-minimum-wages-review-of-the-international-evidence.

11. Manning A. Monopsony in labor markets: a review. *ILR Rev*. 2021;74(1):3–26. doi:10.1177/0019793920922499.

12. Pigou AC. *The Economics of Welfare*. 4th ed. Macmillan; 1948.

13. Hart O, Shleifer A, Vishny RW. The proper scope of government: theory and an application to prisons. *Q J Econ*. 1997;112(4):1127–1161. doi:10.1162/003355300555448.

14. Knutsson D, Tyrefors B. The quality and efficiency of public and private firms: evidence from ambulance services. *Q J Econ*. Published online February 25, 2022:qjac014. doi:10.1093/qje/qjac014.

15. Donahue JD. *The Privatization Decision: Public Ends, Private Means*. Reprint ed. Basic Books; 1991.

16. Rothstein B. *Just Institutions Matter: The Moral and Political Logic of the Universal Welfare State*. Illustrated ed. Cambridge University Press; 1998.

17. Hirschman AO. *Exit, Voice, and Loyalty: Responses to Decline in Firms, Organizations, and States*. Harvard University Press; 1970.

18. Barr N. *The Welfare State as Piggy Bank: Information, Risk, Uncertainty, and the Role of the State*. Oxford University Press; 2001.

19. Vanhuysse P, Medgyesi M, Gal RI. Welfare states as lifecycle redistribution machines: decomposing the roles of age and socio-economic status shows that European tax-and-benefit systems primarily redistribute across age groups. *PLoS ONE*. 2021;16(8): e0255760. doi:10.1371/journal.pone.0255760.

20. Jacques O, Noël A. Targeting within universalism. *J Eur Soc Policy*. 2021;31(1):15–29. doi:10.1177/0958928720918973.

21. Korpi W, Palme J. The paradox of redistribution and strategies of equality: welfare state institutions, inequality, and poverty in the western countries. *Am Sociol Rev*. 1998; 63(5):661–687. doi:10.2307/2657333.

22. Atkinson AB. *Inequality: What Can Be Done?* Harvard University Press; 2015.

23. Diamond PA. *Taxation, Incomplete Markets, and Social Security*. MIT Press; 2002.

24. Bowles S, Gintis H. *Power*. Department of Economics, University of Siena; 2007. Accessed March 29, 2022. https://ideas.repec.org/p/usi/wpaper/495.html.

25. Rothstein J. Is the EITC as good as an NIT? Conditional cash transfers and tax incidence. *Am Econ J Econ Policy*. 2010;2(1):177–208. doi:10.1257/pol.2.1.177.

26. Mason JW. Public options: the general case. Published September 5, 2010. Accessed March 29, 2022. https://jwmason.org/slackwire/public-options-general-case/.

27. Berman EP. *Thinking Like an Economist: How Efficiency Replaced Equality in U.S. Public Policy*. Princeton University Press; 2022.

9. Financing the Welfare State

1. Glennerster H. *Understanding the Cost of Welfare*. 3rd ed. Policy Press; 2017.

2. Barr N. *Economics of the Welfare State*. Annotated ed. Oxford University Press; 2020.

3. Murphy L, Nagel T. *The Myth of Ownership: Taxes and Justice*. Oxford University Press; 2004.

4. Murphy L. How not to argue for tax justice. *Boston Review*. Accessed March 22, 2022. https://bostonreview.net/articles/liam-murphy-how-not-argue-tax-justice/.

5. Anderson ES. What is the point of equality? *Ethics*. 1999;109(2):287–337. doi:10.1086/233897.

6. Scanlon TM. *Why Does Inequality Matter?* Reprint ed. Oxford University Press; 2020.

7. Diamond PA. *Taxation, Incomplete Markets, and Social Security*. MIT Press; 2002.

8. Mirrlees JA. An exploration in the theory of optimum income taxation. *Rev Econ Stud*. 1971;38(2):175–208. doi:10.2307/2296779.

9. Ostry JD, Berg A, Tsangarides CG. Redistribution, inequality, and growth. *IMF Staff Discuss Note*. 2014;14(02):1. doi:10.5089/9781484352076.006.

10. Cingano F. Trends in income inequality and its impact on economic growth. OECD Social Employment and Migration Working Papers No. 163; 2014. doi:10.1787/5jxrjncwxv6j-en.

11. Pigou AC. *The Economics of Welfare*. 4th ed. Macmillan; 1948.

12. Wright A, Smith KE, Hellowell M. Policy lessons from health taxes: a systematic review of empirical studies. *BMC Public Health*. 2017;17(1):583. doi:10.1186/s12889-017-4497-z.

13. Itria A, Borges SS, Rinaldi AEM, Nucci LB, Enes CC. Taxing sugar-sweetened beverages as a policy to reduce overweight and obesity in countries of different income classifications: a systematic review. *Public Health Nutr*. 2021;24(16):5550–5560. doi:10.1017/S1368980021002901.

14. Jha P, Chaloupka F. *Tobacco Control in Developing Countries*. Oxford University Press; 2000. Accessed March 31, 2022. https://econpapers.repec.org/bookchap/oxpobooks/9780192632463.htm.

15. Cohen J. Money, politics, political equality. In: Byrne A, Stalnaker R, Wedgwood R, eds. *Fact and Value: Essays on Ethics and Metaphysics for Judith Jarvis Thomson*. MIT Press; 2001:47.

16. Rawls J. *A Theory of Justice*. Rev ed. Harvard University Press; 1999.

17. Meade JE. *Efficiency, Equality and the Ownership of Property*. Routledge; 2013.

18. Saez E, Zucman G. *The Triumph of Injustice: How the Rich Dodge Taxes and How to Make Them Pay*. W. W. Norton; 2020.

19. Contribution and benefit base. Social Security Administration. Accessed March 31, 2022. https://www.ssa.gov/oact/cola/cbb.html.

20. Saez E, Slemrod J, Giertz SH. The elasticity of taxable income with respect to marginal tax rates: a critical review. *J Econ Lit*. 2012;50(1):3–50. doi:10.1257/jel.50.1.3.

21. Diamond P, Saez E. The case for a progressive tax: from basic research to policy recommendations. *J Econ Perspect*. 2011;25(4):165–190. doi:10.1257/jep.25.4.165.

22. Korpi W. Eurosclerosis and the sclerosis of objectivity: on the role of values among economic policy experts. *Econ J*. 1996;106(439):1727–1746. doi:10.2307/2235214.

23. Atkinson A, Mogensen GV, eds. *Welfare and Work Incentives: A North European Perspective*. Clarendon Press / Oxford University Press; 1993.

24. Dowrick S. Swedish economic performance and Swedish economic debate: a view from outside. *Econ J*. 1996;106(439):1772–1779. doi:10.2307/2235217.

25. Piketty T, Saez E, Stantcheva S. Optimal taxation of top labor incomes: a tale of three elasticities. *Am Econ J Econ Policy*. 2014;6(1):230–271. doi:10.1257/pol.6.1.230.

26. Batchelder LL, Kamin D. *Taxing the Rich: Issues and Options*. Social Science Research Network; 2019. doi:10.2139/ssrn.3452274.

27. Apps P. *Family Taxation: An Unfair and Inefficient System*. Centre for Economic Policy Research, Research School of Economics, Australian National University; 2006. Accessed November 16, 2022. https://econpapers.repec.org/paper/auudpaper/524.htm.

28. Apps P, Rees R, Thoresen TO, Vattø TE. *Alternatives to Paying Child Benefit to the Rich. Means Testing or Higher Tax?* Statistics Norway, Research Department; 2021. Accessed January 18, 2022. https://ideas.repec.org/p/ssb/dispap/969.html.

29. Bivens J, Mishel L. The pay of corporate executives and financial professionals as evidence of rents in top 1 percent incomes. *J Econ Perspect*. 2013;27(3):57–78. doi:10.1257/jep.27.3.57.

30. Frank RH. Positional externalities cause large and preventable welfare losses. *Am Econ Rev*. 2005;95(2):137–141.

31. Corak M. Income inequality, equality of opportunity, and intergenerational mobility. *J Econ Perspect*. 2013;27(3):79–102. doi:10.1257/jep.27.3.79.

32. Gechert S, Heimberger P. Do corporate tax cuts boost economic growth? Vienna Institute for International Economic Studies. Published June 2021. Accessed March 31, 2022. https://wiiw.ac.at/p-5821.html.

33. Tawney RH. *Equality*. 5th ed. HarperCollins Publishers; 1964.

34. Saez E, Zucman G. The rise of income and wealth inequality in America: evidence from distributional macroeconomic accounts. *J Econ Perspect*. 2020;34(4):3–26. doi:10.1257/jep.34.4.3.

35. Saez E, Zucman G. Wealth inequality in the United States since 1913: evidence from capitalized income tax data. *Q J Econ*. 2016;131(2):519–578. doi:10.1093/qje/qjw004.

36. Warren E. Ultra-millionaire tax. Accessed March 31, 2022. https://elizabethwarren.com/plans/ultra-millionaire-tax.

37. Stiglitz JE. The origins of inequality, and policies to contain it. *Natl Tax J*. 2015; 68(2):425–448.

38. Cooper M. Infinite regress: Virginia school neoliberalism and the tax revolt. *Capital J Hist Econ*. 2021;2(1):41–87. doi:10.1353/cap.2021.0002.

39. Gale WG. Raising revenue with a progressive-value added tax. Brookings. Published January 28, 2020. Accessed March 31, 2022. https://www.brookings.edu/research/raising-revenue-with-a-progressive-value-added-tax/.

40. What is a VAT? Tax Policy Center. Accessed March 31, 2022. https://www.taxpolicycenter.org/briefing-book/what-vat.

41. Kopczuk W. Tax bases, tax rates and the elasticity of reported income. *J Public Econ*. 2005;89(11):2093–2119. doi:10.1016/j.jpubeco.2004.12.005.

42. Feldstein M. Tax avoidance and the deadweight loss of the income tax. *Rev Econ Stat*. 1999;81(4):674–680.

43. Brook RH, Keeler EB, Lohr KN, et al. *The Health Insurance Experiment: A Classic RAND Study Speaks to the Current Health Care Reform Debate*. RAND Corporation; 2006. Accessed March 31, 2022. https://www.rand.org/pubs/research_briefs/RB9174.html.

44. Barr N. *The Welfare State as Piggy Bank: Information, Risk, Uncertainty, and the Role of the State*. Oxford University Press; 2001.

45. Slemrod J. Cheating ourselves: the economics of tax evasion. *J Econ Perspect*. 2007;21(1):25–48. doi:10.1257/jep.21.1.25.

46. Rothstein B. *Just Institutions Matter: The Moral and Political Logic of the Universal Welfare State*. Illustrated ed. Cambridge University Press; 1998.

47. Chetty R, Looney A, Kroft K. Salience and taxation: theory and evidence. *Am Econ Rev*. 2009;99(4):1145–1177. doi:10.1257/aer.99.4.1145.

48. Finkelstein A. E-ztax: tax salience and tax rates. *Q J Econ*. 2009;124(3):969–1010. doi:10.1162/qjec.2009.124.3.969.

49. Cabral M, Hoxby C. *The Hated Property Tax: Salience, Tax Rates, and Tax Revolts*. National Bureau of Economic Research, Inc.; 2012. Accessed March 31, 2022. https://econpapers.repec.org/paper/nbrnberwo/18514.htm.

50. Fochmann M, Weimann J. The effects of tax salience and tax experience on individual work efforts in a framed field experiment. *Finanz Public Finance Anal*. 2013; 69(4):511–542.

51. Bruenig M. Why fiscal progressivity discussions are so muddled. Dēmos. Published June 17, 2016. Accessed March 29, 2022. https://www.demos.org/blog/3/26/15/why-fiscal-progressivity-discussions-are-so-muddled.

52. Piketty T, Saez E, Zucman G. Distributional national accounts: methods and estimates for the United States. *Q J Econ*. 2018;133(2):553–609. doi:10.1093/qje/qjx043.

53. Sligar D. The first principle of social democratic tax design is MOAR. Western Sydney Wonk. Published May 20, 2020. Accessed June 7, 2021. https://westernsydneywonk.wordpress.com/2020/05/20/the-first-principle-of-social-democratic-tax-design-is-moar/.

54. Stone C. Fiscal stimulus needed to fight recessions. Center on Budget and Policy Priorities. Accessed March 31, 2022. https://www.cbpp.org/research/economy/fiscal-stimulus-needed-to-fight-recessions.

55. Romer CD. The fiscal policy response to the pandemic. Brookings. Published March 25, 2021. Accessed March 31, 2022. https://www.brookings.edu/bpea-articles/the-fiscal-policy-response-to-the-pandemic/.

56. Dow G, Higgins W. *Politics against Pessimism: Social Democratic Possibilities since Ernst Wigforss*. New ed. Peter Lang AG, Internationaler Verlag der Wissenschaften; 2013.

57. Robinson J. *The Accumulation of Capital*. 3rd rev. ed. Macmillan; 1969.

58. Keynes JM. *The General Theory of Employment, Interest, and Money*. Harcourt, Brace & World; 2016.

59. Kalecki M. Political aspects of full employment. *Polit Q*. 1943;14(4):322–330. doi:10 .1111/j.1467-923X.1943.tb01016.x.

60. Boushey H, Nunn R, O'Donnell J, Shambaugh J. The damage done by recessions and how to respond. Brookings. Published May 16, 2019. Accessed March 31, 2022. https:// www.brookings.edu/research/the-damage-done-by-recessions-and-how-to-respond/.

61. Furman J, Summers L. A reconsideration of fiscal policy in the era of low interest rates. Brookings. https://www.brookings.edu/wp-content/uploads/2020/11/furman -summers-fiscal-reconsideration-discussion-draft.pdf.

62. Mason JW, Karlsson K. Don't fear the deficit: why we can afford a green New Deal. Roosevelt Forward. Accessed March 31, 2022. https://rooseveltforward.org/publications /dont-fear-the-deficit-why-we-can-afford-a-green-new-deal/.

63. Bruenig M. Social wealth fund for America. People's Policy Project. Accessed March 31, 2022. https://peoplespolicyproject.org/projects/social-wealth-fund.

64. Atkinson AB. *Inequality: What Can Be Done?* Harvard University Press; 2015.

65. Lange O. On the economic theory of socialism: part one. *Rev Econ Stud*. 1936;4(1): 53–71. doi:10.2307/2967660.

66. Roemer JE. *A Future for Socialism*. Harvard University Press; 1994.

67. Lansley S. *A Sharing Economy: How Social Wealth Funds Can Reduce Inequality and Help Balance the Books*. Policy Press; 2016.

68. Alaska Department of Revenue. Permanent Fund Dividend. Accessed April 1, 2022. https://prd.pfd.alaska.gov.

69. Piketty T. *Capital in the Twenty First Century*. Harvard University Press; 2014.

70. Oakes J. Slavery is theft. Accessed March 31, 2022. https://jacobinmag.com/2015 /08/slavery-abolition-lincoln-oakes-property.

10. Practice of the Welfare State

1. Barr N. *The Welfare State as Piggy Bank: Information, Risk, Uncertainty, and the Role of the State*. Oxford University Press; 2001.

2. Rothstein B. *Just Institutions Matter: The Moral and Political Logic of the Universal Welfare State*. Illustrated ed. Cambridge University Press; 1998.

3. Brady D. *Rich Democracies, Poor People: How Politics Explain Poverty*. Illustrated ed. Oxford University Press; 2009.

4. Rawls J. *Justice as Fairness: A Restatement*. 2nd ed. (Kelly EI, ed.). Harvard University Press; 2001.

5. Jordan J. Policy feedback and support for the welfare state. *J Eur Soc Policy*. 2013; 23(2):134–148. doi:10.1177/0958928712471224.

6. Levi M. *Consent, Dissent, and Patriotism*. Cambridge University Press; 1997. doi:10 .1017/CBO9780511609336.

7. Hirschman AO. *Exit, Voice, and Loyalty: Responses to Decline in Firms, Organizations, and States*. Harvard University Press; 1970.

8. Cooper M. Infinite regress: Virginia school neoliberalism and the tax revolt. *Capital J Hist Econ*. 2021;2(1):41–87. doi:10.1353/cap.2021.0002.

9. Madsen JK, Mikkelsen KS, Moynihan DP. Burdens, sludge, ordeals, red tape, oh my!: a user's guide to the study of frictions. *Public Adm*. n/a(n/a). doi:10.1111/padm.12717.

10. Herd P, Moynihan DP. *Administrative Burden: Policymaking by Other Means*. Russell Sage Foundation; 2019.

11. Zeckhauser RJ. *Strategic Sorting: The Role of Ordeals in Health Care*. National Bureau of Economic Research; 2019. doi:10.3386/w26041.

12. Unrath M. Targeting, screening, and retention: evidence from California's food stamps program. Accessed February 9, 2021. https://www.capolicylab.org/wp-content/uploads/2021/02/CalFresh-Working-Paper.pdf.

13. Christensen J, Aarøe L, Baekgaard M, Herd P, Moynihan DP. Human capital and administrative burden: the role of cognitive resources in citizen-state interactions. *Public Adm Rev*. 2020;80(1):127–136. doi:10.1111/puar.13134.

14. Barr N. *Economics of the Welfare State*. Annotated ed. Oxford University Press; 2020.

15. Linos E, Prohofsky A, Ramesh A, Rothstein J, Unrath M. *Can Nudges Increase Take-up of the EITC?: Evidence from Multiple Field Experiments*. National Bureau of Economic Research; 2020. doi:10.3386/w28086.

16. Ko W, Moffitt RA. Take-up of social benefits. National Bureau of Economic Research, Working Paper 30148. Published online June 2022. doi:10.3386/w30148.

17. Jacques O, Noël A. Targeting within universalism. *J Eur Soc Policy*. 2021;31(1):15–29. doi:10.1177/0958928720918973.

18. Tullock G. General welfare or welfare for the poor only. In: Tullock G, ed. *Economics of Income Redistribution*. Springer Netherlands; 1997:101–114. doi:10.1007/978-94-011-5378-2_6.

19. Brady D, Bostic A. Paradoxes of social policy: welfare transfers, relative poverty, and redistribution preferences. *Am Sociol Rev*. 2015;80(2):268–298. doi:10.1177/0003122415573049.

20. Atkinson AB. The case for a participation income. *Polit Q*. 1996;67(1):67–70. doi:10.1111/j.1467-923X.1996.tb01568.x.

21. Sen A. *The Political Economy of Targeting*. Annual Bank Conference on Development Economics, World Bank; 1992. https://scholar.harvard.edu/sen/publications/political-economy-targeting.

22. Bruenig M. The problems with means-testing are real. *Jacobin*. Accessed April 5, 2022. https://jacobinmag.com/2020/09/means-testing-max-sawicky-universal-programs.

23. Atkinson AB. *Inequality: What Can Be Done?* Harvard University Press; 2015.

24. Apps P, Rees R, Thoresen TO, Vattø TE. *Alternatives to Paying Child Benefit to the Rich. Means Testing or Higher Tax?* Statistics Norway, Research Department; 2021. Accessed January 18, 2022. https://ideas.repec.org/p/ssb/dispap/969.html.

25. Sligar D. Means testing is a dog of a tax and it will destroy the welfare state. Western Sydney Wonk. Published June 5, 2021. Accessed June 7, 2021. https://western

sydneywonk.wordpress.com/2021/06/05/means-testing-is-a-dog-of-a-tax-and-it-will
-destroy-welfare-state/.

26. Sligar D. Credible tax and welfare reform must tackle the means testing mess.
Western Sydney Wonk. Published October 19, 2022. Accessed December 7, 2022. https://
westernsydneywonk.wordpress.com/2022/10/19/credible-tax-and-welfare-reform-must
-tackle-the-means-testing-mess/.

27. Bruenig M. The folly of means-testing a child allowance. People's Policy Project.
Accessed March 31, 2022. https://www.peoplespolicyproject.org/2021/12/24/the-folly-of
-means-testing-a-child-allowance/.

28. Sligar D. Means testing: bad for efficiency, bad for equality. Western Sydney Wonk.
Published August 25, 2022. Accessed December 7, 2022. https://westernsydneywonk.word
press.com/2022/08/25/means-testing-bad-for-efficiency-bad-for-equality/.

29. Korpi W, Palme J. The paradox of redistribution and strategies of equality: welfare
state institutions, inequality, and poverty in the western countries. *Am Sociol Rev*. 1998;
63(5):661–687. doi:10.2307/2657333.

30. Blanchet T, Chancel L, Gethin A. Why is Europe more equal than the United
States? *Am Econ J Appl Econ*. doi:10.1257/app.20200703.

31. Ferrarini T, Nelson K, Palme J. Social transfers and poverty in middle- and high-
income countries—A global perspective. *Glob Soc Policy*. 2016;16(1):22–46. doi:10.1177
/1468018115591712.

32. Frank RH. Positional externalities cause large and preventable welfare losses. *Am
Econ Rev*. 2005;95(2):137–141.

33. Diamond P, Saez E. The case for a progressive tax: from basic research to policy
recommendations. *J Econ Perspect*. 2011;25(4):165–190. doi:10.1257/jep.25.4.165.

34. Cingano F. *Trends in Income Inequality and Its Impact on Economic Growth*. OECD;
2014. doi:10.1787/5jxrjncwxv6j-en.

35. Okun AM. *Equality and Efficiency: The Big Tradeoff*. Rev ed. Brookings Institution
Press; 2015.

36. Avram S. *Benefit Losses Loom Larger than Taxes: The Effects of Framing and Loss
Aversion on Behavioural Responses to Taxes and Benefits*. Institute for Social and Economic
Research; 2015. Accessed December 28, 2021. https://ideas.repec.org/p/ese/iserwp/2015
-17.html.

37. Apps P. *Family Taxation: An Unfair and Inefficient System*. Centre for Economic
Policy Research, Research School of Economics, Australian National University; 2006.
Accessed November 16, 2022. https://econpapers.repec.org/paper/auudpaper/524.htm.

38. Sligar D. Universal social insurance is sound economics. Western Sydney Wonk.
Published November 1, 2021. Accessed April 5, 2022. https://westernsydneywonk.word
press.com/2021/11/01/the-smart-economics-of-middle-class-welfare/.

39. The tax-transfer system, Progressivity and redistribution: How Progressive is the
Australian transfer system? Austaxpolicy: The Tax and Transfer Policy Blog. Published
December 10, 2015. Accessed April 5, 2022. https://www.austaxpolicy.com/the-tax
-transfer-system-progressivity-and-redistribution-part-1-how-progressive-is-the
-australian-transfer-system/.

40. Skocpol T. Targeting within universalism: politically viable policies to combat

poverty in the United States. In: *Social Policy in the United States*. Princeton University Press; 2020:250–274. doi:10.1515/9780691214023-010.

41. Marmot M, Bell R. Fair society, healthy lives. *Public Health*. 2012;126 Suppl 1:S4-S10. doi:10.1016/j.puhe.2012.05.014.

42. Rose G. Strategy of prevention: lessons from cardiovascular disease. *Br Med J Clin Res Ed*. 1981;282(6279):1847–1851. doi:10.1136/bmj.282.6279.1847.

43. Bruenig M. Why fiscal progressivity discussions are so muddled. Dēmos. Published June 17, 2016. Accessed March 29, 2022. https://web.archive.org/web/20160617093454 /https://www.demos.org/blog/3/26/15/why-fiscal-progressivity-discussions-are-so -muddled.

44. Calnitsky D. The policy road to socialism. *Crit Sociol*. Published online August 8, 2021:08969205211031624. doi:10.1177/08969205211031624.

45. Anderson ES. What is the point of equality? *Ethics*. 1999;109(2):287–337. doi:10 .1086/233897.

46. Gugushvili D, Laenen T. Two decades after Korpi and Palme's "paradox of redis-tribution": what have we learned so far and where do we take it from here? *J Int Comp Soc Policy*. 2021;37(2):112–127. doi:10.1017/ics.2020.24.

47. Blekesaune M, Quadagno J. Public attitudes toward welfare state policies: a comparative analysis of 24 nations. *Eur Sociol Rev*. 2003;19(5):415–427. doi:10.1093/esr /19.5.415.

48. Wendt C, Mischke M, Pfeifer M. *Welfare States and Public Opinion: Perceptions of Healthcare Systems, Family Policy and Benefits for the Unemployed and Poor in Europe*. Edward Elgar Publishing; 2011.

49. Svallfors S, ed. *Contested Welfare States: Welfare Attitudes in Europe and Beyond*. Stanford University Press; 2012. doi:10.2307/j.ctvqsdrs4.

50. Buchanan JM, Flowers, M. An analytical setting for a taxpayers' revolution. *West Econ J*. 1969;68(7):349–359.

51. Marcus MM, Yewell KG. *The Effect of Free School Meals on Household Food Purchases: Evidence from the Community Eligibility Provision*. National Bureau of Economic Research; 2021. doi:10.3386/w29395.

52. Link BG, Phelan J. Social conditions as fundamental causes of disease. *J Health Soc Behav*. 1995;Spec No:80–94.

11. Transfer Income Policy I

1. Sligar D. Basic income, social democracy and the welfare state. Western Sydney Wonk. Published December 11, 2021. Accessed April 12, 2022. https://westernsydneywonk .wordpress.com/2021/12/11/basic-income-social-democracy-and-the-welfare-state/.

2. Anderson ES. What is the point of equality? *Ethics*. 1999;109(2):287–337. doi:10 .1086/233897.

3. Berkowitz SA. The logic of policies to address income-related health inequity: a problem-oriented approach. *Milbank Q*. Published online March 22, 2022. doi:10.1111 /1468-0009.12558.

4. Bruenig M. Technical details for my analysis of 2014 poverty data. Published online

September 16, 2015. Accessed March 12, 2021. http://mattbruenig.com/2015/09/16 /technical-details-for-my-analysis-of-2014-poverty-data/.

5. Kalecki M. Political aspects of full employment. *Polit Q.* 1943;14(4):322–330. doi:10.1111/j.1467-923X.1943.tb01016.x.

6. Barr N. *Economics of the Welfare State*. Annotated ed. Oxford University Press; 2020.

7. Barr N. *The Welfare State as Piggy Bank: Information, Risk, Uncertainty, and the Role of the State*. Oxford University Press; 2001.

8. Scanlon TM. *Why Does Inequality Matter?* Reprint ed. Oxford University Press; 2020.

9. Rawls J. *Justice as Fairness: A Restatement*. 2nd ed. (Kelly EI, ed.). Harvard University Press; 2001.

10. Glennerster H. *Understanding the Cost of Welfare*. 3rd ed. Policy Press; 2017.

11. Rothstein B. *Just Institutions Matter: The Moral and Political Logic of the Universal Welfare State*. Illustrated ed. Cambridge University Press; 1998.

12. McWilliams JM. Pay for performance: when slogans overtake science in health policy. *JAMA.* 2022;328(21):2114–2116. doi:10.1001/jama.2022.20945.

13. Mason JW. Public options: the general case. Accessed March 29, 2022. https:// jwmason.org/slackwire/public-options-general-case/.

14. Sen A. Equality of what? In: McMurrin S, ed. *Tanner Lectures on Human Values.* Vol. 1. Cambridge University Press; 1980.

15. Sen A. *Development as Freedom*. Reprint ed. Anchor; 2000.

16. Beuermann DW, Jackson CK, Navarro-Sola L, Pardo F. What is a good school, and can parents tell? Evidence on the multidimensionality of school output. *Rev Econ Stud.* Published online May 9, 2022:rdac025. doi:10.1093/restud/rdac025

17. OECD. *Improving Schools in Sweden: An OECD Perspective*. OECD Publishing; 2015. Accessed April 13, 2022. https://www.oecd.org/education/school/improving-schools-in -sweden-an-oecd-perspective.htm.

18. Brook RH, Keeler EB, Lohr KN, et al. *The Health Insurance Experiment: A Classic RAND Study Speaks to the Current Health Care Reform Debate*. RAND Corporation; 2006. Accessed March 31, 2022. https://www.rand.org/pubs/research_briefs/RB9174.html.

19. Chandra A, Flack E, Obermeyer Z. *The Health Costs of Cost-Sharing*. National Bureau of Economic Research; 2021. doi:10.3386/w28439.

20. Brot-Goldberg ZC, Chandra A, Handel BR, Kolstad JT. What does a deductible do? The impact of cost-sharing on health care prices, quantities, and spending dynamics. *Q J Econ.* 2017;132(3):1261–1318. doi:10.1093/qje/qjx013.

21. Chandra A, Gruber J, McKnight R. Patient cost-sharing and hospitalization offsets in the elderly. *Am Econ Rev.* 2010;100(1):193–213. doi:10.1257/aer.100.1.193.

22. Baicker K, Mullainathan S, Schwartzstein J. Behavioral hazard in health Insurance. *Q J Econ.* 2015;130(4):1623–1667. doi:10.1093/qje/qjv029.

23. Dusetzina SB, Huskamp HA, Rothman RL, et al. Many Medicare beneficiaries do not fill high-price specialty drug prescriptions. *Health Affairs.* 2022;41(4):487–496. doi:10 .1377/hlthaff.2021.01742.

24. Choudhry NK, Avorn J, Glynn RJ, et al. Full coverage for preventive medications after myocardial infarction. *N Engl J Med*. 2011;365(22):2088–2097. doi:10.1056/NEJMsa 1107913.

25. Card D, Dobkin C, Maestas N. The impact of nearly universal insurance coverage on health care utilization: evidence from Medicare. *Am Econ Rev*. 2008;98(5):2242–2258. doi:10.1257/aer.98.5.2242.

26. Chan DC Jr, Card D, Taylor L. *Is There a VA Advantage? Evidence from Dually Eligible Veterans*. National Bureau of Economic Research; 2022. doi:10.3386/w29765.

27. Silver D, Zhang J. *Impacts of Basic Income on Health and Economic Well-Being: Evidence from the VA's Disability Compensation Program*. National Bureau of Economic Research; 2022. doi:10.3386/w29877.

28. Maynard A, Bloor K. Universal coverage and cost control: the United Kingdom National Health Service. *J Health Hum Serv Adm*. 1998;20(4):423–441.

29. Basu S, Andrews J, Kishore S, Panjabi R, Stuckler D. Comparative performance of private and public healthcare systems in low- and middle-income countries: a systematic review. *PLOS Med*. 2012;9(6):e1001244. doi:10.1371/journal.pmed.1001244.

30. Wray CM, Khare M, Keyhani S. Access to care, cost of care, and satisfaction with care among adults with private and public health insurance in the US. *JAMA Netw Open*. 2021;4(6):e2110275. doi:10.1001/jamanetworkopen.2021.10275.

31. Anhang Price R, Sloss EM, Cefalu M, Farmer CM, Hussey PS. Comparing quality of care in Veterans Affairs and non-Veterans Affairs settings. *J Gen Intern Med*. 2018; 33(10):1631–1638. doi:10.1007/s11606-018-4433-7.

32. Goodair B, Reeves A. Outsourcing health-care services to the private sector and treatable mortality rates in England, 2013–20: an observational study of NHS privatisation. *Lancet Public Health*. 2022;7(7):e638-e646. doi:10.1016/S2468-2667(22)00133-5.

33. Kruse FM, Stadhouders NW, Adang EM, Groenewoud S, Jeurissen PPT. Do private hospitals outperform public hospitals regarding efficiency, accessibility, and quality of care in the European Union? A literature review. *Int J Health Plann Manage*. 2018;33(2): e434-e453. doi:10.1002/hpm.2502.

34. McWilliams JM. Professionalism revealed: rethinking quality improvement in the wake of a pandemic. *NEJM Catal*. 2020;1(5). doi:10.1056/CAT.20.0226.

35. McWilliams JM. Clinician professionalism: "out of the box" thinking to improve care quality. *NEJM Catal Innov Care Deliv*. Published online January 7, 2022. Accessed June 6, 2022. https://catalyst.nejm.org/doi/full/10.1056/CAT.22.0008.

36. Rosenbaum L. Reassessing quality assessment—the flawed system for fixing a flawed system. *N Engl J Med*. 2022;386(17):1663–1667. doi:10.1056/NEJMms2200976.

37. Rosenbaum L. Metric myopia—trading away our clinical judgment. *N Engl J Med*. 2022;386(18):1759–1763. doi:10.1056/NEJMms2200977.

38. Rosenbaum L. Peers, professionalism, and improvement—reframing the quality question. *N Engl J Med*. 2022;386(19):1850–1854. doi:10.1056/NEJMms2200978.

39. Hong CS, Atlas SJ, Chang Y, et al. Relationship between patient panel characteristics and primary care physician clinical performance rankings. *JAMA*. 2010;304(10):1107–1113. doi:10.1001/jama.2010.1287.

40. McWilliams JM. Don't look up? Medicare Advantage's trajectory and the future

of Medicare. *Health Affairs* Forefront. Published March 24, 2022. Accessed May 6, 2022. https://www.healthaffairs.org/do/10.1377/forefront.20220323.773602/full/.

41. MacLean CH, Kerr EA, Qaseem A. Time out—charting a path for improving performance measurement. *N Engl J Med*. Published online April 18, 2018. doi:10.1056/NEJMp1802595.

42. US General Accounting Office. *Health Care Quality: CMS Could More Effectively Ensure Its Quality Measurement Activities Promote Its Objectives*. Accessed June 13, 2022. https://www.gao.gov/products/gao-19-628.

43. Donabedian A. A founder of quality assessment encounters a troubled system firsthand. Interview by Fitzhugh Mullan. *Health Affairs*. 2001;20(1):137–141. doi:10.1377/hlthaff.20.1.137.

44. Press MJ, Scanlon DP, Ryan AM, et al. Limits of readmission rates in measuring hospital quality suggest the need for added metrics. *Health Aff (Millwood)*. 2013;32(6):1083–1091. doi:10.1377/hlthaff.2012.0518.

45. Cook R. How complex systems fail. Published January 1, 2002. Accessed June 13, 2022. https://www.researchgate.net/publication/228797158_How_complex_systems_fail.

46. Stange KC, Etz RS, Gullett H, et al. Metrics for assessing improvements in primary health care. *Annu Rev Public Health*. 2014;35:423–442. doi:10.1146/annurev-publhealth-032013-182438.

47. Berenson RA. If you can't measure performance, can you improve it? *JAMA*. 2016;315(7):645–646. doi:10.1001/jama.2016.0767.

48. Berenson RA, Kaye DR. Grading a physician's value—the misapplication of performance measurement. *N Engl J Med*. 2013;369(22):2079–2081. doi:10.1056/NEJMp1312287.

49. Keating NL, Cleveland JLF, Wright AA, et al. Evaluation of reliability and correlations of quality measures in cancer care. *JAMA Netw Open*. 2021;4(3):e212474. doi:10.1001/jamanetworkopen.2021.2474.

50. Gilstrap LG, Chernew ME, Nguyen CA, et al. Association between clinical practice group adherence to quality measures and adverse outcomes among adult patients with diabetes. *JAMA Netw Open*. 2019;2(8):e199139. doi:10.1001/jamanetworkopen.2019.9139.

51. Krumholz HM, Lin Z, Keenan PS, et al. Relationship between hospital readmission and mortality rates for patients hospitalized with acute myocardial infarction, heart failure, or pneumonia. *JAMA*. 2013;309(6):587–593. doi:10.1001/jama.2013.333.

52. Kwak J. The problem with Obamacare. The Baseline Scenario. Published May 9, 2016. Accessed June 6, 2022. https://baselinescenario.com/2016/05/09/the-problem-with-obamacare/.

53. Cooper Z, Craig SV, Gaynor M, Van Reenen J. The price ain't right? Hospital prices and health spending on the privately insured. *Q J Econ*. 2019;134(1):51–107. doi:10.1093/qje/qjy020.

54. Levinson Z, Qureshi N, Liu JL, Whaley CM. Trends in hospital prices paid by private health plans varied substantially across the US. *Health Affairs*. 2022;41(4):516–522. doi:10.1377/hlthaff.2021.01476.

55. US Department of Health and Human Services, Office of Inspector General. *Some Medicare Advantage Organization Denials of Prior Authorization Requests Raise Concerns*

about Beneficiary Access to Medically Necessary Care. Accessed June 6, 2022. https://oig.hhs .gov/oei/reports/OEI-09-18-00260.asp.

56. Gilfillan R, Berwick DM. Medicare Advantage, direct contracting, and the Medicare "money machine," Part 1: The risk-score game. *Health Affairs* Forefront. Accessed June 6, 2022. https://www.healthaffairs.org/do/10.1377/forefront.20210927.6239/full/.

57. Barr N. Long-term care: a suitable case for social insurance. *Soc Policy Adm.* 2010; 44(4):359–374. doi:10.1111/j.1467-9515.2010.00718.x.

12. Transfer Income Policy II

1. Atkinson AB. *Inequality: What Can Be Done?* Harvard University Press; 2015.

2. Barr N. *Economics of the Welfare State.* Annotated ed. Oxford University Press; 2020.

3. Vanhuysse P, Medgyesi M, Gal RI. Welfare states as lifecycle redistribution machines: decomposing the roles of age and socio-economic status shows that European tax-and-benefit systems primarily redistribute across age groups. *PLOS ONE.* 2021;16(8): e0255760. doi:10.1371/journal.pone.0255760.

4. Jacques P, Leroux ML, Stevanovic D. Poverty among the elderly: the role of public pension systems. *Int Tax Public Finance.* 2021;28(1):24–67. doi:10.1007/s10797-020-09617-2.

5. Arno PS, House JS, Viola D, Schechter C. Social security and mortality: the role of income support policies and population health in the United States. *J Public Health Policy.* 2011;32(2):234–250. doi:10.1057/jphp.2011.2.

6. Barr N. *The Welfare State as Piggy Bank: Information, Risk, Uncertainty, and the Role of the State.* Oxford University Press; 2001.

7. Barr N, Diamond P. The economics of pensions. *Oxf Rev Econ Policy.* 2006;22(1): 15–39.

8. OECD. Inequality - Poverty rate. OECD Data. Accessed January 18, 2022. http:// data.oecd.org/inequality/poverty-rate.htm.

9. People's Policy Project. Family Fun Pack. People's Policy Project. Accessed March 12, 2021. https://peoplespolicyproject.org/projects/family-fun-pack

10. Pascoe JM, Wood DL, Duffee JH, Kuo A, Committee on Psychosocial Aspects of Child and Family Health, Council on Community Pediatrics. Mediators and adverse effects of child poverty in the United States. *Pediatrics.* 2016;137(4):e20160340. doi:10 .1542/peds.2016-0340.

11. Smeeding T, Thévenot C. Addressing child poverty: how does the United States compare with other nations? *Acad Pediatr.* 2016;16(3 Suppl):S67-S75. doi:10.1016/j.acap .2016.01.011.

12. Bruenig M. The folly of means-testing a child allowance. People's Policy Project. Accessed March 31, 2022. https://www.peoplespolicyproject.org/2021/12/24/the-folly -of-means-testing-a-child-allowance/.

13. Apps P, Rees R, Thoresen TO, Vattø TE. *Alternatives to Paying Child Benefit to the Rich. Means Testing or Higher Tax?* Statistics Norway, Research Department; 2021. Accessed January 18, 2022. https://ideas.repec.org/p/ssb/dispap/969.html

14. Rubinow IM. *The Quest for Security.* Arno Press; 1933.

15. Silver D, Zhang J. *Impacts of Basic Income on Health and Economic Well-Being:*

Evidence from the VA's Disability Compensation Program. National Bureau of Economic Research; 2022. doi:10.3386/w29877.

16. Edwards R, Smith S. Job market remains tight in 2019, as the unemployment rate falls to its lowest level since 1969. Monthly Labor Review: US Bureau of Labor Statistics. Accessed June 13, 2022. https://www.bls.gov/opub/mlr/2020/article/job-market-remains -tight-in-2019-as-the-unemployment-rate-falls-to-its-lowest-level-since-1969.htm.

17. Dube A. A plan to reform the unemployment insurance system in the United States. Brookings. Published April 13, 2021. Accessed April 14, 2022. https://www. brookings.edu/research/a-plan-to-reform-the-unemployment-insurance-system-in-the -united-states/.

18. Advisory Council on Unemployment Compensation. Collected Findings and Rec-ommendations: 1994–1996. Published 1996. Accessed August 4, 2020. https://oui.doleta .gov/dmstree/misc_papers/advisory/acuc/collected_findings/adv_council_94-96.pdf.

19. National Commission on Unemployment Compensation. *Unemployment Compen-sation: Final Report*. Published July 1980. Accessed August 4, 2020. https://oui.doleta.gov /dmstree/misc_papers/advisory/ncuc/uc_studies_and_research/ncuc-final.pdf.

20. Anderson ES. What is the point of equality? *Ethics*. 1999;109(2):287–337. doi:10 .1086/233897.

21. Berkowitz SA. The logic of policies to address income-related health inequity: a problem-oriented approach. *Milbank Q*. Published online March 22, 2022. doi:10.1111 /1468-0009.12558.

22. Barr N. Funding post-compulsory education. In: Johnes G, Johnes J, Agasisti T, López-Torres L, eds. *Handbook of Contemporary Education Economics*. Edward Elgar; 2017. Accessed April 21, 2022. https://www.e-elgar.com/.

23. Bruenig M. *The Policy Shop* blog. Accessed April 14, 2022. https://drive.google.com /file/d/1q_IqYXFNJ8yDGSPmU-or8BpmAEeZ6SNm/view.

24. Mehta A, Newfield C. A socialist alternative to human capital theory? *Los Angeles Review of Books*. Published November 19, 2021. Accessed April 21, 2022. https://lareviewof books.org/article/a-socialist-alternative-to-human-capital-theory/.

25. Brown P, Lauder H, Cheung SY. *The Death of Human Capital?: Its Failed Promise and How to Renew It in an Age of Disruption*. Oxford University Press; 2020.

26. Becker GS. *Human Capital: A Theoretical and Empirical Analysis with Special Refer-ence to Education*. 3rd ed. National Bureau of Economic Research; 1994. Accessed April 21, 2022. https://www.nber.org/books-and-chapters/human-capital-theoretical-and-empirical -analysis-special-reference-education-third-edition.

27. Sen A. *Development as Freedom*. Reprint ed. Anchor; 2000.

28. Konczal M. *Freedom from the Market: America's Fight to Liberate Itself from the Grip of the Invisible Hand*. New Press; 2021.

29. Abraham S, Bishop JM, Collier D, Nilaj E, Steinbaum M, Taylor A. The right way to cancel student debt. Jain Family Institute. Accessed May 27, 2022. https://www.jain familyinstitute.org/news/the-right-way-to-cancel-student-debt/.

30. Hoynes H, Rothstein J. Universal basic income in the United States and advanced countries. *Annu Rev Econ*. 2019;11(1):929–958. doi:10.1146/annurev-economics-080218 -030237.

31. Rothstein J. Is the EITC as good as an NIT? Conditional cash transfers and tax incidence. *Am Econ J Econ Policy*. 2010;2(1):177–208. doi:10.1257/pol.2.1.177.

32. Balakrishnan S, Lewis M, Nunez S. Reweaving the safety net: the best fit for guaranteed income. Jain Family Institute. Accessed March 14, 2022. https://www.jain familyinstitute.org/projects/parts/reweaving-the-safety-net-the-best-fit-for-guaranteed -income/.

33. Sahm C, Nuñez S, Balakrishnan S; Jain Family Institute. Model behavior: a critical review of macroeconomic models for guaranteed income and the Child Tax Credit. Jain Family Institute. Accessed December 28, 2021. https://www.jainfamilyinstitute.org /projects/parts/a-critical-review-of-macroeconomic-models-for-guaranteed-income-and -the-child-tax-credit/.

34. Moffitt RA. The negative income tax and the evolution of U.S. welfare policy. *J Econ Perspect*. 2003;17(3):119–140. doi:10.1257/089533003769204380.

35. Bruenig M. Social wealth fund for America. People's Policy Project. Accessed March 31, 2022. https://peoplespolicyproject.org/projects/social-wealth-fund.

36. Gibson M, Hearty W, Craig P. The public health effects of interventions similar to basic income: a scoping review. *Lancet Public Health*. 2020;5(3):e165-e176. doi:10.1016 /S2468-2667(20)30005-0.

37. Greenberg D, Moffitt R, Friedmann J. Underreporting and experimental effects on work effort: evidence from the Gary Income Maintenance Experiment. *Rev Econ Stat*. 1981;63(4):581–589. doi:10.2307/1935854.

38. Greenberg D, Halsey H. Systematic misreporting and effects of income mainte- nance experiments on work effort: evidence from the Seattle-Denver Experiment. *J Labor Econ*. 1983;1(4):380–407.

39. Marinescu I. *No Strings Attached: The Behavioral Effects of U.S. Unconditional Cash Transfer Programs*. National Bureau of Economic Research; 2018. doi:10.3386/w24337.

40. Neuert H, Fisher E, Darling M, Barrows A. Work requirements don't work: a behavioral science perspective. Accessed April 14, 2022. https://www.ideas42.org/wp -content/uploads/2019/04/ideas42-Work-Requirements-Paper.pdf.

41. Ben-Shalom Y, Moffitt R, Scholz JK. An assessment of the effectiveness of anti- poverty programs in the United States. In: Jefferson PN, ed. *The Oxford Handbook of the Economics of Poverty*. Oxford University Press; 2012:709–749. doi:10.1093/oxfordhb /9780195393781.013.0023.

42. Diamond P, Saez E. The case for a progressive tax: from basic research to policy recommendations. *J Econ Perspect*. 2011;25(4):165–190. doi:10.1257/jep.25.4.165.

43. Calnitsky D. Debating basic income. *Catal J*. 2017;1(3). Accessed April 18, 2022. https://catalyst-journal.com/2017/12/debating-basic-income.

44. Social Security Administrative Expenses. Accessed April 18, 2022. https://www .ssa.gov/oact/STATS/admin.html.

45. McCaffery EJ, Slemrod J. Toward an agenda for behavioral public finance. *Behav Public Finance*. Published online August 26, 2004. doi:10.2139/ssrn.590201.

46. Quadagno J. *The Color of Welfare: How Racism Undermined the War on Poverty*. Rev ed. Oxford University Press; 1996.

47. Atkinson AB. The case for a participation income. *Polit Q*. 1996;67(1):67–70. doi:10 .1111/j.1467-923X.1996.tb01568.x.

48. Adkins L, Cooper M, Konings M. *The Asset Economy*. Polity; 2020.

49. Williams P. Public housing for all. NOEMA. Accessed April 14, 2022. https://www .noemamag.com/public-housing-for-all.

50. Ansell B, Cansunar A. The political consequences of housing (un)affordability. *J Eur Soc Policy*. 2021;31(5):597–613. doi:10.1177/09589287211056171.

51. Berkowitz SA, Kalkhoran S, Edwards ST, Essien UR, Baggett TP. Unstable housing and diabetes-related emergency department visits and hospitalization: a nationally representative study of safety-net clinic patients. *Diabetes Care*. 2018;41(5):933–939. doi:10.2337/dc17-1812.

52. Fowler PJ, Farrell AF, Marcal KE, Chung S, Hovmand PS. Housing and child welfare: emerging evidence and implications for scaling up services. *Am J Community Psychol*. 2017;60(1–2):134–144. doi:10.1002/ajcp.12155.

53. Taylor LA. Housing and health: an overview of the literature. *Health Affairs*. Accessed June 3, 2020. https://www.healthaffairs.org/do/10.1377/hpb20180313.396577/full/.

54. Baxter AJ, Tweed EJ, Katikireddi SV, Thomson H. Effects of housing first approaches on health and well-being of adults who are homeless or at risk of homelessness: systematic review and meta-analysis of randomised controlled trials. *J Epidemiol Community Health*. 2019;73(5):379–387. doi:10.1136/jech-2018-210981.

55. Christensen P, Sarmiento-Barbieri I, Timmins C. *Racial Discrimination and Housing Outcomes in the United States Rental Market*. National Bureau of Economic Research; 2021. doi:10.3386/w29516.

13. Factor Income Policy

1. Anderson ES. What is the point of equality? *Ethics*. 1999;109(2):287–337. doi:10 .1086/233897.

2. Tawney RH. *Equality*. 5th ed. HarperCollins Publishers; 1964.

3. Marshall TH. *Citizenship and Social Class: And Other Essays*. University Press; 1950.

4. Kalecki M. Political aspects of full employment. *Polit Q*. 1943;14(4):322–330. doi:10 .1111/j.1467-923X.1943.tb01016.x.

5. Chibber V. *The Class Matrix: Social Theory after the Cultural Turn*. Harvard University Press; 2022.

6. Rawls J. *Justice as Fairness: A Restatement*. 2nd ed. (Kelly EI, ed.). Harvard University Press; 2001.

7. Anderson E. *Private Government: How Employers Rule Our Lives*. Reprint ed. Princeton University Press; 2019.

8. Bivens J, Mishel L. Understanding the historic divergence between productivity and a typical worker's pay: why it matters and why it's real. Economic Policy Institute. Published September 2, 2015. Accessed April 20, 2022. https://www.epi.org/publication /understanding-the-historic-divergence-between-productivity-and-a-typical-workers -pay-why-it-matters-and-why-its-real/.

9. Brill M, Holman C, Morris C, Raichoudhary R, Yosif N. Understanding the labor

productivity and compensation gap. US Bureau of Labor Statistics. Published online June 1, 2017. Accessed April 21, 2022. https://www.bls.gov/opub/btn/volume-6/pdf/under standing-the-labor-productivity-and-compensation-gap.pdf.

10. Acemoglu D, He A, le Maire D. *Eclipse of Rent-Sharing: The Effects of Managers' Business Education on Wages and the Labor Share in the US and Denmark*. National Bureau of Economic Research; 2022. doi:10.3386/w29874.

11. International Labour Organization Organisation for Economic Co-operation and Development. *The Labour Share in G20 Economies*; 2015. https://www.oecd.org/g20/topics /employment-and-social-policy/The-Labour-Share-in-G20-Economies.pdf.

12. Piketty T, Saez E, Zucman G. Distributional national accounts: methods and estimates for the United States. *Q J Econ*. 2018;133(2):553–609. doi:10.1093/qje/qjx043.

13. Barr N. *Economics of the Welfare State*. Annotated ed. Oxford University Press; 2020.

14. Atkinson AB. *Inequality: What Can Be Done?* Harvard University Press; 2015.

15. Robinson J. *The Economics of Imperfect Competition*. Palgrave Macmillan UK; 1969. doi:10.1007/978-1-349-15320-6.

16. Kaufman BE. Institutional economics and the minimum wage: broadening the theoretical and policy debate. *Ind Labor Relat Rev*. 2010;63(3):427–453.

17. Caldwell S, Naidu S. Wage and employment implications of U.S. labor market monopsony and possible policy solutions. Equitable Growth. Published February 18, 2020. Accessed April 20, 2022. http://www.equitablegrowth.org/wage-and-employment -implications-of-u-s-labor-market-monopsony-and-possible-policy-solutions/.

18. Manning A. Monopsony in labor markets: a review. *ILR Rev*. 2021;74(1):3–26. doi:10.1177/0019793920922499.

19. Callaci B. Competition is not the cure. *Boston Review*. Accessed April 20, 2022. https://bostonreview.net/articles/competition-is-not-the-cure/.

20. Posner EA. *How Antitrust Failed Workers*. Oxford University Press; 2021.

21. Neumark D, Shirley P. *Myth or Measurement: What Does the New Minimum Wage Research Say about Minimum Wages and Job Loss in the United States?* National Bureau of Economic Research; 2021. doi:10.3386/w28388.

22. Dube A. Impacts of minimum wages: review of the international evidence. Accessed March 28, 2022. https://www.gov.uk/government/publications/impacts-of -minimum-wages-review-of-the-international-evidence.

23. Cengiz D, Dube A, Lindner A, Zipperer B. The effect of minimum wages on low-wage jobs. *Q J Econ*. 2019;134(3):1405–1454. doi:10.1093/qje/qjz014.

24. Paul S. Charting the reform path. *Michigan Law Review*. Accessed April 20, 2022. https://michiganlawreview.org/journal/charting-the-reform-path/.

25. Blanchet T, Chancel L, Gethin A. Why is Europe more equal than the United States? *Am Econ J Appl Econ*. doi:10.1257/app.20200703.

26. McAlevey JF. *No Shortcuts: Organizing for Power in the New Gilded Age*. Reprint ed. Oxford University Press; 2018.

27. Barr N. *The Welfare State as Piggy Bank: Information, Risk, Uncertainty, and the Role of the State*. Oxford University Press; 2001.

28. Barr N, Diamond P. The economics of pensions. *Oxf Rev Econ Policy*. 2006;22(1): 15–39.

29. Cingano F. *Trends in Income Inequality and Its Impact on Economic Growth*. OECD; 2014. doi:10.1787/5jxrjncwxv6j-en.

30. Ostry JD, Berg A, Tsangarides CG. Redistribution, inequality, and growth. *IMF Staff Discuss Note*. 2014;14(02):1. doi:10.5089/9781484352076.006.

31. Bruenig M. Desert theory, rehashed. Published May 9, 2014. Accessed December 5, 2022. https://mattbruenig.com/2014/05/09/desert-theory-rehashed/.

32. Sen A. Just deserts. Published online March 4, 1982. Accessed April 20, 2022. https://www.nybooks.com/articles/1982/03/04/just-deserts/.

33. Diamond PA. Wage determination and efficiency in search equilibrium. *Rev Econ Stud*. 1982;49(2):217–227. doi:10.2307/2297271.

34. Wolff RP. A wild rant about marginal productivity. The Philosopher's Stone. Published April 27, 2014. Accessed April 20, 2022. https://robertpaulwolff.blogspot.com/2014/04/a-wild-rant-about-marginal-productivity.html.

35. Harknett K, Schneider D, Irwin V. Improving health and economic security by reducing work schedule uncertainty. *Proc Natl Acad Sci*. 2021;118(42):e2107828118. doi:10.1073/pnas.2107828118.

36. Husak C. How U.S. companies harm workers by making them independent contractors. Equitable Growth. Published July 31, 2019. Accessed April 21, 2022. http://www.equitablegrowth.org/how-u-s-companies-harm-workers-by-making-them-independent-contractors/.

37. Bertrand M, Mullainathan S. Are Emily and Greg more employable than Lakisha and Jamal? A field experiment on labor market discrimination. *Am Econ Rev*. 2004;94(4):991–1013. doi:10.1257/0002828042002561.

38. *American Experiences Versus American Expectations*. U.S. Equal Employment Opportunity Commission. Accessed March 12, 2021. https://www.eeoc.gov/special-report/american-experiences-versus-american-expectations.

39. Graf N, Brown A, Patten E. The narrowing, but persistent, gender gap in pay. Pew Research Center. Accessed March 12, 2021. https://www.pewresearch.org/fact-tank/2019/03/22/gender-pay-gap-facts/.

40. Kaufman BE. *What Do Unions Do?: A Twenty-Year Perspective*. Routledge; 2006.

41. Western B, Rosenfeld J. Unions, norms, and the rise in U.S. wage inequality. *Am Sociol Rev*. 2011;76(4):513–537. doi:10.1177/0003122411414817.

42. Unions help reduce disparities and strengthen our democracy. Economic Policy Institute. Accessed April 22, 2022. https://www.epi.org/publication/unions-help-reduce-disparities-and-strengthen-our-democracy/.

43. Freeman RB. *What Do Unions Do?* Basic Books; 1985.

44. VanHeuvelen T, Brady D. Labor unions and American poverty. *ILR Rev*. 2022;75(4):891–917. doi:10.1177/00197939211014855.

45. Muller J, Raphael D. Does unionization and working under collective agreements promote health? *Health Promot Int*. Published online December 13, 2021:daab181. doi:10.1093/heapro/daab181.

46. Leigh JP, Chakalov B. Labor unions and health: A literature review of pathways and outcomes in the workplace. *Prev Med Rep*. 2021;24:101502. doi:10.1016/j.pmedr.2021.101502.

47. Rosenfeld J, Denice P, Laird J. Union decline lowers wages of nonunion workers: the overlooked reason why wages are stuck and inequality is growing. Economic Policy Institute. Accessed April 21, 2022. https://www.epi.org/publication/union-decline-lowers -wages-of-nonunion-workers-the-overlooked-reason-why-wages-are-stuck-and-inequality -is-growing/.

48. Offe C, Wiesenthal H. Two logics of collective action: theoretical notes on social class and organizational form. *Polit Power Soc Theory*. 1980;1:67–115.

49. Cooper R. *How Are You Going to Pay for That?: Smart Answers to the Dumbest Question in Politics*. St. Martin's Press; 2022.

50. Schulten T. The meaning of extension for the stability of collective bargaining in Europe. European Trade Union Institute. Accessed April 21, 2022. https://www.etui.org /publications/policy-briefs/european-economic-employment-and-social-policy/the -meaning-of-extension-for-the-stability-of-collective-bargaining-in-europe.

51. Dube A. Rebuilding U.S. labor market wage standards. Equitable Growth. Published February 18, 2020. Accessed April 21, 2022. http://www.equitablegrowth.org /rebuilding-u-s-labor-market-wage-standards/.

52. Meidner R. Our concept of the third way: some remarks on the socio-political tenets of the Swedish labour movement. *Econ Ind Democr*. 1980;1(3):343–369. doi:10.1177 /0143831X8013003.

53. Dow G, Higgins W. *Politics against Pessimism: Social Democratic Possibilities since Ernst Wigforss*. New ed. Peter Lang AG, Internationaler Verlag der Wissenschaften; 2013.

54. Hall PA, Soskice D, eds. *Varieties of Capitalism: The Institutional Foundations of Comparative Advantage*. Oxford University Press; 2001.

55. Esping-Andersen G. *The Three Worlds of Welfare Capitalism*. Princeton University Press; 1990.

56. Lind J. A Nordic saga?: The Ghent system and trade unions. *Int J Employ Stud*. 15(1):49–68. doi:10.3316/informit.879028458824347.

57. O'Boyle EH, Patel PC, Gonzalez-Mulé E. Employee ownership and firm performance: a meta-analysis. *Hum Resour Manag J*. 2016;26(4):425–448. doi:10.1111/1748-8583 .12115.

58. Jäger S, Noy S, Schoefer B. *What Does Codetermination Do?* National Bureau of Economic Research; 2021. doi:10.3386/w28921.

59. Jäger S, Noy S, Schoefer B. Codetermination and power in the workplace. Economic Policy Institute. Accessed April 21, 2022. https://www.epi.org/unequalpower /publications/codetermination-and-power-in-the-workplace/.

60. Mason JW. Alternative visions of inflation. Accessed December 28, 2021. http:// jwmason.org/slackwire/alternative-visions-of-inflation/.

61. Mason JW, Karlsson K. Don't fear the deficit: why we can afford a Green New Deal. Roosevelt Forward. Accessed March 31, 2022. https://rooseveltforward.org /publications/dont-fear-the-deficit-why-we-can-afford-a-green-new-deal/.

62. Tcherneva PR. *The Case for a Job Guarantee*. Polity; 2020.

63. Mitchell WF, Watts M. *Investing in a Job Guarantee for Australia*. Center of Full Employment and Equity; 2020. http://www.fullemployment.net/publications/reports /2020/CofFEE_Research_Report_2000-02.pdf.

64. Mitchell B. Michal Kalecki – The political aspects of full employment. Bill Mitchell – Modern Monetary Theory. Published August 13, 2010. Accessed April 21, 2022. http://bilbo.economicoutlook.net/blog/?p=11127.

65. Rothstein J. Is the EITC as good as an NIT? Conditional cash transfers and tax incidence. *Am Econ J Econ Policy*. 2010;2(1):177–208. doi:10.1257/pol.2.1.177.

66. Jones MR, Ziliak JP. *The Antipoverty Impact of the EITC: New Estimates from Survey and Administrative Tax Records*. Center for Economic Studies, US Census Bureau; 2019. Accessed December 29, 2021. https://ideas.repec.org/p/cen/wpaper/19-14.html.

67. Bruenig M. The myths of the earned income tax credit. People's Policy Project. Accessed April 21, 2022. https://www.peoplespolicyproject.org/project/the-myths-of-the -earned-income-tax-credit/.

68. Mason JW. Public options: the general case. Accessed March 29, 2022. https:// jwmason.org/slackwire/public-options-general-case/.

69. Linos E, Prohofsky A, Ramesh A, Rothstein J, Unrath M. *Can Nudges Increase Take-up of the EITC?: Evidence from Multiple Field Experiments*. National Bureau of Economic Research; 2020. doi:10.3386/w28086.

70. Kleven H. *The EITC and the Extensive Margin: A Reappraisal*. National Bureau of Economic Research; 2019. Accessed April 21, 2022. https://ideas.repec.org/p/nbr/nberwo /26405.html.

71. Adkins L, Cooper M, Konings M. *The Asset Economy*. Polity; 2020.

72. Bruenig M. Social wealth fund for America. People's Policy Project. Accessed March 31, 2022. https://peoplespolicyproject.org/projects/social-wealth-fund.

73. Paul S. On firms. *Univ Chic Law Rev*. 2023,90(2):579–621. https://live-chicago-law -review.pantheonsite.io/sites/default/files/2023-03/09_SYMP_PAUL.pdf.

14. Civil and Political Rights

1. Rothstein B. *Just Institutions Matter: The Moral and Political Logic of the Universal Welfare State*. Illustrated ed. Cambridge University Press; 1998.

2. Brady D. *Rich Democracies, Poor People: How Politics Explain Poverty*. Illustrated ed. Oxford University Press; 2009.

3. Iversen T, Soskice D. Electoral institutions and the politics of coalitions: why some democracies redistribute more than others. *Am Polit Sci Rev*. 2006;100(2):165–181.

4. Persson T, Tabellini G. Constitutional rules and fiscal policy outcomes. *Am Econ Rev*. 2004;94(1):25–45. doi:10.1257/000282804322970689.

5. Offe C, Wiesenthal H. Two logics of collective action: Theoretical notes on social class and organizational form. *Polit Power Soc Theory*. 1980;1:67–115.

6. Fried BH. *The Progressive Assault on Laissez Faire: Robert Hale and the First Law and Economics Movement*. Harvard University Press; 2001.

7. Goldman L. *The Life of R. H. Tawney: Socialism and History*. Illustrated ed. Bloomsbury Academic; 2014.

8. Boyd RW. The case for desegregation. *Lancet*. 2019;393(10190):2484–2485. doi:10 .1016/S0140-6736(19)31353-4.

9. Massey DS, Denton NA. *American Apartheid: Segregation and the Making of the Underclass*. Later Printing ed. Harvard University Press; 1993.

10. Williams DR, Collins C. Racial residential segregation: a fundamental cause of racial disparities in health. *Public Health Rep.* 2001;116(5):404–416.

11. Politicians target LGBTQ kids in national erasure campaign from classrooms to sports fields. NBC News. Accessed April 27, 2022. https://www.nbcnews.com/nbc-out /out-news/book-bans-dont-say-gay-bill-lgbtq-kids-feel-erased-classroom-rcna15819.

12. Gabbatt A. Bills to ban US schools' discussion of LGBTQ+ issues are threat to free speech – report. *The Guardian.* https://www.theguardian.com/world/2022/feb/15/lgbtq -rights-ban-us-schools-republicans. Published February 15, 2022. Accessed April 27, 2022.

13. Ray R, Gibbons A. Why are states banning critical race theory? Brookings. Published November 2021. Accessed April 27, 2022. https://www.brookings.edu/blog/fixgov /2021/07/02/why-are-states-banning-critical-race-theory/.

14. Bouie J. Democrats, you can't ignore the culture wars any longer. *New York Times.* https://www.nytimes.com/2022/04/22/opinion/red-scare-culture-wars.html. Published April 22, 2022. Accessed April 27, 2022.

15. Roeder O. Just facts: quantifying the incarceration conversation. Brennan Center for Justice. Accessed April 27, 2022. https://www.brennancenter.org/our-work/analysis -opinion/just-facts-quantifying-incarceration-conversation.

16. Pettit B, Western B. Mass imprisonment and the life course: race and class inequality in U.S. incarceration. *Am Sociol Rev.* 2004;69(2):151–169.

17. Clegg J, Usmani A. The economic origins of mass incarceration. *Catalyst.* 2019;3(3). Accessed April 27, 2022. https://catalyst-journal.com/2019/12/the-economic-origins-of -mass-incarceration.

18. Wacquant L. Class, race & hyperincarceration in revanchist America. *Daedalus.* 2010;139(3):74–90.

19. Wakefield S, Uggen C. Incarceration and stratification. *Annu Rev Sociol.* 2010;36(1): 387–406. doi:10.1146/annurev.soc.012809.102551.

20. Travis J, Western B, Redburn S. *The Growth of Incarceration in the United States: Exploring Causes and Consequences;* 2014. doi:10.17226/18613.

21. Massoglia M, Pridemore WA. Incarceration and health. *Annu Rev Sociol.* 2015;41(1): 291–310. doi:10.1146/annurev-soc-073014-112326.

22. Desmond M, Western B. Poverty in America: new directions and debates. *Annu Rev Sociol.* 2018;44(1):305–318. doi:10.1146/annurev-soc-060116-053411.

23. Johnson C. The Panthers can't save us now. *Catalyst.* 2017;1(1). https://catalyst -journal.com/2017/11/panthers-cant-save-us-cedric-johnson.

24. Use of force standards. National Conference of State Legislatures. Accessed April 27, 2022. https://www.ncsl.org/research/civil-and-criminal-justice/use-of-force-standards .aspx.

25. Wacquant L. *Punishing the Poor: The Neoliberal Government of Social Insecurity.* Illustrated ed. Duke University Press Books; 2009.

26. Deshpande M, Mueller-Smith MG. *Does Welfare Prevent Crime? The Criminal Justice Outcomes of Youth Removed From SSI.* National Bureau of Economic Research; 2022. doi:10.3386/w29800.

27. *Miller v Johnson.* 515 US 500 (1995). Accessed April 27, 2022. https://www.law .cornell.edu/supct/html/94-631.ZS.html.

28. *Rucho v Common Cause*. 588 US __ (2019). Legal Information Institute. Accessed April 27, 2022. https://www.law.cornell.edu/supremecourt/text/18-422.

29. Gilens M. *Affluence and Influence: Economic Inequality and Political Power in America*. Princeton University Press; 2012. doi:10.1515/9781400844821.

30. Gilens M, Page BI. Testing theories of American politics: elites, interest groups, and average citizens. *Perspect Polit*. 2014;12(3):564–581. doi:10.1017/S1537592714001595.

31. Bartels LM. *Unequal Democracy: The Political Economy of the New Gilded Age*. 2nd ed. Princeton University Press; 2016. doi:10.1515/9781400883363.

32. Rawls J. *Justice as Fairness: A Restatement*. 2nd ed. (Kelly EI, ed.). Harvard University Press; 2001.

15. Conclusions

1. Mills CW. "Ideal theory" as ideology. *Hypatia*. 2005;20(3):165–184.

2. Táíwò OO. States are not basic structures: against state-centric political theory. *Philos Pap*. 2019;48(1):59–82. doi:10.1080/05568641.2019.1586573.

3. Krieger N. *Ecosocial Theory, Embodied Truths, and the People's Health*. Oxford University Press; 2021.

4. Rawls J. *Justice as Fairness: A Restatement*. 2nd ed. (Kelly EI, ed.). Harvard University Press; 2001.

5. Scanlon TM. *Why Does Inequality Matter?* Reprint ed. Oxford University Press; 2020.

6. Dworkin R. *Sovereign Virtue: The Theory and Practice of Equality*. Trade Paperback ed. Harvard University Press; 2002.

7. Anderson ES. What is the point of equality? *Ethics*. 1999;109(2):287–337. doi:10.1086/233897.

8. Anderson E. *Private Government: How Employers Rule Our Lives*. Reprint ed. Princeton University Press; 2019.

9. Anderson E. The fundamental disagreement between luck egalitarians and relational egalitarians. *Can J Philos*. 2010;40(suppl 1):1–23. doi:10.1080/00455091.2010.10717652.

10. Sen A. *Development as Freedom*. Reprint ed. Anchor; 2000.

11. Rothstein B. *Just Institutions Matter: The Moral and Political Logic of the Universal Welfare State*. Illustrated ed. Cambridge University Press; 1998.

12. Tawney RH. *Equality*. 5th ed. HarperCollins Publishers; 1964.

13. Marshall TH. *Citizenship and Social Class: And Other Essays*. University Press; 1950.

14. Dow G, Higgins W. *Politics against Pessimism: Social Democratic Possibilities since Ernst Wigforss*. New ed. Peter Lang AG, Internationaler Verlag der Wissenschaften; 2013.

15. Esping-Andersen G. *The Three Worlds of Welfare Capitalism*. Princeton University Press; 1990.

16. Korpi W, Palme J. The paradox of redistribution and strategies of equality: welfare state institutions, inequality, and poverty in the western countries. *Am Sociol Rev*. 1998;63(5):661–687. doi:10.2307/2657333.

17. Lynch J. *Regimes of Inequality*. Cambridge University Press; 2021.

18. Sen A. Equality of what? In: McMurrin S, ed. *Tanner Lectures on Human Values*. Vol. 1. Cambridge University Press; 1980.

19. Rawls J. *A Theory of Justice*. 2nd ed. Belknap Press of Harvard University Press; 1999.

20. Sen A. *Inequality Reexamined*. Harvard University Press; 1995.

21. Jacques O, Noël A. Targeting within universalism. *J Eur Soc Policy*. 2021;31(1):15–29. doi:10.1177/0958928720918973.

22. Rothstein B. Managing the welfare state: lessons from Gustav Möller. *Scand Polit Stud*. 1985;8(3):151–170. doi:10.1111/j.1467-9477.1985.tb00318.x.

23. Bruenig M. *The Policy Shop* blog. Accessed April 14, 2022. https://drive.google.com/file/d/1q_IqYXFNJ8yDGSPmU-or8BpmAEeZ6SNm/view.

24. Kaufman BE. Institutional economics and the minimum wage: broadening the theoretical and policy debate. *Ind Labor Relat Rev*. 2010;63(3):427–453.

25. Murphy L, Nagel T. *The Myth of Ownership: Taxes and Justice*. Oxford University Press; 2004.

26. Fried BH. *The Progressive Assault on Laissez Faire: Robert Hale and the First Law and Economics Movement*. Harvard University Press; 2001.

27. Jordan J. Policy feedback and support for the welfare state. *J Eur Soc Policy*. 2013; 23(2):134–148. doi:10.1177/0958928712471224.

28. Pascoe JM, Wood DL, Duffee JH, Kuo A, Committee on Psychosocial Aspects of Child and Family Health, Council on Community Pediatrics. Mediators and adverse effects of child poverty in the United States. *Pediatrics*. 2016;137(4):e20160340. doi:10.1542/peds.2016-0340.

29. Saez E, Zucman G. *The Triumph of Injustice: How the Rich Dodge Taxes and How to Make Them Pay*. W. W. Norton & Company; 2020.

30. Batchelder LL, Kamin D. *Taxing the Rich: Issues and Options*. Social Science Research Network; 2019. doi:10.2139/ssrn.3452274.

31. Diamond P, Saez E. The case for a progressive tax: from basic research to policy recommendations. *J Econ Perspect*. 2011;25(4):165–190. doi:10.1257/jep.25.4.165.

32. Bruenig M. Social wealth fund for America. People's Policy Project. Accessed March 31, 2022. https://peoplespolicyproject.org/projects/social-wealth-fund.

Index

Figures and tables are indicated by "f" and "t" following the page numbers.